Hate
Don't
Make
No
Noise

Hate Don't Make No Noise

Anatomy of a New Ghetto

by Etta Revesz

A RICHARD SEAVER BOOK

The Viking Press / New York

039053

A Richard Seaver Book/The Viking Press
First published in 1978 by The Viking Press
625 Madison Avenue, New York, N.Y. 10022
Published simultaneously in Canada by
Penguin Books Canada Limited

LIBRARY OF CONGRESS CATALOGING IN PUBLICATION DATA
Revesz, Etta.
  Hate don't make no noise.
  "A Richard Seaver book."
  1. Slums—California—Case studies. 2. Housing—California—
Case studies. 3. Urban renewal—California—
Case studies.   I.   Title.
HT176.C3R48   301.36′3′0926   77-16164
ISBN 0-670-53359-9

Printed in the United States of America
Set in Videocomp Times Roman.

To all those
who live in projects,
yet dream of castles,
and to special people—
Pat Miller, Marc Havoc,
James Thomas Jackson,
and Plowboy's Johnny—
who believed.

PRIVATE HOMES

FLOOD

PLAY AREA

McDONALD'S
DRIVE-IN

BASEBALL FIELD

PLAY AR

ROOSEVELT ROAD

FENCE

CHEMICAL PLANT

STORAGE
BARN

① Edith Bentwood's Social Service Ce
② Action For Tenants Office
③ Ben Hamilton's Office
④ Community Hall
Ⓟ Parking Lot

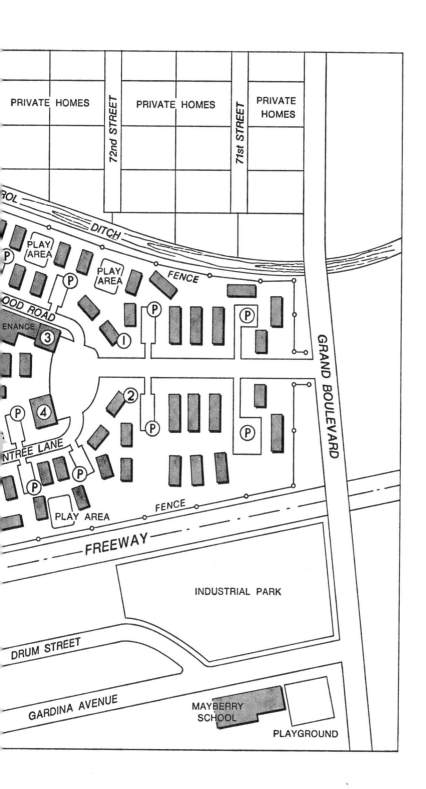

Hate
Don't
Make
No
Noise

1

He lay half inside the entrance to my office. The door with the stenciled sign, BUENA VISTA HOUSING PROJECT—SOCIAL SERVICES CENTER, was pushed wide open. The lower part of his body sprawled over the stoop and hung down the walkway. His legs curled crazily, like the limbs of a rag doll. Scuffed black calf-high boots anchored his feet.

Now I moved. One hand reached toward me—crawling along the floor like a drunken crab. I bent down. His face was hidden. He moaned into the bent arm folded under his head. I kneeled beside him. Touched him.

"What happened?" I knew the answer.

That morning I had come to work early. Paperwork had piled high, and I wanted to catch up. Running feet crunched across the driveway, pounded past. A shadow fell across my desk and I looked up. Dude Muggins. Behind him was Harry the Shoe, fat and squat, waddling in baggy pants. Harry's trademark was his shoes—an endless supply of cloddy Navy rejects, all several sizes too long. His lope reminded me of a caneless Charlie Chaplin as he padded after his tall skinny black friend. Whenever petty crimes were reported by one of the 3500 tenants in the project, the complaints often mentioned these two youths—one black, one Chicano.

What were they up to now, I wondered.

The telephone rang. It was Annie Flunk. Annie rarely talked; she orated at the decibel level of a jet plane. Distracted, I watched Dude and Harry the Shoe spring across the project street, Flood Road, then stop. A short huddle, and they took off in different directions and disappeared.

Annie's voice softened to a yell. I listened as she shrilled out the details of her problem.

She had washed early that morning, hung out her wet laundry, and someone had come along and cut the wire clotheslines. All her clean wash had landed on the ground and was covered with dirt. She knew who the culprits were! My ear was deafened by the blast as Annie described her intentions toward the project children.

"When I get my hands on that son-of-a-bitch Billy Goochen, I'll cut his balls off!"

"Mrs. Flunk! Annie! Wait a minute—please!" I screamed to make myself heard.

"Miz Bentwood, you gotta do something about those rotten kids!"

"OK, but listen—are you sure it's Billy Goochen? He's only ten—he couldn't reach that high. Besides, it probably was an accident."

"Shit! It weren't no accident. I run them off yesterday when I caught them swiping stuff outta the liquor store. They're bastards! You wanna hear more what those goddamn kids did? Billy an' his gang? They brung all them loose-running dogs over and let them crap on my clean laundry!"

Her voice boomed. I pictured her three-hundred-pound body vibrating with anger. She itemized tortures to be applied to Billy and his gang when she caught up with them. I was holding the receiver away from my ear, only half listening, when I heard it.

A different sound. Close by. A low, dark-brown moan. Then a thump—like something being thrown, or falling. The door from the outside to the front room was always kept open, as a "welcome" gesture. My office, with desk and telephone, was in a back room. I listened, waited. Nothing.

I heard it again. Then a whimpering, a voice, words.

"Oh, Christ . . . please . . . someone . . . ohhhhhh!" A gurgle.

My stomach tightened, relaxed, quivered. I cut Annie's hysterics short. "Annie! Look, I'll be down to your place and we'll talk about it. I have to go—someone came in!" I hung up before she could object.

That's when I ran into the outer room and found him.

Who was he? His dead weight made it difficult, but I moved his head around. It was the young man living with Betty Lou Lupke—the boy just out of county jail. I knew him only as Doug.

I felt his hand tug at my skirt. He grabbed a fistful of cloth, and then his hand went limp and dropped to the floor. I looked down. He had smeared blood on my dress.

Now I knew. He was cut. I half shoved, half yanked him over so I could brace him against the open door. The top of his jeans and part of his shirt were ripped. His middle was oozing blood like a miniature whirlpool. His eyes opened and rolled back. Sweat dripped under my arms and down my sides. My fingers were tentacles of ice.

"Wait . . . please! I'll get an ambulance."

I stumbled, knees weak, and ran back into my office cubicle to the telephone. My mind blocked. The police . . . fire department . . . paramedics . . . ? I ran my finger down the emergency list I had pasted on top of my desk. Dialed. Yes. They would dispatch a vehicle immediately. Address? Buena Vista Housing Project . . . off of Grand.

The woman at the end of the line hesitated. I yelled at her. "What do you mean you won't send help without police protection? I don't care what you've been told! A man is bleeding to death on my doorstep!"

She repeated the address then—254 Flood Road #37.

I ran back to the dying man, leaned over him. His right hand lay over his wound. His fingernails were manicured in blood.

"Doug . . . you're Doug." Should I try to get him down flat? "Just hang on. I called for help. Hang on!" I demanded.

Chattering children broke through the silence. Oh, God! School must be out! I looked out the door and into the faces of four youngsters. They stood on the walkway watching me and the caved-in figure of the man. They moved in slowly . . . closer.

"Stay away! Go, go!" I waved them back, but still they came. Very deliberately, fluttering their crayoned school papers against their bare legs. Not frightened—just curious.

"Wow!" The boy was about eight. "Wow, man, someone sure messed over that sucker!"

"He gonna die, Miss Bentwood?" a girl asked.

My lips moved dryly. My teeth seemed too large for my mouth. "Kids, go home. There is nothing for you to see."

"Hell, this ain't so much. You ever seen someone with their ears cut off . . . jus' little holes left?"

I had seen this child before on the playground. She looked about eleven; sullen, pretty, with thick black hair, dressed in torn jeans and sneakers that had the eyeholes ripped out.

"I bet I know who bossed this. I bet Tommy Gun bossed it. He did the other time, but no one would tell on Tommy Gun."

"You don't know what you're talking about," I said. Her blatant uncon-
cern frightened me.

"The shit I don't. You got a lot to learn, lady." The sneer came naturally.
"C'mon, kids, let's find Betty Lou and tell her Doug's been knifed."

She galloped off and the others followed. I watched them run down the
sidewalk and around the curve of Flood Road. They disappeared among the
apartment buildings. Their voices calling out "Betty Lou" drifted back and
echoed against the cement-walled buildings until the wail of a siren took
over. It grew deafening as the ambulance squealed in from Grand Boulevard, up Flood Road, and braked to a stop in front of my office.

The news spread. Doors opened. People ran over, some carrying infants,
others with clinging children. One group of tenants ringed the ambulance
and circled my office. I saw Billy Goochen and two of his gang off to one
side. The white-coated attendants looked nervous as they opened the rear
door and took out the gurney. One of them walked up, glanced at Doug,
and went back. He passed the other attendant and spoke one word.
"Shock."

He brought out two blankets, unfolded them.

Now a woman was wailing . . . screaming . . . shoving her way through
the crowd. They made a pathway. I saw the long blond hair and belly-ripe
figure of Betty Lou Lupke. I knew she was due soon with Doug's baby. I
had taught her how to knit at our weekly Mothers' Club.

She flayed the air, tripped once, and was caught, held up, hand-passed
by other tenants toward the bleeding man. No one asked any questions.
They just stood and watched . . . waited.

I moved aside as Betty Lou came closer. She tried to lean over Doug.
Couldn't, her unborn child a barrier.

"Doug . . . Doug, goddamn it to hell!"

She hit out at one of the attendants who was trying to lift the man. She
screamed at them. "Do something, you bastards!"

"Lady, get the hell out of our way. You're hanging us up!"

The swarthy attendant jerked his arm free from Betty Lou's grasp. He
looked around. His eyes shifted over the crowd that was milling around,
foot-shifting, silent. He turned to me.

"We're not supposed to come into this cesspool without police escort.
Where in hell are the black-and-whites?"

They came—three black-and-white police cars, followed by the unmarked car that meant Lieutenant Hank Garrison. They lined themselves
up like dominoes, blocking the street and hemming in the ever-larger group

4

of onlookers. The crackling of police radio calls punctuated the low rumbling of the tenants' voices now.

Betty Lou leaned on me, sobbed hard in sucking gasps. I watched as Hank Garrison walked in our direction. He unbuttoned his jacket. He moved his hand to feel for the gun tucked in at the small of his back. His eyes held a question for me. My eyes and nod indicated the ambulance. He wheeled around and forced his way over to the orange-and-white van. He pushed away the two attendants, who had slid the gurney with the blanketed Doug halfway into the rear section. The tall officer leaned over the still face of Doug. A voice from the crowd called out.

"Hey, man, you holdin' up the works! Let the cat get to the hospital!"

One of the uniformed cops now reached Hank Garrison. His hand was on the butt of his .38. He scanned the tightening crowd.

A woman's bitter voice. "You pigs trying to make sure he croaks before he gets to a doc?"

Another opinion. "Lousy mother-fuckers! Protection, hell! This what we pay taxes for?"

A snigger. "Who you jivin', man?"

Like a slow-motion nightmare, two more uniformed cops ring Hank and the bleeding man. The static on the police cars grows louder. I look over to one side. Across Flood Road a tentlike figure approaches.

Starlet Jones waddles her bulk across the grass, dragging Bitsy, her two-year-old. With her hair in curlers, she looks like a radar installation melted down. She plows her way past everyone until she reaches Betty Lou and me.

"C'mon, honey. Doug's going to be all right." Starlet's look to me contradicts her words. Already I had learned how shrewd these tenants were when it came to judging life—and death. Starlet takes over, transferring Betty Lou from my arm to hers and steering her into my private office.

Reality returned.

I edged around the pool of blood on the faded rug and made my way toward Hank Garrison and Doug. A policeman's arm barred me.

"No, you don't, lady. Get back and mind your own business!"

His voice said I was dirt . . . less than dirt. I shoved him away, protested. Hank heard and looked up. Beckoned.

"She's OK. Let her through. She works here."

The cop stood aside and let me pass, then resumed his stony glare at the brooding tenants. The paramedics exchanged uneasy looks, shuffled their feet. Their hands twisted at the metal tubing of the gurney, as if polishing it with fear. Questions went through my mind. What makes a guy take a job like that? Is he a sadist? Someone who likes to see mangled bodies? And what about a man who becomes a cop—is he someone who needs a legal right to inflict misery, even deal out death? Does a person's choice of occupation reveal a secret shame or need? What about me? What had landed me in this island of hopelessness? Forget it. This was no time to explore myself. Another time maybe.

The blanket-covered man was breathing hard—too hard. His eyelids flickered. Lieutenant Hank Garrison, the pride of the City of Crestview Police Community Relations Department, prodded the dying man, and his eyes opened. Garrison leaned his ear close to the young man's mouth. I watched spittle run out one corner of Doug's lips and down his unshaven cheek.

"Come on, talk! Who did it? Goddamn it, who cut you? Give me a name, fellow!" Hank's voice was low but clear—urgent.

A rattle from the man's throat. His lips were blue.

I spoke quietly, clipping my words. "Can't you wait? My God! Let them get him to a hospital. You can question him later."

Hank tilted his face toward mine, hard-eyed. "Yeah, how're you going to question a dead man?"

"Maybe he wouldn't die if you quit playing Kojak!"

He ignored me, grabbed a hunk of Doug's hair, and jerked his face around. "Son-of-a-gun! Try, damn you, talk! Who did it? Just one lousy name! I know you bastards know! Why don't you help us catch these animals?" Hank's voice rose. It carried.

"Hey, man, you trying to make sure the dude can't cut it?" a hard-case voice shouted out.

The theme was picked up.

"Stinkin' cops! Quit shitting on us. You just playin' games instead of helpin'."

Another voice. "Get him to a doctor! Move it, you mother-fuckers!"

A chorus of "yeah"s and "right"s followed. The mood was ugly. The young cops locked their knees into post stances. Hank Garrison ignored the rumblings, grimly tried to rouse Doug again.

Behind us, from my office, came Starlet's voice trying to soothe Betty Lou. Maybe it would work. Certainly it was worth a try. I shoved Hank's face away from Doug's head. A strand of sweat-limp hair slashed across Doug's face. I picked it off and leaned low.

"Listen, Doug . . . for Betty Lou's sake . . . and the baby's . . . whoever did this to you may go after her . . . them."

His eyes slit open, glassy. His lips quivered. No sound came out. I felt rather than saw Hank shake his head. I tried again, my lips to his ears—already he smelled of death.

"Doug, did you hear me? Try . . . just one word . . . one name."

Crazy. He started to sing. "Happy Birthday . . . God . . . happy . . ."

He died.

"Get him out . . . fast." Hank spoke low to the attendants. They nodded. One man began to pull the blanket over the dead man's face. Hank gripped his arm and the man winced.

"What the hell's the matter with you? He's dead!" He elbowed Hank back.

"Shut up! What the hell's the matter with *you?* This mob'll turn on you if they think he's checked in. You jerks want another Watts on your hands?"

Hank pulled the blanket down as the two men slid the stretcher gingerly into the ambulance, pretending that any jiggle might harm the man on it. Slam went the double doors. The medics raced for the cab and climbed in. The motor churned, idled, as the driver waited for the police cars to unblock the street. Once freed, the ambulance cut short, one wheel humping over the curb, and headed for Grand Boulevard. I wondered why no one questioned why the emergency siren wasn't blaring urgently.

The people drifted off. A few children were left roughhousing on the ground. A couple of dogs chased each other. Starlet Jones and two other women tenants half led, half dragged the now quietly sobbing Betty Lou toward her own apartment.

The last police car pulled away. It cruised around the Flood Road curve and continued deeper into the project. Hank and I were left standing alone on the sidewalk outside my office. He pointed, and I looked down at my skirt. The starfish shape of Doug's blood, where his hand had reached out for help, stained it.

"Makes one wonder." I stopped. "I mean . . . why wouldn't he tell us who stabbed him. It had to be someone in the project—someone he knew."

"Some day you'll find out . . . maybe accept it. Buena Vista is like . . . like quicksand. You go near it and hands reach up, pull you in. Chokes any decency a person may have when they move in. What remains is filth . . . perversion." He buttoned his jacket and shrugged himself back into duty. "Maybe he had it coming to him. Who knows? It's nature—like animals in the wilderness. These people eliminate their own diseased."

"That's a lousy thing to say. No wonder you cops are afraid to come into the project. If you keep poking a stick at an anim—"

"Animal! Go on, say it. See, you get all mush-mouthed about your precious tenants, but the truth is just that! That's exactly what they are, wild animals. Wild animals roaming around in the middle of civilization, a threat and danger to everyone, even to themselves."

"Maybe to you, but not to me! This was a senseless killing. Doug had just gotten out. He was trying to make it for Betty Lou."

"Well, we'll never know. If he would have made it, I mean."

"Or care."

I turned away and went up the stoop to my office. Garrison made me sick —everything made me sick. I had one foot inside when I looked down. The pool of blood was now black—most of it had soaked into the old rug. To walk on the dead man's blood would be obscene. I backed up and started for the end of the building. I would go around the back to the kitchen door. I passed Hank now in his unmarked car. He rolled down the window and asked me to go have a cup of coffee with him. I shook my head and kept going. I knew if I said anything I would start bawling.

"Don't take it so to heart. Like I said—these people have thick skins. You'll see, next year this time your Betty Lou will be knocked up by another stud."

Anger stopped my tears. I snapped my head away. I heard him drive off. The grass was high and my feet pressed a path across it. I made a mental note to tell maintenance to get on the ball and trim the grounds oftener. Also to ask them how to get the bloodstain out of the office rug. And my skirt? Should I deduct the price of a new dress on my tax return? Job-related expense? Like tools of the trade? I wanted to laugh. Couldn't. I wanted to cry. Couldn't. I realized I didn't even know the dead man's last name.

My eyes picked up a trail of evenly spaced roundish spots. I stooped and touched one. It was still wet. Blood. There were more. I followed them to the center of the parking lot. They stopped at the rim of a larger puddle, glistening on the tar paving. This is where it had happened. A broken pool cue lay on the paving. Its splintered end was dipped into the blood. I picked it up. Blood dripped. A drop fell on my shoe.

2

The root cellar was dark. I stumbled down the uneven dirt steps in a blinding shaft of sunlight, which changed to sudden blackness as the wooden trap doors slammed shut behind me. The slidebolt rattled as it was shoved into place. My mother's steps faded. I was alone.

Hands outstretched, I dared a few steps into the moldy air of the underground storage room. My foot hit something. I leaned over. My hand touched a rough surface. Potato sacks. The lumpy shapes felt cold under the burlap. Shuffling in choo-choo steps, I moved on.

The side walls were braced with posts. My hands fumbled along the dirt intervals until I reached the shelves, with their rows of home-canned food. I knuckled one hand and xylophoned a rhythm on the metal-capped jars. I rapped too hard; one glass jar tipped and fell. It landed near my foot. I nudged it. It rolled. Relieved that it hadn't smashed, I backed up, turned in another direction. Sharp pain at my shinbone told me I had tripped over a carton of canned goods.

Sprawled half over the box and half on the ground, I let myself go limp. My head dangled downward; my pigtails pointed stiffly, like a hunting dog's tail.

I was hot. The dank coolness suddenly choked me. Loose strands of hair got into my mouth. I spit, pushed my tongue into the space still open from my missing baby teeth. Saliva dribbled past my chin. I sucked it back, became busy making spit bubbles.

The box corner pressed into my stomach. It hurt. With my hands braced against the dirt, I shoved free. Now I sat on a rope-mesh bag of onions, legs crisscrossed. I plucked at the straggly hair on my face, smearing dirt into mud as I wiped my hand across my wet chin.

The darkness became heavy. It moved around in big balls. It bounced against me and I kicked out at it. An arrow of light slanted through the thin center crack between the trap doors. It fell across the shelves. Each jar turned into a glittering glass eye boring through the blackness. A drum beat in my ears; I covered them, held my head down. The drum was my heart. I crossed my hands over my chest to keep it from tearing up my new blouse, the one I was to wear my first day in second grade.

The cloth of my play shorts bunched between my legs and cut me. It hurt, sent shooting pain up my middle. I considered crying. Maybe shouting, screaming. No one would hear me—I knew that.

When our cat had been trapped down in the root cellar, no one heard *her!* Only when the delivery man brought the winter supply of potatoes and opened the cave cellar doors did the cat get out. I remembered how crazy she looked, not at all like the soft, purring cat I cuddled, but crazy-eyed. She almost tripped the man, hissing cat screams and clawing at anyone who came near. She ran away and never came back.

What if no one came and got me out of this dirt pit? Would I be forgotten like our cat? Now I cried—screamed—shouted. I scrambled on my hands and knees, not caring what I bumped into. A rip of pain made me grab at my left leg. A half-pulled nail in the rough wood of an open crate was the attacker. I kicked at the crate, once . . . twice . . . When my toes hurt I stopped. Something warm and sticky trickled down my leg. I was afraid to touch it.

Now careful, I fumbled my way along the floor until I reached the steps. I crawled up and pressed my eyes against the thin crack of light. A branch with reddish autumn leaves waved against the blue sky. Out . . . out! With the palms of my hands I slapped at the trapdoors—knocked—beat—banged against the slats. A splinter ripped into my finger. I pounded. Screamed louder. The root cellar mocked me. My voice came back hollow. Then only a death-stillness. I heard nothing until the doors opened away from my face. My mother stood looking down at me.

"Well, have you had enough? Do you think you can behave? Not be impolite? Be a nice little girl and say 'please' and 'thank you'? Only when you're polite will people love you."

10

She reached her hand to me. I didn't take it. I wished I were a cat so I could run away. But when you're not quite seven, you stay. But you remember.

Later that day my mother scrubbed at the stain left on the sneaker where the nail gash dripped blood.

Winter comes early in Maine; the ground hardens with overnight frost, and breath makes brittle clouds. Pigtails flying, I galloped to school in my sneakers until snow started; then I got heavy-soled shoes. The sneakers were tossed into my closet, but each time I noticed them, the round brownish stain on my left shoe reminded me of the root cellar and the moldy smell —and fear.

During the years of growing up, I often raged within myself when forced to mouth false "please"s and "thank you"s in return for acceptance as a civilized person. Finally I made it a game. "Please" really meant "You're ugly and I hate you." And "thank you" meant "Shut up, or I'll put you in the root cellar."

The game worked until I stopped caring. By the time I entered college, I didn't care if anyone loved me. Not on that basis, at least. It took me a long time to get over the fault of politeness.

In my third year at the university I became an orphan. My mother, widowed when I was three, died in August. I cried bitterly. I walked along the stony Maine beach and begged the heavens to give her back to me. For once I said "please" honestly, but the greenish-black waves beat over the granite boulders and washed my cry away on the wind. I remembered only the sweet things about her. The songs she sang, the Sundays of listening to symphonies together, and her concentration as she practiced her cello. And the pleasure she took each time she polished the silver to a star-bright gloss. She was a polite woman in an unpolite world. There was a new aloneness for me, the aloneness that comes when there is no other person to blame for your mistakes. It makes you crawl into your personal root cellar and bolt it shut from inside.

There was money left for me to finish my art degree. That last year I did numerous self-portraits; all made me into a Medusa-like witch. I even went back to tight-lipped "please"s and "thank you"s at crazy times . . . like when I bought stamps, or reached for a Jell-O at the school cafeteria. It didn't help. No one knew they were supposed to love me.

My pre-ancient-history art seminar dealt with excavations, archeology, and dead civilizations of the Middle East. Carl Bentwood sat in on the class. His mouth squared his lips when he smiled. His hands were large, blunt, with stiff hairs bristle-rubbed where his multitalented watch reported the time, the weather, and the day of the month. It fascinated me and I watched it whenever he sat next to me in class. Leaving the classroom, I trailed inconspicuously behind his tall square shoulders. At first I was sure he was a football player, but, after he asked me to have coffee with him one day, I found out he was a graduate student, sponsored by an oil company to specialize in research on drilling and oil-discovery methods.

We started dating, taking trips to nearby attractions. I introduced him to art galleries and country auctions. He made me dream of going to foreign countries, of roaming the world! We sat for hours in the local coffee shop while Carl, with intense determination to teach me, illustrated with a fork or spoon how a drill pushed through the ground. I was very stupid but faked understanding.

What I didn't fake was a need—a need for Carl's solid caring, a need to wrap myself up in something besides my self-portraits. I loved Carl and wanted to share his sensible approach to life.

We were married the week before I was graduated. Carl said it was silly to go through the graduation ceremony. Who cared? Since I had no relatives to come and take pictures, I agreed to skip the last official student duties. My diploma was sent care of General Delivery to the town where Carl had his first job—a dusty crossroads in East Texas which had oil fields and a modern lab for Carl. I was back in the root cellar, this time trapped by drabness, a cultural desert, and a sly prejudice toward Northeasterners.

A year later life improved. We were transferred to Oklahoma. There was less dust but more cold; fewer tent revival meetings but more stiff social gathering with local old-guard wheeler-dealers. I didn't fit in.

What had happened to hot desert sands? To gauchos, swinging lariats while they rode on silk-black ponies? And what had happened between Carl and me?

Carl's precise engineering brain never could accept my untidy desk or random housecleaning. In his world, laundry had to be done on Monday. In my world, it was sandwiched in between rug-weaving and star-gazing. We hung on to our lukewarm marriage for nine years, neither hot nor cold in love—or hate.

When Carl accepted a job in the Middle East among sand dunes and oil fields, I packed up our bric-a-brac marriage, had a huge garage sale, and moved to California. Crestview City, on the coast, within ninety minutes' driving distance of Los Angeles, convenient to museums, concerts, and beaches, seemed the logical place to settle.

The apartment I found was near the beach. I moved in, hung pictures, learned to work the dishwasher, and, after six months, filed for divorce. It was simple to get through the legal matter. It was not so simple to admit I had exchanged one root cellar for another.

Six months of mornings with the "Today Show," afternoons with Mike Douglas, and evenings spent with The Fonz, Kojak, or Mary Hartman ended. The car needed a tune-up; my instant coffee and my money ran out the same day. Job hunting became a priority. The problem was that a degree in art history and advanced psychology prepared me for Culture Crazies and little else. The positions I wanted didn't want me. Not even when I said "please." I was broke just at the wrong time: The economy was in a slump.

Thanksgiving Day was spent alone. The prospect of a lonesome Christmas and no money haunted me.

The *Los Angeles Times* Positions Offered section had a small notice between "Housemother for Delinquent Girls" and "Investigator for Skip-tracing." It read, "Housing: Cultural Director." It asked for someone with "human behavior" understanding and "willingness to adjust." The clincher was the location of the job—Crestview City! It was made to order for me! A quick telephone call and a short description of my talents (I lied a bit) led to an interview at the central office of the Housing Agency in Los Angeles.

After I passed the preliminary screening, I was taken to the plush office of the head of the agency, a Mr. Albert Lottman. Silver-haired, cigar-smoking, oozing competence, he described the Housing Agency organization. It was an autonomous agency, authorized by the county and monitored by a Board of Advisors, to supervise public housing for low-income citizens. The funds came from the Federal government through the Housing and Urban Development Department.

It sounded rather complicated but I tried to look intelligent. Mr. Lottman's bearing was military, from his toes to his cropped hair; a carefully tended goatee gave his face a satyric expression, while china blue eyes looked innocent. The paradox of his appearence disappeared as I was captivated by his avowed concern for the 3500 low-income residents in the public housing complex in Crestview City.

"We are looking for someone with refinement, someone who can bring beauty and the joy of living to our tenants."

Silently I yelled, "That's me!" Aloud I said nothing, but nodded and smiled a lot. A chorus of "please"s and "thank you"s circled in my head: Love me . . . love me . . . give me the job, please—please! Get me out of my root cellar!

Toward the end of the interview, Mr. Lottman tapped his inch-long ash onto a silver ashtray. He offered me the position.

3

I spent the next days doing last-minute tasks. I wanted to be free to devote all my time to my new position, one that would involve my professional and educational background. To bring appreciation of art, literature, and music to a culture-starved population promised to be exciting and challenging! Visions of art history sessions, discussions of contemporary literature, introducing classical music by using the lighter Mozart operas danced in my head. Besides doing what I loved, I would be paid! I could hardly wait to start.

A week before Christmas, I drove into the Buena Vista Housing Project to report to the project manager, Ben Hamilton.

The door to the housing office was scarred, paint-sprayed in curlicue squiggles, and topped with a single glass window, cracked. Persistent knocking finally brought a response—a woman who introduced herself as Gloria, the bookkeeper. With her armful of slave bracelets clinking, she towed me into the manager's office.

A broadly smiling, almost bald, youngish man got up and extended a moist hand to me. Before he spoke, he used his tongue to shift something from one side of his cheek to the other.

"Mr. Hamilton?" I broke the silence. "Hi! I'm Edith Bentwood."

"I see you came." He sounded ominous, as if he meant to add ". . . in spite of being warned."

"Yes," I said.

Since he didn't offer me a chair, I looked around his office. The walls were a faded army green; venetian blinds with torn cording hung slanted across two iron-barred windows. A blazing orange-and-black poster tacked on a ratty bulletin board demanded LOOK, for safety when climbing a ladder. On the wall behind Ben Hamilton's desk was a fly-specked map showing in detail the Buena Vista Project, its 147 buildings with 952 units. Its streets, Flood Road and Greentree Lane, met in a wishbone shape before they divided and circled the project. Large indentations between every two buildings were lettered "Parking." Each block-shaped building was honeycombed into sections, and each cube had a number which identified the apartment address. I studied the map while I waited for the manager's next words.

He scratched one side of his face, opened his left desk drawer, reached in, and handed me a cellophane-wrapped licorice ball. "Take it. You'll need it around here. Gives you energy."

"Thank you." I unwrapped it. Should I tell him I hated licorice? It always reminded me of Halloween.

He watched me carefully, like a mother whose child is about to take its first step. I placed the licorice in my mouth, trying not to chew out the black coloring.

"That's it. I tell you . . . it's all that keeps me going." He noticed my blank expression. "I mean, it helps to stop me from telling off these . . . these . . ." I helped him out.

"Tenants."

He nodded. "I make it a policy to chew ten times before I respond to one of those impossible people's complaints. Keeps me from losing my temper."

"Sure, I understand," I said. I wanted to ask, what about your mind? I didn't.

He shoved out of a creaking, spring-swivel chair. "Come on. I'll show you around."

We returned to the reception area. Gloria was in a tight conversation with another woman. They parted as Ben Hamilton introduced me.

"Mattie Weatherby is our occupancy clerk. Been here for fourteen years!"

Mattie raised her pencil-thin plucked eyebrows. Blue eyeshadow and white-rimmed eyelids stretched to give her a smeared Star Trek mask. She clicked towards me on knee-high plastic boots; her stick legs and stringbean body fit in with the sparseness of the shoddy surroundings. With a tight smile, she extended her hand. "Pleased," she said but didn't sound it.

"Edith will be working with us as cultural director. She'll do counseling —help our tenants with their problems." The manager's tone denied any confidence in that goal . . . or approval of it.

"If you're here to help the tenants, find them jobs so our taxes go down. All this welfare to those women who sit around . . . lie in bed till noon. And those little half-nigger babies!" Gloria's voice rose. She puffed smoke from her dangling cigarette.

She clearly did not believe in mixing the races, or, I suspected, in sex for welfare mothers. I also suspected that she wished sex stickers could be issued like food stamps. What would they be called, I wondered—Intercourse Permits? And what would qualify a woman? Loneliness? Need to share? Share what? Love? Warmth? Passion? Or belonging—the feeling of belonging to something, to someone? To be part of another's world, even if that world was imperfect!

I panicked!

What was I doing in this shabby room with these caricature people? A longing for Carl—even with his overly neat top drawer and his carefully tabulated bank stubs—started a hurt somewhere inside. What in the world had I done with my life?

That old urge—to run away, to escape—filled me. But again reality clobbered me: I was broke, I needed this job, and I needed people, any kind at this point, to let me know I was not alone in another root cellar. Besides, I *did* have something to offer!

A small, sweet-voiced, over-rouged, past-sixty woman hung on my arm. She gushed. "I think it's just wonderful that you're here to help these poor, poor, dear people. They do so need help, you know!"

"Cut the crap, Bernice." Gloria cackled as she flicked her ash onto the faded linoleum floor.

Bernice Homel was the "annual girl," Ben Hamilton explained. "Once a year each tenant has to come in with their verified income and Bernice does a redetermination on them."

It sounded on a par with a Wassermann test—one that always came out positive! Redetermine people? As what?

"It means I check their income, welfare grants, Social Security awards or pay-record stubs—but not many of them work! You would be surprised at all the white lies that are told to cover up their black deeds just to keep the rent low. But I don't get fooled often! Like if they have a man living with them, an illegal man, and they try to hide it!"

"How can you tell?" I asked.

"Babies! They report each baby so they get more welfare and lower rents.

You can't have babies without men, can you?"

I said nothing.

"Bunch of bastards, that's what we have in Buena Vista," blurted Mattie. "Bunch of lazy, dirty spongers living on taxpayers' money." She left out the words "my money," but that's what she meant.

Gloria disappeared into her bookkeeping cubicle and Bernice, with a squeeze and wink, trundled into a backroom office and closed the door. Ben Hamilton shuffled from one foot to the other, as if undecided whether to stay or go. Mattie was back at her typewriter, but she looked up and winked at me as Ben Hamilton spoke. "I suppose you want to tour the project?"

"It would be helpful . . . you know, to give me an overview." I hoped I sounded efficient.

"Sure, why don't you show Ms. Bentwood around?" Mattie's eyes had a wicked gleam.

He reacted as if touched with a live wire, stuttering as he found reasons not to accompany me. His unexplained fear was obvious enough to be embarrassing to me. I helped him out. "Why don't I explore on my own? Maybe get acquainted with tenants. I could introduce myself . . . tell them why I'm here."

He was so grateful I thought he would cry with relief. I was half out the door when Mattie called after me. "Just stay away from Ernestine Trotmartin! If she thinks some hoity-toity dame is running around trying to culturize her folks, she'll smash you, make mincemeat of you, blow you away! Get me?"

Ernestine Trotmartin: That was not the only time I would be warned about her. Still, that morning she meant little to me. I wanted to get away from the dreary atmosphere of the office and its gloomy staff.

The main office building had a yellow stucco exterior. Behind it was a maintenance department and a barnlike dome designated as a community hall. After I went down the broad steps of the entrance, I was faced with a choice of directions: Flood Road and Greentree Lane began at either end of the huge football-sized parking lot in front of the office. I turned left on Flood Road.

My heels clicked along the cracked sidewalk that curved toward the interior of the project. I avoided dog droppings, moldy trash, wind-torn paper scraps, and smashed pop bottles. The day was still early, the sky overcast. It matched my mood. The place was strangely quiet. Where were the 3500 residents? Were they all asleep? Had someone, a wicked fairy, cast a spell on these ugly dwellings? Were the people waiting for a prince? A princess? Me?

I continued, past pitted, black-tarred parking lots with hulks of old cars, some without wheels, others with engines ripped out like disemboweled war casualties. I turned away from the stench of rotted garbage, soiled paper diapers, puddles of grimy oil, scattered and broken windowpanes. Ragged garments drooped on wire clotheslines. A lean cat gnawed on a chicken bone, only to be chased away by two equally emaciated dogs.

Traffic rattled and clattered along the freeway. Somewhere to my left I heard trucks grinding along one side of Buena Vista. Between the apartment buildings I saw cars flash by over an elevated dirt-banked road. The air was thick and smelly from the gasoline fumes.

I was ready to turn back, to resign before I began. A child's crying sent me across Flood Road and an unkept grass lawn in the direction of the sound. Ripped mattresses scattered cotton balls over scuffed ground. I detoured around large open bins stuffed with trash, some overflowing onto the ground. An acid smell turned out to be eucalyptus trees; they smelled like cat piss. The crying got louder. I almost cracked my foot on a broken bicycle part as I hurried along.

A cyclone fence ran along the far side of the property, and huddled against it, half hidden in stubbled, sun-dried grasses, a small dot of a child wailed its misery. It was a small boy in a tattered shirt, without any pants, blue-legged, pinch-faced. He dug his fists into shadowed eyes; a scratch along his cheek showed red and puckered with blood. When he spotted me, he scrambled and tried to run away. I overtook him, my feet sinking in the calf-high weeds. He fought me, flailed his arms as I held him.

"Shush, shush. It's all right. Don't cry." I felt him relax, turn his dirty face to me. His ribbed chest heaved with dry sobs and he buried his head in my shoulder. He was about three years old, sandy-haired. "Do you know your name?" I asked him when he quieted down. "Where do you live? If you tell me, I'll take you home to mama."

"Mama don' want me." Muffled words against me. "Mama say get out . . . get out! Don't no one want Swenson."

"Don't cry. I want you. Let's go see your mama. I bet she just got angry. I bet she really wants you, loves you a lot."

His face turned up. "I love you. Don' go 'way," he said.

Holding his hand, I followed his lead toward one of the paint-scuffed apartment doors. As we reached the walkway up to the entrance, he broke away from my hand. I noticed his small, naked bottom was bruised as he raced to the door, jiggled the knob, and disappeared inside.

I hesitated. Part of me wanted to confront the uncaring mother; another part said, "Wait! Mind your own business." Just before I turned, my eye was caught by a movement inside the glass-topped door. Swenson's small hand shoved away a curtain, then rapped on the glass. He kissed his hand, blew on it, and smeared his kiss onto the windowpane.

Pantless Swenson decided me. There was no turning back. That morning, when I took my first steps through Buena Vista Housing Project, I entered another world.

Just two months later, I stood looking down at my shoe. The drop of blood was already stiff on my leather pump. And I remembered. The moldy darkness of the root cellar returned, the nail stabbing my leg, the pain! Me ... crying to be let out. And the brownish stain on my sneaker that wouldn't wash out. It too was round, like this drop of blood. Doug's blood.

4

I shook loose my memories. I needed people—alive, moving, complaining perhaps, but people with warm flesh and blood running tidily in proper streams, not emptying on grimy tar surfaces. I swerved away from my office door and headed for the main office. Besides, I had to report to Ben Hamilton. He had to be told what had happened.

Mattie was on the telephone as I walked in, so I bypassed her and went into Ben Hamilton's office. It was empty. Bernice trotted up behind me. I asked where Ben was.

"Gone!" Bernice simpered. "When he saw the police cars come into the project, he said he had to take care of some personal business and he left."

I returned to the outer office. Mattie was off the phone now. She opened wide her frosted eyelids.

"Ben Hamilton is a nervous wreck! He got so upset with Starlet Jones this morning when she screamed at him about the sewer backing up in her bathtub that he broke out in hives."

"Starlet Jones is an ass!" Gloria yelled out to us from her bookkeeping alcove.

Gloria disliked the pink-and-gold Starlet, mainly, I suspected, because Starlet had copulated with one of the very black maintenance men who worked in the project and the cute tan-skinned Bitsy was the result.

"Hey, lay off Starlet! She did a great thing today. She's got a big heart," I said.

"Yeah, as big as her behind!" Gloria wagged her new red wig and retreated into her cubicle.

"Didn't anyone hear the ambulance come in and see all the commotion?" I asked.

"So? What else is new?" Mattie acted bored.

"Doug, the fellow who lived with Betty Lou Lupke, was stabbed."

"Who? What happened?" Bernice picked up what I said and came running in. I repeated my news.

"Oh, dear, how dreadful! What hospital is he in? I'll send him a get-well card."

"He's at the morgue," I said.

"I'm not surprised. I knew something would happen when he came back into the project." Mattie sounded almost pleased.

"What are you talking about? You knew what would happen?"

"Ask Bernice. She knows all, tells all."

I turned to Bernice.

"Now, I hate to get anyone into trouble . . ." She cast her eyes down and fiddled with her pen.

"He's dead. A man is dead. He was stabbed and died on my doorstep." I heard my voice rise and then break. "Now if you know who did it . . ."

"It was something I heard. Before Betty Lou's boyfriend got sent to jail." Bernice stopped.

"What did you hear?" I hated to play her game.

"Some of the tenants . . . Josie Mansfield, for one. She's Go-Boy's and Raquel's mother. Anyway, the story's around that Tommy Gun was out to get Doug."

There were two residents in Buena Vista about whom I had heard gruesome tales. Ernestine Trotmartin was the first. She was touted as a combination of Lady Macbeth, Ma Barker, and Gloria Steinem. The second was a young black, Tommy Gun. His reputation seesawed between Jack the Ripper and Abe Lincoln, with a little of Gable's charm for spice. So far, I hadn't met either one.

"You're not making sense, Bernice. I keep hearing about this Tommy Gun . . . but that's all. I've never seen him," I said.

"Oh, he's around." She evaded my eyes. "Well, I'll just have to send the condolence card to Betty Lou instead."

She tripped into her office; I heard her desk drawer open. Bernice and her everlasting cards! Once Mattie and Gloria had corralled me and told me it was a fetish with Bernice. She kept cards for each situation; a maintenance man delivered them to any tenant she deemed deserving of her attention. Annoyed, I turned back to Mattie at her desk.

"What is with this Tommy Gun? What is he, some kind of ghost? Holy Ghost? No one wants to talk about him but everyone knows him. Except me."

Mattie inserted paper in her typewriter and rolled it into place. Her manner said she hoped I would shut up. I waited at her side until she felt forced to answer me.

"Tommy Gunther Matthews is a young black, and an illegal resident. He shacks up with all kinds of different women. He's a stud." She flushed lipstick red at the word. "He's no good. He's trouble. He's rotten."

She started typing. I waited.

"Everyone thinks he's special. Like a leader. Like a spokesman for the people."

"Even if he's no good?" I asked.

"What's good for nothing is sometimes good for someone." She started pounding the keys furiously.

I was lost. I had come in needing a responsive ear and consoling arm, a place to unburden my sadness, and what I got was snatches of negative attitudes . . . and no real answers. Suddenly, tension scrambled my reasoning powers. Names and faces superimposed themselves: Betty Lou's face dissolved into Hank Garrison's hard-cop look, until his twisted into the becurled Starlet's head, only to melt into drawn-skinned, blue-lipped Doug's. Now the image was Ben Hamilton, sugary spittle gluing the corners of his lips together. Hate gagged me, made my eyes burn, became double-visioned hate—for myself, for all the mannequin people of the world. Weak-kneed I leaned against the counter; looking down, I saw that the bloody starfish from Doug's hand had dried on my skirt, like a logo of the Buena Vista Housing Project.

I let myself out and went home.

I woke up to sunshine, the flip side of yesterday's bad record. The ceiling of my bedroom shifted with leaf patterns cast by the jacaranda tree outside my window. My mind backed up years and I was twelve again, summer scarred, lean as beef jerky. A small-girl body under tightly tucked blankets lay asparagus-straight, sunwashed by an early morning Maine sky. Soft wind messages sent by trembling leaves flickered on the walls and white-washed ceiling of the cottage bedroom. Clusters of red cherries tied with a flowing green ribbon marched across the wallpaper. Small sounds—crickets, a lone fly buzzing against the screen—rubbed the sleep away. A pine-tree branch teased the window screen. The sweet sounds of the world met in a symphony and I, the girl-child, rubbed sleep away from dreams and listened.

What had happened? Where along the way had I exchanged my white ceiling for a blood-stained skirt? Maine summers for California's Kodachrome winters? A cricket's love song for a cry of horror?

Day noises began outside my window and the sun slanted across my face, a golden, beckoning finger. It was time to get up.

As I dressed, I waited until hot instant coffee cooled. I gulped it down, splashed water into the empty cup, and set it upside down in the dishwasher. I debated about fixing a sandwich for lunch, decided against it, and grabbed an apple instead. Then I remembered. I unfolded a brown paper sack and put the soiled skirt in it. Sometime during the day I would drop it off at the cleaner's.

Today the pastel buildings bordering the beach city's streets looked bright under the smogless sky. I turned onto the freeway ramp and got into the middle lane. As I drove I cataloged the priorities for that day. Certainly Annie Flunk was one. Then Betty Lou. I would check with Starlet Jones to see how the pregnant girl was taking the loss of her child's father. Hank Garrison's cynical words came back to me. Damn him! What did he know about a woman's feelings in a situation like Betty Lou's?

I remembered the day I first met Hank Garrison and Herbie Brent. I had been at the project only a week when the office door opened and two men walked up to the counter. They were dressed casually in slacks and sports jackets, with soft shirts and no ties. The younger man had a conventional short haircut. The older man had shaggy dark hair which fell uncombed over his forehead. He looked about forty, was taller than his companion, and appeared to be in charge.

Mattie trotted over to them as they waited at the counter. I glanced up at them, dismissed them. They didn't look like tenants or even potential tenants. I was on the telephone trying to appease an irate tenant who was threatening to slash another tenant's car tires over a disputed parking space when Mattie clicked over and shoved a business card at me.

"They want to talk to you!" she announced.

The card read:

After I introduced myself to both men, the younger one grinned and said, "Director of Cultural Programs, huh? I'd like to program this garbage heap and its maggots right out of the city!"

I was tired of it, the snide remarks, the crude jokes.

Just that morning an old lady at the local senior citizens' agency went hysterical when I invited her to meet me in the project to discuss a music program for our older tenants. "Oh, my dear!" she had gasped. "You must be very brave to work there. The last time someone from our office went to Buena Vista, they had their purse snatched and were knocked down! No, no, I will not go out there!"

She had hung up before I could even respond.

Stalling, I looked at the card carefully, trying to keep my temper down.

"As members of the police force and as public servants who are paid by the taxpayers, you have no right to make such remarks." I hoped I sounded convincing.

The younger police officer flushed but the other one laughed. "Herb, I think we got a fighter! Just what this place needs—a real scrapper. If you think you can last after the first round!" He leaned over and patted my arm.

I jerked away.

"I'll last!" I read his name from the card. "Lieutenant Garrison."

"And this is my partner, Herbie Brent." He touched the other man's shoulder.

"Look, I didn't mean anything," Herb Brent said. "It's just that this place has given the city nothing but trouble. We have more crime here than in all the rest of Crestview."

"Well, that's your job. You're the police. You stop it," I told him.

Hank Garrison turned hard-faced suddenly.

"We'd like to. You haven't been here long enough . . . but you'll find out. Find out that these damn tenants yell for the police, but then are too scared to press charges. Until they get fed up with their situation and cooperate with us"—he threw up his hands—"there's nothing we can do."

I wanted to argue that day, to defend the project, like a mother defending her child.

"We just stopped in to let you know if you have any problems or . . . information . . . well, call us," Hank had said.

"Especially if you hear anything about guns . . . machine guns." Herb Brent then looked sharply at his boss.

"If you can't reach us, you can always call Intelligence." Both turned to leave.

"It's nice to know that you police have intelligence," I said, "but it's sad it's only in one special department."

After they left, I felt very smug. Still, the look in Herb Brent's eyes when he said "machine gun" scared me.

Weaving in and out of traffic on my way to work, I reluctantly admitted to myself that I understood what Hank had meant that day about being helpless. My daybook was filled with crime reports made by fearful tenants. Each time I urged them to report it to the police, they backed out. I was sure that someone in the project knew who had killed the young white man. I pushed Doug's last words, "Happy Birthday," out of my mind. I resolved to set up a meeting between the police, Ben Hamilton, and myself. Something had to be done.

As I drove into the project from Grand Boulevard, children were already walking the three blocks to school. Like bright-colored marbles they rolled against each other, sometimes in friendly puppy ways and sometimes with a sharp yell, followed by a tearful wailing.

Two little black girls waved for me to stop as I coasted down Flood Road toward my office.

"Hiya, Miz Bentwood. You got any candy for us?"

"Not this morning, Georgetta Liana." I smiled.

"How come a rich white lady like you don' get us kids candy?" Doreen said.

"Easy! Because I'm not rich, and besides, candy will make your teeth rot out and drop into your soup."

They considered that for a moment, then giggled.

"You heard about Annie Flunk?" This from Georgetta Liana.

"Annie Flunk's apartment got flooded last night!" Doreen was not to be outdone.

"Flooded! That's too bad. Probably her water heater burst." We had three heaters go bad last week.

"Shit, it warn't no water heater. It was Billy Goochen an' Romeo Curtis an' Go-Boy Mansfield. They stuck a water hose into Annie's mail slot and turned on the water!"

"NO!"

Both little girls bobbed their heads up and down, pleased that they had been the first to bring me this delicious news. They galloped away as I parked my car.

Even before I unlocked my office door I heard the insistent ringing of the telephone. I knew who it would be.

Annie Flunk's voice was hoarse but loud. In X-rated words she informed me how she was going to redesign the three boys' anatomy. It was very graphic. I finally screamed back at her. "Don't you dare do anything! I'll be right down." Annie had told me that she had the three youngsters captured and that they were under control. Her control!

I took my keys and a note pad and started down Flood Road, rounded the curve, and went deeper into the project.

Even in mid-February the large shade trees still had leaves. They dripped with night mist waiting for the sun to burn off the moisture. The project looked deserted. The children who went to school were already on their way. The mothers who didn't bother to get their children ready slept until noon. There was an eeriness about the place, as if a huge hand had scooped up all the people, leaving only hulks of dwelling places, like ghost ships.

My footsteps crunched gravel on the cracked sidewalk. The sound hung suspended like a sigh about to become a scream. I started to cross the parking lot toward Annie's place when a rock crashed at my feet. I jumped back and looked around to see where it had come from. Nobody around. I started walking again. Another rock. This time I caught a head ducking down inside one of the partly demolished cars at one end of the parking lot.

I hesitated. Good sense or maybe lack of courage decided me. I made a cautious detour around the rear of the car, up to the driver's side. The person inside was ready to heave another rock from the passenger side. I reached in and collared the neck before the hand let fly its missile.

It was the dark-haired girl who had sassed me the day before, the one who told about the holes left by the cut-off ears.

"What do you think you're doing?" The child squirmed; she released her hold on the rock. It fell dully to the ground.

"Who wants to know?"

"You almost hit me."

"So? If you can't cut it, get your ass outta here."

"Why aren't you in school?"

"Because I ain't."

I had let go of her and she shriveled into the far corner of the front seat. She leaned against the ripped side panels. The grime on her cheeks had a clean path down to her chin from old tears.

"What are you doing out here? It's too damp for the way you're dressed."

"Yeah! Well, I been here all night."

She looked very young, very thin in her washed-out cotton blouse and thready boy's jeans. And very old. A whisper of womanhood showed through her movements. There was a sweet roundness to her cheek, a hidden gloss under her dirty tangled hair.

"What's your name?" I asked.

"None of your goddamned business!"

She moved quickly, heaved herself up and through the broken car window, barely missing the jagged edges. I watched as she ran barefoot, weaving around scattered trash, tin cans, dog droppings. Her black hair was a bouncing dot as she disappeared around the end of the building.

I felt bitter. Another one of the army of stay-at-homes! Every day small groups of youngsters roamed the project when they should have been in school. Instead, they made trips to the liquor store to exchange empty pop bottles for candy or potato chips or more pop, or to shoplift. As I continued toward Annie's apartment, I decided to contact the schools. Maybe this truancy could be stopped.

5

Annie Flunk lived in Building #87. Since each apartment building looked like the next one—square, graffitied, and bleak—brass numbers were imbedded in the second-story corners to identify one structure from the other.

I passed the playground, a sorry pit of scuffed ground and seatless swings, their chains dangling like the entrails of some mechanical monster. The jungle gym had no crossbars. The slide was tilted and twisted for instant disaster. Two dogs were relieving themselves in the sandbox as I passed.

A handful of toddlers squatted around a point of interest. They jumped away when I walked over. It was a dead cat. I shooed them away and found a cardboard box to cover it until a maintenance man could dispose of the body.

Two buildings over I reached Annie Flunk's door. I pounded on it, to make myself heard over the loud stereo music blasting from the next apartment. Finally, after much rapping and yelling, Annie let me in. From the kitchen I could see past her into the living room. Three boys sat on a red crushed-velvet couch. Two of them had their pants around their ankles; the third was crying noisily and rubbing the snot away with one hand.

"There seems to be a problem," I began diplomatically.

"You bet your sweet ass. Come right in, Miz Bentwood. You is finding yourself in the home of Mrs. Marcus Welby an' you is about to witness a miracle of medicine in Annie Flunk's Medical Center!" Annie smiled broadly and wickedly; her gold tooth glittered in the darkened living room. I followed her. The small, square room was crowded: A large color TV occupied one wall, components of a stereo were on top of the TV, and speakers were set on the shelf above. A companion chair to the red velvet couch faced the window. A bulbous amber-glass hanging lamp dipped on linked chains over an ornate Spanish-type coffee table. As Annie waved her arms at the three youths, I saw a butcher knife in her hand. Mattie had told me about Annie and her fondness for knives. She had warned me that Annie used them on people if riled up.

"I sure hope you boys is ready to give up tom-cattin' for ever an' ever, 'cause old Annie Flunk is goin' to make you pure from here on in."

Annie slapped the broad side of the knife against her buttocks as if they were a razor strap. I recognized the largest boy as Go-Boy Mansfield. He was almost fourteen, with a shag of white-blond hair over his forehead, pink cheeks, and an angelic expression. His specialty was stomping the smaller children as they crawled through a hole in the flood-control fence which was the shortcut to the liquor store across Grand Boulevard. Twice last week I had had frantic calls from mothers reporting that Go-Boy had robbed their kids when they had been sent to buy milk.

Go-Boy looked green enough to fit his name. He cupped his hands over his vital parts, encased in very dingy jockey shorts. In the curtain-drawn room, his face was ghostly. "She's crazy. What in hell's she think she's doing?" he said.

He shuffled his feet, entangled in his dropped jeans. I watched one hand creep downward and hook itself in a loop, ready to drag the pants up and cover his nakedness, when a wild whoop from Annie made Go-Boy panic. He fell back next to his buddy in crime, Billy Goochen.

Billy was ten but looked younger. His impish face, with an Irish grin, was difficult to associate with all the horror stories told about his deeds. His knobby knees were bruised in various shades and scabbed with cuts. Frightened, he still showed his defiance by banging his knees together, opening and closing his legs like a bellows. "You mess with my dick, Crazy Annie, an' my mama'll tell Tommy Gun. He'll whip your ass!"

"Mebbe so, young fellow, but when you go running home to your mama, you be holding your ass in your han'."

Billy stopped moving his legs, quickly pressed them tight as if to close the door to mayhem. He looked in my direction and kept his eyes on me as he answered Annie. "She won't let you mess with us. She'll call the cops, you start messing with us."

Annie twisted the knife like a screwdriver under the small upturned nose of the boy. "Be too late then. Your name is going to be Betty instead of Billy!" Annie liked that. She looked over at me to make sure I caught her joke.

"An' you . . ." Annie poked the knife at the third occupant of the sofa. The boy's black skin was shiny with sweat. He still had his pants on but under the sleazy white T-shirt his chest heaved with short, careful breaths. He bored into the far corner as if he hoped the shadows would absorb his blackness and make him invisible.

"Nigger boy . . . you are goin' to wish you been born a yeller dog, 'cause a yeller dog, he got a tail to put between his legs, an' you ain't going to even have a stump left!"

Annie reached across the coffee table, her left hand stretched toward the boy's modified Afro. Now I recognized him. It was Romeo, Freddie-O's twelve-year-old brother.

Romeo made the mistake of leaning forward, and Annie's man-sized hand nested in the boy's hair. He yelled with pain as she dragged him into a standing position. Like two dolls on a weather vane, the big woman and the boy rotated in an awkward dance. Annie sliced the air with her knife while she let the boy twist under her iron grip on his hair. He cried and cursed at the same time. The other two huddled together, still big-eyed, obviously glad attention was focused away from them.

To break the stalemate, I moved across the room; my footsteps sank into the shag rug, squishing wetly with each step. I had forgotten . . . the flood! The fiber carpet was instep-deep in water.

I looked toward the front door of the apartment. It led directly into the living room. A sliver of light showed where the metal mail slot had been ripped out from the paneled door. The inside of the door was water-stained, and a trickle of water oozed out from a section of limp garden hose dangling through the opening.

Go-Boy called out to me. His voice was brittle. "You better tell her to let us go. She got no proof we stuck the goddamn hose in her mail slot."

"Fat bitch, we shoulda shoved it up your ass." Billy got into the act.

Romeo was lucky. Annie dropped his head and advanced on the younger boy, her huge breasts swaying. She stabbed the air toward the sitting child. Annie cackled. The knife was held throat high. "Here comes Dr. Welby!"

"Shit! You look more like Wolfman!"

"All you mother-fuckers! When I get finished you never going to stick your cocks in a hole again!"

I got worried. One stumble or slip and blood would be mingled with the

---

30

water on the rug. Before I could act, Go-Boy sprang up and jammed the coffee table against Annie's legs. As she lost her balance, he poked his fingers into both her eyes. Now Annie screamed! She dropped the knife and covered her face. Boys and woman were shouting and swearing.

I bent over and picked up the knife. I wished I were a sword swallower. Instead, I ran over to the mail slot and poked it through; I heard it drop onto the cement porchway.

Annie stumbled to her oversized and overstuffed red velvet chair. Her flesh spilled onto the arm rests. Her mumbled curses were lost as she nursed her painful eyes. Now it was my turn to get tough.

Their tormenter out of commission, the three boys tried to run by me, but I blocked their path. "No, you don't! I'm not through with you!"

"Lady, get your ass outta my way. You want I should get Tommy Gun to whip yours?" Go-Boy was in top form again.

"Yeah, who do you think you are, po-lice lady? Huh?"

Billy and Romeo were crowding me.

"Move, lady!" Billy's "lady" meant "bitch."

It was now or never. To back down in Buena Vista was to be backed out. To save my neck I had to save face first. I took my stand.

"You guys are not leaving until you clean up the mess you made. Go-Boy, you and Romeo pick up the rug and hang it on the clothesline. Billy, get her mop and pail and sop up all the water on the floor. Then you all can sweep the dirt tracks from the kitchen floor and wash and wax it."

I hoped I looked ninety-three feet tall and dangerous. "Or . . ." I let the "or" drift on a laser beam of legal entanglements which Buena Vista kids knew meant a visit to juvie, and seventy-two hours of being "detained."

Billy poked a toe into the soaked rug, glanced over at the subdued Annie, then back at me. The youngest of the three, he was the leader. I could feel him weighing the evidence, the consequences, and the benefits of cooperation.

"What the hell, let's get the fuckin' rug out!"

They hustled. Go-Boy and Romeo moved the furniture, then dragged out the water-heavy carpet. Billy mopped and all of them waxed. Romeo even returned the knife to Annie. Their animosity disappeared as the satisfaction of accomplishment took over. Annie got into the spirit and, after the boys finished, she offered them store cookies and let them split two soft drinks.

Before they left, they promised to return and replace the dried-out carpet for her. Since it was almost noon now, Annie insisted I try some of her homemade chili. So, over a bowl of red beans and soda crackers crumbled like snowflakes in the pepper-hot food, I pumped Annie. "Annie, I keep hearing about a Tommy Gun. What about him?"

"Why you askin', Miz Bentwood?" Eyes down, cautious.

"Every time something happens . . . a fight . . . burglary . . . ripoff . . . sooner or later his name comes up. Like today. Even these boys use his name."

Annie took several spoonfuls of her chili, sprinkled more crackers. Decided to answer me. "It's kinda like this. Tommy Gun is one bad cat. He is a mess, you know what I mean, Miz Bentwood? He is a number-one double-trouble for women. Yes, ma'am! One big trouble. But then, he's one big pleasure, too!"

She smiled broadly, started to wink, didn't. Instead shoveled another mouthful of beans.

"Doesn't make sense." Did I sound offhand enough?

"It do if you know Buena Vista. See, this project . . . it's like a country . . . apart . . . with its own rules and laws. Now Tommy Gun could be likened to a chief, or mayor. Sometime the mayor do good, and sometime he do not so good. But messin' with them women is his own thing. That don't count on either side of the scorecard."

"Not even if he takes their money?"

"Could be Tommy Gun's got his reasons. One thing for sure, you need something done an' you get word to him, he delivers."

I took a wild guess. "Like Doug?"

Annie tilted her bowl up, scraped the sides with her spoon. The noise made goose-pimples on my arms. She raised one corner of her apron and wiped her mouth. I pretended to rescue the last few beans floating in the sauce, and crammed a cracker after them to neutralize the hot spices. Her tone changed. She said one word. "Maybe."

"You're saying that Tommy Gun had something to do with Doug getting stabbed."

"I'm not sayin' anything, an' you better not run your mouth off and say I did."

My usefulness and welcome were over. Annie Flunk wobbled the table as she pressed down on it and boosted herself out of her chair. I got up and waited as she undid the complicated lock arrangement.

"Be right smart of you to recall what I said about Buena Vista. About it havin' other kinds of ways."

I looked back once. She still stood at the door, watching.

32

6

The morning had gone quickly. It was afternoon before I started back into the project, this time down the Greentree Lane side. Betty Lou had no telephone, or I would have called to inquire how she was after yesterday's sad event. Few tenants had telephones; the extra expense was not allowed for in their welfare grants. This lack of instant communication made my position a training camp for long-distance walking. The few tenants who splurged kept the service until everyone in their parking lot had made all the out-of-state calls they wanted; then the original subscriber refused to pay the bill. Strangely, the telephone company cut off service but never picked up the instruments. The result was that each time a tenant moved out, the maintenance men delegated to clean and paint the apartment in anticipation of a new family ripped out the phone cords and dumped the telephones in the maintenance office. A huge crate held over two hundred tangled and chipped telephones in black and assorted custom colors. Alfred, one of the wittier maintenance men (who was also Starlet's Bitsy's father), joked to me one day as we both looked at the mess.

"Beats all, don't it, Miss Edith, this box here, with all dem ruined machines? Dey look jus' like this here project, don't it? All dem phones . . . all different colors mixed in together!"

On my lunch break, I bought a sack of oranges for Betty Lou's two other children, Joey and Dolly. The rumor was that each child had a different father, but I learned one never asked about parentage in Buena Vista. If a woman volunteered, OK. If not, keep your mouth shut!

I neared Betty Lou's building and was checking out the numbers to find the correct apartment when an accented voice called to me from an open doorway. "Hey, you! Lady!"

She was blond and pretty, about twenty-seven. Her hips were thrust forward as an admission of her sexuality. I turned and faced her.

"Ya, you! You got a minute?" A man's shirt was knotted under her breasts, cupping them loosely. Her middle was bare; her tight pants were low on her torso.

For an answer I walked over. She stepped aside and held the door open so I could enter first. Then she closed it behind her and moved toward the stove.

"Sit down, please, I fiz you some caffee into a mug." The accent was Slavic. "You da lady that's in charge?" It was a statement.

"Not exactly. Ben . . . Mr. Hamilton is the manager of the project."

"Huh! Manager! That man, that nothing! He shit in his pants when he zink he got to walk the project. He is . . . what you call a . . . jelly bean!"

"Fish," I corrected her.

"Ya . . . you right. That fellow is fish . . . cold fish."

I considered correcting her slang terms. Instead I looked around. The kitchen was spotless, curtains crisp, floor polished. Daisy-patterned Con-Tact paper was pasted on the cabinet doors and behind the open shelf where a row of shining glasses was lined up. A wash basket was piled high with neatly folded children's clothing. It was a pleasant room. The smell of the steaming coffee that she poured into a yellow mug relaxed me. I cupped my hands around its heat. I was unprepared for her next words.

"Listen, lady, ven zat cocksuckin' broad don't get offen my back, zer is going to be a murder around here!"

I stalled by taking a sip of the coffee. It went down like molten lava, bringing tears to my eyes. My hostess ignored my suffering. She sat down, pulled her chair knee to knee, and leaned her Marlene Dietrich features tissue-paper close to my face.

"Look, lady, I'm not makin' the foolin'."

"My name is Edith . . . Edith Bentwood. What's yours?" I wondered if my next line should be "Let me entertain you, let me make you smile." Still, Baby June I was not.

Her eyes short-circuited their anger; she softened her tone. "OK, so Bentwood, I tell you. Lisa Fritzle. I come from behind Iron Curtain. Maybe you can tell from my talking, uh? I been married wit a G.I., but son-of-a-beech, he dump me and go back to some jerky broad. Me an' my keeds, Janos and Eva, he forget about. Now I got two more, Lavinna Pearl and the leetle one, Jefferson . . . Jeffy we calls him. Dey gut keeds. No trouble . . . no trouble at all dey give me."

"That's good . . . great." I took a big swallow now. The coffee had cooled off.

"You bet your bottom dollar."

We sat quietly for a moment. Then Lisa gripped the edge of the dinette table. Her hands went board stiff. She started to tremble. "Lady, you got to help me. That lousy son-of-a-beech, that robber, that teef, that ass-chasing bastard. I git my hands on zem both . . . Tommy Gun and that whore . . . I keel them!"

The Holy Ghost again.

"What did he do?"

She was crying, wringing her hands, pacing her neat kitchen. "You believe me when I tell you? No, you find it impossible to believe. I can tell." She slammed herself back into the chair again, leaned over toward me. "He come to my house las' night and say, 'Don't forget, baby, on fifteen I come for the check!' Such nerve dat nigger have! Who he tink he dealing wit'? Some nigger broad?"

"What check are you talking about?"

"Der welfare check . . . what else check I get?"

"Why would Tommy Gun demand your welfare check?"

"Why? Because I throw him out when I find out he fuckin' dat bitch Yvonne."

I finished the mug of coffee before I answered. "The easiest thing to do is the next time he comes around asking for the money, tell him no," I advised.

"You keedin'? You must be crazy . . . tell Tommy Gun no? You tink I vant my toothes kicked out? He keel me, for sure Tommy Gun send over someone to beat me up."

"Then you call the police. No man can beat you up and get away with it."

The terror drained; cunning replaced it. Behind her long lashes was a cold, impersonal look. She pulled back, teetered on the back legs of her chair.

"Oh, no, lady. You don't catch me rat-finkin' on my man. I take care of my business my vey, ya understood? My vey. You lousy government people, juz like the Communists, snoopin', alveys snoopin'."

Lisa jumped up and yanked the kitchen door open.

"So now you go, huh?"

She held the door for me. I passed her and went out. Just before she slammed it shut, she yelled after me. "Listen, lady, you find dat bitch Yvonne dead, don't come lookin' for me, you hear?"

I wanted to shake that scene out of my mind. What was it all about? Did Lisa want protection from Tommy Gun or not? I decided to make a concentrated effort to find this superman, this mythical black man, this Tommy Gun who held so many of the women tenants in his pants pocket, along with their welfare checks.

I located Betty Lou's apartment and found her looking at a sympathy card that Bernice had sent over with a maintenance man. Almost illiterate, she asked me to help her read it. The front had a bluebird sitting on a branch with apple blossoms. Musical notes were escaping from its open red beak. "Sorry" was written out in an escalating arc. Betty Lou stood the card up on the television next to a sack of corn chips. The funeral would be back in Arkansas, she told me as she took the oranges from my hand.

"Doug had a brother back there. The police called him and he said to send Doug back home."

I was glad she was so calm.

"Are you going too?"

"Shit, no! You think I got the bread to blow on something like that? Not on your life. Besides, I got Joey and Dolly."

On cue the two children ran into the apartment. Joey was kindergarten age and Dolly was toddling. Her diapers were sopped and Betty Lou placed the little girl on the couch as she changed her. Dolly kicked out and hit the swollen belly of her mother. Joey reached for the chips and sat contentedly on the floor eating.

"This will make it hard on you, won't it? With Doug gone . . ."

"I guess. In a way. He was a good guy, you know what I mean, Miss Bentwood? He kinda protected me."

Dolly twisted herself down and ran over to get her share of the chips from Joey. Betty Lou picked up the half-finished baby sweater I had helped her make. She knitted quietly—stabbed the yarn back and forth as she worked the needles in and out.

"That's why he was killed, you know. He took up for me."

"No. No, I didn't know." I know I sounded shocked.

Slowly and very carefully, she picked her words. They sounded like a recitation—like a foreign language one learned without understanding the full impact.

36

"See, Doug didn't like niggers, coming from Arkansas like he did . . . and you know how it is around here. Those black bastards think every white woman's got the hots to be laid by them. Well, last Fourth of July, that was before Doug went up for that bum rap, a bunch of us here in the parking lot had us a party. Beer and stuff, and us women made a barbecue. It was cool. Everything was movin' nice and easy and we were getting ready to get it on a little, dance and . . ."

Her voice got hard. "Then these two black fellows come up an' they seen we had drinks an' were dancing. They were strangers, or so we thought, from outside the project. Doug and me were dancing and one of the blacks cut in on us. He come between Doug and me and shoved Doug and grabbed me. I smelled trouble an' I told Doug it was all right with me—the guy just wanted to dance an' I told Doug to leave it alone . . . you know . . . cool it. It didn't mean nothin' to me, but Doug being from Arkansas took exception and it got to be a big hassle. The pigs come an' bust it up. They hauled Doug away because someone got hurt. One of the black guys got in the way of a flying bottle and it ripped his head open. Doug being on parole already got sent back for six months' county time."

Dolly was crying because Joey had kicked her in the face. Betty Lou leaned over to pull Joey away from his sister. I waited. I knew there was more to come . . . more about Tommy Gun. I was correct.

"When Tommy Gun heard about how Doug put the nigger boy down, he let it out as the dude was a cousin of his. Everyone black is a cousin or brother . . ." Her voice drifted off.

"So Tommy Gun arranged for Doug to get killed." It was a statement from me.

"Yvonne, she's Tommy's woman now, she told me last night it was meant to be a warning, but the knife went too deep."

Deep enough to end a life, I wanted to yell. I watched the pointed needles click another row of yellow wool onto the small garment before I spoke again. "Do you know who did it?"

"Maybe."

"Tell me."

The look she gave me was half pity, half disbelief. "You must be kidding, Miss Bentwood. Don't you know yet that talking out of turn can get you messed up? Messed up bad! You forgetting I've got Joey and Dolly to look out for and now this one . . ." She looked down at her middle.

Suddenly she smiled broadly. "At least I'll get a bigger welfare check as soon as the baby gets here—that's one good thing about this whole deal.

7

Albert Lottman had neglected to mention the other duties of my position the day he sat back in his walnut-paneled office, letting his cigar ash grow to two inches, and in a kindly voice asked me if I could bring Culture to the tenants of Buena Vista. He forgot to mention tiptoeing among dog droppings, dodging knives, mediating between murderers, or retrieving stolen guns, cars, welfare checks, and assorted household furnishings.

After the first three weeks I resigned myself to promoting one main program—helping the tenants stay alive. Maybe it wasn't Culture with a capital C, but it did demand cleverness to the nth degree. It also demanded the stamina of a Rams football tackle, the deviousness of the CIA, and the iron stomach of the Bionic Woman.

Lottman had also forgotten to mention Ernestine Trotmartin.

Besides bringing gusty winds down from the snow-covered Southern California mountains, March roared into my life not like a lion, but with a tigress! Her name was Ernestine Trotmartin.

Shortly after I started at Buena Vista, Ben dragged me into his office and after fortifying himself with a fresh licorice ball told me about the Terror —Ernestine Trotmartin.

"She's an awful woman . . . nothing but gutter talk. Dangerous . . . mean. She's got one son, who should be chained to a battleship and dragged out to sea. They call him Tank, because he runs over everyone, just like his mother. Plus she's the chairman of the Action For Tenants."

"So?" I said. After all, Mattie had mentioned her that first day, but so far she was still as invisible as the elusive Tommy Gun.

"So watch your step. She's in Oregon right now because her father is dying, but when she gets back . . ." His voice faded in sepulchral tones.

"When she gets back . . . ?" I encouraged him to continue.

"She's a troublemaker. You'll see. She called a rent strike about a year ago and caused us a lot of problems."

"So do most of the tenants," I reminded him. "What's so special about her trouble?"

"For one thing, you weren't supposed to be hired unless the Action For Tenants group approved. That means Ernestine. She runs the show."

"Well, I'm here now, so she can't do anything about it."

"Except that under the agreement and guidelines of the Housing and Urban Development Department, the tenants have a right to have a voice about who is hired in their project. And you weren't approved by Ernestine."

Ben made it sound as if I brought every virus since the Black Plague into Buena Vista.

"When she gets back, I'll meet her and work things out."

"Good luck." That was all Ben said.

Since I had started work at Buena Vista, none of the tenants to whom I mentioned Ms. Trotmartin seemed anxious to discuss her personality or philosophy. When I mentioned the Action For Tenants and asked when it met, either silence or some offhand remark passed for an answer. What was obvious was that Ernestine held the reins of the Buena Vista wagon in the matter of housing policy by the tenants.

The first of March I came to work early and was in the main office to check on some tenant addresses before the official opening of my social service office at nine o'clock.

A manic pounding on the front door shook the paper shade which covered the top glass section. The violence indicated an emergency, some disastrous event to a tenant, who needed help immediately. I ran over, snapped up the shade, and unlocked the door.

A large, light-skinned black woman was beating on the glass. Dressed in a wildly printed caftan, she moved her wide-sleeved arms in a flying-bat movement. Before I could properly let her inside, she knocked the door out of my hand, shoved me aside, plowed over to the counter, palm-banged on the top, and shouted her question. "Where the fuck is that goddamned manager?"

She kept slapping on the scarred wood counter as I walked past her, around the end, and finally stood before her, face to face. The pounding stopped. Grayish eyes squinted angrily; her bust was half over the dividing barrier, her arms spread out, braced on the edge. That's when I saw her left hand—the fingers twisted and stubbed, gnarled by fire. The skin on the forearm above was scarred in puckered ridges . . . evidence of a childhood accident. I noticed she had great teeth. A thin scar started from her left ear and curved around under her chin. Wiry reddish hair escaped from a skinned-back ponytail. Only the broad flaring nostrils and mocha skin stamped her background as integrated.

I knew whom I was facing.

So did she.

"So! So! You're the fink the goddamned Housing Agency sent down here? Thought they could screw around while I was away? Let me tell you right off, you better get your ass outta Buena Vista before someone buys your travel ticket! And it won't be to no Holiday Inn."

"I don't think we've met. I'm Edith Bentwood."

I hoped I sounded like Grace Kelly; I wished I was Dracula's wife and could aim for her jugular.

"I don't care a shit who you are. I know *what* you are! You're illegal! You took this job away from a tenant and I'm going to make damn sure that the community boycotts you!" She dismissed me with her eyes and looked past my head. "I want to see Ben Hamilton."

Steady there, I told myself. Two can play the game. "May I have your name?"

She caught my verbal Frisbee and tossed it back. "My name?"

I stepped back, half expecting flames to shoot from her nostrils. Instead the Lane Bryant Dragon Lady bellowed, "My name?"

"Yes, may I say who is here?"

"Who's here! *I'm* here! Ernestine Trotmartin, chairman of the Action For Tenants, that's who's here! And you better get your ass in there and tell that sorry excuse for a manager that I'm not letting any two-bit fuckin' Housing Agency keep me waiting!"

Ben Hamilton was at a central office meeting that morning with the Board of Advisors and Albert Lottman, the head of the agency.

"Mr. Hamilton isn't in this morning. He's at a meeting in Los Angeles. I'm sorry, Mrs. Trotmartin."

"Sorry? You will be before it's over, and so will the whole damn mother-fuckin' bunch. Bastards!"

"May I take a message." My jaw ached with correctness.

"Goddamn right you can take a message!"

Her fist hit the counter. The slam made all the "Opportunities for Senior Citizens" pamphlets quiver like green leaves. From some place in the folds of her garment, Ernestine pulled out a paper. It had black letters in bold writing. She threw it at me. It flew across and fell down behind the counter.

I waited until she yanked the door open with her good hand, stormed out, and slammed it before I bent over to pick up her message.

Gloria and Mattie had been in the back maintenance office having their morning coffee. They came up as I was reading the flyer.

"I heard that old bitch blowing off steam. What is she up to now?" Gloria walked up behind and read over my shoulder.

ALL TENANTS

LET'S GET OUR SHIT TOGETHER!

STAND UP FOR YOUR RIGHTS

STOP PAYING RENT

WE DEMAND NEW STOVES

DECENT PLAYGROUND EQUIPMENT

BETTER POLICE TREATMENT

WE GOT TOO MUCH BROKEN GLASS

TOO MUCH DOG SHIT

TOO MUCH CRIME

WE DEMAND JOBS

WE DEMAND ILLEGALLY EMPLOYED PEOPLE BE FIRED

GET THE RAT-FINK OUT

COME TO THE A.F.T. OFFICE

SEE ERNESTINE TROTMARTIN, CHAIRMAN

"She's after you, that's for certain," Mattie sighed. She had learned to like me.

"Bitch! Someone should shoot her!" Gloria threw the paper onto Mattie's desk.

I picked it up and placed it on Ben Hamilton's desk before I returned to my own office.

The traffic into the main project office increased after tenants began to trust me and ask my help. My corner of the room had no privacy and I soon discovered that most of the people were paranoid when it came to making complaints about their neighbors. With good cause! Complaining often resulted in fire-bombings, beatings, or slashed tires. Since the parade of tenants frightened Ben anyway, he moved me into an empty two-bedroom apartment, with living room, kitchen, bath, a front entrance, and a back door.

42

While glad to get rid of me and my "nuts," as Gloria put it, all three women expressed concern for my well-being.

"I wouldn't be caught dead sitting alone in any apartment in this project," Mattie warned.

"Oh, do be careful, dear! You never know what these dear, dear, dear people might do if they get angry!" Bernice happily saw disaster in everything.

"The hell you don't! Tell her about that welfare worker that got beaten up in here last year. Go on, tell her!" Wigged Gloria was in a dark-haired Elizabeth Taylor that day.

"Now, Gloria, we don't want to worry our Edith, do we?" Bernice was aching for me to find out.

"She was more than beaten up!" Mattie blitzed me with her ghoulish eye makeup. "Crippled her, that's what! Caught her as she was leaving some slut she was investigating as a welfare fraud case. I heard the woman resigned when she got out of the hospital. Heard she's still in a wheelchair."

When Hank Garrison suggested the extra telephone to Ben as an instant means of communication with the main office, I didn't resist. It was a dialless instrument. The slightest tipping of the receiver would make it ring in the main office, signaling trouble. I also used it for direct communication with the office girls, much like an intercom system, without tying up my outside line.

When Ben returned from his meeting in Los Angeles, he rang me on my hot-line and insisted I come over immediately to see him.

When I walked into his office, he closed the door grimly behind me. Ernestine's announcement was still centered on his desk. He beat the flyer with both fists, groaned, then buried his head in his hands.

"It's too much! She's starting up again . . . agitating. Getting the tenants to withhold their rent . . . causing trouble. Edie, that woman is impossible!"

"But she's right about some things, like the playground stuff and the broken glass."

"It's her fault that we don't have the playgrounds improved. She won't OK the purchase order."

"Why does she have to approve a purchase order?"

"The Feds . . . HUD . . . the Department of Housing and Urban Development demands we have tenant input and OK before a public housing project can make decisions. If they only knew what a headache they cause us! They're safe in Washington. It's us who have to cope with all their dumb regulations."

"I still don't understand—even if those are the conditions, why won't she OK the playground equipment?"

"Because she's crazy! She says that the price is off and that someone is getting a cut. She says *she* can get more for *our* money. All she really wants to do is make trouble."

"Is someone getting a kickback?"

"How should I know? When you're dealing in millions, who knows? Or cares if someone gets a little on the side? Besides, I don't want to get mixed up in that kind of stuff. You get too nosy and first thing you know they abolish your job."

Ben popped another licorice ball into his mouth. He had learned that I didn't care for them. I reread the flyer.

"Most of the tenants accept me, so I'm not worried about her threats, and I can't believe tenants would take a chance of being kicked out of their homes. They'll pay their rent." Like a mother, I patted down Ben's fear.

"Don't count on it. She's got some of the people fooled and the others are afraid."

"Afraid?"

"You heard me. Afraid. She threatens tenants who oppose her orders. They get fire-bombed, robbed, have their car windows smashed, get beaten." Ben played with his key ring.

"I don't believe that," I said. "She may be a thorn in the Housing Agency's side, but that's blackmail. It's coercion. Conspiracy. It's against the law. It's criminal!"

"Wait and see."

"How can one woman do all those things?" I scoffed.

"She's got influence—friends—inside and outside Buena Vista. And she's got Tommy Gunther Matthews. They have an 'arrangement.' "

Tommy Gun again. I saw my chance to tie loose ends together. "How come this Tommy Gunther is so powerful in Buena Vista? Every time a crime is committed or solved, every time something happens, somewhere along the way this man's name comes up?"

Ben Hamilton rocked back in his chair, unpeeled three more licorice balls, and stuffed them into his mouth. He crunched up the papers, crammed them into his shirt pocket.

"Forget about Tommy Gun, like I do. I forget about him."

"That's OK for you. You sit in here, but I go into the project. I hear about all the complaints the tenants have. I can't find out where this guy holes up."

Ben rocked faster and faster in his swivel chair. If it had taken off and shot through the ceiling I wouldn't have been surprised.

"Listen . . . take my advice. Don't try to find him. Let well enough alone."

"Well enough for you, but not for the women who get robbed of their welfare money, and not for the babies he makes."

"That's none of your business. Matthews is trouble for anyone who interferes. He's power. He's the connection."

"Connection to what?"

"Just do your eight hours and go home. Like me. I put in my time and then leave. It's a job, a paycheck. That's all."

I walked out.

That evening I watched a family comedy on TV. The Dior-dressed teenager argued with her executive-type father in a split-level home just as her mother returned from winning an election for state senator. Younger brother came in dripping wet from the swimming pool to announce he was tired of making gold records with his sixth-grade band. To the soundtrack of uproarious laughter the show faded.

The commercial with screaming singers offered hamburgers with or without pickles, and a perverted store clerk squeezed toilet paper instead of a woman's behind.

The next show could have used that squeezed toilet paper. Four feather-boaed females jerked in spastic contortions as the camera dissolved and sank into the limpid eyes of the swishie male balladeer. I turned down the sound and watched the pictures and people move across the screen.

The swallow of instant chocolate was lukewarm. I put the mug down on the lamp table. Flecks of undissolved grains floated on the pallid surface of the chocolate. Ben Hamilton's colorless voice replayed itself. His words— a job . . . a paycheck—was that all? He was wrong.

They were all wrong! Hank Garrison, Ben, Mattie, Gloria, Bernice. Well, maybe Bernice had a heart. But still.

The television screen showed a dialogue taking place among the star, a toupeed, past-tense cowboy actor, and a flat-chested, gaunt-eyed women's lib comedienne. The camera turned on rows of laughing people. Diffused kliegs made crosses over the heads of bowling-ball faces.

Before me was unreality.

Reality was the project . . . the people. The project boiled with life, however foul, however criminal. That was where it was at. And I was part of it.

I cut off the television, carried the chocolate into the kitchen, and dumped it. I turned off the living room light. In the dark I went over to the sliding door that opened onto my narrow balcony. I watched the moving lights of the passing cars and, farther away, the moving ocean. Carnival lights, meant to camouflage the oil islands, bounced on the cresting waves. The chill wind of the March night fluttered the ninon curtains. Midnight rang from a nearby church. The next second would be the new day. I made a commitment: I would stop looking under my own pillow. I would be the tooth fairy for others.

I pulled the drapes and shut out loneliness.

8

Southern California has no spring. One day is dreary with fog-stacked mornings and evenings and the next day sparkles in cartoon colors. March 15 was a picture-postcard day. I turned on the gas wall-heater in my office to dispel the overnight cold. Next I checked over my notes from the day before to see which "emergency" could be delayed so that the "critical" would get first priority.

A thunder-roll rat-a-tatted on the front office door. A rattle of the door-knob, and Gussie McClure shuffled into view, blocking my back office entrance. She was dressed in sapphire blue stretch pants that reached only to mid-calf, topped by a shabby pink satin quilted bedjacket left unbuttoned over her Twiggy chest. Her dirt-cracked feet wobbled in thirty-nine-cent zoris (a slab of rubber with straps for toes); with her Modigliani features, she reminded me of a racehorse gone berserk.

Gussie churned her arms, waving a child's sand pail as if flagging a train. "That does it, Miss Edith, that does it! I've had it!"

"Come on, Gussie, sit down. What's wrong?"

"Now you know, Miss Edith, you know very well I go jogging every morning and that's when it happens. Every morning now for the last week it's happened."

She pitched the sand pail onto my desk. It tilted, and scraps of garbage and coffee grounds oozed onto my blotter. I sopped up the mess with a tissue as Gussie jogged around my office. When one of her zoris flew under the loveseat along the far wall (I had inherited it from the last tenant who lived in the place), Gussie stopped. As we struggled to move out the heavy furniture and reach the rubber footwear, Gussie aired her complaint.

For the past ten days some bastard had been messing with her garbage, Gussie wailed. Every night she put out her trash in an old, crunched-up garbage can. One morning she went out on her usual jogging run. When she returned home, someone had swiped her can.

"So I went out and bought a new one, orange plastic with a good tight cover." She stretched her arms wide and high to show me the size. Her new can was still outside by her back door when she started jogging around the project the next morning. When she returned, that can was gone. In its place was a smaller, drab-green, rusted and dented metal can.

"I went all around, Miss Edith, looked in every trash bin and couldn't find my new can. So I said, maybe I was mistaken, imagined it, you know, about buying a bigger orange one."

Gussie sat down on the loveseat and put her zori back on. I placed her sand pail on the floor and sat next to her on the loveseat. She continued in a puzzled voice. "Then that evening, I put my garbage in the green can, half deciding I *had* dreamed up the orange can. The same thing happened—when I got home from jogging the next morning, there it was again . . . gone from my kitchen door."

"You probably misplaced it, Gussie. Did you look by your front door?"

"Misplaced it? Miss Edith, you think I'm so stupid I forget where I put my can? Just listen. This time the green can was gone and this time I found a white diaper pail, with a cracked cover. So now I had a clue. I went all over this damn project looking for some girl who had a baby."

She stopped. Her fingers picked on a crust of food hardened on the knee of her capris. Her voice changed, became flat-sounding. "I had my suspicions. Someone was trying to drive me crazy. So the next night I decided to fool them. I got me a bag of dog shit an' filled the diaper pail. Just let that son-of-a-bitch rip me off again, he'd get a snoot-full."

Gussie's watery blue eyes pleaded for approval. I wanted to laugh at the situation. Instead, I nodded seriously.

"So now, this morning, what do I find? The diaper pail is gone and all I have left for my garbage is that cracked red sand pail! Do you think that's fair?"

Both of us looked at the bucket almost expecting it to rise up and defend itself as a special pail. Too bad it wasn't an Aladdin's lamp pail. Buena Vista could use a genie!

"I don't know what to tell you, Gussie. Maybe you got into an argument with a neighbor and this is a joke they're playing on you."

"The joke's going to be on them. I know what their game is. Tomorrow they'll take away my last bucket and then what will I do? See, they want to force me to eat my garbage—that's their plan."

Gussie became louder. Her mouth twisted. Her tongue repositioned her false teeth behind her thin lips. A new voice took over. "I'm going to contact the F.B.I. After that I'm going to order my men to beat hell out of those Commies."

"What men?" I watched her closely.

"In the attic, of course. The men who live in the attic." She leaned close and put her gnarled fingers up to her lips; her blue eyes shifted secretively from window to door. "You've got to promise you won't tell, but the men in the attic are getting ready to move! That's right, as soon as they get my signal, they're going to kill all the goddamn Commies in the project. That means Lisa Fritzle, and Alpha Washington, and Ben Hamilton. He's the ringleader, you know. He thinks he can fool me—tried to drug me with one of those candies he's always handing out, but I outsmarted him. I wouldn't take the paper off. I swallowed it whole with the paper on it and all."

I was dealing with a crazy.

Gussie suddenly lurched toward me and put her arm across my shoulder, rested her head on me. The leanness of her facial bones cut into me. She spoke differently—softer, cultured . . . Southern.

"Sometimes I think I'm going insane. I ask myself, 'What are you doing in this place, Augusta Kingston?' Back home in Virginia the name Kingston was hyphenated with 'God.' I grew up in money. Back home we say 'in money,' not 'with money.' There is a difference. We had stables and our horses won ribbons and I was presented at eighteen in a white dress made in Paris. I was pretty. My hair . . ." She stopped and pulled on the dangling dried yellow wisps.

I was silent. The picture of a pretty girl in a white dress took the place of this scarecrow next to me. I reached over and covered her other hand with mine. My touch was rewarded by a turned-up palm and a desperate handclasp. We sat entwined.

"I made a brilliant marriage. Brilliant."

We both saw the handsome young man.

"Then . . . something happened. I keep trying to remember what happened. He left me, you know, and took the children."

There was a long pause. Her fingers traced my hand.

"You understand now, don't you, why it upsets me so when my garbage can keeps disappearing. It's like it's happening all over again. Little by little, everything I had was taken away from me. The worst thing is that I can't remember what I had. If you don't remember what you lost, how do you know what to cry for?"

She sobbed now. Her arm across me tightened, drew me closer. I loved Gussie McClure. I told her so.

"I love you, Augusta Kingston McClure. I remember when you were the prettiest girl in Virginia."

She pulled away. I sat still, watched Gussie get up and shuffle to the door. The sand pail was held in both hands, tightly to her chest. She started to leave—turned.

"The slip was pink . . . and showed through. I mention it just in case you forgot that. And I was . . . the prettiest."

She left quietly, whispering her feet along on the old rug. I watched from my window as Gussie McClure jogged down Flood Road, the red bucket swinging from one hand, but I saw Augusta Kingston in her white dress, dancing in moonlight.

Gussie's traumatic experience of disappearing garbage pails was almost on a par with Gloria's disappearing rent collections. The long line of tenants that snaked from the rent-paying window in Gloria's cubicle dwindled that month to a handful. The less money she took in, the more she cussed and smoked. She finally bought an Afro and said she looked like Barbra Streisand. Even Mattie confided to me that she thought Gloria was going as batty as that crazy Gussie McClure.

"Next thing you know, she'll be wearing two wigs at once. Be a regular hairy ape!"

"More like King Kong!" I suggested. "I wouldn't be surprised if she didn't try to demolish every building in the project just to get back at the tenants."

"Fools, they're fools!" Mattie said. "If they think they can get the best of the Housing Agency, they're crazy too." She went back to her book work.

Ben Hamilton had another opinion when I went to talk to him. He told me that Albert Lottman was deeply distressed.

"He's deeply distressed . . . disappointed. In fact, he asked me to call Ernestine in and lay down the law." Ben looked pitifully at me. "You know how Ernestine is, how . . . loud!"

"What did he want you to say?" I asked.

"He expects me to tell her . . . warn her . . . demand! He wants me to make her call off the rent strike." With that, Ben collapsed.

"Well?"

"I can't do that. Why, she never even gives me a chance to talk. She's always hollering. Maybe it would be better if a woman . . . if you . . . You're always saying you can handle the tenants—so here's your chance to prove it!" Ben half begged, half dared me.

So far Ernestine and I had avoided each other. Like two dogs after the same bone, we carefully circled each other without creating any actual confrontation. Remarks she made about my ability, honesty, and ancestry were tattletaled to me by other tenants. I knew that the residents of Buena Vista wanted a head-on, no-holds-barred fight. Well, maybe this was the occasion to challenge her position. I left Ben's office without making a commitment, except to say I'd let him know. It came without my having any say-so about it.

The matter of playground equipment had started before I came to Buena Vista. Ernestine's demands about decent areas for the project children were not unreasonable. The play-designated sections *were* disasters. Ben's explanation of why no improvements had been made threw the blame directly on Ms. Trotmartin's fleshy shoulders. The trouble was that she effectively shrugged it off.

I was in a shocked state twice that week. The first shock came when I made a trip into the project in answer to a terse telephone call predicting instant disaster to the "shit-faced slut" who dumped her "shitty washwater" over the caller's dog, Poodles! I knew Poodles to be a leg-lifting, urine-yellow, runny-eyed pest. In fact, not long before Poodles had nipped me as I passed on one of my rounds. Most of the dogs in the project were on good terms with me: Cats and dogs found me a sucker for their wistful eyes and grateful responses to my petting. Cutting across Greentree Lane toward the trouble spot, I passed one of the playground areas in the project. I stopped, stunned!

A conglomeration of brightly enameled play equipment was anchored in concrete foundation posts—complicated and intriguing jungle gyms, slides, seesaws, swings, along with whimsical free-form animal shapes with openings for children to crawl in and out of. It was a child's paradise!

Finally! I felt like crowing! Now let's see Ernestine shoot her mouth off about lack of good faith on the part of Albert Lottman and the Housing Agency! Here was the proof. I continued to Poodles's master's pad feeling very smug.

My smugness lasted two days. The third morning I got my second shock. As I pulled up to my social service center, a frantic Ben Hamilton tore toward me, so fast I almost ran him down. When I got out of the car, he tugged at me to follow him. Incoherently, he sputtered, moaned, and, if it's possible to gnash one's teeth, well, Ben did! Expecting at least a massacre of one hundred, I stumbled after him. He led me to the playground area, this one on Flood Road.

Disaster! Either a bomb had fallen during the night, or some mad sculptor had revenged himself on society. All that remained was a twisted mass of pipes, tumbled-over structures, ripped metal from the slides, swing chains wrapped around and through the animal shapes as tug-lines. Ruts of car tracks showed where the forms had been ripped off their foundations and cracked apart. Added insult was that the entire ground was flooded to create a gigantic mud puddle. To complete the picture, two very small children played happily in the mud.

"My God!" I managed.

"No," said Ben. "Ernestine."

"That's impossible . . . one woman . . . do all this?" I waved at the scene. "And why? What in holy hell would make her want to destroy the very thing that she's been bitching about?"

"To show us . . . Albert Lottman . . . me . . . you. Let us know her power. She's got a regular army—mob—she controls. She and . . . that Tommy Gun." His voice was sad as he wiped his bald head.

I was sad, too, but more—mad.

"OK, Ben, you still want me to tell Ernestine to knock off the rent strike? Well, watch me take on that fu——"

"Hold it, Edith," Ben interrupted. "Don't take on the gutter ways of these scum, or let them drag you into their mud. It's easy to let it happen. I fight against it all the time. It's not in my nature . . . to change things." His expression was odd. For a moment I wanted to ask him what he meant. The moment passed. He was right. It was a temptation to return tit for tat.

"I won't, Ben. I'll remember I'm a lady . . . or at least trained to be one!" I tried to make a joke, to cheer him. Suddenly I liked Ben very much.

That afternoon I invaded the Ernestine's holy of holies. I walked across Flood Road to the building that held the Action For Tenants office. It was an apartment the same size as my office space and had been given to the tenants' organization for their headquarters. Ernestine could usually be found there, behind a desk in one of the bedrooms turned into an office.

I knocked to be polite but shoved the unlocked door open immediately and barged into the front room. A few tenants were lounging on the tattered chairs and couch. I recognized them as Ernestine's cronies. Their faces as I walked past and into Ernestine's area expressed blank shock at my appearance.

Ernestine had a mug of coffee in her hand as I walked in on her. Her surprise showed by the few drops that spilled as she brought it to her mouth. To her credit, she calmly drank the coffee down first. Her eyes bored into me until she finished. She carefully positioned her mug on a trivet, then spoke.

"What the hell do you want, honky?"

"I want to talk to you about: one—the rent strike, and two—the playground equipment . . . or what's left of it after you and your criminals got through with it!"

"You keep your goddamn ass offa my pisshole or you won't have a job or an ass or be enjoyin' very good health for long!"

"Are you threatening me?"

"Are you callin' me a criminal?"

She got up, shoved her chair backward. It tipped and crashed. I felt, rather than saw, the tenants crowd in the doorway. They watched silently.

"If the shoe fits?" I crooned.

Toe to toe.

"Let me tell you something, smartass: That playground crap that fool Lottman crammed down our throats is illegal! Us tenants are supposed to have a say-so in approvin' whatever goes on in Buena Vista. It's in the agreement after the last rent strike. It's a contract that's official from the government HUD office and it says the Action For Tenants group gotta sign their OK. And I never signed any OK on that kid stuff—so that makes it all illegal!"

"What's the difference? Who do you hurt? So you didn't OK it, so what? The kids in the project are the losers, not you or Lottman. The kids!" I yelled as loud as she did.

"You know why Lottman passed over the AFT? Over me? I'll tell you. We were the last project to sign, 'cause I held up the deal—the fuckin' crooked deal. Know who got the two-hundred-and-fifty-thousand-dollar order, at fifty-three thousand a crack for each of the five projects under Old Bert's agency?"

She came toward me, her index finger pointed at my chest. She prodded. As she continued talking, Ernestine poked me backward, out of her office, back into the front room where the others had hastily retreated. "His buddy! Some prick—Gregory! That's who got the contract for over a quarter of a million dollars."

"That's ridiculous! How do you know? Can you prove it?"

Could it be true? My mind jackrabbit-jumped back to Ben's words about "getting a cut." Who was Gregory?

"And that's not all." She stopped short. "Shit, no, I can't prove it

. . . but I know what I'm sayin' is so. Someday, someone will come along with enough guts and brains to stomp out those vermin—that's all they are —sitting big-assed on their cocks, getting rich off us poor folks. They got fancy lawyers and crooked politicians to cover up for them. Someday, maybe someone will come along . . ."

Her passion simmered to a murmur. This calmer Ernestine encouraged me to broach the subject of the rent strike.

"The rent strike you're proposing will bring more trouble to everyone," I began. "Mr. Lottman is very concerned about what's going on in Buena Vista. Maybe if you and he got together and you submitted your grievances, some kind of deal could be worked out. Compromise . . . you understand?"

Ernestine recovered. She was Tiger Lady again. Fangs bared, she snarled, "Fuck you! Who you think you are—Dear Abby? You come waltzin' in here with your stinkin' nose in the air, and your prissy puckered ass-lips and Big Mama attitude, an' think you're hot shit? Well, that's jus' what you are—SHIT!" She screamed now. "Get your mother-fuckin' ass out of MY office!"

I had taken a bite out of a green apple . . . and besides getting a sour taste, I'd left my teeth stuck in it. I had struck out with Ernestine in a big way now. I struggled to save whatever face I could. I spoke sternly. "I'm very busy, so I'll have to go, but I'll arrange free time for you whenever you are ready to discuss this matter again."

I ducked out quickly.

My report to Ben Hamilton omitted the accusations Ernestine had made against the Housing Agency. The rent-strike situation was a stalemate, Ben conceded. He thanked me for trying, but I left him too depressed to unwrap his usual licorice ball.

9

After Carl and I parted, I had to get accustomed to my mail being addressed to Edith Bentwood instead of Mrs. C. Bentwood. Lonely moments brought fleeting regrets, guilt. I played the game of "what if." What if I had shown more interest when Carl explained his theory of forcing oil out of sand. He spoke about creating caverns underground, allowing the oil to seep into them. Perhaps if, on the field trips we made into the desert lands of Texas, I had not complained about the sand sifting into my shoes . . . I hated the metal rods plunging into the ground. The pulsating grinding of the pumps appeared obscene to me as they bore into the earth—Mother Earth. I was the earth and I was being robbed—left empty, unfulfilled.

That night in bed, listening to the zinging buzz of the air-conditioner in the small town's only motel, Carl and I had made love. Later, lying apart with the clammy stagnant air drying our sweaty bodies, I told Carl I wanted to have a child.

What if . . . ? What if we had made a child that night? What if Carl hadn't made a joke out of my plea? He said a child wasn't on his drawing board yet. What if the days hadn't become long and meaningless, the nights strangers to intimacy? The only touch between us happened as we reached for the salt at the same moment. What if my dreams, my need to love, my desire for a child had been transmitted to another woman? Perhaps the child of my loneliness had been born to another. Could I recognize it? Would there ever be a coming together?

My second encounter with the dark-haired girl, the day she stoned me, had left me disturbed and curious. As I walked my rounds in Buena Vista following up complaints, carrying messages, or checking the vacant apartments for squatters, I caught glimpses of her. Always dressed in odd combinations, always grimy, always uncombed, she would watch me. Like a wild animal stalking a prey, she would taunt me with her presence. When I called to her, she disappeared. I wanted to find out her name, who her mother was. I asked other children, but my description brought only blank stares. Which dark-haired, dirty, eleven-year-old girl did I mean? It nagged at me and annoyed me that I could not reach this child.

Therefore, when I saw a group of children playing around the steps leading to the office entrance one day, I was surprised to see her remain as I approached.

There she was: matted hair, black eyes, a soiled boy's shirt, ripped bell-bottoms, bruised and bloody toes, a dirty face, and her usual filthy mouth. She was standing on the top of the broad concrete steps and greeted me by throwing an empty whiskey bottle past me against the sidewalk. It broke with an explosion, scattering glass which barely missed my legs.

My insides contracted and expanded like a traveling snake. My instincts were as deadly; my common sense took over. Don't blow! I told myself. Control! Remember your Advanced Psychology II.

"You threw a bottle," I stated.

"Prove it!" Bloody Toe said.

"You were angry, so you threw a bottle." I plowed along.

"You're crazy, lady!"

"An action like that could cause physical injuries."

"Yeah, prove it!"

She looked uncertain. I tried again. "Broken glass can cut feet, and you have no shoes on."

"Mind your own damned business."

"You should be in school."

"You some spy for the lousy school? You go tell that fuckin' principal I hate his crappy school."

She stood defiantly, her hands resting on either side of her thighs, like a fighter ready to attack at the starting bell. She squinted and chewed on her lower lip. A red trickle penciled its way down one arm. A piece of flying glass must have cut her. She dared me, jaw jutting, but I was silent.

"You can't make me do anything."

Her arrogance made my hand itchy. I ached to slap her. Instead, I resorted to animal cunning. "Oh, no? That's what you think. Just try me, go ahead, just try me." I hoped I had a glint in my eye, an evil one.

The other youngsters watched our confrontation. There were five: two boys, two girls, and a toddler who could be either sex. One boy, about eight, poked me. "Let's see you make her do something," he challenged. His tone told me he knew who would win the dare. It wasn't me.

I had to come up with something. My success or failure with these disenchanted children depended upon my next few words. I was a threat, evil and frightening because I was unknown, and worse yet, because I represented that vast "outside." I decided, if given the name, why not play the game?

I raised one hand and pretended to spit on my palm. I rubbed both hands together.

"Why you spittin' on you?" One of the five-year-olds crowded me.

"Getting ready. Ready to put a spell on you!" I hoped my expression was terrifying.

Questions came now.

"How come? What we done?"

"Who are you?"

"I'm a witch!" I spoke low and hissed.

There was a silence, then nervous twitters.

"Hey, she says she's a witch." A giggle from a small girl.

"I'll bet!" This was from Bloody Toe.

"Let's see you be magic then." The small black boy shivered happily.

"She's not magic and she's no witch." Scornfully, Bloody Toe dared me again.

My audience was big-eyed, half scared, half hoping it was true. Even Bloody Toe seemed intrigued.

"You're a goddamn liar." She hesitated. Then, "Prove it! Let's see you do something witchy," she said.

I turned around three times, almost falling off the steps. Then I clapped my hands three times and scowled, one eyebrow raised higher than the other.

"Icky-Micky-Ticky-Toe! I will turn you into a purple frog!" My voice was spooky, quivering.

The children huddled; they looked at each other with delight.

"Me," the eight-year-old boy demanded. "Me first."

"No. Me. Get out of my way, you creeps!" Bloody Toe shoved her way forward until she faced me.

"Go ahead, let's see you do it. Make me a purple frog." Bloody Toe was the center of attention. She made a face at me as she gave me the finger.

"Carrots and peas and turnips and mice! This spell will last until the sun becomes ice!" I waved my hands over her head. "Tomorrow morning when you wake up, you'll be a purple frog . . . if you pick up the glass."

Bloody Toe smirked. "You're screwed. I don't believe you. You're a fucking liar. You're not magic. I'm not going to pick up any of your dumb glass."

She backed up, avoided me, ran down the remaining steps to the sidewalk. "Phony . . . you're just a phony!"

She started down Flood Road at a gallop, still screaming. I watched as she stooped and picked up another discarded bottle. As Bloody Toe pitched it over her shoulder, she twisted enough to make sure I saw her actions. Glass flew as the bottle broke in the street. She ran between two buildings and was gone.

Hate drummed against her. I hated that kid. I hated her for not being a child, for not being able to make-believe, for deflating my ego, and for not crying as her blood hardened on her thin arm.

The other children scrambled for the glass and tossed it into the trash barrel by the steps. One girl pulled on me. "I think you're a witch."

"Me, too. Turn me into a purple frog." The boy's eyes were marble-round in his dark skin.

I made my witchy face and promised they would be purple frogs and green kangaroos and yellow anteaters. But it wasn't the same with Bloody Toe gone.

My witchcraft was somewhat rusty; they were the same grubby children the next morning. Still, from then on, I was met by a growing number of the project children every morning on their way to school. They would dance around me and shout out their demands. "Witchy, witchy, what will you turn me into tomorrow?"

I defied nature and Darwin and turned them into orange hippopotamuses or polka-dotted rabbits or blue tigers, as they giggled and nudged each other in our delicious conspiracy against reason. As they trotted toward the school, I also wondered what would they turn into . . . and what kind of a tomorrow they would have.

March was almost gone, and still I did not include Bloody Toe in my faithful make-believe zoo. My failure with her gnawed at me. There were more attractive children, more neglected ones, and even more delinquent ones in the project, but she touched something within me that I could not explain. Somehow she was "my" Bloody Toe, my unconceived child, my other side that rebelled. She bubbled anger and spewed it out; like a pan of boiling farina, she popped up in volcanic explosions. I had to know who she was.

Late one afternoon I found her stretched out on a greasy spot close to the cyclone fence separating the housing project from the flood-control ditch. She jumped up when she saw me approach, but she was trapped. I spoke kindly and asked her what her name was.

"If you're so goddamned magic, find out for yourself." And she was gone again, in zigzag leaps over shrubs and the junk rotting on the ground.

That day I asked Mattie if she knew who the girl was. I described her and her ways.

"That one? That girl? The wild one? Her?" She waved me toward the row of files which contained the tenant records. "Look it up yourself," Mattie said and then proceeded to run down the family background for me. "Her mother is Angelina Hernandez Gorman Linden. Right now she's using the name of Jones. She's lived in the project eight years and has shacked up with a dozen guys and has two or three—I can't keep track of how many— bastards. She runs with the bikers. She's trash and so are her kids."

As Mattie talked I took out the file and made note of the address.

"They say she sells narcotics and gives the kids pills to shut them up when those bikers flop at her place."

"Why don't you report her then?" I was tired of hearing horror stories and finding that no one wanted to get involved and stop the abuses.

"You'll learn." Mattie gave me her superior look. "What good would it do? You think people like that have any intention of doing right? Forget it!"

The housing application of the family file showed that my black-haired girl was Dellie Gorman, almost twelve. Three other children in the home were younger. One was a full brother. His name was Norman Gorman. Then there was a boy about six and another girl of four. Angelina, the mother, was only twenty-seven. I wanted to meet her. I wanted to talk about Dellie.

It was a busy week, with two robberies and a hair-pulling fight between Hilda Franks and her neighbor, Grace Smidt. Harry the Shoe stole a car that week, and with too much liquor in him he hit the side of one of the steel-reinforced buildings and split the car in two. Nothing happened to Harry. Herbie Brent came out and cussed because he couldn't get any witnesses to say that Harry was driving.

When Friday came everyone was tired and left early. I was in the main office and promised to flip on the alarm switch and raise all the blinds (so that cruising police cars could see inside) before I went home. It had been a dreary day, overcast and raw. Now March fog rolled in, cutting the chill night into sections, making mesas of the buildings in this urban Grand Canyon.

The project looked forlorn—deserted—when I let myself out and looked around. From habit I looked over at the playground next to the community hall. Dellie usually hung around there, even though Hermita Dalton, the city's recreation director for the project, had banished Dellie from any activities. In frustration, Hermita had recited Dellie's sins to me. The circle of keys attached to the loop of her gym pants jiggled as Hermita dug her thumbs, manlike, through her belt. "You saw the outside wall? Holes she dug with a screwdriver and then pitched eggs into them! And the drinking fountain—it's bust! She rammed a coat hanger into the spout, and I know . . . I would bet that Dellie's the one who cut all the swing seats off again . . . not to mention the motor oil in the sandbox!"

Defending Dellie was useless. Hermita had her own solution. "Another chance? Are you kidding? Take her along on the trip to Marineland? The only trip I'd include Dellie in is a trip to jail. She's impossible. No one can reach her." After that, Dellie defied the recreation leader and tormented her by just being visible.

I pulled my jacket closer as I searched my purse for the car keys. Once more I strained my eyes in the grayish dusk. The playground was empty. No Dellie around. The steps were slippery. I moved carefully. Heavy dampness and the smell of moldy leaves combined with the odor of burning wood. Another smell, a sweetish pungent one, unidentifiable, made me wonder subconsciously which trash bin had been set afire. Setting the trash bins on fire was fair game and one of the routine occurrences at Buena Vista.

The smell sickened me. I walked slowly toward my car parked in front of my office. Suddenly I was weary of this place, its people, all the problems. The ugliness of the past two months overwhelmed me. I was tired. Bone tired. Soul tired. Mind tired. A weekend with no complaints or tensions was what my body hungered for, as well as my psyche.

There she was! Hunched over, sitting on the curb by my car, wearing a too-large and misshapen sweater, her usual jeans with frayed bottoms, and her boy's ragged black high-topped sneakers.

I stopped, secretly pleased to see her. She raised her head and spat out, "Get fucked!"

I wanted to hit her, to abuse her, this nemesis I could not shake, control, conquer. Then anger left me, drained through the sieve of my own doubts. Her dark eyes, usually so shiny, were sunken into cavern hollows. One side of her cheek was washed with faded colors of an old bruise. She shivered but her eyes held steady on my face. They implored . . . what? I had to know.

My mood and the wistful loneliness of the child moved me wordlessly to her side. I sat down next to her, feeling the cold, rough curbstone through my skirt. We sat quietly, she with her knees pulled up to her chin, I with my legs sprawled out, my purse placed between us. Absently, I jingled the car keys loosely on their chain.

Window lights came on in the growing darkness, giving the scene a deceptive coziness. A few children's voices came through the night, punctuating the blaring sounds of rock music. An old car rattled past us down Flood Road without stopping at the stop sign. It roared away, with defective muffler, around the curve.

I wanted to say something to Dellie. What? I felt drained, inadequate to cope with this child I felt so drawn to. Impulsively I placed my hand on her bent head, feeling the roughened and uncombed hair. Like a flame her arm darted out, and her hand caught me across my chin. The sudden blow staggered me. I drew back. I heard her words only as a background to the sting I felt.

"Get your asshole hands offa me!"

Adrenaline flooded my body, hate lumped in my mouth. The shriek of police sirens stopped me; I was distracted. Before us, three black-and-white police cars peeled around Grand Boulevard and tore past. A yellow county ambulance, ding-donging its bells, followed closely.

Doors opened, making square shapes of light, like suddenly opened mouths. Antlike forms poured from the caravans. Some tenants ran, following the sirens; others gathered into clusters, black against the paler ground. The sirens stopped and now the air was thick with that odd smell—a dead root-cellar smell! Then screams came, loud male voices rising and falling. A man shouted. His voice drifted toward Dellie and me. "He's in there!"

Gunshots. Then a female voice, hysterical. "He's got two of the kids in there."

Again, voices, male voices, harsh, ordering, through a bullhorn. Police. "Come out with your hands over your head."

Another shot.

The smell burned my throat.

Women's hysterical voices were mingled with brutal male curses, orders.

"Move back. Move back!"

My anger drained. I looked down at Dellie, who, like me, was stunned. We forgot our conflict. She got up first. As three more shots kicked out, she threw herself at me. My impulse was to ward off another attack when her arms encircled my waist. I felt her head bore into my rib cage. A long horrible groan vibrated against me. Her words were lost. I gently embraced her and, after a moment, moved her head around so I could see her face. Her eyes were squeezed shut but large tears rolled over the bruised flesh.

In the background I listened to the noise of what was going on around the bend of Flood Road. More men's voices, excited, and then a small child's crying. Women's voices and then the child cried louder and ended with a shriek.

The shrill voice of the child made Dellie release her tight hold on me. She opened her eyes; even in the black night, they glistened.

"That was my little sister," Dellie said. Flatly.

"Your sister? Why do you say that? How do you know?"

"He killed Normie."

"What are you talking about?" My voice was stretched thin, like tissue paper over a comb.

"Fat Al said he'd kill Normie, and I guess he did."

Inside I hurt, cut in two by the pain. I felt myself screaming. "What in God's name are you talking about? Who is Fat Al and why would he kill your brother?"

"Mama got pills from him . . . and other stuff and sold them and Fat Al . . ." She stopped, then recited blandly, by rote, an alphabet of horror. "Fat Al said she held out on him and so he beat her . . . twice he beat her and last week he burnt her back. He made a knife hot and burnt her back."

I grabbed her. "Stop! I don't believe you! Why didn't you tell someone? Me?"

"He said if I told anyone he would rape me."

It was my turn to close my eyes, as if by doing so I would also close my ears. I wanted to cry but no tears came, only that pain, a rock of pain that pressed against my lungs. I couldn't breathe. We were still holding on to each other when Dellie pushed me away.

"I'm going to see."

"No."

"Yes. You don't have to come, but I gotta see what happened to Normie . . . and my mom."

She started, and after a few steps I followed. When Dellie ran, I stumbled after her. We arrived at the parking lot for her building together.

Ambulance attendants were bringing out a stretcher from Dellie's apartment. A man's feet protruded from under the sheet. The body was snuggly tucked in and strapped on. Fat Al. I was glad he was dead.

The groups of people standing around were silent, encased in fright. Even the youngest children were still, and the usually rank-mouthed teen-agers, who abused any police who entered the project, were slit-eyed and subdued. All of us were watching the door of the apartment.

This time another policeman came out carrying a child. A boy. The man's hands were large and white against the child's dark clothing. They trembled and then tightened as he held the body closer. He stopped a moment, dipped his head to the boy's blondish hair, and rested his face on it a second. He continued toward us; then, as he stepped on a broken toy on the grass, he stumbled. His knees almost gave way.

I had forgotten Dellie until I saw her rush to the policeman carrying the boy. She blocked his path and pulled on the child's hand that hung limply and swayed with the motion of the walking man. When Dellie kicked at him, he accepted her blows; when she clawed at her dead brother, he balanced himself against falling. Dellie's epithets lost their foulness in the despair of her agony. I turned away and cried silently.

The man broke away and carefully crossed over to the ambulance. When I looked up, Dellie was racing for the door of her home.

Tenants had gathered in tight groups in another area of activity. At the far end of the parking lot where the trash bin stood, more police and another ambulance pulled up. Rumbles of voices rose, then hushed. A riot-helmeted cop walked to one side and vomited. He leaned against an old Chevy with only three wheels and placed his hands on top, like a youth being rousted in a police search, legs apart, helpless. He bowed his head onto his hands.

I felt sick again. Other people had their hands over their noses. Some had pulled clothing over their faces like masks. The ambulance men backed away from the bin. Curls of grayish smoke rose and bits of blackened paper floated up and then drifted to the ground like dead blackbirds.

A fire engine geared its way through the crowd and pulled up at the bin. It shrilled to a stop. Firemen with gas masks jumped off. I moved toward that end. Before I heard the whispered words of the ambulance man, I knew. He shifted his eyes, wet his lips, pulled his lower lip in and bit down on it. Said the words. "He musta stabbed her first and then . . . and then dumped her into the trash. Covered her up with garbage."

A hushed voice added, "Someone must not have known . . ."

"Damn fool kids, always settin' fire to sumpin'," a black man grumbled.

The firemen demanded the area be cleared. Everyone moved to the fringe of the parking lot. I was conscious of people on all sides when a young boy, half crying, frightened, right behind me, spoke. "But you told me . . . Ma . . . you said—"

"Shut up, fool," her voice ordered.

"I didn't know. I never looked in," he whimpered. "How could I know . . . I didn't see nothin'."

"Can't you keep your goddamn mouth shut?" Desperation in her voice. "Ma . . . Ma—"

"Ma, nothing. You didn't do anything wrong. All you did was burn some old trash. What happened weren't any of your fault. Now shut up!"

I saw her take the boy's arm and lead him away. He stopped hanging back when she promised him, "We get home and you can have some change for a Pepsi and some tacos. Just you forget about what you seen. It don't concern us."

They disappeared down the street.

The firemen took charge of removing the body from the smoking bin. The people drifted away. The police cars thinned out. The sick smell that hung in the air was less noticeable. The ambulance and fire truck left.

I walked back. I looked for Dellie and saw her huddled on the stoop of what had been her home. A small girl hung on to her hand. I knew it was her half-sister, Sally. A boy about five was crying wildly. This was Tonto, the half-brother.

An unmarked car drove into the parking lot and a trim policewoman got out. She approached the two cops still left and they pointed toward the three children. I saw Dellie look up and then jerk away as the woman gently reached down to take Sally's hand. One of the officers lifted Tonto and carried him to the waiting car.

Dellie grabbed at her sister and for a moment I thought she would fight to hold her, but she gave up. Sally was led, barefoot and dirty, to sit beside Tonto in the back seat.

The policewoman came back. She stood silently near Dellie and I saw her worried face and sensed her hesitancy. A few more steps and she was at the girl's side. Dellie had her head down but as she felt the touch of the woman's hand on her shoulder, she jumped up and dodged to one side. "Keep your dirty hands off me!"

"You have to come with us, honey." The policewoman sounded tender.

"The shit I do!"

"C'mon, kid." One of the men spoke low and kindly. Both men moved in closer.

64

Dellie backed away. I shifted my place. She looked up and saw me. She raised her head and jutted out her chin as she looked straight at me. Her voice started low. "Well, witchy-poo, let's see you do some magic! Let's see you make it all go away! Let's see you change me into a purple frog!"

She was crying now—screaming and shaking her fists. The woman and two men grabbed her arms and tried to steer her toward the car. She slid out of their grasp and ran to me. She beat on my breast with both fists before they dragged her away. She flung herself to the ground and thrashed as they tried to pick her up and stand her on her feet. Holding her upright they moved clumsily toward the car.

They shoved her into the back seat next to the other children and barely had time to close the door before Dellie, still screaming, clawed at the half-open window.

Suddenly she stopped yelling obscenities and became stone-still. Even the police turned to see what caused the change.

Dellie was motionless and expressionless. Her eyes stared, like black bugs pinned against white paper. Her look started a shiver up my back. The others must have felt panic, too. One approached the window, bent down, and asked, "Are you OK, kid?"

Still no movement. Dellie's fingers were curled over the glass of the open window in a death grip—white icicles that burned into one's memory.

"Looks like she's in shock," one said sorrowfully.

"Let's get her the hell away from here!"

One of the cops started for the driver's seat and got in. The other two went around to the passenger side. That left only me still facing Dellie.

She was staring at me but I knew she did not see me. Her small face was marble-veined from the cold air. Dellie's question revolved in my mind: "Witchy-poo, where is your magic now?" I looked again at this child-woman, whose suffering had frozen her soul.

I took a step closer; her face was inches away. The car motor started, half drowning out my words. I screamed right into her ears. "Get fucked! Get fucked!" I was trembling, unable to control myself. "Get fucked! Screw you . . . screw you!"

Then, as the car moved off, I saw it. First there was a flicker of her eyes and then her fingers loosened and Dellie flipped me off. She gave me the finger—a salute to her god. Her words screamed over the car noise. "Get fucked, witchy-poo! Get fucked yourself! Screw you . . ."

In that moment my unconceived child was born, grew up, and left me, and I would love it forever. Amen.

10

The hot-line telephone jingled. It was Gloria Cogsville from the main office. She dripped venom.

"Go down to Carmen Sanchez's and tell her if she doesn't boot out those three 'cousins' with their three wives and their twenty-seven kids, I'm going to bill her for three hundred dollars a month rent." She took a deep breath. And her Harpo Marx wig sizzled.

Tenants were allowed to have guests for two weeks. After that they were "illegals." Illegals were a no-no and when they were discovered, the machinery of pressure started. Gloria Cogsville, as bookkeeper, collected the rents at the first of every month, when the tenants lined up at her cubicle and doled out part of their welfare checks for their apartments. Whenever a child was sent in with the money, Gloria immediately decided that it was because the adult had something to hide. In her mind that could only be an illegal. Her questions snapped at the young person and sometimes brought out the truth. Most times the project kids adhered to the rule of survival: When in doubt, keep your mouth shut!

The Sanchez home was the modern equivalent of the underground railroad, except that it was for Latins up from Mexico. The reason these small, brown men with friendly smiles, shy-eyed women, and their teddy-bear babies became visible was that they couldn't shut up. I became convinced that with the birth of every Chicano baby, a guitar is delivered with the afterbirth. One or two guitars may pass detection, but Carmen Sanchez's visitors played and sang in relays all day and all night.

Ben Hamilton's name for the musicians was "jumping beans." Herbie Brent named them "cockroaches" because, as he said, "they multiplied just as fast."

I looked up Carmen's address, slipped my key ring into my jacket pocket, turned off the heater, and went to see Carmen.

The sun felt mint-warm on my back as I turned down Greentree Lane. A breeze lifted my hair and my heels ping-ponged on the sidewalk. There was a young feeling, a hopeful zest, in the air. Buena Vista responded with a new spring greening. I walked along, dream-clouded, my eyes riveted by the sparkle of sun on a high-flying silver plane—a metal skygull.

Jean-clad legs sprawled across my path. I almost tripped. My gasp and balancing act brought a snicker from the group of five men assembled at the end of Building #103. I recognized three of them. Stupp Hankerson was the beltless, bulging, sloppy white man who stayed with Velma Washington. Stupp had one wooden leg and carried a trimmed-down two-by-four as a walking support. The crisply clean Velma did not fit with the sour-wine, dirty-socks smell of Hankerson.

It was Junior Hernandez whose legs had stopped me. He had a reputation for scoring with the women and verified his reputation by twisting his head so he could peek under my skirt. He was handsome; his soulful Latin eyes expressed intense hostility—or was it fear? Junior was about twenty-five and married to Carmen Sanchez's daughter Anita. Last week I had stopped in to see Anita and their two children, Rosie and Gregorio. Rosie was three, the boy was two, and a new baby was expected soon. Rumors were that Junior was pushing hard stuff, along with "reds." The teen-agers called Junior the "red-and-white man," and then ignored my questions.

The third man I recognized was Ti, short for Tiger, I had been told. His real name and background remained obscured by various tales. Ti could have passed; his gold skin and brownish hair were said to be the result of a mating between a high-ranking politician and a beautiful black actress. Only his chiseled lips and melting black eyes showed his African bloodline.

That was one story about Ti. The other story had Ti the former lover of a Hollywood male star, marking time in the project until a front-page murder of the actor cooled down. Whatever the truth, Ti didn't seem short of cash or flashy clothes.

The other two men, both black, both Jack Sprat lean, both in their early twenties, were strangers to me. One fingered a silvered knife handle.

Junior rolled back onto the grass and leaned up.

"Hey, Mees Bentwood, you tell that dirty son-of-a-beech Hamilton he's one dirty bastard!"

"Yeah, man, who that goddamn fuckin' Housing Agency think they jivin' with? They supposed to give us tenants jobs. An' what do they do but mess over us!" the unknown holding the knife said.

"We can't hustle us a job an' some of us stand to go back in the slammer." Junior again.

I knew that he had applied to Ben Hamilton for a job in maintenance. Ben had turned him down because, Ben told me, Junior was under surveillance.

"The joint ain't no place to grow sweet peas, but it ain't no place for men neither." Stupp hitched up his pants. He moved closer, pointed a liver-spotted hand toward Junior.

"Name me one good solid reason why that fat-assed white manager don't hire a good boy like Junior," Ti said.

Now I was hemmed in by Stupp and the elegant Ti. Junior was still at my feet on the grass. The two other blacks were off to one side. The one with the knife squatted. He kept jabbing the knife blade into the ground. The other man spread himself next to his partner. For the first time, he spoke. "I'll give you one good solid reason, nigger. Maybe the Man knows about . . ." He stretched out his forearm and used his index finger in a poking motion toward the inside vein. His voice was soft.

"Man, you're full of bullshit!" Junior's voice was harsh.

"The fuck he is. Gun says you're shootin', man, then you're shootin'." Stupp prodded Junior with his two-by-four.

"Yeah, where'd he get the bread, huh? Who ya jivin', you mother-fuckin' honky?" Ti said.

"Now who's jivin', nigger? What you think we're sittin' here for so early?" Stupp wiped his face with a square of dirty cotton, then stuck the rag into his back pocket.

"Man, it sure is hell getting outta the sack so early with no liquid refreshments to sort of carry a dude along."

Everyone laughed. Stupp kicked at an empty wine bottle at his feet. I wondered why they were out so early. Usually the project males never showed themselves before noon. I asked.

"What are you all waiting for—a ride or something?"

"Waiting for the Government Man, lady. You might even go so far as to say you are right. They *are* waiting for a ride—a free ride!" Ti slid a sly grin at the others and flipped his wrist.

"Hey, man! Jet, tell the lady 'bout our special club," Junior coaxed.

Two names clicked in my mind. Gun and Jet! Ben Hamilton told me that Tommy Gun operated with another young black as a sidekick. It must be this Jet! His face smiled but his voice was steely. "Yeah, man, we got this here fancy club, lady, just like you dis-ting-uished so-ci-ety people. We is waiting for our di-vi-dends. See, we got it made, lady!"

"Tell her like it is, baby!" Junior butted in.

"Yeah, we is like all them other rich bums. We jus' clip our coupons. Right? You fuck over us, we say OK! You don't give us jobs? Shit, we just do our thing . . . an' someday we'll get ours. You dig my meaning?"

"Lay it on her, man! The gravy train come twice a month!"

Looking at Stupp's clothing, I decided the gravy train came every day and dumped over on him. Of course! The Government Man was the mailman and he delivered the women's welfare checks on the first and the fifteenth. I let them know I understood.

"You men are waiting for the welfare checks."

None of them looked embarrassed.

"Sure is nice of you folks to give us coke money!" Junior flipped over on the grass and ha-ha'd. The others watched to see if I caught the meaning of "coke."

"What's stopping you from going outside the project to get a job? Stop waiting for people to hand you everything. I bet you haven't even tried . . . really tried."

Junior dragged himself into a sitting position. His dark eyes were glazed, his voice shook. "Hell, yes, Mees Bentwood. I try . . . all over I try. The P.O. say go to work or I send you back. Back. You know what the 'back' is? Quintan, the big joint . . . hard time. I got a five-to-twenty hangin' over me. I go back an' my kids . . . they be grown . . . Anita . . ." His eyes brimmed. "Can you help me?"

I turned away. My excuse was Jet. He was pegging the knife into the grass with the ferociousness of a man raping a woman. He kept his eyes down as he spoke. "I had me this job, it was a bitch, see? Not much bread but no-how . . . it was a job. At this drive-in food joint. Dig? Hot dogs— sour-smelling hot dogs with sauerkraut hair. I take the orders and pack the slop. Doing fine. Everything was cool . . . sliding along . . . nice and easy . . . son-of-a-bitch!"

He stopped stabbing, looked at the dirt-crusted knife, turned it over and over. "Two fuckin' weeks an' the boss calls me over. He says, 'Sorry. You got a record. You're an ex-con an' our insurance don't cover cons handling cash an' besides'—he puckered up his pig-jew eyes—'you lied!' "

Jet spoke to the other men. "Hell, yes, I lied. I move in on the dude.

70

'Would you of hired me if I told you right off I done time?' Know what his answer was? Sure you know—it was no. Just a sweet asshole no. Round and firm and oh so fully packed."

No one spoke. It was up to me. "He fired you?"

"Lady, don't let us discuss it no more. Someday we boy scouts will start us a marshmallow roast."

He stood up and wiped the knife on his pants. I saw the glint as he held the blade by the tip. A snap of his hand and the knife spun across the street into a tree. It hung like a silver arrow.

The sun was hot. Still, a shiver started up me and spent itself at my hair-roots. The men were motionless, a Gordon Parks photograph. Would rubbing scorched minds together start a holocaust? Unsaid words held me there.

The silk trees creaked and two mongrel dogs ran past. A child cried out; then the squealing rubber of a speeding car cut into the silence. The dogs growled and jumped each other, a tangle of hair and teeth.

Jet leaned over and reached for the empty wine bottle. He pitched it at the dogs. It exploded like a bomb and broke up the tableau. One dog let out a yelp and ran. The other one hobbled off, blood dripping from a gash where the flying glass had ripped him open.

I was enraged. Anger crawled, hung in each vein, acid droplets burning in millions of pinpricks.

"Why? Why did you have to do that? Why did you have to hurt them?" I swayed with the violence of my anger, with the helplessness of it.

I felt a hand on my foot. It lay on my shoe, anchored me to the ground. I looked down. It was the hand of the soft-spoken young black. I felt his warmth through the shoe leather.

"We don't have much choice. You see, hate don't make no noise, but blood . . . now blood . . . blood screams!"

He moved his hand away. The warmth was gone. Truth took its place. I had heard it and he was right. When hate is simmering and silent, death stands and waits. It slowed my words.

"Is violence the answer?"

"We give what we get." Said flatly. "Violence?" His chest expanded, filled out, then collapsed back into rib-cage leanness. He gathered cigarette butts from the dirt and laid them in a neat pyre. "Violence." He said it again and wrote a book with the word. He left the pages blank for me to fill in.

"It's ugly, but then we're an ugly people. We are poor and we are black and we are shit. Black is beautiful is shit. It's like saying cancer can be fun . . . and going hungry is good for the figure. Cancer is not fun an' hunger is bad . . . my, oh, my, but hunger is bad for the soul!"

He looked straight at me. "You know about the soul, don't you?"

I knew about the soul: Hail, Mary, full of grace, pray for us sinners, now and at the hour when we get a bellyache from those damn little green apples God made. Rearrange "soul" and you get "louse" without the *e;* Webster defines louse as a parasite on man and other warm-blooded animals.

"You and your lousy soul talk." I knew I was talking with Tommy Gun. In the name of the Father, the Son, and the Holy Tommy Gun Ghost. Who did he think he was kidding, trying to palm himself off as a good guy?

Someone spit and the blob passed between us and landed on the sidewalk. It spattered.

"Maybe I'll go hit a liquor store tonight. Lame me a white ass." Jet's eyes grinned a threat.

"Tommy Gun. Tommy Gun." I repeated it.

"The one and only. You know me?"

"Only by what I heard."

"Heard? What? C'mon, baby, don't bounce me no rubber check!"

The men regrouped, blocked off my path, nudging each other, waiting, listening.

I had a choice: keep quiet or let loose. Either way I was putting myself on the line—a very thin line. Buena Vista destroyed the timid. If I backed down, it would be a defeat. Once defeated I would be fair, or unfair, game. I really had no choice.

"I heard that you are a junkie—a dealer of hard stuff, carry a gun and use it. Rob welfare checks which should be used to feed kids. You father children and desert the mothers.

"You're the contact for getting jobs done—twenty-five dollars for a beating, two hundred for a killing and alley dumping. You're a no-good bastard! That's what I heard."

Stupp swished the overgrown weeds with his stick; Junior whistled softly. Neck cords vibrated. Ti turned his head sharply to catch Tommy Gun's reaction. I forced my eyes to hold on his. I knew the others would take their cue from him.

The tension broke. Tommy Gun slapped his thigh, laughed. "Man, woman, cool it! Hold on, you can't believe that crap!"

"Is it true?"

"Hell . . . some of it maybe. But you are way off on one thing. I don't mainline. I'm clean!"

He shoved his arms out for me to inspect. Working in Buena Vista, I had become an expert on terms. "You *could* be conning me. Maybe you skin-pop or shoot between the toes . . . under the tongue."

Tommy Gun looked away, pretended to shake his head with disbelief and frustration. "So I'm down in your little black book!"

"Black, red, and rotten! There are other stories."

"What other stories?"

"She's not buying your con, nigger-baby!" Jet said.

"Shut yo' mouth, boy!" Tommy Gun kicked at Jet's rear, but the other moved to avoid the push.

"Go on, white lady, what else have you heard . . . what other stories?"

"Crazy things. Like . . . like you stop fights. That you can handle the kids—they follow you . . . trust you . . . respect you. That when trouble comes—bad trouble—the word is 'get Tommy Gun.' That you give back, as well as take away. They call you the Mayor . . . and Peacemaker . . . the Peacemaker of Buena Vista."

I looked at him closely. His face was smooth except for a small goatee. The crinkled Afro was molded gracefully around his skull. A blue tattoo of a bird in a cage was on one forearm. A loop of gold hung from his left earlobe. It was his eyes that held me—black as they were, behind their blackness was a golden sheen. Like the sun just before it bursts through a storm cloud. We stalked each other with visual search warrants.

"Is the other part worth it?" I said. I knew he understood what I meant.

"Your freeway got no entrances for my brothers and sisters. Our maps have only exits."

"Freeways go both ways. Exits are entrances. You road-blocked them off with whines and cop-outs! Black! That's your magic word, isn't it? Your plea bargaining? Your all-purpose excuse . . . your password? Give that man a year's supply of bullshit!"

My voice was shrill. I felt shame that I had let myself be drawn into this passion of feeling. Useless, helpless, stone-ground despair. More painful because the anger was toward myself for denying their truth. But I went on.

"And you . . . you could help . . . but you don't. Chickenshit, that's what you are, Mister Tommy Gun, Mister Pop-off Gun!"

I backed up. The men opened a path for me. My heels hit the sidewalk again. I picked my way around the green glass of the wine bottle. Behind me, the voices were loud.

"Son-of-a-bitch!"

Then, "That broad got you by the balls, Gun!"

"That's layin' it on! Heavy, man, heavy!"

And, "You gonna sit still for that crap, Tommy?"

I expected it when it came.

"Hey, hey, lady!" It was an order.

I looked back.

Tommy Gun stood up, legs spread apart. His hands cupped his mouth as he shouted at me. When he saw me stop he dropped his hands, resting them on his hips. He was grinning.

"Hey, lady! Bentwood, baby! You is one nigger-lovin', white mother-fucker!"

I knew we were both on the same freeway. What I didn't know was where we were going and who would get off first.

Carmen Sanchez and her millions of relatives were eating when I got to her place. The music was soft, the children crawled all over the floors, the men politely offered me a chair and listened with their un-English ears. Carmen nodded a lot and said, "*Sí . . . sí,*" as I explained the problem—too many nonpaying relatives.

"You no understand, Mees E-dot, all family come up from Tecate to see Sharlie—our 'elative dot beeg singer. You know, Sharlie!"

"Sure, sure, but when your singer is through with his song, they go back Tecate! OK?" I insisted.

Happy, she grabbed my hand for a kiss as I backed out of the garlicky kitchen. The children waved and I knew that not a word of what I had said or threatened would change the number of tenants in the Sanchez home. Next month there would be another "Sharlie." Let Gloria send her $300-a-month rent bill. There would be the same smiles and nods, other faces but the same smells. Nothing would change . . . except maybe Gloria's wig.

11

The rent strike took on momentum. Ernestine Trotmartin held several meetings in the community hall with her Action For Tenants. The local newspaper sent a reporter and the resulting article did nothing to recommend Buena Vista. The project was described as a "blighted" area. The management was declared "inept," the tenants' actions "criminal."

The putdown brought out the best or worst in Ernestine, depending on whose bleachers you sat in. Twice during the week following the article I had heard Ben Hamilton on the telephone with Bert Lottman. Ben had mainly nodded and punctuated Lottman's pauses with "yes, sir"s and then returned to twiddling the telephone cord around his thumb. On direct orders from Lottman, I had stayed away from the evening meeting Ernestine called. Since Lottman spoke through Ben, I didn't have a chance to ask why. I nailed Gloria one morning after the third rent-strike meeting.

"I don't understand why I'm told not to attend the AFT meetings. Shouldn't I know what's going on?"

"Why?"

"Why? Because I'm involved with the tenants! It's my job to keep things moving along smoothly."

"You stick your nose in Ernestine's pot and your goose will be cooked. Take my advice . . . she's dangerous." She dismissed me and bent over her records. I walked away when she called out to me again. "And so is Lottman."

Everyone in this crazy place was infected with paranoia!

A week later my hot-line buzzed. It was Mattie. In doom-and-gloom tones she told me to get over to the main office right away or I might find myself out of a job. Before I could ask her what she was talking about, she slammed the phone down.

The office was crowded when I entered. Besides Gloria, Mattie, and Bernice, seven of the maintenance crew were gathered around a large poster taped to the office wall. In bold letters it told its message in blunt terms.

!BIG RALLY!

ALL TENANTS MUST COME

SHOW HOUSING THEY CAN'T

SCREW US NO MORE

HOLD YOUR RENT—DON'T PAY!

LET'S GET RID OF THAT FINK

BENTWOOD—RUN HER OUT!

GET YOUR ASS OVER TO THE

COMMUNITY HALL—FRIDAY—7 P.M.

ERNESTINE TROTMARTIN: CHAIRMAN

ACTION FOR TENANTS

"She's after you." Gloria wore her own hair today and looked like Marjorie Main on one of her worse days.

"Better start looking around, Edie, for a new job." Mattie scratched her head with a pointed pencil.

"You gonna let that sow chase you out? Hell, I'd cut her water off so fast she'd dry up and blow away!" Chuckie was our master plumber and a specialist in unclogging sewer lines.

"No one can get the best of Ernestine. They've tried before." Gloria challenged anyone to disagree with her.

To everyone's surprise it was Bernice who did.

"Maybe if the police knew what Ernestine's kid was doing . . . that Tank . . . maybe she would simmer down if she was scared someone would tell." She stopped and ran back into her rabbit-hutch office.

Alfred, who ran the tractor lawn mower, hitched up his pants and tightened his belt a notch. Alfred drank, and watching him whip around the trees on the mower when he had had a few was better than Evel Knievel risking his neck. "You mess with Ernestine and you're messing with Tommy Gun. An' you mess with Tommy Gun, you got big trouble." Alfred meant those words for me.

"I know Housing will stand behind me. After all, Bert Lottman told me when I was hired I had nothing to worry about, from anyone. He said it was a permanent job."

"Don't count on Lottman's word!"

George Tree was the project's head painter. He was a tall, slender black man and better educated than the other workmen. When I made my rounds in the project, I often stopped in where he was repainting an apartment and we talked about the day's news and the people. I respected this thoughtful man. His comment about Bert Lottman could not have been made without some basis. I felt uneasy. First Gloria, then the painter, George Tree. Did they know something I didn't?

Another one of the workmen spoke. "I been working at Buena Vista eight years now and I tell you somethin' is going on."

"Yeah, maybe . . . I don't understand why they let seven guys go last week. How they expect us to keep the place up with such a small crew?" Chuckie sounded worried.

Heinie was the carpenter. A fat, short Germanic-looking man, he wore thick glasses and rubbed his bald head with an oil which made it glisten. He had bladder trouble; his work pants were often dotted with wet spots. Once Gloria joked about asking Chuckie, the plumber, to put a washer on Heinie's faucet to keep it from leaking. His speech was pedantic.

"I would say that the powers that be"—he looked balefully around—"the powers that be are not too concerned. They don't care how Buena Vista looks any more. In my opinion . . ." Again he stopped. His look dared us to disagree with him. "In my opinion the project is in danger!" He took off his thick-lensed glasses, spit on them, and rubbed around the wetness with a stubby forefinger. He repeated, "In considerable danger."

"And when hasn't it been?" Mattie snubbed Heinie. Her voice still remembered ration stamps.

"OK, smart lady, wait and see!"

The men left to start their daily chores. Mattie and Gloria got down to work. Bernice could be heard making her calls to set up her annual rent-review appointments. I returned to my office.

Heinie's statement about the "powers that be" set me thinking. The powers, I had been told, were Bert Lottman and the Board of Advisors, the overseers of the total Housing Agency. The politics of the agency were unknown to me, but Bert Lottman's sincerity when he "welcomed me aboard" on the "rough waters of public housing" impressed me with his dedication to and concern for the low-income tenants who were helped by subsidized rents. I remembered how Lottman leaned forward, his tennis-tight body encased in his well-cut clothes, the masculine whiff of smoke floating from the cigar held in manicured fingers. His thick, silver-layered hair emphasized his sharp blue eyes. Was he a sleek cat that would purr if rubbed the right way but held its claws quivering, ready for any threatening move? My mind replayed his description of the position, which captivated me.

"You'll be responsible for helping our tenants in Buena Vista. Any problem . . . any complaints they have, you are to help with . . . make their lives better. If it means taking their side against us . . . against the administration . . . well, I want you to be frank. And not afraid to speak out, or ask questions."

Well, I had questions. Why were maintenance men discharged when the grounds and apartments already showed neglect? Why didn't the administration try to meet with Ernestine Trotmartin and the AFT and mediate some of the complaints? Were the "powers that be" encouraging the rent strike by ignoring the problems? Perhaps I should try to brave the Tigress in her AFT den again. If I could remove only one of her claws . . . I considered it as I walked back to my office. Since that other time, we had avoided each other by an unspoken mutual agreement.

That afternoon, for once, my telephone didn't ring. I caught up on entering my daybook memos. Later, I called various wholesale meat houses to get donations of free hot dogs for the Teen Club cookout. It was too good to last. I answered the telephone on the first ring. The loud sobbing lasted a full minute.

It was Judy Nickel. Judy was the project's Avon Lady, Tupperware party-giver, Beeline Fashions outlet, and Royal Jewelry supplier. The one time I had been in her apartment, it was stacked with boxes of sold goods, promised goods, and samples. Judy had swiped a Safeway grocery shopping cart and used it to deliver her orders around the project. Annie Flunk had named her "J. C. Penney" and swore that Judy "nickeled and dimed" the gullible women and kept them broke with useless items.

Judy was incoherent. The few words I understood gave me a partial indication of what had happened. Judy and her two girls had gone to Chino to visit her husband at the correctional facility. While she was away, her place was ripped off. Everything was taken: furniture, clothing, her girls' toys, a secondhand washing machine, and worst of all, all her merchandise. The boxes of Avon products had been ready for delivery and now . . . ? Her last wail triggered hot anger in me. Damn it, here was a woman who tried to make it on her own, worked hard, kept her nose clean, and some rotten people . . . ! Disgusted, I calmed Judy down by telling her I would be right down to see her.

Her story was correct. I looked around the small rooms and wanted to cry with frustration. After promising I would round up some bedding, a table, and a few chairs, I left. Someone must have seen what happened. Judy's possessions didn't just float away. I decided to investigate.

I made the rounds of her neighbors. Everyone clammed up. Dark glasses of forgetfulness screened their comments. It was from two youngsters of seven or eight that I finally got scanty information.

"Yeah, we seen a truck pull up to Judy's pad."

"Kinda old . . . torn up on one side . . . maybe gray or green."

"Naw . . . I don't 'member no license number . . . wouldn't tell you if I did."

"You askin' for misery, Miz Bentwood, if you get too nosy."

I took a wild guess, closely watching their eyes.

"Tommy Gun have anything to do with this?"

The young faces tightened into masks, smooth, blank. Backward shuffles, sideways glances, and then they were gone. I knew better than to expect an answer. Frustration! I wanted to hit out at something. A torn sack stuffed with empty beer cans blocked my path as I started out of Parking Lot #7. The temptation to kick had to be released. I toe-connected with one silvery can and gave it a boot worthy of a Rams player. It clattered and rolled to a stop at the same time as a male voice shouted to me. "That'll be a five-hundred-dollar fine for kicking the can around. Don't you know littering is against the law?"

I looked across Flood Road and saw Herbie Brent driving the unmarked police car. Hank Garrison sat shotgun. I walked over. "Too bad it's only a beer can!" I said.

Hank reached back and opened the rear door for me to get in. Herbie drove to my office and cut the motor. I told them about the burglary and Judy Nickel's dilemma.

"What do you expect us to do? Taking a report is a waste of time if you can't come up with a witness," Hank said after I complained of lack of interest on the police's part.

"Two kids told me what the truck looked like . . . but it was after dark. They saw the stuff taken out."

"Fine. That's just fine. Now, can you get me one adult to agree to testify who they saw?" Hank demanded.

"No, I can't and you know that I can't."

Something about Hank Garrison usually had me between despair and anger. He could get under my skin with his objectivity. Why couldn't he feel the same outrage and involvement that I felt after some hideous incident happened in the project.

"You have to forget it then. There's not going to be any change in this cesspool until the people themselves want it to change," Herbie said.

"That's crazy! You're the police. You're paid to catch criminals and you keep giving me this garbage that you can't do anything. What good are you then? You know it must be the same goons that pulled those other burglaries . . . old lady Slattern's place and Grace Paxton's stuff." I was mad.

"I know that, and you know that, and all the damn tenants know that, and no one—I repeat, no one—will step forward and press charges. They just won't show up in court to testify. Why can't you get that through your stupid head?" Hank was yelling.

"Both of you make me sick! I bet I can get more action from Tommy Gun than from the whole dumb Crestview police goon-squads."

I yanked open the car door and went into my office. I heard their last words. "Great! Just great! Don't call us . . . we'll call you!" That was Herbie.

"Let her stew in her own juices!" Hank sounded like a superior number-one ass!

Once inside and at my desk, I realized I had bitten off a hunk of trouble for myself. I had boxed myself in, with the tenants in one corner, the police in the second, the project's criminal element in the third, and me in the fourth! Stupid Edith Bentwood, the crusader for the underdog, the big-mouthed, overaged Joan of Arc was lighting her own fire.

The rest of the day was lost in hours of petty problems and routine tasks. The stinging remarks of the community relations police returned like the itching of a big mosquito bite. It probably would have gone away if I had left it alone, but since I scratched at it with the sharp fingernail of stubbornness, it became inflamed and spread.

So they thought I would be defeated! Ha! And ha again! I decided to test the mystique of Tommy Gun's power. My first problem would be to make contact—to locate his present accommodations.

The next day I put out the word to Billy Goochen and Go-Boy Mansfield. "If you should happen to see or talk to someone who knows where Tommy Gun is, get the word to him that I'd like to talk to him."

"Tommy's gone," Billy said.

"He's left the project?" Disappointment showed in my tone.

"Oh, he'll be back . . . he's jus' gone to visit his daddy."

Daddy! Somehow, Tommy Gun having a daddy seemed surrealistic, like

Bluebeard going to sleep with a teddy bear.

"Yeah, his folks live in Washington. Daddy's a judge or sumpt'in'."

Go-Boy thought it was funny and the boys rocked against each other as they ha-ha'd.

"But he'll be comin' back," Billy promised. "Anyway, here or gone, he'll get the word. Tommy Gun keeps in touch."

They raced away.

The information that Tommy Gun's father was a judge opened new questions but answered others. I wondered about his background. While his talk was rough and he used the customary four-letter words—which by now had lost their meaning through overuse—I sensed he had gone beyond high school. Perhaps coming from a professional home gave him that smattering of rhetoric that lent authority to his words. More than ever, I was intrigued by this black man's charisma.

The week ended without any special emergency. The Mothers' Club met on Friday morning and Betty Lou finished the sweater for her baby. So far I had no news about Tommy Gun. Three angry calls (from owners of houses that bordered on the project) about juveniles crawling through a hole in the flood-control fence prompted me to insist that Ben Hamilton inspect it with me. Reluctantly, he went with me to the far end of the project where the passageway was cut across the slime green drainage ditch. On the way I told Ben of all the burglaries committed by project kids in the houses that abutted Buena Vista, and that one man who had called me swore he would shoot the next black kid he saw climbing the fence into his yard.

"Let him" was Ben's response.

We found a break in the chain link fence where clippers had opened a hole large enough for a small body to sneak through. Two makeshift ladders were placed against each cement wall banking the drainage ditch. Stagnant water was blocked by old tires, broken furniture, cans, and whatever the tenants found surplus. Across the ditch were the private homes with neat yards and patio barbecues. It was easy to understand how "our" children got over to rob these houses.

"I wonder if God would answer my prayer? Let me create a miracle ... like a tidal wave that would wash this place away." Ben Hamilton poked his foot through the hole and tipped the ladder over into the slime.

"You mean like parting the Red Sea, only in reverse?" I asked. I hoped my scorn showed.

He didn't answer me. We returned to the office and he left word for the maintenance crew to repair the hole in the fence. He said it wouldn't do any good. He was right. Later that day it was fixed; the next morning I had another furious telephone call. The clippers had done their work. This time the break was three feet away from the first hole. There was no use in reporting it to Ben again. He was jumpy enough.

All that week there was unusual activity at the AFT office across from my social service center. Tenants went inside in groups, came out looking smug and gleeful. By Friday Ben fell to pieces. He reacted to the Friday night rent-strike rally by calling me every half hour. He wanted me to look out the window across to the AFT office and report who was going in and out. When I asked him what difference it made, he said that Bert Lottman wanted to know who else besides Ernestine Trotmartin were the ringleaders.

Despite Ernestine's aversion to me, I felt that spying on the tenants was underhanded. If they were entitled to an organization, then they should be left alone. The withholding of rent was a legal problem and surely the Housing Agency could deal with that. The third time Ben called me, I told him that I couldn't recognize people from across the street and hung up.

Ernestine's remarks about me and her words in the poster concerning my position irked me. Maybe she couldn't fire me, but it did make my daily work more difficult. Mentally, I flipped a coin to decide if I should attend the evening meeting that night. It came out yes. I gave in and rang Ben in his office. I didn't expect his reaction. He sputtered, argued that it would create more of a platform for Ernestine's ranting. *He* wasn't going; I shouldn't go. "If you show your face, Ernestine'll try to show her muscle and it will create a situation."

In my mind the situation was there already, but I finally promised I would stay away. Before I went home for the weekend, the tenants had nailed a large banner made from old sheets over the community hall entrance. It said UNITE—RENT PROTEST in broad black letters. Groups of residents were gathered in each project parking lot as I drove out. The smell of anger smogged the project.

12

The silence after Ernestine's rent rally was ominous: Questions brought no answers. Ben Hamilton begged me to find out what tactics the tenants were planning. I couldn't. *No* one would talk!

One early morning two stern-faced, cropped-haired men in suits and shiny shoes walked into my office. They badge-streaked me, hitched up their razor-edged pants, and sat delicately at the edge of the loveseat. They were from the United States Treasury Department, Bureau of Narcotics, Alcohol and Firearms Division, I was informed, and they were working on a drug-smuggling ring about which they had an undercover tip. The tip indicated that Buena Vista Housing Project was the ring's headquarters.

Since I had started work in the project, there had been minor drug incidents: a few overdoses (only one fatal), several instances of property damage due to "loaded" drivers not making the Greentree Lane curve, and strong smells of marijuana floating over other pungent project odors. Drug ring? I shook my head in response to their Elliot Ness prodding.

"Not unless you consider twelve-year-olds passing a joint between them," I told them.

They did not reply, either by word or by facial expression. I sensed I was being sized up, but for what? Finally the nitty-gritty of their visit came out. They had a lead on a "buy" going off in the project within the next days —a big transaction.

"Now, what we need is information from you," one man said. He sounded as if he was demanding my last pint of blood, which I could not refuse.

"You have been checked out," the second man said. He took out a small notebook, three-ringed, in black grained leather. He mumbled, turned a page, snapped it shut, and bared teeth. I felt like Little Red Riding Hood facing the wolf.

"And now you want me to check *in?*" I hoped I sounded funny. They didn't laugh. Instead, they scared hell out of me. Both men stood up as if riveted together by an invisible steel bar. I debated if I was supposed to hold my hands out for them to snap handcuffs on my wrists.

"Definitely. We would hope for your cooperation," one man said.

I kept nodding, like one of those toy dogs that perch in a car's back window. That's me, the perpetual smiling, nodding, agreeable please-and-thank-you gal. Except that the project was my root cellar now. I noticed the men's eyes. They looked like oysters—gray-shaded, clouded, obscure.

"What we want you to do is be on call when we make the raid. You see, in a"—he groped for the least offensive word—"place like this, unless one has an insight into the various relationships and possible combinations of individuals associated, an operation of this magnitude is hampered to a successful conclusion. The subjects under surveillance usually are located in one dwelling or easily contained locality, but in this situation, we cannot be certain—"

I unwound him. "What you're saying is that you don't want to be caught shooting the wrong people in this rabbit hutch, you don't know your way around, right?"

"Put crudely, yes!"

"And you want someone who knows the tenants and their habits to save you from making a massacre."

The word "massacre" hit the bull's-eye; their pupils dilated, then contracted.

"You will be available." It was not a question, even though his eyebrows shot up.

Relieved that I was not to be arrested for refusing to cooperate, I folded my hands behind me, shrugged.

After they left in a one-two gait, I remembered they had not told me exactly what the deal was or when the raid was to be. And who among my tenants were involved.

Thursday evening I was at home, puttering around on my balcony, sweet-talking a fern that had crumpled its leaves and gotten brown on the edges, when the telephone rang. It was one of the men. It would be "handy" if I were "around" this evening in the project. At ten.

"Around where . . . and handy for what?"

He would not expand. Instead he was sarcastic. "Oh, come now, Miss Bentwood, let's not play games!" He hung up.

"Look who's playing games!" I told the room.

At nine-thirty I drove into the project, parked behind my office, and quietly let myself in. The day sun left the cement-block walls still damp at night. I stumbled in the dark into my back-room office. The window let in semilight from the street light down Flood Road. Strange shadows, the stagnant chill air, and the knowledge that somewhere out there among the square block buildings were men with guns, probably gas bombs, even sharpshooters, started cold sweat. Who did they suspect? Hope to capture? Who were they prepared to maim or . . . kill? I had no patience with drug users or dealers. Still, if the Federal agents knew who had the drugs, why did they have to resort to a S.W.A.T. episode? Why not go in with a search warrant, take the dealer, get the drugs, and do it in daylight? That would be honest, professional.

I kept my mind working to shake off the eeriness I felt. When the phone rang, I collapsed over it, both hands holding down the receiver. It rang three more times before I grasped it with both hands and steadied it near my ear. I whispered, "Hello."

"Yes, Treasury here. Ready there?"

"Yeah . . . sure. Say, wait a minute . . . listen . . . Treasury—what am I supposed to do? I don't mind telling you that this whole caper sounds ill advised and . . . "

Treasury cut in. "Don't talk any more—just listen to your orders. Start walking towards area seventeen, due southeast after reaching clear space on the right. Wait under the overhang at the end building. You will be contacted when we need you. Got that?"

"Sure, I heard what you said but . . ." The line went dead.

For a moment, I considered calling the city police. Maybe ask them to contact Hank. Then I reconsidered. Can one call local cops on the Treasury cops? This is madness, I decided, but a madness I was also caught up in.

Area seventeen was where Junior Hernandez, Carmen Sanchez, and Lisa Fritzle lived. I carefully let myself out and moved across the grass instead of the sidewalk. The night wetness made my leather soles slip soundlessly. I angled around the building, rather than taking the direct route down Greentree Lane. It was a dark night; a lopsided moon sulked behind clouds. I looked for evidence of activity, police cars or crouching men. Something

—anything except this strange emptiness. Not even liquor-provoked fights or blasting music interrupted the silence. Accidentally, I kicked a beer can over a curb. It rattled, sounding like a cannonball to my ears. I slinked next to a wall, moved toward the overhang at the end of the area-seventeen building.

I saw them! Men, dark figures. Dressed in knit caps, loose jackets, narrow pants I assumed were jeans. They huddled, softly argued. The tone carried, not the words. I watched as one man moved away, as if angry, only to be pulled back by a second man. It looked like a modern ballet, a version of Dante's *Inferno* à la public housing. Now another figure joined the group. His Afro gave away his race. Voices got louder, rougher; then three men started across the parking lot.

I scrunched into a little ball, squatted down, found a prickly shrub to hide behind. Fury thumped my heart valves. Insane . . . what in God's name would I do if those men found me?

They passed me. The one with the Afro leaned closer—it was Jet. My eyes, now like a cat's, could see the forms walk across the grassy sections, turn. I glanced back at the other two men. One stood rigid, military straight. I knew he was a cop. The other man slouched, took out a cigarette, and a flicker of light from his match lit his features—Junior Hernandez!

Curiosity got me. I wanted to see where Jet was leading the other two men, who I suspected were also Treasury cops. I crept on hands and knees, got scratched by twigs, and had made it around the corner when all hell broke out!

A Chinese New Year is an exercise in meditation compared to the fireworks that erupted in Buena Vista.

Shots came from thirteen directions. Hooded hangman figures darted across the open spaces, bullets crisscrossed. Heavy footsteps—someone zipped past me. I recognized the jacket. It was Junior Hernandez. Behind him streaked the hippie-dressed Treasury man. As he sprinted past, he spotted me, a dark blob against the lighter building wall.

"C'mon, follow me. We have to know which apartment they're headed for. We're going to blast those mother-fuckers' heads off! They've ripped off our front dough!"

I followed, muttering about dirty mouths and clean soap. From tenants, yes—from Treasury, no!

Ahead of us, I saw Jet leading the other two men in a zigzag path into one vandalized apartment, out of the second-floor bedroom, along the ledge, through another window and out the rear door. Panting behind me were the hooded S.W.A.T. team. I felt like Top Cat leading the local tomcats, all midnight black!

Junior Hernandez cut off in a different direction. That produced another huddle as my Treasury man took part of my tomcat brigade and spread out. Junior Hernandez had disappeared.

Suddenly the project came alive. Like bears stretching after a long winter's hibernation, the buildings shivered themselves awake. Tenants spilled out, dressed in night clothes and odd garments, carrying wailing babies, raising fists, cussing kids. They startled the law enforcement agents.

A few overzealous agents kicked in a door looking for their escaped quarry. Annie Flunk came out, a knife in her hand. The wrath of Buena Vista descended. More stray shots were fired. Treasury men went from door to door; one stayed outside, two others spear-gunned their way in, came out empty-handed.

Elongated yellow light, like birthday candles tipped over on a chocolate cake, streamed across the yards as lamps were snapped on by angry people. I knew what would happen. I had seen tenants work their intimidation on others. I backtracked, deciding to chase down the other two Treasury men with the balance of my tomcats.

It wasn't difficult. The next parking lot over was covered with armed men. I caught up with one of the undercover agents. He was breathing hard and limping.

"Sir, about that man you're hunting for, what did he do?"

Even in the darkness, I sensed he paled. He shook his head heavily, shifted his lame leg, moaned a little. I knew he brain-cussed before he finally answered. "That . . . that S.O.B. took off with ten thousand dollars of our drug-bust fund. Ripped us off! We had him . . . all set up . . . and that S.O.B., that goddamn mother . . ." He stopped before he cried in frustration.

"That's too bad!" I said. "Ten thousand dollars is a lot of money. Did you get the drugs?"

He winced as if I had struck him or asked if he'd voted for McGovern. "Nothing, we got nothing." Something occurred to him. He sharpened his words, accused me. "You know these damn crazy-house people. C'mon, you're going to take me house to house until we nail that nigger!"

He grabbed my arm and steered me toward an occupied building. I knew it would do no good but humored him. After all, that was a lot of money to have ripped off . . . taxpayers' money. And I was a taxpayer also, wasn't I?

We canvassed two buildings and found no Jet. At the third, Building

#64, a white-garbed female figure came fluttering, shrieking toward me. My companion raised his gun but when he saw me advance with my arms open, he let his hand drop. Gussie McClure buried her head on my shoulder. After she slowed to an understandable verbal pace, her problem came out.

"They did it again, Miss Edith, they came down out of my attic and ate all my stew. I made it with baby lima beans and cooking sherry and now it's all gone. Those men are trying to starve me . . . just because I won't give them my favors!"

The agent looked disgusted at me for listening to Gussie. "She some kind of loony?"

"Gussie McClure has boarders that live in her attic," I told him.

"And they don't pay rent, and try to force favors from me, and eat my food." Gussie was glad of a new ear. "Tonight I sat up—to catch them— but they escaped back to the attic again."

"Well, send them a bill." To me, "Lock her back in her cage and let's hit the next building."

Gussie still hung on to me, still talked. "And now they're even bringing in their slaves, colored boys. Those men in my attic have lost their pride, sharing it with colored folks."

"Lady, I said let's hit the road!" The agent moved ahead of me.

"Listen, I think she's trying to tell us something. Maybe she's telling the truth about men in her attic. It just could be . . ."

"It just could be you're as nuts as that old dame. Now come on!"

I led Gussie back to her door, then followed the leader. Time would tell, and money might talk, but I knew that Gussie wasn't as off as she appeared sometimes. My gut instinct told me that Jet was in that attic with ten thousand dollars. Well, I tried, didn't I?

The project bedded down after the search turned up neither Junior Hernandez nor Jet. The last official car drove away to yakking laughs and hoots. It was past 3:00 a.m. before I got home again.

I slept late that morning and came to work at noon. Ben immediately called me and asked why I was late. I explained, and heard him hiccup twice and hang up.

13

Two weeks of relative calm passed. Easter was the next big holiday. The women were saving for new outfits for themselves and their children. It was a status thing in Buena Vista, I learned. New clothing for that holiday came before food, rent, traffic tickets, or even beer. The Mothers' Club put on a spurt of sewing to get ready. I had received donations of new fabric in dress-length yardages from an outlet house. The ladies came to my office three days a week to use the sewing machines set up in the back bedroom. Usually one of them brought cookies or a cake, and gossip and chattering made a pleasanter background than the usual trouble calls and crime reports. Even Gussie McClure made a new apron for herself.

The days were long now. Leaves had unfolded and clumps of daffodils dotted unlikely areas in the project. I found wilted offerings of flowers on my office steps when I returned after a trip into the project. I knew the children had stolen the blossoms from homes on their way back from school.

A collection of misshapen bunny rabbits and wildly colored ovals of paper eggs decorated my office walls. Grimy, uncertain hands of kindergarten children had drawn them and cut them out. Proper ohs and ahs toward each work of art satisfied, and a penny lollipop was the expected reward for the gift.

Spring brought other changes. Gloria studied travel folders of places to go when her yearly vacation started in May. Mattie switched her blue-and-white eye makeup to green-and-white, no doubt in honor of the greening of the season. Bernice restocked her dwindling supply of sympathy cards.

April Fool's Day and the silly tricks that adults indulge themselves in were over. Rent-collection day came, and a tense office staff watched and counted off each tenant who paid and totaled up the number who did not pay. Gloria snapped at everyone more than usual and Ben Hamilton rammed his car into the project pickup when he got the results. Ernestine Trotmartin had been successful in her appeal. Over seventy-five percent of the tenants had not paid their monthly rent.

On the fourth morning I was buzzed in my office by Gloria. "Watch out, you got a crazy woman on the way over. Sadie Handle has blood in her eyes —says she's going to kill Amelia Goochen. Just thought you should know—Sadie beat up two girls last year and sent them to the hospital." The telephone went dead, but the screaming that flowed into my office was alive! And its name was Sadie Handle.

Sadie was the project's fortune-teller. She had long tangled hair, generous hips, unshaven legs, and many beads and chains around her neck, and she affected fringed shawls, which she used like a bullfighter's cape, to entice, provoke, and lead the bull to disaster. In Sadie's case, the mysterious gypsy quality of her appearance convinced her clients that Sadie was truly gifted with occult powers. Also lung power!

Sadie's breasts heaved, her shawl-fringe wiggled, and her words quivered at the end of each bellow. Since the words "crap" and "shit" were applied to various situations and events in Buena Vista, it was not until I got Sadie quiet and seated on the loveseat that I found out what her problem with Amelia Goochen involved. It *was* crap! Dogs' crap! Sadie's complaint was that Amelia Goochen's three dogs were tied to the clothesline pole used by both families. The rope reached Sadie's back door and yard, and that is where the dogs relieved themselves.

"I am goddamn sick of cleaning that dog shit from my kid's feet!" The gleam in Sadie's eyes was evil. "One more time and I'll . . . I'll . . ."

"Cast a spell on them?"

Sadie took me seriously. "Worst! I'll put a curse on the whole family!"

Before Sadie went home, I promised I would have a talk with Mrs. Goochen. She promised to wait with her spells and curses.

Later that day I looked up the Goochen address. Often I knew the children in a family but not their parents. This was the case here. Billy Goochen and I had many run-ins but I had not met his mother yet.

When I got to the correct building and apartment, I was stopped at the walkway up to the door. Three dogs made an effective barrier with their toothy grins and unwagging tails. The grass was littered with the results of their restricted freedom on the chain leashes. The smell was ripe.

I waited, hoping that someone inside would investigate the barking dogs. No one did. I called out several times but got no answer. Next I picked up a beer can and threw it at the door. That brought results. The door opened and a white woman, bone thin, dressed in a flowered cotton dress, faded and styleless, stuck her head out. Her hair was gray brown and caught into a bun low on her neck. She would have looked at home on a piney-woods farm in East Texas. She inspected me before she spoke. "You from the welfare?"

"No, from the office. Are you Mrs. Goochen?"

"Who are you?" It was an accusation. One thing I had learned about the tenants in Buena Vista was that they rarely admitted being anyone until they knew that acknowledging their own existence would not get them into trouble.

I answered her. "I'm Edith Bentwood."

"What do you want?"

"Just to talk to you a moment." I smiled my "trust me and the world is yours" smile.

"About what?"

This was getting me no place. I made my "look here, this is serious" look and my "do you want the rest of the project to hear" frown.

"We seem to have a problem," I said.

That phrase was the best approach I had found over the past months. It got me into most of the apartments without too much stalling. One thing that the tenants all understood was problems. It worked again.

When the owner accepted me, the three dogs stood aside and allowed me to pass into the apartment. I sat down on the torn upholstered dinette chair which was indicated for me. Its rips were taped together with Band-Aids. Mrs. Goochen remained standing, her arms folded across her skimpy chest.

"Well?" she said.

"Yes. Well, the problem we seem to have is your dogs."

"We don't have no problem, lady. My dogs is fine."

The smell was overpowering: cat smell. Besides the three dogs, the Goochens had cats. I tried to gulp air through my mouth instead of breathing through my nose when they came in. All five of them.

Cat lovers must send out a signal; cats always come to me fully confident that I will pet, scratch, and purr for them. This time was no different. One cat jumped on to my lap, two rubbed against my legs, and the other two positioned themselves on the kitchen table staring into my face with round green eyes. I reached out and massaged a matted ear.

"You like cats." It was a statement.

"Cats like me."

Mrs. Goochen pulled out a chair and sat down. She leaned her head on a leathery palm and stared at me just like the cats.

"I say when cats like a person, they must be good people."

So we forgot about the defecating dogs and talked about cats. From the cats we talked about the project and Mrs. Goochen. Like salt pouring in dry weather, the details of her life poured out. As each of us scratched one cat's ears, I learned that Mrs. Goochen (or Amelia, as she asked me to call her) had lived in the project five years. She had come to California from a town on the Texas side of the Texas-Louisiana border, with her four younger children, because her oldest son was in a government hospital in Southern California. He had had both legs shot off in Vietnam and she came to be close to him. Her next son was now in jail for armed robbery. Amelia's lip trembled as she told this. "He was a good boy," she said softly. It was this place, this life. Her hand rested on the smooth fur of the cat. Her fingernails had ridges, and knuckle-bumps indicated arthritis would soon cripple her hands.

Her middle child was a girl, and retarded. The state hospital was going to move her into a private place. Amelia confided her fears about that. "It ain't right, to move them poor things. No private place is goin' to care like the state does. I wanted to bring her home, but they wouldn't let her come."

She brightened when she talked about Celia, the next child. Celia would be graduated this spring from high school. "She's smart—smart and pretty. She'll make it, she and Billy. Billy's my baby. He's eleven . . . gets sassy sometimes."

I could see that Billy was the joy of his mother's life. She had gotten up to bring me a picture of Billy at three years old dressed in a cowboy suit. The Billy I knew wasn't like this cute baby! I was saved from making ohs and ahs when Billy walked in the kitchen door.

Billy's thick overlong hair drooped on the old army jacket he had on. I wondered if it was his wounded brother's. Under it, he wore the usual T-shirt and jeans. The sleeves of the jacket covered his hands. His kid look was spoiled by a bloody mouth which was twisted bitterly. Mud was streaked over his face. He limped as he walked over to the sink and took a drink from the faucet. His mother sighed and shook her head at him.

"You been fightin'," she said.

"Goddamn bloods!"

He wiped the blood from his mouth. It smeared. His lips were purple.

"Mama, I ain't going to school no more. You can't make me."

He was close to tears; hate made them stay back. When he saw me, he stopped. His face tightened up. He kept his eyes on me as he questioned his mother whether the school had sent me down. Amelia told him I had come down about the dogs. It seemed to satisfy the boy. I was the one who asked Billy what had happened to him. Before he answered, Billy picked up a rag from the floor and spit into it. A mouthful of blood came up.

"B.T. and that Danny Gree and Buttons Lewis grabbed me and beat me on the way from school. Sons of bitches got me behind the fence and pounded me."

Now the tears came and smeared into the blood.

Amelia coaxed him over to her. She held out a doughnut she took from a half-open box on the table. I noticed a small cockroach crawling on it, but I kept silent. As Billy took it, the insect dropped off.

"The kids around here are awful." Amelia helped herself to a doughnut and shoved the box toward me. I ignored it.

"I sent Billy to the store last night and those same Negroes robbed him and then stole his shoes."

I looked down at Billy's feet. He had on sneakers with big rips. They were girls' shoes, his sister's, I assumed. I wondered if Amelia knew that her son wasn't lily-white either. Billy crammed the doughnut into his mouth. The powdery sugar stuck to the wet blood on his lips.

"Those damn niggers think they can mess over me any time they get the notion, Mama. I'll show them, the lousy bastards."

His voice cracked with anger and he started into the living room, peeling off the jacket. We heard him stomp up the stairs. The loud purring of a cat was the only sound. Amelia's fingers brushed the doughnut crumbs into a little heap, then mashed it down flat. One cat leaned over to sniff at it, passed it up, and settled in the woman's lap. Suddenly Amelia threw the cat off, jumped up, and headed for the other room. The other cats scattered. I heard her shouting up the stairwell.

"Billy! What are you gettin' into? Billy! You hear me?"

A muffled exchange took place and Amelia came back to me. She braced herself against the back of a chair. We heard the boy come back downstairs. I faced him as he stood in the doorway. A gun was in his hand. I shrank back. It was ugly; despite all the TV shows of detectives and police chases and assorted criminals, I still did not know one gun from another. It just looked wicked and deadly.

The boy stopped. His hair fell over his forehead; the dried blood across his face made a crooked slash on his white skin. He swayed and his hand trembled as he shifted the gun from his left hand to his right. I looked up at his mother.

Amelia sagged. Her sparse flesh traced the narrow face-bones into a hollow-eyed skull. She lifted one hand and pulled out a thin wire hairpin. With it she scraped loose hairs into a branch which she twisted and then poked back into the bun with the hair-prong. Her words straggled out, a strand at a time.

"Where did you find my gun?"

"I know where you stash it."

"Here, give it back. I don't want no trouble, no more. I got enough already. Give me that gun, Billy Goochen." She held out her hand toward her eleven-year-old son.

He ignored her outstretched hand. His eyes narrowed, evaluated his mother. Then he walked by the table and threw the gun down. It skidded toward me and I jumped. His mother reached over and picked it up. Billy started for the outside door. She ran after him and grabbed his arm.

"Don't go back out. They'll catch you again. Let mama talk to some people. You gotta listen to mama, Billy. Not all Negroes is bad . . . maybe if Tommy Gun knows what's goin' on, he'll make them stop. He's a fair Negro. I'll go put out the word he's to come by."

Tommy Gun again.

"Go to hell!" the boy shouted.

He pulled away from his mother, ripped open the door, and ran outside. The tin curtain rod over the glass-topped door fell. The dingy fabric hung crookedly. Mrs. Goochen plucked at the curtain and replaced the rod before she turned back to me.

"He didn't mean it. He's just upset."

She looked down at her other hand still holding the gun. Her casual handling of it made me nervous. I asked her if it was loaded.

"Yes, it's loaded."

"Aren't you afraid? I mean . . . to have a loaded gun around?"

"I'd be afraid if it wasn't loaded. I sleep with it under my pillow. Every night."

She picked up the same rag that Billy had spit into and started to polish the metal.

"As long as it gets out a woman's got a gun in this hellhole, an' ain't afraid to use it, they let you be."

"Have you ever used it?" I asked.

"Not yet. But if I have to . . . Well, if I have to, I can and I will."

Amelia sank into her chair again; she spit on the barrel and continued rubbing it. My eyes never left her hands. The gun held the center of attention. I questioned her about the attack that Billy had complained about. Did it happen often?

"All the time. Sometimes worse than others, then it slackens off. It's the dropouts . . . the big kids that jus' hang around . . . mostly the colored kids."

"Then the school authorities must be notified. They are responsible for seeing that a child gets safely to and back from school."

"The school authorities!" She looked up, her hand still, her voice bitter. "What do they care? Moment a child comes from Buena Vista they peg him as a bum. They don't care what happens to our children. The school—all they need is an excuse to run them out. Half the kids that pull this stuff have been kicked outta school already. Just get them out . . . get rid of them. Then they wonder why they turn bad!"

She returned to her polishing. She blew breath on one side, scrubbed harder. A quivering sigh rattled from her corded neck. I watched two more cockroaches crawl over the table headed for the doughnut box. Her hands rested. The rag was dropped and the gun lay naked between us, fat barreled. She kept her eyes on it as she spoke.

"Sometimes I think to myself that they wish they could call the dog pound an' just have our kids picked up and put in cages and then after a little while, do them like they do the cats and dogs—gas them. We is just nuisances."

"That's not so! Children are important, no matter where they live or who they are. You'll see! I'll contact the police . . . the community relations officer and the juvenile authorities."

She picked up the gun.

"They won't do anything. This . . . this is authority."

I tried to convince her that the police were caring, would do their job of protecting everyone. Amelia kept shaking her head.

"No, ma'am. The cops are scared. Like roosting guinea hens, they raise up a fuss when danger comes, but you take notice where they holler from —high up in the tree where they're safe."

I was starting to leave when I realized nothing had been settled about the three Goochen dogs. Suddenly the dogs barked wildly. The door was knocked open and two teen-aged girls shoved their way in. One was Hilda Franks's girl Joyce—overweight, thick-ankled, a candidate for the ugly award.

"Mrs. Goochen, you better get out there . . . quick! Something's happened to Billy!" Joyce pulled on the seated woman.

"They're beating Billy up!" Tami Jewel—pinched-faced, skinny, over-perfumed. The other girl was bug-eyed.

The mother reacted; her face went white, then flooded red. She stood up. "Who?" It was a demand.

The girls were silent. They pulled back, looked at each other. Fear made their voices low as they gave her names . . . Danny Gree and B.T.—mainly Danny.

"They're using a chain—a biker's chain."

"It's bad . . . please . . . you better come quick," Tami said.

The mother used the gun in her hand to sweep us all aside. She followed the girls, who were running ahead. I followed behind. We rounded that building and crossed Greentree Lane. In the next parking lot a crowd had gathered. A group of children and adults formed a semicircle. The girls fell back as Amelia made her own path by knocking people aside until she got to the center. I heard her scream and then curse. My heels slowed me as I ran up behind her. As I passed several tenants I screamed at them to call the police. Someone answered me. "You call 'em yourself, lady. We call the cops on those dudes, maybe our kid'll be next."

I passed an open apartment door. Old Mrs. Papadakis, a constant com-plainer, was watching. Now her face was welcome. She had a telephone! I mumbled something as I pushed her aside and ran in the direction she pointed. I called the emergency number and shouted for help at the bland voice that answered. Satisfied that the message had gotten across, I ran back out.

The crowd was larger. I looked for Amelia Goochen. I parted my way past onlookers until I spotted her, collapsed on the ground. In her flowered print dress, she looked like a neglected garden. She was bending over Billy. Close by her, I recognized Dude Muggins and Harry the Shoe. Lisa Fritzle was holding her baby, Jefferson. The crowd watched silently. Small children toddled between the legs of the adults. Over hushed murmuring of the tenants the guttural cursing and crying of the woman could be heard. I watched as she put her arms under her child's form and tried to stand up. He was dead weight and she sank under it to her knees again. I rushed over to help. My heel caught and I almost tripped. I looked down, tried to shake loose. My heel had slipped into one of the oversized links of a huge steel chain. Like metal intestines, it curled at my feet. It was red with blood. The crowd parted just as I looked up and saw Billy's head.

I was hardly conscious of my first scream; I retched out another scream and plunged toward the child. I saw Amelia lift her hand with the gun. She pointed it into the air. My next scream was split as she fired. Once into the air. Twice into the crowd. Wildly the shots rang out with a boong-boong. Like wind down an alley, a sucking sound of drawn-in breath came from the stunned spectators. A trio of teen-agers shifted and moved outside the circle. A passageway opened up and caught the figure of Danny Gree exposed. He seemed riveted, like a rat when a light shines in its face. I tried to reach Amelia before she could take aim. I was too late. She was back in the swamplands of the border lakes of Texas. The head of Danny Gree was the head of a black moccasin and Amelia was protecting her rights. She shot and hit. A thin screech, then running. People milled, shoved. Shouts. Then tires making a curve, flashing red lights, a cherry on top of an ice-cream sundae. The police arrived.

A voice said, "Split!"

Another voice, "The pigs! Move it!"

More police cars came; I counted six. The squad cars blocked the parking lot. Uniformed men piled out. Some had guns drawn, some stoked their billy clubs. They moved in a sweep. I tried to wave at them to come over to where the injured child lay on the ground. I found myself moving protectively between the police and the mother with her child. I wanted to explain to them what had happened, before they arrested the mother. The police neared, then parted and detoured around the three of us. No one stopped to take the gun from Amelia's hand. No one glanced at the bleeding child. Most of the tenants had taken off, melted into the buildings. When the area was swept clean, silently, the white-helmeted police backed up. The scene had a macabre feeling, like a film run backward—except these were no Keystone Kops and this was no comedy.

Now the police turned to us. One cop approached me. He still had his gun drawn. He was curt. "Sergeant Fuller, ma'am. You work here?" His voice said he knew I did.

"Yes."

"What happened?"

I turned toward Billy and Amelia. Somehow she had managed to pick him up. She staggered under his weight. His arms hung limp and his feet dangled in their ragged sneakers. Amelia had tucked the gun into his belt. It lay heavy on his stomach hollow. I said nothing. I pointed to the boy in his mother's arms and then at the heavy chain. It told the story. Another policeman came up. He toed the chain to move it. It assumed another shape. The policeman wiped the blood off the toe of his boot by scuffing in on the ground.

"See who did it?"

I repeated the names that the two girls had called out. The sergeant nodded.

"Punks. I know them. Lousy little punks."

Amelia Goochen swayed under her burden as she came up to us. I wondered what the police would say when they saw the exposed gun. Did they know she had hit someone?

A shout from the far side of the parking lot. Another cop.

"Hey, Fuller, we got a pool of blood here. She hit someone."

"I hope to God I did!" Amelia said. "Bastard!"

The sergeant did two things at the same time. He took the gun off the boy's still figure and reached behind and unhooked his handcuffs. Amelia backed, twisting away and out of range. He spoke over his shoulder to the younger man and told him to flush out Danny Gree. He turned to me and asked me which apartment was the Gree place. I pointed toward the end of the building.

"Take a squad and bring him in."

I watched as four men started down in that direction; their walk was stiff, their heads swiveled, carefully scanning the empty area.

A dog barked.

A stereo blared hard rock.

The sergeant forgot about Amelia as he watched his men get close to the Gree place.

A sharp whistle, the kind a kid makes between fingers.

The doors opened and tenants streamed out. In seconds over a hundred people ringed the four policemen. Silent, unsmiling, they watched: black, white, Chicano; men, women, children.

The men continued firmly to the front door. I turned and looked over to where the other cops were waiting by their cars. They shuffled, adjusted their gear, fingered their guns. Their white helmets bobbed like beach balls on water as they talked softly among themselves.

Staccato raps turned me around and I saw that Sergeant Fuller had joined his men at Danny Gree's door. Three separate times he banged on the door. Like shots, each rap bounced between the concrete buildings. The door stayed closed.

"Open up. Police! Open up or we'll kick it down."

The door opened. Slowly. A thin black woman barred entry with her arms.

"What you botherin' me for?" Angry, shrill, her voice carried.

"Ma'am, we're looking for Danny Gree. You his mother?" The man's voice was low, not quite steady.

The woman looked out and over the heads of the uniformed men standing lower than she. I followed her gaze. The tenants merged and now a ring of people slowly pressed forward. I started over and felt Amelia behind me, drawn closer also; no one spoke, as if they were waiting for another signal.

The woman in the doorway spread out her arms and gripped the sides of the opening. She said nothing. Another voice broke the silence.

"Go home, pigs!"

To punctuate the demand, I saw something fly through the air from behind me. It crashed on the stoop where Sergeant Fuller was standing. It was the chain. It made a dark curved line at his feet.

The signal!

Other voices took up the obscenities. Everyone joined. Chants started. Like the chain, the words were hard, heavy, hate-filled.

This wasn't real, I told myself. Sweat ran down my neck, under my arms. I wanted to get out of this place, but there was no way to leave. I was too afraid to be afraid.

The policemen drew their guns. Sergeant Fuller moved back and away from the door, against the stucco wall. He faced the crowd. His face looked flushed. He swallowed hard and I saw him look toward his other men by the cars. He nodded slightly.

He slid his hand over the handle of the gun strapped to his hip. He pulled it out.

A boy about seven stood next to me. He was shoeless and wore pants too large, rolled up. A woman's dress belt wrapped twice around his wasp waist held them up. He pushed forward into the clearing and ran close to the policeman. He laughed wildly and stuck his thumbs into his ears and wiggled his fingers.

"Mister Po-liceman, you gonna shoot me?"

Then, running in circles, he imitated the classical call of insult: "Oink . . . oink!"

The tension broke. People snickered at the child's antics. The sergeant wet his lips and raised his hand, palm flat, a signal to his men in the background to move back. The four cops near him let their guns stay in the holsters. The crowd made a hole through which the men drifted toward the squad cars. The sergeant stayed back until he saw them safely in the cars, then turned to the black woman in the doorway. I saw him lean close to her and speak. Whatever he said brought roaring curses from her. She flayed her stick arms like a spider climbing its web. The cop went for his handcuffs hooked at his belt.

The mood of the tenants had relaxed; it changed. It was tombstone still. A distant ambulance scream grew louder. Someone kicked a can. It rattled off the curb. I forgot about Amelia until I heard her voice behind me.

"Get the hell out! You're no damn good to us anyway! All you cops do is cause more trouble and then take off." Her voice broke. "Look . . . look at my kid. Not one of you bastards even stopped to look at my boy. You don't care nothin' 'bout us . . . any of us . . . white or black."

Amelia Goochen turned her back on the sergeant and walked in a seesaw way toward her own apartment. She arched her back under the weight of the boy. When she vanished behind the building, it was all over.

The crowd dispersed again, this time in small groups. Sergeant Fuller let the handcuffs dangle from one finger while he and the black woman faced each other down. As if by mutual agreement, both acted at once. The woman shut the door and the man turned his back and walked away. He passed me, stopped.

"Someone should burn this place down." His jaw twitched.

"And the people?"

"The best way to get rid of roaches is to pour gas on them and light a match."

I clamped my mouth together so hard my teeth hurt. Then I said, "Like the lady said, you better get the hell out of Buena Vista—now!"

I was shocked to hear myself. I turned and walked away.

Billy Goochen made the evening papers, and, for a month after that, Amelia carried the clipping enclosed in a plastic folder. The ambulance had taken him to the hospital. After three days he was back holding court in his front yard, growling dogs, smells and all. Even Sadie Handle forgot to complain about the "crap" and loaned Billy her transistor radio. Billy basked in the project's recognition.

Danny Gree was the most attentive. The bullet had grazed his head and the scalp wound had bled a lot, but under his Afro, the mark was unseen. He carried Billy in and out and kept him in steady supply of Pepsis and barbecued corn-taco chips.

One afternoon I went into the main office after seeing Billy hold court. I mentioned to Ben Hamilton how strange it was that, after first almost killing Billy, now Danny was playing nursemaid. Ben's tongue, black from his licorice candy, prowled his sticky lips.

"You got to realize that you're not dealing with rational, normal people." I watched his black tongue flick in and out. He continued. "They don't react like we do. You know, have feelings and suffer. They're almost like fish . . . cold fish . . . bloodless, no emotions. Just welfare checks and booze." "You forgot about sex. You know about sex?" He flushed, then laughed. "Oh—that! Like animals, you know. It's an instinct, not love!" I just nodded. Ben Hamilton was the perfect example of the desensitized, deodorized man: a can for a heart and a nozzle for a head, expelling lethal black spray, like smog. Ben Hamilton *was* the Right Guard man of the year.

14

The next afternoon, bitchy Mrs. Fairchild, an older tenant, presented me with a petition signed by twenty-seven senior citizens. It stated they objected to the words of the song that Alfred sang as he whipped around the project on his I. J. Case commercial lawn mower.

I took off to track down "Hi-Ho" Alfred on his metal steed, "Trigger." Alfred rode with the aplomb of a black Roy Rogers. He wore a straw hat and dashiki shirt, and he sang a lot better than Roy. His appeal for the ladies in the project was legend, and Starlet Jones's Bitsy was not the only small face that resembled Alfred's.

Finding anyone in the seventy-eight acres of Buena Vista was a task for a Sherlock Holmes on a skateboard. I usually walked, but today I limped. A new pair of "comfortable walking shoes" gave me a heel blister. Just as I spotted Alfred across Greentree Lane and waved for him to stop, he vibrated around the corner of Building #73 and disappeared. I began to run, then stopped, leaned against the front fender of a car, and took off one shoe. While I was rubbing my heel and wriggling my cramped toes, I heard an apartment door open behind me. I turned. It was Debby Nickel. Children in Buena Vista had a built-in radar antenna that separated dangerous nosy people from those not to be trusted but easy to con. Debby Nickel, who was nine and not bright, finished her evaluation of me: not dangerous, just dumb.

"Mama got our furniture back and all her samples."

"She did? That's great! What happened? I mean, how did you get it back?" I kept my eye on her as I put my shoe on.

"They brought it back."

"Who brought it back?"

"Oh . . . some people."

Her eyes shifted to the grass and she pretended to pick up something buried in the ground. It was her way of saying "get lost." The body English of tenants in Buena Vista was a graduate course in silent communication. I was learning. Persistence was one of the prerequisites.

"What people?" I repeated her words.

Her mother's voice reached us from the open door of her apartment. It was unfriendly. Judy Nickel chastised her daughter for talking to me—and me for listening.

"Shut your damn mouth and get yourself in here."

She started toward the girl, hands outstretched. To me she said, "An' you, you want to cause trouble?"

The project's Avon Lady anchored her fingers in the child's hair like one of those claw hands in penny arcade candy machines that almost—but never quite—come up with the prize your engineering plots. Debby twisted her head, ducked. Obviously she had long practice in evading her mother's tactics. She ran to my side.

"I ain't doin' nothin' wrong! You said yourself, Ma, that Tommy Gun got the word and fixed it up so's we got our stuff back."

Mrs. Nickel pulled her flowered kimono snugly around her waist. Clenched the cloth tighter at the neckline. She looked like a moth in her cocoon—one that would never turn into a butterfly.

"I got my stuff back . . . I don't ask no questions."

I knew she hoped I would go away, but I had learned to fence with my tenants for information.

"I thought Tommy Gun was gone—was out of the project. Nobody's seen him . . . that I know about." I watched her as she answered me.

"He don't have to be here to get things done. He jus' have to send the word."

Her tone was softer, conciliatory. She extended one arm toward Debby. The girl understood she was forgiven. She moved away from my side toward her mother. They reached a pact of silence.

I hobbled off, wondering where I could find "Hi-Ho" Alfred and his X-rated songs.

Later that week the word was out—Tommy Gun was back! A scarlet 1964 T-bird thundered in from Grand Boulevard, circled the project, zipped down Flood Road, raced up Greentree Lane, and disappeared somewhere in the project.

Finally our paths crossed. I was in a hurry to leave the office and was locking up when the insistent honking of a car horn made me look up. Tommy Gun was driving the T-bird. The honking stopped when he saw me notice him. He dipped his broad-brimmed hat encircled with an Indian silver band at me. Grinning, he used one hand to slap against the side of the car in a rhythmic jungle-drum beat. The tinny sound echoed.

"Hey, nigger-lady! Keep it cool! Stay with it, baby!"

I bent down to see who was sitting next to him. It was a heavyset black man, older, dressed in a suit—certainly not a project tenant. Now was my chance to ask Tommy Gun about the Nickel deal. I had almost reached the car when the driver gunned the motor and they roared away, chrome pipes billowing oil clouds.

"Hey! Hey . . ." I yelled and waved my hand but they were gone.

So much for Tommy Gun! I was piqued at his arrogance. I knew he had gotten the word that I wanted to talk to him. Somehow he cleverly divined what I wanted from him. Sure, he granted my wish—getting the Nickels' stuff back—but he denied me the pleasure of feeling I had some authority over his actions. I wondered who the well-dressed black man was with Tommy Gun.

Driving home that night, I mulled over my resentment toward Tommy Gun. A tickertape string of insults spewed through my mind. I ended up angry that I could get angry about this really nonimportant person in my life.

That night I had a class at State University. I rushed through a boiled hot dog and a glass of tomato juice. The lecture was two hours of dull statistics on the "sociological aspects of concentrated low-income residents disseminated into upper-class areas in a one-to-one placement factor." All of which meant, if you take ghetto slobs and put them into decent neighborhoods, will they keep the lawn trimmed next to the house belonging to good old Joe Smith who has paid into Social Security for 193 years?

I raised my hand three times during discussion period. I wasn't called on once.

It had been a rotten day for me—even a rotten week. In fact, the whole damn month wouldn't have won a box of Cracker Jack on "Let's Make a Deal."

I went to bed that night with a thick headache from jungle drums beating out the words "nigger-lady!"

At 8:01 the next morning the telephone rang itself into a Cher frenzy. I stumbled into my office in time to get the last ring. An old-lady voice quivered, "You have to do something about that noise. All night long, slamming doors, playing the Victrola, and the people . . . all kinds. Black fellows, white gals, screaming! I can't sleep now for two nights. You just got to do something, Miss Edie."

She gave me her building number and apartment address and said the offending tenant lived next door to the left. No, she didn't know her name but she was white and had one white child and one . . . Here the old voice sputtered and died.

I hung up and called over to Mattie on my hot-line. I asked her to look up the tenant's name according to the information I had. She hooted and snapped it back.

"Building eighty-nine and next to Tillie Thompson? Ha! You got a winner in that girl. That's Raquel . . . Raquel Mansfield."

"Hey, don't make the funnies with me."

"Who's making funnies? That's her name—Raquel. You know—Go-Boy's sister! The Mansfields are one of our three-generation families—grandma Maybeline, mama Josephine, and Raquel, with her two brats!"

My mind accepted the connection. Mattie rambled on.

"Raquel Mansfield has no business being in the project. I warned them. I told Ben Hamilton not to let her back in after all that trouble we had with her and her bunch . . . drugs and stuff."

"Then why did he?"

"Ernestine."

"Ernestine Trotmartin?"

"The same. She and her Action For Tenants. She put the pressure on poor Ben and you know how scared he is of her. I am so sick of that woman! We never had any trouble until she came along with her AFT! If you ask me—"

I didn't. I thanked her and hung up.

I turned left when I came out of the office and strolled under the dipping spring-green, hair-thin branches of the pepper trees. The air was still. Earth smells mingled with night mist. Buena Vista rested in morning freshness; sighs and sorrows and dragging feet were still chained to sleep.

I passed the first parking lot and turned into the second. The usual broken pop bottles, pools of brackish car oil, rimless axles, soiled paper diapers, and evidence that the Colonel (Kentucky, that is) beat out Jack-in-the-Box slowed my progress.

Building #89 was ahead of me. All doors in the project looked alike. Only by checking the small metal numbers over each entrance could one find the correct dwelling. I found number 845. Door 845 had one cracked windowpane, one broken-out windowpane. One square had cardboard taped over the hole; the fourth section was intact. The lower part of the wooden paneled door had spattered egg yolk dribbled into octopus fingers that had dried in waxy strings. Cracked eggshells, like plastic snowflakes, dotted the cement stoop. I felt that I had been at this apartment before—when? I couldn't remember.

I knocked and waited. No answer. I peeked through a hole in the ripped plastic curtain held together with a safety pin. Nothing moved inside. I knocked again. This time I heard a noise; then the doorknob rattled. A young child's voice said, "Come in."

"Where's your mommy?" I called into the hole.

"Mommy bed."

"Can I speak to her?"

"Come in."

The door opened and I was looking down into blue eyes set in a bright little face topped by a mop of blond hair. Dressed in dirty shorts on backward, a T-shirt which exposed his belly button, and barefoot, he looked like a Kewpie doll. He was all of three. It was Swenson. Swenson of my first day at Buena Vista. Swenson, whose mother said, "Get out."

"Hi, aren't you Swenson?"

"Uh-huh."

"I'm so glad to see you again. Do you think you can get your mommy?"

"I see."

He ran from the kitchen into the living room while I waited at the open door. I heard his scrambled progress up the stairs. My eyes wandered over the kitchen.

The drainboard was stacked with dirty dishes and pots. Heaped sacks of garbage with greasy bottoms made a totem pole against the stove. A soiled diaper lay on the dinette table; flies tick tack toed over it. Potato chips spilled from a ripped bag. A plastic spoon stood upright in a dash of hardened cereal. The dish was on the tray of a high chair encrusted with Gerber's finest. A loose nipple protruded from a heap of blue-specked soap powder. The box had tipped over from a basket of dirty clothes. They smelled.

I was struggling with my middle-class attitudes when Swenson came back with a young woman. He tugged on her fleecy nightgown. One side was ripped, showing a skinny upper leg. The untorn part barely concealed a skeleton body. Stringy hair hid most of her narrow face. Thin lips, dime-sized freckles, and an underdeveloped bustline spelled out "Mommy." The name "Raquel" was misleading!

What would be a more appropriate reason for a tenant to use a gun than being addressed as a sex symbol, when one glance in even a cracked mirror lets her know she is Ma Kettle's stand-in? Taking no chances, I positioned myself behind the door and only poked my head in. I smiled, I think.

"Raquel? Raquel Mansfield?"

"Yeah. Who're you?"

"I'm from the office. I'm Edith Bentwood."

"Yeah, so? You here about the rent?"

"No."

It looked safe; I hadn't been shot at yet. I decided that Raquel's near-nude appearance would cause further gossip if we talked at the open door. I took a chance.

"Can I talk to you—inside?"

She nodded, lifted one leg, and kicked away a wheelless toy truck that blocked my path. She stood aside.

"Sure. Come in."

Swenson led the way, his mother followed, and I trailed her into the living room. Suddenly I felt I had drowned in deep ocean water. The one window was darkened by heavy blue drapes. The only light came from an aquarium tank. Mysterious bubbles swirled and popped in the greenish water. Fish swam royally through china castles and tickled themselves on waving plastic seaweed. A lopsided couch was draped with a tapestry.

I shoved my feet through the litter on the floor: worn clothing, empty bread wrappers, beer cans, more broken toys, and a pebbled trail of Cheerios. I made my careful way to the couch under the poster eyes of Martin Luther King, Jr., Snoopy, and George Wallace. George's smiling face was covered with the scrawled instruction, "Kiss My Ass."

The couch cushion slanted and I braced myself against the arm. Raquel had gone upstairs. The blasting cry of an unhappy infant stopped and Raquel came back a moment later cradling a girl baby about eight months old. Her gown was soiled and she was sucking a rubber-nippled empty baby bottle. A perky red ribbon was tied in her blondish, kinky hair. Brimming black eyes, a flattened nose and caramel skin told that her father was black.

The mother curled up in the only chair in the room, a ripped platform rocker. She put the baby on the floor, where it immediately exchanged the nipple for some Cheerios.

My eyes could distinguish what was going on now. I saw the television set, stereo and speakers, and flat tapes stacked like cards on a massive Spanish-type bookcase. I felt I was in a poor man's version of Captain Nemo's Cosy Cabin. I watched Raquel as she fumbled for a cigarette, scrubbed a match on fire, and sent out the first long smoke cloud. After the second drag, she raised her hand and brushed the hair away from her face.

Raquel had only one eye!

I had adjusted to ripe garbage smells, blond black children, deep-sea living rooms, and Snoopy for President, but a one-eyed tenant was more than I had bargained for! Still, I had a job to do. I firmed up my voice.

"We seem to have a little problem." (My old standby.)

Raquel kept smoking. She closed her good eye. That bothered me, because I remembered my mother explaining life to me when I was ten: "Never trust a person who won't look you in the eye when you speak with them." What do I do now, Mama?

I tried again. "Did anything special happen last night?"

The eye opened. "Like what?"

"Oh, like an emergency?" I waved my hands like Cloris Leachman.

"Nope."

The eye closed. The smoke went upward. Swenson dragged in a puppy from somewhere. The puppy was whining, and, as Swenson passed his mother's chair, she stuck out her leg and tripped him, cuffed him on his head when he landed on the yelping dog, and then kicked him.

"Goddamn! I told you to leave the fuckin' dog alone! You hurt that puppy and I'll skin you alive!"

Swenson got up without crying and rolled away behind his mother's chair out of sight. The puppy crawled under the couch by me. I wanted to yell back. Instead I said, "Children that age can be trying."

Her good eye flickered a moment, then shut again.

"The reason I'm here is because we had a complaint about you."

There. It was out. Not Swenson, the girl baby, the puppy, or Raquel's sometimes open eye would prevent me from dealing with the problem. I waited for a response.

"So? I got complaints, too. Big ones."

Raquel kept her eye open. This was headway. She took a deep puff from her butt and blew the smoke out slowly, teasing the already foul air to accept the last dregs.

"Yeah. I want a new stove. Like Ernestine says, they ain't nothing but old junk and don't cook no way. And—I got bugs."

It was my turn to close my eyes. Bugs! I itched all over. I wanted to scratch something, anything. Where were they? On me! I starched my voice. "What kind of bugs?"

"Cockroaches. What kind do you think?"

My scalp stopped tingling but now my legs twitched. I knew if I looked down I would see quarter-sized creatures marching up my shoes. I looked, but all I saw were circles of dead cereal. I wanted to say, "You dumb broad, no self-respecting cockroach would be caught dead wandering over this mess!" Instead, I stuck to my task.

"What time do you go to bed?"

That was a mistake! I knew it as soon as I said it. Raquel opened her good eye Cyclops-wide and the blue light turned to red.

"What's it to you?"

"The complaint that I received was that you and your guests make noise all night long. It disturbs the other tenants."

"Bullshit!" The eye closed again.

The battle of the century—Eye against I.

Swenson crept past me and escaped up the concrete stairs leading to the bedrooms. I wished I could follow him. Anything to get out of this waterlogged situation. The sound of other feet coming down the steps made me turn my head. It was a young black girl. She was massaged into skin-tight pants and topped with a halter of wild colors. Long, dangling gold earrings hung under a modified Afro. Close at her heels was a young black boy. Also in tight faded jeans, he wore a muscle shirt in purple edged with yellow binding. I recognized Freddie-O. Just last week Freddie-O and I had a run-in. It was a matter of his having a BB gun and the vacated apartment's having six broken windows. His mouth was bigger then my staying power and finally I let him off. Now what was he doing here? Freddie was only sixteen and lived with his mother, Honey Curtis, and five brothers. His home was two parking lots and four buildings away.

The black girl ball-footed silently past both Raquel and me and went into the kitchen. I heard the refrigerator door open, then slam shut, and then a *ping* of something metal hitting the floor. She returned, sword-swallowing a giant Pepsi. She stopped and took a long swig, then passed the Pepsi to Raquel, who copied her actions. In turn, Raquel handed the drink to Freddie-O. I wondered if some tradition or ethnic policy of public housing would stamp my refusal to share this hospitality a grave sin leading to slashed tires or sugar in my gas tank. My fear fled. Freddie-O finished the bottle.

Freddie-O sat yogi-fashion. He had kicked away assorted junk to clear off a section of floor. Now he rolled the empty Pepsi bottle under the couch. I watched as he combed and fluffed out his hair with a lethal steel-pronged comb. The high-stepping black girl disappeared upstairs again without saying a word. I wondered who she was.

The only movement for a minute or two was Freddie-O ratting his hair, the fish maypoling, and me surreptitiously scratching my ankle. I took the plunge; I landed like a high diver in a tar pit.

"Raquel, is your friend living with you, because if she is, you know that unless she's on your lease, it's against the Housing Agency's policy."

"What?" Her blue eye opened.

"I was just explaining—"

"Fuck the Housing Agency."

A smoke-sword dissolved before it reached me. Behind it, the eye shuttered itself. Since she was so forthright and frank in her feelings, I tried the same direct approach.

"Look, who's that girl that went upstairs?"

"Alpha."

Short and to the point. I decided I had found the correct technique in dealing with Raquel Mansfield.

"Alpha Washington?"

"Who else?"

"But she lives with her mother, doesn't she?"

Begrudgingly. "Building forty-two."

"What's she doing here?"

"Her boyfriend beat her up last night."

"Where?"

"All over."

"No. I mean where, at her house or here?"

"Both. He started at her ma's place and then she ran over here an' he followed and beat on her some more over here."

"Didn't you call the police?"

Raquel's eye popped wide open. Freddie-O burped loudly. He stopped fussing with his hair and left the silver metal comb locked in the fuzzed-up hair like an antenna. He started low. "The po-lice! We call the cops—and what they do? Nothin'! Know what that shitass said? Alpha was spread out on the floor an' Dude was kickin' the shit outta her an' you know what that shitass cop said?"

Freddie-O was screaming now. I shook a "no." He mimicked. "Why don't you people do me a favor and beat yourselves to death and save us all a lot of trouble?"

Freddie-O stood up. He toed a beer can at the wall. It climbed three feet and fell back with a clatter.

"That's your lousy cops for you."

The resentment and distrust of the police was an established fact in Buena Vista. Yet the complaints were never specific. This was different. If I could get to the facts in this case, perhaps I could show this boy that he was either exaggerating, misinterpreting the officer's remarks, or plain lying.

"They took a report, didn't they?"

"Hell, no! The lousy cops didn't do nothin'." Raquel stubbed out her butt and lit another cigarette. Small angry smoke rings circled the room and died in mid-air.

"You mean to tell me that two policemen came by, saw a man kick and beat a young woman, and didn't even take a report—or arrest him?"

"Lady, I mean to tell you just that!"

Freddie-O was rooting out all the empty beer cans and flattening them. Every time his black scarred feet smashed a can, I felt he saw a cop instead of a piece of metal. I refused to swallow his story.

"You expect me to believe that the man who was responsible for this assault wasn't picked up?"

No one answered. Freddie-O squashed the last Coors can. Raquel leaned her blond head back on the chair and continued to blow neat rings. I noticed she had buttoned the gown in a concession to modesty. Her face was turned to one side and, in profile, her pale skin and flowing hair against the rich shadows of the darkened room made her look like an angel by Raphael.

I wanted to leave. I started to get up, then stopped. They had sidetracked me with Alpha's problem and the gripe about the police. I realized that I had not settled the complaint about last night's noise.

"Let's get back to the noise complaint. Whatever the reason was this time, you have been reported for excess noise before. Now, what guarantee will you give that it won't continue?"

A voice from behind answered. It was Alpha. "Get off her back!"

She walked by me toward Raquel and took the cigarette from her hand, puffed on it twice, and then gave it back. Her bruised face showed up as the colored lights from the fish tank highlighted her bronze skin. The room became a voodoo cave, the girl, a primitive princess of black magic.

We posed as still life.

The rattle, then slam, of the kitchen door started action. I turned my head as a young man walked in. At the same time, Alpha bolted in front of me and pounded up the stairs. It was Dude Muggins! Of course! The name Dude had been said, but then "dude" was a common way in Buena Vista to refer to any male.

Dude entered limping. He leaned on a broken pool cue for support of one knee. A wide porkpied hat with a beaded band sat on his stockinged Afro. An unbleached muslin shirt decorated with sunbursts and peace signs was cut low to show his lean belly. A tooled belt with silver buckle held up his low-hipped pants. Sandals slopped under elongated toes.

His graham-cracker skin had a deep cut down the left cheek. One eye was closed in a plum-colored circle. He limped past Freddie-O, the baby crawling on the floor, and Raquel, who still had her good eye shut. He reached the couch, pushed off junk, and sat next to me. He stretched his thin legs out and banged out taps on the floor with the end of the cue stick.

I watched as Raquel opened her eye, moved it over the man's face, and then smiled. It showed in her voice. "Hey, you OK?"

"I'll make it."

"Right on, brother!"

Freddie-O had resettled himself on the floor, braced against the bookcase. Dude used the tip of the pool cue to shove his hat back on his head. He nodded sideways toward me but spoke to Raquel.

"What's she doing here?"

"Her? Oh—she's from the office. Someone's been bitchin' about me."

Raquel covered her empty eye socket as she looked in my direction. This was my cue to say my piece. I let Dude know that he was part of the noise problem.

"Him! Dude? Hey, tell the lady you're no problem, Dude." Freddie-O cracked up. "It's the chick who's screwed—Alpha!"

I protested. I repeated what I had heard. That Dude Muggins had assaulted the woman.

"You is so right! I a-salted and I peppered the bitch!" Manly pride showed in his voice.

"Who you puttin' on, Dude? Kinda looked like it was th' other way 'round!" Raquel came to life, animated.

Dude maintained he whipped Alpha as Freddie-O crawled to the stairwell and shouted up for Alpha to "get her ass down."

"You let that chick know she come down here, I'll tear her up!" Dude slapped the pool cue on a throw cushion lying on the floor. Dust flew. He speared the cushion and tossed it.

Clumping feet announced Alpha. She charged into the room. She did not mince her words nor make idle threats. She told Dude to get his "mother-fuckin' ass out of there quicker than a crow could piss" or she'd "lame his other leg." I ducked as Alpha took a swing at the seated Dude.

This was it! I had had enough. My attempt to solve the noise problem had taken second place to last night's continuing battle. I edged myself off the couch, ready to bolt at the first opening. It came when Dude got up, grabbed Alpha's arm, and spun her down on the couch. One of her kicks landed on my leg and I jumped up and ran for the kitchen door.

But I turned and then I saw it. The back of Dude Muggins's shirt was decorated with words. The words were "Happy Birthday, God." It came back to me. The dying man, the three words choked out by death, the pool of blood, and the broken cue-stick. And Dude Muggins's shadow across my window that day. His whispered conference with Harry the Shoe and then their dash to disappear.

I let myself out. I heard the baby cry, then Raquel scream. Something inside hit the wall with a loud boom. Freddie-O's wild laugh. Offhand I wondered which one was winning, the man or the woman. I didn't care. Suddenly I realized why the police hadn't done anything. Still, the anger in Raquel's voice and Freddie-O kicking the beer cans stayed with me, filed away in an album of fear.

Each step I took toward the main office was walked to the beat of those three words, "Happy Birthday, God." My discovery lay heavy, like sinkers on a fishline. What would my knowledge hook? Justice? For whom? And who would listen? Hank Garrison? And believe? I doubted it, but still I would try.

I reached the main office and went in. Mattie looked up from her work.

"Well, did you solve Raquel Mansfield's problem? She promise to stop the noise every night?"

I busied myself with Raquel's file—made notations. Hell, I could be as cryptic as everyone else.

"What else!" I told her.

I slept badly that night. I dreamed of garish birthday cakes and trying to blow out candles that relit themselves. And Carl, dressed like Charlton Heston as Moses, carrying tablets that said, "You'll never make it, kid!" And my mother crying on my ninth birthday because she had no money to buy me a birthday present. And me crying.

I was glad to go to work the next day.

15

The first thing I did the next morning after I got to my office was tear apart the place. I knew I had poked the broken cue into some box or behind some bag of craft material. I found it rolled back on the top shelf of the storage closet in the bedroom that we used for sewing. I carried it into my office. I put it down on the desk. The splintered end was a ruddy brown.

The police operator answered my call and put me on hold after I asked for the community relations department. Excitement crawled in my stomach. It made its way into my voice. (Mrs. Sherlock Holmes, that's me.) Hank's voice was curt, professional, as he identified himself. As soon as I spoke I could feel him relax. No irate taxpayer, just that dingbat from Disasterland.

I started out nice.

"Hank, remember a couple of months ago when that young guy, Doug, was stabbed? And remember what he said just before he . . . he died?"

I gave him a chance to back up his mind.

"Well, I think I know who did it."

I heard paper rustling as if he was only half paying attention to me, like a parent pretending to listen to the babbling of his child. Hank spoke slowly, distracted. "So? What do you expect me to do? Run out and nab someone on your say-so?"

"I expect you to investigate, if nothing else. That is, if it's not too much trouble finding a murderer!"

"You don't know a damn thing about how police work. Sure, maybe you got suspicions, but suspicions don't get convictions. If I went to the D.A. with a loose-goose case, he'd laugh me out of his office!"

"Great! That's just swell—equal justice under the law! If Doug were some rich man's son or a cop's brother, you'd go all out—"

"Save me from a crusading female—they're worse than a crooked politician! All right! I'll have Herbie cruise by and take your information and we'll go from there. OK? That satisfy you?"

"It's a start!" I hung up.

The next day Herbie Brent appeared at 8:00 a.m., alone. When he traveled with Hank Garrison, Herbie faded into the background. Now, faced with dealing with the younger plainclothesman, I considered him more closely.

Herbie was tall and slender. His well-cut clothes indicated his salary was spent on himself. I realized I knew nothing about his personal life. Our relationship seesawed: I acted or bitched; he reacted or justified.

He flopped on the loveseat, long legs cocked up on a straight chair against the wall by the window. He reached up and patted his hair from his forehead. His wrists looked bony, like a very young boy's—like unfeathered wings of baby birds. Vulnerable. Crackable.

"Does your wife let you put your feet all over the furniture?"

"Don't have a wife . . . any more."

"No wonder, if you aren't housebroken!" He didn't smile; I made amends by showing concern. "What happened?"

"She gave me a hard time."

"And you didn't? Give her a hard one . . . hard time, I mean?" Trying to be funny again. Me.

"She found another guy. With money."

Herbie looked away, out of the window. He dropped his feet with a clump and stood up. Both hands dug into his pants pocket. The butt of his gun showed where his jacket hiked up. As he stood shadowed against the morning light, his Jack Armstrong features outlined sharply, I watched a quiver. It traveled past his chin and rolled down his throat. It ended in a sigh. We were separated by a double-pointed knife: There was pain at both ends. I wondered what the girl had been like.

We spoke at the same time, dismissing the moment.

He said, "Well, what d'ya have?"

I showed him the pool cue and told him about Dude Muggins and the shirt he wore with "Happy Birthday, God" on it and the fact that I remembered seeing him and Harry the Shoe cross in front of my window just before Doug collapsed at my door step. It cut no ice. Herb was all cop.

"It's not good enough."

"But aren't you even going to check it out?"

"Sure, I'll check it out. I'll go find Dude Muggins and say, 'Hey, Dude, did you do a number on Doug what's-his-name?' and Dude will spit carefully three inches away from my newly polished shoes and look past my shoulder to where sixteen of his soul brothers are holding a prayer meeting. Then Dude will grin and do a jive dance step and shout to his backup gang. He'll say something like, 'Hey, man, you hear what the Law's askin' me? A fine up-standin' young citizen like me?' Then the Greek chorus behind me will say 'Screw you' to me in sixteen different ways and the Dude will pick his nose and tell me to arrest him."

"And will you?"

"I'll pretend it's all just a big joke and stand back and watch him take off."

"And that'll be the end of it!" I tasted sour anger.

"However, if I should happen to discover Dude Muggins in a compromising situation and I should happen to call out, "STOP!" and he should happen not to hear me because I didn't say it very loud, and then I should happen to think he was fleeing an officer's command, well—accidents do happen, you know."

Herbie had turned to me. The light behind him obscured his expression. He was a shadow, a cardboard shape. Does the devil play Scrabble with people's lives?

"That makes you as rotten as him."

"You can't have it both ways, baby." Blank eyes, black as gun muzzles, frightened me. I was silent. Awed by evil.

He felt my fear. He moved around so that light fell on his face again. He wanted to make me feel better, laugh.

"Happens all the time. All the time—accidents. After all, justice is supposed to be blind and what's more blind than a cop on a dark night?"

Dark night. Lying awake in my darkened room and listening to my mother's voice singing. First Brahms, then Schumann, and often a special song just for me. My mother knew that I stayed awake until then. Full and tender her voice reached me as my eyes fluttered and ached to stay open . . .

"The night has a thousand eyes,
And the day but one;
Yet the light of the bright world dies,
With the dying sun. . . ."
. . . and I would flow into sleep on that melody.

"The night has a thousand eyes and a million crimes . . . but whose heart will die when you shoot in blindness."

He looked puzzled. I could not explain. He walked out and I watched through the window as he got into the unmarked four-door sedan that everyone knew was a cop car.

After Herbie left, I sat and studied the pool cue. Could I let this be the end of Doug's murder? It became the symbol of everything that was wrong in Buena Vista—apathy. No one followed through on any of the terrible things that happened. Misery was shrugged off. Not me, I vowed. This was one time I would dig until I had enough to hand over the murderer to Hank and Herbie. I remembered the information Betty Lou had given me and Tommy Gun's part in the fight that night. Tommy Gun! He was back. I decided I would track him down. This time, I asked for no help.

Buena Vista during the working-day hours had relatively little activity. Tenants walked down the sidewalks and out of the project. Fights started; kids vandalized. Cars rattled in and out. The staff did their thing with paper work, and the maintenance crew tried to keep up with repairs. But the few times I stayed after hours, I noticed that, as the last employee's car left, a new aliveness crept over the place. A nervousness vibrated—gradually doors opened, groups of tenants clustered in parking lots, children ran pell-mell from deserted dwellings, climbing in and out of broken windows. Coarse laughter, male shouts, sometimes gunshots, broke over the descending light. Whatever and whoever could move crawled out of their shells and became visible. The real life of Buena Vista's residents began after dark.

That night I stayed over. There was plenty to do as I waited for the dusk, then the twilight, and finally the first darkness. When the telephone rang, I wasn't surprised. My office light indicated I was still in the project. No one answered my repeated hellos. I hung up, annoyed. A tense moment followed, but I shoved it down. I put on my car coat, took my purse, and, after securing the windows and back door, went out into the project.

My presence was telegrammed ahead. I should have realized that the second I went around the bend of Greentree Lane, secrecy would be over.

I walked blindly on, acknowledging a few casual greetings, lots of quizzical stares. Several off-color remarks drifted behind me as I passed two parking areas. I was headed for Velma Washington's apartment in Building

#42. Rumor had it that Tommy Gun was staying there with Yvonne Washington, Alpha's sister and the same Yvonne whose life hung on Lisa Fritzle's Slavic fury.

As I approached the door, a group of tenants shuffled off; some went into the next apartment, some melted into the shadows behind cars. Two men remained. I recognized Tommy Gun and Ti.

Ti was dressed in supersharp clothes: wine suede pants and matching jacket. Holding a suitcase, he bent down to flick a dirt spot from his Gucci shoes. Tommy Gun, in his usual jeans and silver-banded hat, leaned against the stucco wall. He was finishing a soft drink and hamburger bun.

"Why, hello, nigger-lady. I been expecting you!" Tommy Gun crumpled the waxy paper wrapping of the hamburger into a ball and tossed it over my head.

"You're a hard man to locate," I said.

"Only for some people."

"Why didn't you wait that day . . . why didn't you stop the car?"

"Wasn't nothing else to say."

"I had something to say . . . that's why I'm here looking for you tonight."

Ti straightened up, bounced on his feet, feinting like a fighter impatient to get into the ring. Tommy Gun glanced at him, then at me.

"Come go with me. I've got to carry Ti, here, to the airport. Things is gettin' a little too hot for our man." He laughed as he emphasized the word "man." "You can rap your piece to me comin' back."

My face showed my apprehension.

"You scared! Shit-scared! Lady, you got no guts. If you can't hack it here in paradise, go to hell!"

I dug my fists deep into my coat pockets; my arms held my body together. This black man's assessment of my reaction was correct. I *was* afraid. I looked for a way out.

"Sure, why not? But I'll drive," I said.

"Careful, aren't we, nigger-lady? Someone advise you not to get into a car wit' a black man? And him driving at that?"

"No."

"Then we'll go in *my* car . . . wit' me chauffeurin'."

I was between the stone and the wall. My answer was to turn and follow Ti and him to the red T-bird.

The ride to International was taken up with talk between Tommy Gun and Ti. Their patter was nonunderstandable to me. Street expressions and slurring accents hid the meanings of their conversation. I sat cramped in back. Ti got out at the airline terminal, took his bag, and, after a complicated handshake with Tommy Gun, disappeared into the lobby. With one flip of his hand, Tommy Gun instructed me to climb next to him in the front seat. I did. We drove around the airport circle, and out toward the San Diego freeway.

I broke the silence by asking about Ti, and what "getting too hot" meant.

"The heat is comin' down . . . the dude who got his throat sliced was Ti's connection."

I let the word "connection" sink in. It could mean a dozen different things: sex, drugs, blackmail . . . Tommy Gun read my mind.

"Ti was the gofer for movie people . . . between them and Las Vegas . . . and border runs. You get my meaning?"

I nodded. Ti was gone from the project; he was a poisonous plant—let him blossom someplace else.

The car moved steadily in its own lane. Traffic hum lulled me. I struggled with how to open up the matter of Doug's death. Plunged in.

"I understand that you had something to do with Doug's death. That you gave orders to get him."

"You've been listening to tales."

"Well, is it true?"

"Yes . . . and no."

Game-playing. I already knew his tactics. This time I outplayed Tommy Gun. I was silent. A long time passed. I watched as he glanced at me sideways. His eyes squinted and he picked at his goatee. Go ahead, you bastard, I told him silently, let's see you squirm a little. I waited. Finally he spoke.

"The Dougs of the world got to learn . . . they have to stop taking up all the room on this earth."

"So your answer is to put them under the earth?"

"You're a clever woman, Edith Bentwood. That'll be your downfall. Anyone who's clever and honest and has . . . guts . . ." He smiled big. "Yeah, I hate to admit it, but, nigger-lady, you got balls!"

"Don't worry about my downfall. What about Doug's murder?" I persisted.

"It was an accident. Just like a slip of the tongue can hang a man, so a slip of the knife can kill him . . . even when neither is meant to happen."

"You're telling me that Doug was only meant to be scared . . . that Dude Muggins and Harry the Shoe loused up your orders?"

"I'm not telling you anything . . ." Hard-voiced.

Silence. Lights from oncoming cars ping-ponged across the divider. The car windows were open and the gassy smell from industrial plants along the freeway choked me. I was stupid to have gone on this ride. What in the world was the matter with me? Here I was with a man whom I knew to be involved with a grocery list of criminal acts, in a car traveling along a freeway where any off ramp would take the car into a deserted business section. That's where bodies were found every week, shot, raped . . . stabbed.

Breathing became difficult. I let air out slowly, feeling the tightness of my muscles. The car swerved. I hung onto the door handle. Tommy Gun's right hand left the steering wheel and reached for the radio knob. Assorted music, news, commercials came on in short spurts as he moved from one station to the next. To my surprise, he bypassed the heavy rock and settled for the one classical music channel. A delicate melody spun out, "The Girl with the Flaxen Hair."

I turned in my seat. Looked directly at his face. Tried to see if it was a put-on or . . . put-down. A flicker of his eyes indicated he was aware of my scrutiny. I saw his hand reach over. He covered my hand resting on the car seat. It felt warm and strangely comforting, a "don't worry" kind of gesture. His eyes stayed on the road as he spoke.

"Yes, I know about Debussy . . . and van Gogh . . . and Hegel and Hamlet and Hitler. And Christ."

"I can believe the others, but Christ? No," I said.

"Christ was an agitator. Christ was a symbol . . . still is . . . what can be done if one's crazy enough or determined enough. See, Hitler and Christ are the same . . . just different sides of the coin."

"And you? Which side are you?" I wanted to end it on a joke.

"I'm the edge. I can be set up . . . and twisted by an idea. . . . Then I'll spin. A spinning coin travels farther than a coin laid on either side."

"Where did you come from . . . I mean . . . grow up? What brought you to Buena Vista?" I rattled out the questions I had stored up ever since I first heard this black man's name. And what had happened to his black slur— his street language?

"That man in the car—the day you wanted me to stop. That man is my father. He's got a high post in Washington . . . one of the first to make it. He went through college by working in a Chinese laundry. Yeah, how does that grab you? A nigger working for Chinks. He used to tend the huge vats of hot, soaking clothes. But he got there—on top—where he wanted to be." He stopped.

"And you?"

"I'm on the bottom."

"Is that where you want to be?" I asked.

"You ever have an hourglass? You know, the kind where sand sifts from the top to the bottom?"

"A three-minute timer, an egg timer?"

"Right. Then you know that when it's turned over, what was on the bottom . . . gets to be on top."

"Like the flip side of a record. You expect to replace your father . . . equal his success. Seems to me you've sprung a hole in that hourglass. Your sand may be running out. . . . There'll be nothing left to be on top."

"My father said if I'd change—use Right Guard and remove the gold earring—he'd get me a job in Washington." Tommy Gun laughed dryly.

"So what's so bad about that?"

"He came to L.A. for some high-level convention and I made him drive back to Buena Vista with me that day. I wanted him to see that things were bad . . . not just for us but for anyone who was down . . . buried . . . locked in."

"Root-cellared," I murmured.

"What?" he asked.

"I think I understand," I answered.

"How can any white middle-class man or woman understand?"

"Conceit is your big fault. A root cellar is dark. . . . The color of your skin doesn't show and the fear is the same inside."

"Before long . . . all of us who are victims will become avengers. The heartbeat has stopped in this country . . . and what do you do when the heartbeat stops? Give it a shock . . . a jolt. The heart of this country has died. We need to get it a pacemaker."

"Pacemaker . . . or peacemaker. Isn't that what the tenants call you? Peacemaker of Buena Vista?"

No answer came, except he moved his hand and put it back on the steering wheel.

When we pulled down Flood Road, Tommy Gun waited until I eased my car toward Grand Boulevard. In my rear view mirror I watched as his red back light traveled down Greentree Lane and back to Yvonne Washington. Strangely, I felt jealous!

Should I hate him? Fear him? Respect him? How can one respect a thief . . . blackmailer . . . child corrupter? Chameleon emotions tumbled through my brain. Rationally I indexed his crimes, his behavior, his control over these 3500 people. People caught in a stagnant pool, like tadpoles, hoping to survive, consuming their own bodies. The ultimate incest! Would they start on others . . . as Tommy Gun predicted?

Home, I slammed the dark out when I entered my apartment. For once, being enclosed, locked in by a door, was security. I felt safe. Tonight the outside world became a root cellar for me.

16

Easter with its jelly-bean time was over. The bunny-rabbit drawings came down from my office walls. Easter outfits were washed and hung in balloon colors on the wire clotheslines. Apartment doors were left open to the May sun. Daffodils shriveled into twisted brown stems, male dogs ran in packs after each bitch, cats had kittens, and the women sat on the narrow cement back porches waiting for Sammy the Breadman to toot his ten o'clock morning whistle

Sammy the Breadman had pullout drawers of doughnuts, cookies, and sticky Danish. Layer cakes sat on cardboard squares with plasterlike icing in poster-paint colors. His yellow van was set at a half-mile-per-hour speed and stopped at the merest indication that a customer was near. He would hop out and have his back door open and drawers pulled out before his car key stopped vibrating in the ignition. Sammy was a hustler.

Like birds flocking to a feeding station, the ladies of Buena Vista Housing Project would gather, chirping, around Sammy for their midmorning snacks. Sammy was moon-faced and loose-lipped; his pants were baggy, and hair grew in his ears. Rumor had it that Sammy had made a fortune in the twelve years that he had had the sole franchise in the project. Rumor also had it that Sammy had run off several other vendors by contacting Tommy Gun. One thing for sure was that Tommy Gun never seemed to run up a bill with Sammy. Holding a well-fingered sales pad and licking the stub of a yellow pencil, Sammy had more charge accounts than Neiman-Marcus and probably fewer bad debts. A tenant might go several months without paying but in the end, Sammy always got his money. Those who were not on Sammy's credit list missed most of the good things in life—at least, life as it was lived in Buena Vista.

I used to watch, amused, when I stopped to chat with the ladies as they made serious decisions about jelly-filled crullers or glazed angel-food doughnuts. Sammy always made a display of offering me a free, day-old pastry—which I always turned down. Both of us understood it to be a ritual, but still he offered and I refused, leaving us free from obligations on both sides.

The day that Starlet Jones forced a powdery ring of greasy dough on me, I declined by saying I was on a diet. Several of Sammy's best customers choked laughs while they glanced sideways at their fleshy shapes. They kept stuffing.

"Hello, Miz Edie, what you got to diet for? You're like a chewed-off chicken bone." Annie Flunk picked fallen pink icing from her bosom and popped it into her mouth.

Heather Jean Johnson took her change from Sammy but didn't help herself to one of the cream puffs she bought.

"I sure wish I could drop me a few pounds."

"What we need is an exercise club." Vanessa Van Platzen jiggled the Bronze Medal on the black velvet ribbon she always hung around her neck. The project's only Olympic champion—a 1952 shot-put medalist—Vanessa flexed her biceps the way the other women ran off their mouths: too often. Her life-motif was this one success.

"Yeah, my figger has gone to pot!" Starlet handed Bitsy the rest of her apple turnover.

The many extraordinarily overweight women who lived in Buena Vista secretly amazed me. One day, after a three-hundred-pound tenant left the main office, I asked Gloria if there was a quota on a tenant's weight. I should have known better. Gloria rattled off her opinion of "fat asses" that did nothing but stuff their "fat" faces and never got off their "fat" butts to clean up their places. Her "fats" ran up and down the scale of anger until I left and went into Bernice's back room. She looked up as I spoke.

"Don't you wonder why so many of the women are fat? Even the pretty ones have let themselves go."

"Well, darling, don't you see? Don't you really understand? They're unhappy, the poor dears." Bernice's eyes teared.

124

"Sure, I'd be unhappy if I looked like a hippopotamus . . . a pregnant one!"

"It's so sad. They're just eating their little hearts out." Bernice wiped her eyes, blew her nose into a flowered tissue. A sigh, like the sound of air escaping a leaking tire, shook the papers in her hand. I backed out.

I bit my tongue for asking that question. I knew the reason behind their grotesqueness. Their lives, their loves, and their futures were as misshapen a comment on poverty as the distortion of their bodies.

Vanessa's suggestion about exercise and Starlet's comment about dropping pounds got the Take-It-Off Club into high gear.

Starlet Jones and Fannie Hupp designed a flyer and we had it run off free at the central office. Debby Nickel and two other little girls were pressed into delivering the flyers by Judy Nickel. As Avon Lady, Judy foresaw a small fortune in selling beautifiers to suddenly slim women.

Wednesday morning at 10:00 a.m. was the agreed time to meet at the community hall for the Take-It-Off Club. The flyers and the word of mouth had worked; Wednesday, nine ladies of assorted ages puffed their way up the steps and into the hall. The flyer had mentioned that each person bring a quilt or old blanket to lie on while exercising. It had not suggested they wear pants.

The blankets were spread out. The ladies got on their hands and knees and gradually eased their yard-wide butts onto the floor. Their flesh oozed, bulged, and quivered as they spread out like gingerbread men waiting to be baked.

I had taken gymnastics in school and had made a tentative plan of exercises that seemed mild enough for the first session. I lay down on my grass mat, raised my head slightly, and called out my directions.

"All right, now, ladies," I screeched. "Raise your right leg, hold it up, and let it down slowly to a count of three. Then raise your left leg and we'll do the same thing."

I lowered my head and dutifully obeyed my own orders. I was scissoring the air when I heard assorted whimperings. I elbowed myself up and looked at my ladies.

Two women—one of whom was Vanessa—had managed to get their legs off the floor; the others were prone. I pretended it was time to switch to a different exercise, rather than embarrass the others.

"Turn on your sides," I bellowed. "We'll move our legs back and forth. Like we were walking. Great for the hips! Ready? Start."

I turned on my side and illustrated. My ladies had a hard time; they looked like mountain ranges under attack by an earthquake. Their dresses had hiked up; in the interests of modesty, I called it quits.

"That was super!" I said. "Next time let's all wear capris and really kick high!"

Released from their torture, the ladies tried to get up. The spirit was willing but the flesh just couldn't make it. Like turtles on their backs, they flayed the air, trying to grab on to each other to heave themselves into a sitting position. Starlet finally made it by grabbing Helen Jimmer's leg, who in turn pulled herself up on her knees by bracing herself on Annie Flunk. This was giving them more exercise than my one-two-three-kick routine. Finally with an added tug from me they were on their feet again.

Now I made my announcement. I had contacted the local junior college and made arrangements for one of their home economics teachers who specialized in nutrition to come once a week. She would teach the ladies of the Take-It-Off Club how to plan nonfattening meals. Great! My ladies were gung-ho for it.

Ms. Joan Takaki arrived. A four-foot-eleven-inch, petite, tight-skinned doll glided in with a canvas bag of inspirational recipes. She set up her show on a table and, after a little bow, went into her act. Annie Flunk and Heather Jean Johnson fell asleep and almost tipped over in the metal folding chairs we had lined up for the meeting.

Ms. Takaki happily hopped in her size-four shoes, measuring bean sprouts and wheat germ and dumping them into a bowl of unsweetened shredded and squeezed-dry pineapple. Starlet and Fanny Hupp and Denise Dopplemyer wrote down the directions step by step in the folder that Ms. Takaki had given to each lady. Helen Jimmer voiced her antagonism. She insisted upon bringing up questions: How in hell did Mrs. Tacky (as she pronounced our gourmet guru's name) think welfare mothers were going to buy imported food with food stamps? (Welfare regulations said imported foods were a no-no.)

Ms. Takaki ignored all adverse comments with a wide smile, a few more hops, and a graceful waving of a delicate hand. The mimeographed recipes for diet meals were passed out and all my Take-It-Off members promised to put them to use.

The diet club caught on. The next week there were fifteen bodies climbing the steps into the community hall. It was a Jack LaLanne dream come true. None of them was under two hundred and fifty and a few were at least three hundred.

The second meeting went better. This time old-timers like Starlet and Helen Jimmer took over the blanket-spreading. When I got there, the community hall looked like a Head Start school at nap time, or an exercise in disaster-alert training. Lane Bryant must have had a run on extra larges in their capri department. All my ladies wore stretch pants. Annie Flunk's were electric blue, gussied up with three rows of white ball fringe braceleting the legs.

I had planned to start my ladies with a few bends and touch-toes maneuvers, but they were already spread flat out like willing virgins. Nothing to do but follow suit. As I counted out "one-two-lift your right leg," the ladies moaned and groaned, but most of the crew got their legs off the floor at least nine inches.

This time the getting-up was coordinated. Everyone rolled on her side and grabbed the ankle of the woman directly in back. Slowly the linked bodies pulled themselves to their knees. There was some hand-and-knee crawling, but eventually all the Take-It-Off Club sat on the metal chairs, with dangling feet and red cheeks.

Ms. Takaki arrived exactly on time—fresh and smelling like jasmine. This time she prepared a tantalizing meal of sliced raw broccoli stems sprinkled with wheat germ, celery stalks dipped in egg and rolled in wheat germ, and bamboo shoots tossed with wheat germ; for dessert and to supply natural sugar and iron, we had ground-up raisins rolled in marble-sized balls and sprinkled with wheat germ.

At this point someone (I suspect it was Helen Jimmer again) muttered loudly that it was like eating dog crap. The dainty Ms. Takaki ignored the remark, continued sprinkling wheat germ as if it were fairy dust, and promised that next week she would have a special treat (it sounded like "feet") for the ladies.

After the club members finished their Dixie cups of wheat germ with various additions, the meeting broke up. I watched as one lady smeared her raisins-and-germ mixture on the underside of her chair.

Ms. Takaki stood at the door as the women left and passed out leaflets with meals planned around shredded Chinese cabbage, ginger root, dried fish, and wheat germ. She did it with elegance, a small bow from the waist, a whiff of jasmine, and, I suspected, the Oriental equivalent of "get with it, you slobs." Her performance lacked only one thing—an aria from *Madame Butterfly*.

The third week there were twenty-three ladies—even some who were under two hundred pounds—and everyone was chattering away as I entered the hall. I was surprised to see Annie Flunk's mortal enemy, Louise Cawlwell, and Annie in a peaceful conversation. Maybeline Mansfield (Go-Boy and Raquel's grandmother) was laughing with Juanita Lechuga; only last week the police had been called in to settle a dispute between them. I realized that even if fat didn't disappear, the club's common goal might stop a few beatings and fire-bombings.

That morning the building shook and the floor trembled as the ladies swung their legs and rolled back and forth on their hips. Mattie peeked in once to see what was happening.

True to her promise, Ms. Takaki brought her special surprise—really two surprises. Number one was her assistant, a blond Mark Spitz type. He flashed his Mah-Jongg teeth and dynamically dumped a fifty-pound sack of wheat germ on the table. Then he carefully placed a pink bathroom scale on the floor.

My ladies watched with interest as Ms. Takaki introduced him as Flank Weskenowski. She explained that Flank was a defensive guard on the football team who had enrolled in the home economics department because he felt he owed it to the deserving girl he would marry one day.

While our Cio-Cio-San cataloged Flank's assets, Flank fascinated the ladies with blushes, nervous twitchings of his hips, and much tossing of his mane of blond hair.

There was vigorous applause when Ms. Takaki finished and lots of laughter when Billie Goody yelled out that Flank didn't have to take any classes as far as she was concerned. She'd like a chance to play on his team and break down *his* defenses! Flank swelled the wrinkles in his pants smooth and Ms. Takaki pretended not to hear.

The second surprise Ms. Takaki planned was to parcel out a lunch sack of wheat germ to each lady, courtesy of the Zen Health Food Emporium. She also announced her program to set up a weight chart for each lady to keep track of her progress. Her hummingbird flutters acted like Black Flag spray on green horseflies: The ladies were stunned but not dead. They reacted. They refused to be weighed.

Vanessa Van Platzen was the only one who stepped onto the delicate pink scales. When the indicator shamed her, Vanessa blamed her athletic career, saying that her weight was "just solid muscle." Her "solid muscle" wobbled on the tiny scale platform and to steady herself, Vanessa grabbed Flank Weskenowski around the neck. The young man was swallowed into the fleshy arms and bust of the shot-put champion. Entwined like Hercules fighting the Hydra, Flank and Vanessa toppled over and sprawled before the delighted Take-It-Off Club.

The following week Ms. Takaki didn't show up. No one mentioned her absence and no one complained. Each week we met and did our exercises —knee bends were steady, and fingers dangled close to toes. There was no question that my ladies were getting agile, but no one lost any weight.

Shortly after our club broke for the morning, I walked Helen Jimmer back to her apartment. I was headed for another tenant's place just beyond her parking lot.

Helen wore men's pants and a knit golf shirt with embroidered tiny golf clubs stretched across her massive breasts. The pants zipper was at half-mast and a peek of pink panties showed. We chitchatted as we walked. I asked her if she had used up the wheat germ Ms. Takaki had handed out on her last day.

"Wheat germ, hell! What do I need wheat germ for?"

"It's a high protein food with low calories."

"Shitttt! You think I need some half-ass Jap bitch with her prissy ways coming in here an' jawin' at me to eat wheat germ?"

We reached the parking lot and turned in. The yellow van with Sammy surrounded by female tenants made a flower-garden color spot. Splashy cotton muumuus on the women fluttered in a light breeze and gossipy voices singsonged over rock music escaping from an upstairs window. Small children whined for treats as the mothers considered and evaluated their selections of bakery goods.

Helen surged forward, leaving me to follow. She hurried toward the van, her large buttocks jiggling. Suddenly she stopped, turned. As I caught up with her, she put her heavy hand on my arm. A naked look of agony showed in her face. She dropped her eyes and spoke softly, like someone in a confessional hoping that the darkness would ease the shame of the deed.

"Miss Edie, it don't make no difference. You understand what I'm saying? Who in hell cares how I look? So I'm fat, so what?"

The sadness in her voice was heavier than her weight on my arm. She looked toward the other women still surrounding Sammy. Some had white sacks filled with bakery goods in their hands.

"Someone who cares how I look—that's what I need. We all need. A man . . . who doesn't use us . . . who cares. Who don't desert us an' our kids."

Her hand dropped from my arm and she moved from my side and joined her peers.

The Take-It-Off meetings continued for another three weeks, but gradually the ladies dropped out. Sammy and his sweets won over self-pride and social prejudice, and the toot-toot of his whistle became the dirge for the diet club.

At odd times Helen Jimmer's words haunted me. Maybe I wasn't like the ladies; my size-nine dresses fit over a well-proportioned frame, my hair was shiny and thick and framed my face, and my face . . . ? It was OK, or so I had been told in different ways—by steady stares from men in coffee shops, or by quick glances from male drivers as our cars were stopped abreast at a traffic light. Then what was wrong? Or—what was wrong with me?

Insulation from any emotional involvements after parting from Carl had protected me from disappointment. Sure, my social life included occasional dates with nice men who attended some of the classes or lectures I found listed in the "Calendar" of the regional edition of the Saturday *Los Angeles Times*. But I found it easy to turn them down . . . and turn them off. Somehow, they seemed sterile, too bland. Trying to focus on their conversations about insurance, teaching, or IRS injustices made me crosseyed with boredom. Their faces faded before my tight smile, and I saw Buena Vista residents, heard shouts and curses, remembered arguments with Herbie Brent and Hank Garrison.

Hank Garrison!

His stubbornness exasperated me. His blasé acceptance of violence in the project made me hate him. Still, I found myself thinking about him almost as often as about my tenants. I told myself it was because he was part of the total picture related to my position. I told myself that. I didn't quite believe it.

One evening after work as I drove back to my apartment, I postponed going up. Instead I parked along one of the short streets that dead-ended at the beach. I slugged across the sand. It seeped into my shoes until I pulled them off and continued barefoot. Near the wet part of the shore, I flattened a dry spot and sat down. Legs outstretched, I let the nearly-night wind blow my hair wild. It chased under my dress, like an insistent lover's delicate fingers, that probe yet desert all too soon, when a new temptation winks and beckons.

Immense emptiness made me light-headed. I became Peter Pan flying back to Never-Never Land. I wanted to be small again, buying penny candy and unwrapping a small square of white fudge, hoping for the occasional pink piece. Finding the pink candy entitled one to five free penny candies. I remembered the powerful feeling the day I got the pink one. I studied the free selection so long that the old man who ran the shop finally yelled at me to hurry. Too bad life wasn't a penny-candy store, where one had a chance for a pink candy—a special sweet, a treat, unexpected and therefore more precious. So far I had paid my pennies, but as I unwrapped my life I never found the prize. Suddenly I felt very alone. The sky became gray, then grayer, then black. A Brillo wind scoured holes into the sand. The sand soaked up evening mist and I curled my legs and rested my head on my arms folded over my knees.

The oil islands floated in the bay like black-encrusted birthday cakes disguised by primary-color floodlights. They beamed ribbons into the sky. I squinted. The ribbons unfurled, frayed, then faded. Only a thin line zagged, like a single loose strand of hair. Like a fissure—as if God had cracked the sky open like a huge egg to let a streak of heaven spill down to us. Was it a warning—or a promise?

I had to laugh to save myself from tears. God busting eggs from above and the devil earthquaking from below! What chance did any of us have! I went home.

17

There were times when I felt like an octopus: eight hands in eight different pots of trouble. One pot was labeled "schools." Part of each day was spent on the telephone with some member of the grammar school, junior high school, or senior high school staff. A working relationship with the city's educational institutions was necessary to keep "our" children in the system. Dropouts were all too numerous. Laziness, poor nutrition, medical problems, and parent apathy made attending school a hit-or-miss deal. There were exceptions. Celia Goochen was one, and, strangely, Danny Gree was another. Danny was the star basketball player for the Gordon High School team. Agile, quick-thinking, and ruthless in execution, Danny excelled in sports. Twice I had frantic calls from his coach to round Danny up and chase him over to practice. As disruptive as he was in the project, he settled down and performed in a competitive situation.

Most of the calls from the school offices involved health problems. Epidemics of head lice always brought terse instructions from the elementary school nurse. She intimated that all the lice started from Buena Vista children's heads, and she was outraged that the careful instructions she had sent home with each child were not followed. She proceeded to give me directions: shampooing with Selsen, careful combing, and daily inspections of each child's scalp and hair. Only after the all-clear signs were noticed could the child return to school. As she talked I felt that she expected me to administer this cure as part of my "responsibilities."

"Just providing a roof over their heads isn't enough. We have to keep those heads sanitary, too!" She rattled her R.N. degree at me as she gave me the names of students on the infected list. All of them came from the project.

That same morning the junior high vice-principal, Mr. Winsted, called and asked me to locate Mrs. Goochen, since they had no telephone number for her listed in the school file. I asked for the message he wanted delivered.

"Billy Goochen was just stabbed by a classmate."

My gasp brought the added information that it was nothing serious. Just that Billy had crapped in his pants and needed a change. The other kid was in the hospital, under intensive care.

"What other kid?"

"The one Billy shot."

"Shot!"

"Miss Bentwood"—the man's voice was weary—"this week we have already confiscated three handguns, six switchblades, one iron pipe, three sets of brass knuckles, two tear-gas grenades, a box of dum-dum shells, one electric-shock stun gun, and three bottles of birth-control pills. Oh, yes, I almost forgot the dynamite. We found that behind the cafeteria."

"What's going to happen to Billy?" I chose not to comment on his recital.

"He's going to smell up my office until someone brings him a clean pair of pants. How about it?"

"Sure. I'll tell his mother, but what about the police? Are they taking him in?"

"Police! Listen, if I called the cops every time something like this happened, the city'd need another three hundred police. The taxpayers can't afford it. *I* can't afford it. *You* can't afford it! Do you know that my house taxes went up to . . ." He stopped. "What the hell. About those clean pants . . ."

"What about the gun?"

"Don't worry. I took it away. See, you've got to understand something—it was self-defense. So if I make a big thing out of this . . . incident, the newspapers will pick it up. Maybe even the networks. The principal will be called downtown, and the school will look bad. Then the community will start hollering about the scummy kids from Buena Vista, and some half-ass politician will call in the press and give a grandstand interview blaming the Department of Education and I'll be transferred to an inner-city, piss-smelling, earthquake-cracked, seventy-five-year-old death trap—either the plaster will fall on my head or a Saturday Night Special will make a widow out of my wife! Now, you still think I should call the cops?"

"I get your point. Honest! Except . . . what about the kid Billy shot?"

"Don't waste your time on that pervert. He had it coming—a real sickie." He paused. "Nabbed the younger kids on their way home—just the boys. You know . . ."

"Beat up on them?"

"Hell no—blow jobs."

"Oh!" Stupid me. He hung up. I wanted to throw up.

A second later the phone rang. It was Mr. Winsted again.

"About those clean pants—hurry! We haven't been issued gas masks . . . yet!"

Neighborhood squabbles between adults also occurred regularly. Usually I was summoned by a hysterical child or woman to "come see what happened!" Mayhem, murder, and/or torture would be sworn by each of the complaining parties against the other. I learned how to steer between the fighting tenants. In private conversations with individuals involved I would point out: one—the absurdity of the fight, two—the possible legal repercussions, three—the racial overtones, or four—the possibility of intervention by Tommy Gun. Number four usually calmed the situation down into a simmering but introverted hate.

One morning Ben Hamilton asked me to investigate a fire-bombing at Geneva Lane's apartment. He informed me that these fire-bombings had to stop. It was costing too much maintenance crew time to repaint and clean up the messes that resulted. He neglected to mention any possible people damage.

It was a beautiful day and I trotted down to Parking Lot #14, where the problem had originated. It turned out to be "just a friendly disagreement" between Geneva and her neighbor, Lottie Thomas, over which parking space Lottie's boyfriend could use. (The boyfriend was an illegal tenant, or shack-up job.) Naturally, no one admitted seeing or knowing who did what. Geneva's original complaint of the bombing was forgotten. She was in tears because the fire department had responded to the bombing by flooding her place.

When I arrived at her building, there was Geneva outside, her furniture dragged onto the grass, water oozing from all corners. Under her directions three young children were jumping up and down on the waterlogged couch cushions. The water squirted into the parched lawn.

Geneva was wringing her hands and adding to the wetness with big tears down her brown face. She leaned on me and sobbed out her despair. The furniture wasn't even paid for yet, and it was ruined—ruined! (It was.)

I felt sorry for her even though I knew that Geneva would find some way to even up the score. Revenge was the spice of project life, and I wondered if I should warn Lottie Thomas to play it smart and stay away from Geneva. Mainly, to keep her mouth shut!

I wasn't wrong and it didn't take long.

Two days later I was met by Geneva's little girl, Violet, as I drove into the project. It was already close to eighty-five degrees and promised to go over ninety-five.

As I got out of the car she handed me a note, folded over. I unfolded it and read to myself: "Please, Mrs. Bentwood, will you take Violet home wit you. I am in jail." It was signed, "Ever gratful in God we trust, Geneva Lane."

Violet followed me inside the office, sat down on the loveseat, and watched me get settled behind my desk. Feet properly together, hands in lap, she followed my actions. Now I looked at her. She was dressed in mismatched shirt and shorts, and her hair was plaited in tight sections arranged in circular designs on her well-shaped little head.

How does one discuss a mother's stay in jail with a seven-year-old child? Violet helped me out.

"Mama shot Lottie."

We stared at each other. Then: "Honey, do you want to talk about it?"

"What do you want to know?"

Everything, I said to myself. To her I said, "When did it happen?"

"Last night, I guess. Me . . . I was stayin' overnight wit' Betty Sharp— she an' me are in the same class. Betty stays wit' her mama in Building Sixty-one. Anyway, thi' mornin' someone come over an' give Betty's old lady this here note an' say it come from my mama and it's to give you."

That explained why the Juveniles hadn't picked up the child when the mother had been taken away. Children in a situation like that were placed in foster homes until arrangements were made with relatives. Buena Vista had its own method. It hid its children in an underground of protection. Tenants knew that when a child was removed, the parent had little chance of getting it returned without long court proceedings. I wondered how long Geneva would be detained. The only way to find out was to call downtown.

"Well, let's see how serious your mom's case is." I hoped I sounded encouraging.

I dialed, and the voice wanted to know if I wanted homicide or assault to kill with a deadly weapon. It could be either, I told her. I certainly couldn't ask the seven-year-old! When the booking department line was busy, I asked for Lieutenant Garrison. He answered crisply and we discussed the situation. I was cagey and he got exasperated because I had no real facts. After a five-minute hold, he came back with the information: "Geneva Lane, twenty-six, black, two scars on left arm, one burn mark on lower right leg. Five feet six inches, date of birth September nineteen, nineteen forty-three. Place of birth Amarillo, Texas.

"Call came at one twenty-six to proceed to six thirty-seven Flood Road for emergency aid and shooting incident. Victim, Lottie Thomas, was found lying in front yard of six thirty-seven Flood Road. Victim was apparently shot. Weapon not recovered. Said victim was removed by paramedic after being treated for bleeding. Suspect Geneva Lane was apprehended while attempting to flee. Witnesses refused to give any information as to circumstances of shooting. Suspect Geneva Lane was arrested and transported in custody of police matron Grace Norton to city jail. Charge of resisting arrest; assault upon an officer; illegal possession of dangerous drugs, to wit: three ounces of hashish; attempted murder and assault with a deadly weapon. Arresting officers G. Helm and P. Hadden. Victim removed to county hospital."

"How bad is Lottie Thomas?" I asked.

"She died." He sounded flat.

Silence on my end. Then I told him about the note Violet had delivered. I wanted to sound objective. I failed. My voice broke. When I finished reading Geneva's note to him, Hank exploded. "Don't be a fool! You can't take that kid home. Her mother will be up for murder now. Best place for her is a foster home. You *have* to turn her over to Juvenile."

He was shouting and I looked over at the child to see if she heard. Her pinkish lips closed tightly to keep her chin from shaking. She had heard. I got rid of Hank Garrison in a few words.

Violet's sneakered feet scuffed the floor back and forth. Her fingers twisted like brown velvet ribbons against her shorts. The small head with its geometric hairstyle bowed lower and lower, and still no sound came from the child.

"Violet, do you have any relatives? An auntie, or grandmother? Cousins? Father?"

She looked up at me. "No one. No one but you, Miss Bentwood."

Me. What would I do—what could I do with one small black seven-year-old girl whose mother had just killed another woman over a parking place for a half-junk car?

"I'll be good, Miss Bentwood."

"I know you would."

Our eyes met and spilled over. I rushed to the loveseat and scooped the child against my chest. My arms folded double around her narrow body. My face was roughened by her coarse braided hair. We rocked back and forth, moaning softly, our hearts wailing silently at the injustice. We rebelled against the helplessness of the defenseless. We sat melted into each other. We were chiseled by grief.

The telephone rang.

I disengaged Violet's arm and answered the phone. The voice said, "Don't you turn over that baby to nobody. She'll make out jus' fine."

"Who is this?"

"Never you mind. That don't concern you. You heared me? You jus' turn her loose and she'll find herself mos' welcome."

I didn't answer. I tried to recognize the voice. It sounded familiar.

"Look, lady, you got the message, I hope, 'cause we don't want to see that baby put out like a dawg!"

I responded. "*You* don't understand. What do you expect me to do? Just let her wander away and not worry about her? That's crazy!"

I was shouting now. My voice cracked. The other voice softened.

"No need to fret. Jus' you do like we say, you dig? Let the little lady go."

"Lottie Thomas died."

"The word come through already. It don't make no difference. Can't no one hold Geneva. The pigs got no gun an' no witnesses. So you just turn loose on her baby."

"You're saying that the police can't make the murder charge stick?"

"Now you got it!"

I looked at Violet, so little, a small nut-brown pixie.

"OK, OK. I'll let her go. But you better know one thing—you better take care of her . . . good!"

"We take care of our own." She hung up then.

I found half a roll of Life Savers and gave them to Violet and told her to go out and play. She knew what to do. I watched as she skipped down the sidewalk and then ran with arms outstretched toward a woman down the way. They walked hand in hand around the curve of Greentree Lane.

Late that afternoon Herbie Brent and a policewoman drove up. I knew they were here to pick up Violet. The policewoman looked annoyed when I told her that Violet had run out on me when I was in the rest room.

"It's really too hot to go chasing the kid." She shifted the gun at her waist. A sweat mark showed.

"You're sure you don't have her stashed away someplace? Like maybe your apartment?" Herbie had been coached by Hank.

"Want to take a look?" I threw my keys across the desk toward him.

"Crap! One more nigger broad turned loose on society. How old is she —ten, twelve?"

"Violet is seven and in the second grade and she draws purple cats and believes in the Easter Bunny."

"Yeah, well, she better be able to pull a rabbit out of her hat or she'll be down the drain like the rest of the Buena Vista brats."

It was too hot to fight him back. I let them leave.

Seventy-two hours later Geneva Lane returned to Buena Vista. The voice on the telephone had been right. With no gun, no witnesses, and a loudly outraged Geneva denying any knowledge of Lottie's demise, the district attorney's case was too weak to file on. Without "probable cause" the search was illegal, the drug charge invalid.

But we knew—all of us in Buena Vista knew—that Geneva Lane had killed Lottie Thomas over a pitted, tarred section of oily ground. I pushed away the idea that I might be guilty of concealing information in a felony case. I only knew one thing. I was glad Violet had her mama back. Maybe Geneva was a murderess—but she was also a good mother. Good mothers are not to be sneezed at, nor shut away from girl children who need them.

Everybody went to Lottie's funeral. It was very nice. Ben Hamilton returned to work the same day. He was still captive in his mind-made prison.

On Friday the Mothers' Club met and the discussion was how to get infant clothes and baby furniture for the new babies who were always being born in the project. I had arranged for a lady to come out and lecture on family planning that day, and some of the mothers had dragged their teen and pre-teen girls along. Ms. Felicia Moxie came from the city Health Department. She had pepper-and-salt hair, trimmed up to her earlobes.

Dressed in early-shirtmaker, her shape was as up and down as the stripes of her dress. I hoped that she would not moralize. I didn't have to worry. Not only did she promote "sex is fun" but she also left everyone with the glowing knowledge that "sex is necessary." The ladies loved it; the young daughters grew embarrassed at the frank answers to the hesitant questions of their mothers. I learned a lot—mainly to check my speakers from now on to make sure they weren't X-rated.

Often calls came into my office from people outside the project wanting to donate items. Many times when I went to pick them up, I was faced with leavings from a general garage-cleaning spree. I learned to ask pointed questions before I ended as trash man. Today the offer of childrens' and baby clothes came from a woman. It sounded good. I got directions, reported to Mattie where I was going, and took off.

I returned with my car trunk and back seat piled high. The prospect of unloading the clothes depressed me. It was hot and I was tired. I pulled in behind my office and parked. I noticed that the old green van, reported to the maintenance department as abandoned, was still parked crookedly, taking up two parking spaces. A flat made it tilt. A smashed window sugared glass on the ground. A sweetish odor drifted out.

I followed the smell, peeked into the van, then poked my head through the broken window. Two boys shifted and squirreled around in a haze of sweet air when they noticed me. I recognized Freddie-O and Danny Gree. I schemed! Made my voice deep and threatening.

"OK, you're busted!"

"Hey, Miz Bentwood, you crazy? We ain't doin' nothin'." It was Danny Gree at his most charming.

"You're so right. You don't ever do nothin! Get out, I'm taking you in." I yanked open the dented rear door.

"Shit! How you figger you kin do that? You ain't no pig!" Freddie-O eased himself out after Danny.

"Watch me!" I said.

The boys exchanged anxious looks. Freddie-O's mouth grinned but his eyes flicked hate under his dropped eyelids. He slouched against the dusty car.

"Man, you don't really mean you're takin' us downtown? Hey, man, that ain't cool! You wanna be cool, don't you? You wanna take it easy, Edie baby!"

I kept a straight face.

"I got the message. In fact, the best way *I* know how to keep cool on a hot day is to have two fine strong men like you and Danny to unload this stuff for me."

I waved my hand at my cramped car. Danny doubled over. Slapped his head. Punched Freddie-O.

"What a ripoff! C'mon, you black mother—" He loped over to my car and yanked open one door. Freddie-O watched, standing back. He looked relieved; now his eyes were friendly but his mouth had an ugly twist.

"You know, lady, you shouldn't mess around like that. I mean pull this kinda act. Makin' out you gonna bust someone. It can be unhealthy, like, man—the wrong people might think you aren't jivin' and pow!"

Freddie fashioned his fingers into a child's imitation gun and pointed it to his own head. His tongue clicked, once, twice. He aimed his fingers at me and held still.

"Iffin I tol' you there's enough ammo in here to blow a lot of folks up, would you believe me?"

"Shut up, nigger. You fulla crap!" Danny held out a box to the other boy. Freddie-O ambled over to my car but turned back and looked hard at me.

"They never did find the piece that Lottie Thomas met up wit' either, did they?"

I got his message. I stood back as they unloaded the car. We spoke only necessary words as I directed them where to stack the boxes in the extra office rooms. What started out as a joke on my part to get the boys to help ended up with a uncomfortable me—scared. This was not the first time I had heard rumors that the project was also an arsenal. That, and the memory of Herbie Brent asking about machine guns, chilled me.

18

Spring ended; summer started. July began with sun-scorched days, and trouble exploded like popcorn over a hot fire. It began with Ernestine Trotmartin sending double-page flyers condemning the Housing Agency, Bert Lottman, the head of the agency, Ben Hamilton, and me. The wording was terse. A morning meeting was set up at the community hall for a big rally. Again, tenants were urged to withhold their rent. And again they did.

Gloria was burdened with sending out delinquency notices and she resented the extra work. She growled in her cubicle, shaking her newest-style wig and waving her cigarette holder. "They oughta evict every one of those damn bastards!"

Mattie bobbed her head; Bernice twittered and spoke too loudly as she offered Gloria sympathy.

Bert Lottman drove down in his Lincoln Continental. He and Ben Hamilton huddled in Ben's office for hours. After Lottman left, Ben went home sick and stayed away for three days. Gloria made a joke and said Ben was home with his period.

Ernestine Trotmartin and I rarely met. My knowledge of her activities came from sly hints dropped by different tenants in my daily rounds of trouble spots. I knew that she kept up with my actions through the same gossip grapevine. Indications were that the latest rally planned by the Action For Tenants included a big surprise. Speculation included: an invasion of blacks from the downtown area, an invasion of bikers (white) from the uptown section, a riot of disgruntled tenants, a march on Town Hall, or provoked mass arrests by S.W.A.T. policemen for publicity.

It was none of these. Instead, on the day of the rally, I came to work and immediately got buzzed on my hot-line. It was Ben Hamilton; his speech was a fast Donald Duck quacking, like a record playing at the wrong speed. When I got him slowed down, I learned that Ben, Albert Lottman, and I were hung in effigy in front of the community hall and within view of the office door.

I walked over to find a crowd milling around the steps leading into the hall and main office. The mood was festive, almost like an Iowa picnic. Something big must be in the air, I decided, if it got so many women up, dressed, and out by 9:00 a.m. Even senior citizens were parked on the steps, their stockings twisted, their purses clutched under arms, safe from snatching. The men shuffled and stood around in baggy pants, some with sweaters hiked up by hunchbacked posture.

Giggles and grouping greeted me as I approached. There, bigger than life, three stuffed dolls dangled from ropes that were attached to the rafter beam of the overlapping eaves. Two male forms wore cast-off men's clothing. Placards identified them as Bert Lottman and Ben Hamilton. The third stuffed body represented me: high heels, ripped hose, a buttonless blouse revealing an overstuffed chest, and an uneven skirt hemline. My sign read, "Get rid of Bitch Bentwood."

On the top step, positioned below the lynched dolls, Ernestine Trotmartin was in her glory. A Captain Bligh in dashiki, she snarled out her demands. Waving her arms, pointing at each of the hanging figures, she itemized their sins through X, Y, and double-Z.

"This here meeting is held to let the goddamned management know they ain't gwanna fuck over us no more."

Loud cheers.

"The mother-fuckers think they can mess over us, because we're poor. Well"—she waited until roars stopped—"well, when we get through with them they'll be kissin' our asses!"

Whistles, clapping, hoots.

"Right on, you tell 'em, Ernie!"

Ernestine again. "We gotta stand together—all of us! We gotta let them cock-suckers know they can't shit on us no more!"

The crowd knew the rules of the game. Everyone shouted support. The old people looked embarrassed, gave approval with grins.

"We is behind you, Ernie!"

"Tell it like it is!"

"You got it together, baby!"

"Now I promised you a surprise—an' here it comes! Our state senator is going to check into our complaints!" She pointed over all our heads toward Flood Road and out to Grand Boulevard. Everyone followed her announcement and turned. A caravan of cars pulled into the project toward us. The first car was driven by a chauffeur. The other two were less imposing. One had the insignia of a television channel, NBC, and the other was a paneled van from ABC. Behind them, two compact cars ended the invasion. What event in Buena Vista could make NBC, ABC, and the *Los Angeles Times* send their people? Ernestine let us know.

"Everyone—let the man through! Right up here, sir, where the people can hear you, Senator."

The crowd parted; the man started up the steps toward Ernestine, who stood like Caesar receiving homage from conquered lords. It was State Senator Buford Joseph, his florid face worked into a nervous smile. An aide trailed—birdlike, young, sallow. Jaybird chattered as he flicked tenants away from the older man. When the senator reached Ernestine on the top step, he held his hands high in a fighter's grip, smiled, bowed, and would have slipped off the step if Jaybird hadn't blocked his fall.

I was watching the TV cables being set up by men who worked in silent efficiency. Ernestine's bellow cut in again. "We got a state senator here, the man who's supposed to fight our battles! Right, Senator? OK. Senator Joseph, you got a chance to let the people see you at work. You tell the people of Buena Vista what you're going to do to help us. We may not have fat bank accounts but the senator knows we got votes! Right?"

It hit me. This was election year.

The crowd applauded. The senator looked sick. The tenants streamed in from all sides and the cameraman cat-moved over lines and around people to get a clear view. Another man edged up and held a mike close to the politician. This was big time and Ernestine had pulled it off! The crowd hushed as the senator spoke.

"I want you to know what a pleasure it is for me to be able to address you fine people . . . fine tenants . . . yes. Fine, fine citizens. Your wonderful leader, Mrs. . . ."—Jaybird whispered—"Mrs. Trotmorton."

Jaybird whispered again, but the senator brushed him away.

"Yes, Mrs. Trotmorton, your chairperson, tells me you people have serious complaints. Justified complaints, as I understand it . . . against some of the conditions in your homes."

Spontaneous encouragement met the senator.

"Damn right!—You said it, man!—Right on!"

"I was asked to come and let you know I am very concerned about the situation as it was presented to me . . . and I pledge . . . I absolutely pledge you fine people that I will take all steps at my disposal to remedy the problem and find a solution when I return to Sacramento . . . after the coming election."

It sank in, then.

"That's four months away, man—we want action now!"

The voice was masculine. Loud. The last word was picked up in a chant.

"Now . . . now . . . now!"

The crowd became restless, shoved. The man with the mike was trying to make his questions heard above rumblings. Someone knocked him aside and he scrambled to his feet, the wires twisted around his neck. I looked over and saw the cameraman backing up, his eye glued to the camera's view-finder. Jaybird had the senator's elbow cupped in his hand and he was tugging at him to start down the steps. The steps were blocked by tenants.

Ernestine roared out. "Screw you! What in hell do you mean—*after* the election? We want action—not some goddamn mealy-mouthed bastard fartin' goddamn piss-words! We are sick of crooked politicians! If you can't do no better than that, get your ass outta here!"

The senator got red, then white. He pretended it was a clever joke, that it was all in fun. He put a hand on Ernestine's arm to show they were friends. She almost knocked him down. The mood was ugly. Another aide was shouting, trying to worm his way up the steps to reach his boss. The crowd meshed into a fence, held him back.

It was Ben Hamilton who saved the situation. He opened the office door and poked out his smooth, pleasant face. That did it! The tenants surged forward; a new toy! They razzed him.

"Hey, Ben, come out! You chickenshit? You scared you gonna be raped? You don't get us new stoves, we'll have your ass on the hot seat!"

In their delight at flushing Ben out, the crowd forgot the senator. He shoved past me, half-stumbling, his heavy jaw slack with fear as he was pushed into the long black car. Jaybird and the other man crammed next to him in back. The driver eased the car forward but he was stopped. Ernestine shouted some orders and now the people surrounded the car, jammed up against the windows, climbed on the hood. Sweaty handprints marked up the polish. The driver inched forward, carefully. I could see the people inside the car. The senator wiped his face. The younger men had their hands on the inside locks. Now the horn was blown. The tenants grew tired of the sport. They let the driver ease ahead. I turned away, back to

Ben, who was trying to get back inside.

Suddenly a squeal of braked tires, then a scream, shouts. The senator's car stopped cold. I ran down as I saw Billy Goochen spread-eagled on the ground before the car. Headlines raced before my eyes: "SENATOR'S CAR RUNS OVER PROJECT CHILD." The newsmen scrambled to see what else had happened. I screamed my way to the center. I clawed my way through smelly bodies just in time to see Billy jump up, stick his tongue out at the shaking driver, and give them the finger. Then he ran off, roaring with delight at his trick.

Relief made everyone agreeable. The senator's car finally pulled out of Buena Vista. The newspeople suctioned their cables into the van, the crews moved out, the tenants drifted away, Ben had made it back to his refuge, and only Ernestine and I were left.

Our smiles were tight. Our eyes stalked each other. The three effigies dipped and spun on their ropes. Ernestine reached out and gave my form a jerk. It danced. She spoke first.

"You know you're an interfering son-of-a-bitch."

I waited.

"You know something is going on—they're out to screw the tenants. All those empty apartments . . . and no maintenance men to fix them up. And hiking the rent."

It was said quietly. In a worried voice. Like a mother whose child had not come home at the expected time.

"I know," I answered her concern.

"You know? But you don't care a shit! You're nothing but a stoolie, aren't you?"

I shook my head. I watched her walk away. Later that day someone cut down the three dolls.

The evening newscast had forty-five seconds of Senator Joseph's talk and included a fleeting glance of Ernestine before panning the crowd and ending. The project was mentioned by name and described as a local hotbed of crime. The rally had not been beneficial for anyone.

One result of the event was that Bert Lottman called three times a day from the central office. Ben Hamilton ran out of licorice twice in one week, and arrangements were made to consult an attorney to cope with the increased withholding of rent money.

The first week in August, Ben Hamilton asked me to come over to his office. A lawyer, Edgar Salmon, was expected at the project. Since I was so closely involved with the tenants and knew the mood of the people, I was asked to sit in during the legal discussion.

Mr. Salmon was short and fat and wore a red vest with one button missing. His jacket was too tight under his arms, and his pants too long over his wing-tipped shoes. While I was explaining some of the factors behind the rent strike, he was twiddling his glasses and looking absently out of the window. I finished and there was a long silence. Had I been talking into a void? I knew Ben had no legal knowledge, but Mr. Salmon didn't appear to have much either.

Public housing projects that received Federal money did not come under the ordinary landlord-tenant rules. Safeguards for low-income residents were spelled out in Housing and Urban Development guidelines. Eviction could come only after a grievance hearing requested by any tenant who got a P/Q notice. The Action For Tenants was aware of that, and I was positive that Ernestine Trotmartin knew every last technique for delaying the Pay or Quit procedure. The formal calling of a rent strike put all unpaid rents in limbo. Except—and that was a big except—if the tenant had been delinquent in rent before the strike was called. I had made it my business to borrow the HUD manual from Mattie and had found in the fine print that the Federal agency had left itself a loophole.

While I wondered if I should mention what I had found, the silence was snapped by a *ping*. Mr. Salmon had twiddled his glasses too long. One ear-brace dropped off and fell on the floor. Immediately, the man crumpled over in his chair and twisted his head to find the part. A stubby finger pointed under my seat. As I bent to pick the ear-brace up, Mr. Salmon threw himself off his chair and was on his knees.

"Let me get it for you." I scooted my chair over and reached for the eyeglass part. He snatched it away. Instead of getting up, he started patting the worn brown linoleum like a child making mud pies. I looked at Ben, but he was all concern.

"Is something missing?" Ben asked.

I wanted to scream, "Yes, his marbles," but I kept quiet as the lawyer patted under my chair. Mr. Salmon had his ample rear turned toward us. His words were muffled. "My screw! My screw is missing!"

I resisted an impulse to butt him with my foot and push. What are the penalties for butting an attorney? Life?

Ben's expression said there was nothing strange about a fat lawyer crawling around a dirty floor of a Buena Vista office looking for a screw. His bald head glistened with sweat.

"It's really not a screw. It's a pin that holds the glasses together. It must be here someplace." He pivoted and faced us.

"Let me help." Ben eased himself to his knees. Now he was crawling and patting the floor. I felt I was on an island surrounded by frolicking seals. Flap-flap; honk-honk; slish-slish-splash! Ben was still trying to make the meeting meaningful. As they crawled, he discussed the legal matter. "Now, about the procedure of setting up grievance hearings. Do you suggest we allow the tenants one or two postponements, Mr. Salmon?"

They were playing follow the leader now. Seal Salmon crawled under the kneehole of Ben's desk. His voice was hollow. "Where in hell could that damn thing have rolled?"

I watched Ben make a ninety-degree sweep. My usefulness was gone; I walked out of Ben's office. I heard Mr. Salmon banging into something, then his angry voice. "I'm stuck! Christ, get me out of here!"

Ben gurgled, "I've got it! I found it, Mr. Salmon!"

I closed the door behind me. Gloria stopped me with her raised hand like a traffic cop. "Well, when do we start booting out the deadbeats?"

"They're searching for a solution. Any day now."

I left.

The next month involved more meetings with Edgar Salmon. I attended another one; the loophole had been found by Mr. Salmon and it spelled P/Q notices with no chance of a grievance hearing.

I was in the main office when Gloria was given the go-ahead on the Trotmartin rent account. Ben and Gloria studied the billing card minutely, reviewed it, and then re-reviewed it. There could be no mistake that would allow Ernestine to holler "foul!" At last it was determined that, including the charges for replacing broken windows and for repair of the front door after her son, Tank, had used an ax to gain entry, the unpaid balance was $943. At the rate of $43 a month, that meant that over a period of about two years the lady had lived rent free!

Ben showed the final accounting to us. He held it high and fluttered it like a fan.

"We've got her! We've got her! Now let's see what she does!" He grinned like Wolfman Jack.

The eviction notice was lovingly typed by Mattie with Gloria looking over her shoulder. Since Ben had been ordered by Bert Lottman to make sure everything was done legally, Mr. Salmon's process-server was hired to hand-deliver the P/Q order.

The day the big event was to take place, Mattie buzzed me to look out of my window. Mattie said that the young man would serve Ernestine at the AFT office across the street. Her voice shivered happily.

I watched as a robust young man jogged down the main office steps and casually crossed the area toward the AFT office. It was a muggy day. He stopped halfway over to remove his jacket, then checked for the legal writ. He kept it in one hand as he knocked at the door with his other hand. No one answered. He turned, used the legal paper to fan himself, and rapped knuckles again on the door frame.

It happened very quickly. The door opened and Ernestine emerged in a shocking-pink dashiki. She braced her arms on both sides of the door frame —a Samson bringing down the temple in an old Cecil B. De Mille movie! The young man backed up. I saw his lips move as he obviously asked if she was Ernestine Trotmartin. Her answer was loud enough to crack pillars.

Somehow he got the document into her hand while at the same time ducking to avoid her other hand that came up to hit him. Half-stumbling, then galloping, he made his way to his Toyota, got in and roared away.

Ernestine's cussing flowed like soap bubbles from a child's pipe. In a stream of glittering adjectives her heavy insults rumbled through the immediate area. Doors opened, the usual crowd formed, and Ernestine performed.

Holding the unfolded white paper high overhead, Ernestine ripped it into confetti and scattered it. The last sound was the slamming of the AFT door as Madam Chairman disappeared. One glass pane fell out and shattered on the stoop.

Now began the waiting period. Thirty days from now, Ernestine Trotmartin should be nothing more than a bad memory. Ben cheered. I could have told him better.

The next week went by with no special incidents. There were the usual complaints about dirty dogs, dirty stoves, dirty cockroaches, and dirty-mouthed neighbors, in that order. Only one stabbing was reported, and that didn't really count because it was just JoJo Wallace who was high on "reds" and had mistaken his pal Horace for a cop. Horace considered it a "spat." Mabel Dawes came in furious because Scatter Armbruster stole her new Firebird and, while joyriding, wrecked it on the curve of Greentree Lane. He hit a telephone pole. Mabel insisted that the Housing Agency was responsible and that their insurance should pay for the damage. Her logic was that since we let "no-good bums like that bastard Scatter" into the project, we assumed liability for his actions. It took me an hour to convince her we would not pay her repair bills. I wanted to ask her how she could afford a new car on welfare grants, but it was a delicate subject. I knew how. She was one of Grand Prix Papa's "girls" and the Navy base provided plenty of customers. There was also a rumor that Grand Prix Papa had an "in" for "hot" cars. I mentioned that to Mabel. She shut up and left in a hurry.

148

Toward the end of the week, I had to deal in genetics. LuEllen Lincoln brought her youngest baby into the office. LuEllen was white, and had seven other children, the last two from "casual" relationships, according to the welfare records.

The seven-month-old baby boy snuggled on her lap as his half-brother of two wiped his snotty nose on LuEllen's faded cotton jumper. The older child was white, sandy-haired, pale-eyed.

We made conversation. LuEllen's Arkansas twang rattled along about her child-raising problems. At twenty-seven, she had found the secret to getting the most out of life. Babies! With a welfare grant of almost $500 a month and rent at Buena Vista no more than $45 including all utilities, LuEllen should have worn Gucci shoes instead of plastic sandals that showed her cracked toenails.

Finally she came to the point of her visit. She turned the baby in her lap squarely around to face me.

"Miz Bentwood, kin I ast you a question? What does my baby look like?"

"Like a healthy, cute, bright little boy." I lied.

"No, no! You don't understand what I'm astin'. I mean does he look Mexican or black?"

I hedged.

"You'll have to check with his father."

"That's jus' it. I been wondering myself. José Perez say the baby not his, 'cause it got kinky hair, and Willie Cotton slapped me 'round when I tell him it's his. I got them both to agree to let you decide who's the daddy."

The baby reached out toward me. The gold necklace I wore attracted him. I took it off and let him play with it as I tried to come up with an answer.

His hair was crinkled but his features showed no Negroid structure. How in hell did this dumb female expect me to know who impregnated her? And really, what difference did it make? LuEllen's welfare grant would increase whether the child was José Perez's or Willie Cotton's. Her thirteen-year-old daughter would stay home from junior high to babysit the newest infant; and LuEllen would lose two more teeth from the everlasting soft drinks and candy she bought with her food stamps.

"Does it really matter?" I hoped I sounded kind. "Just as long as you love him and you're happy with him."

LuEllen turned the baby to her and looked him over like a grapefruit.

"I guess you're right, Miz Bentwood. But I tell you one thing—I learned my lesson. This time . . ." And she patted her belly. "This time I put it down on the calendar an' I'll know who the daddy is." Her look was triumphant.

"LuEllen, honey," I tried. "Remember when Felicia Moxie talked to the Mothers' Club? About terminating unwanted pregnancies? You know that with your medical card it will be easy for you—"

She wouldn't let me finish. She stood up, chin pulled in tight to her neck, one baby clutched to her breast, the toddler clinging to her dress. "I'm surprised at you, Miz Bentwood, trying to get me to commit murder. Trying to get me to do something wrong! I'm truly surprised at you, yes, I am!" She trundled out with her children.

It was a confused and subdued Edith Bentwood who let herself into her apartment that evening. I had left in a hurry that morning and the place was untidy. I threw my evening paper on the couch and slipped off my shoes.

There was a hopelessness within myself. What change had taken place in me since I started to work at Buena Vista? Stabbings, beatings, stolen cars, starving children—starving for love and for decent food; vandalism, foul words, foul deeds, despair, and fear, always fear. My first frantic effort to right each wrong, to bring justice, compassion, hope—even love—had dwindled now to accepting the horror. I compromised, ready to accept misery for others as their due. Had I copped out?

I flicked on the stereo and the sweet tones of the Mendelssohn violin concerto lulled me as I went about changing and tidying up. The project was far away, in another world. Dusky light drifted, slanted across the rug. A haziness crept over me. I was between two worlds . . . and I wanted neither one. I felt torn, as I had been when the decision to leave Carl had to be made. Maybe it was time I left Buena Vista, went on to something else. Something sane.

I ate. With the evening paper to distract me, I postponed answering my question. The headlines were comforting. Some gangster had been blown up in his car and the police had no lead. A state assemblyman had been arrested for accepting a bribe; a father had killed his retarded son; and Disneyland announced a great new exhibit: Billy Graham sitting on a replica of the *Jaws* shark reciting the Ten Commandments. In Spanish, yet!

Perhaps, I told myself, the world is all a big project, the real thing, while my little nest, with melody and needlepoint cushions and thin china teacups, was the unreal, imaginary spot. Flickering, fast-fading, like firebugs when they fly too high, my dreams had become small lights lost in the brightness of diamond-hard stars.

Then the telephone rang. Shrill. Insistent. I didn't want to talk to anyone, but I picked up the receiver. The man's voice sounded unfamiliar.

"Edith—Edith Bentwood?"

"Yes."

"This is Hank Garrison."

"How did you get my number?" It was unlisted. He knew that. "The phone company cooperates with the police." He sounded urgent and businesslike. Since we had parted antagonistic the last time we talked, his contacting me at home was strange.

"How were things when you left the project tonight?"

"What do you mean, 'How were things at the project?' " I wanted to hang up. That was a stupid question! Hank's voice was hard, cold, not what I needed with tears so heavy, ready to flow.

"Why don't you answer me?" He was irritated.

"Everything was fine. The tenants were busy mixing their five o'clock Molotov cocktails, after which they will dine on cockroaches under glass. Then when the children are tucked into bed with their dear little .38s safely under their pillows, the Buena Vista Book Club is discussing 'Invest Your Food Stamps and Make Millions'!"

"I am calling you on an official matter." His voice was early-bastard. "We got word that another rent-strike rally has been called by your friend Ernestine for tomorrow morning. There could be trouble."

"What kind of trouble?"

There was silence. I thought he had hung up.

"We got word that outsiders . . . 'brothers' from the central city might move in—with guns."

I didn't answer.

"Did you hear what I said?" He pressed.

"Yes. What do you want me to do about it?"

"Hell! What do you think I called you for? I want you to take care of yourself!"

He hung up first, but suddenly I felt much better. The words of one of my diet ladies—Helen Jimmer—came back to me. Words about caring. The record finished, the sun had set, and the room was summer-night dark, but I felt much better.

19

I slept restlessly all night. When the telephone rang I answered on the first ring. It was Ben Hamilton. He rollercoasted his words.

"Edith, there's a rough day coming up. The city police intelligence department called me last night and said there might be trouble—big trouble. Guns!"

"I know."

"Seems like that damned Ernestine is organizing another rent-strike rally. She's mad about her eviction notice, I guess."

"So I heard."

He sounded miffed that I didn't seem surprised.

"Well, since you know already, I won't go into details, but I think you should come in the back way to the project. Leave your car parked at the McDonald's drive-in across the street."

As he was talking, I got up and trailed the telephone cord. I reached for my robe and in the process knocked over my bed lamp. It crashed with a bang. Suddenly I heard Ben screaming hysterically at me over the telephone.

"What happened? Is someone attacking you? Oh, my God, did they throw something through your window? Hang on, don't panic! Hang up! I'll call the police! Relax—don't get excited!"

"Ben, shut up!" I screamed back at him. "No one is doing anything to me. I just knocked over my lamp."

So this was the kind of day it would be, I told myself as I had my coffee and got dressed. Driving to work I almost had an accident. I crossed an intersection when I should have stopped. A stake truck swerved to avoid me. The driver balled his fist at me. After that, I decided to take Ben's advice and park at the drive-in behind the rear section of Buena Vista and walk through the project until I reached the front and my office. I couldn't afford a Molotov cocktail exploding in my front seat.

I made a deal with the girl attendant at the drive-in, locked my car, and moved toward the back entrance of the project.

I chose to walk the shorter route, between the buildings, rather than along the cracked sidewalks.

Summer mornings the project was usually active with children, women getting out early washloads, and lots of dogs running loose. And music—rock, country, blues. The dogs were out, but otherwise the grounds were deserted and quiet. The echoing silence made me hurry. I noticed that more cars were parked at erratic angles than usual—cars I had not seen before. Some were pulled tight against the back doors, parked on the grass. Parking on grass was illegal. I made a note to myself to have the maintenance men ticket the cars.

The uncommon stillness puzzled me. I bolstered myself by telling myself that I shouldn't let that stupid Garrison or hysterical Ben Hamilton scare me. I hummed under my breath to show my confidence as I picked my way through the usual dog piles, loose food-smeared papers, and broken glass. Then it happened!

I heard the glass shatter before I actually felt the blow strike my back. I almost fell but caught onto one of the metal clothesline pipes and braced myself. A stinging ache started. I looked around but saw nothing. Only the early morning white sun reflected on the paned windows. I ducked my head and ran toward one of the vandalized and boarded-up apartments. I waited under the small roof-overhang. My knees were wobbly, my hands cold. I felt sweat bead on my forehead. I held my breath and hoped that made me smaller. I waited. All was quiet. I took one step and poked my head out to look up and down the building front. Nothing. The project looked like a deserted movie set waiting for the actors to take their places. I waited another few minutes, then stepped away from the building. Nothing happened. It was just some dumb kid acting up—tossed a bottle out! It had hit me by accident—a mistake. I told myself that. A mongrel dog ran by me and stopped. He was a young animal; instinctively I put my hand out. He trotted over and muzzled it. It felt good to have a living thing with me— even a stray dog. I tempted him with a hurried ear-scratching and he followed me happily. We had passed two more vandalized apartments when it happened again. A low growl by the dog at my side made me look upward at a darkened window. Two squares were broken out. There, in a half-light and partly hidden, a hand held a bottle. The oblique sun-ray caught it with a glint as it was released and spun toward us. I felt anger, then outrage. A bitter bile taste seeped into my mouth, burned my throat.

"Cut it out, you idiots!" The strength of my voice surprised me. "Who is up there? Stop it!"

The bottle landed on the grass with a thump. The dog ran over, sniffed at it. I walked slowly, keeping my eye on the window. Now I *was* frightened. I moved in next to another building and hugged the wall. I was light-headed with fear. I wondered how many bottles they had up there. The dog had finished investigating the first bottle and spotted me. He started over at my soft whispered command, "Come here."

As I watched, he was hit. It was a beveled green wine bottle with a rounded belly. It seemed to hang for a moment as if nailed to the dog's head, and then it dropped with a hollow sound. The stunned animal yelped once and then his legs caved in, and he fell. Blood gushed from his mouth.

I ran now, to the dying animal, my friend, my companion. He was immeasurably dear to me. I bent over him and my tears mingled with his blood. He was so young, still with his soft puppy fur. He would have grown to be a large dog. I held his limp paw to my chest. He was large already and heavy. Somehow I picked him up and carried him like a wounded child. My purse slapped against my thigh with every step I took.

Once I turned and in a voice that didn't seem to come from me, I screamed back at that black hole. "Goddamn lousy murderers!"

The dead weight of the dog lay heavy against my chest. My arms ached. I dragged my feet and almost stumbled over a broken toy.

I was not conscious that anyone was close until a black hand reached from behind me and braced my sagging arm.

"Nigger-lady, you're a fool to walk here."

It was Tommy Gun.

"They killed the dog!" I sobbed.

"Better the dog than nigger-lady." He pried the dog out of my arms and carried him to the nearest trash bin where he laid the dog down. I looked at my dress. It was bloody. Blood had dripped down my hose and onto my shoes. I ran up to Tommy Gun.

"Don't leave him there. He caught it instead of me. They meant it for me." I had a deep hurt someplace inside.

"The dog died like a man." He hesitated. "He played his part. Once you have played your part, death can be the reward—the applause."

He stopped me from going to the animal, a scrap of matted fur, wine red with his own blood. The black man elbowed me back to the walkway.

"The dog died good, see, nigger-lady." He matched his nervous strides to my heeled hops. "You're too soft, too tenderhearted. In my world men live like dogs and die like dogs. They end up lying in the street and *no one cares!* No one cares at all."

His voice shook—vibrated like a tuning fork. His tone was metal hard. Bitter. "He made out pretty good, that dog. You cared, and you'll remember. Someone to remember you—what more can anyone ask for?"

We walked quietly. Together. Side by side. As we reached the main office building, rumbles of voices were broken by shouts, then shrill screaming of playing children.

Hank Garrison had been right, then. Something was going on. We turned the corner and were met by a large crowd already assembled. Women with placards were milling in groups. I read signs that said "P/Q—HELL! P/U TO THE HOUSING," and "GET RID OF HAMMY HAMILTON, BENTWOOD IS A FINK-FINKS STINK!" and "TELL LOTTMAN TO SHOVE IT." The women started to move in a circular pattern, with small children hanging on, running between, yelling and fighting. The mothers yelled at them to shut up or they'd knock their teeth in.

Ernestine Trotmartin had the largest sign. It dipped, top-heavy, with each step she took. Her voice bellowed abuse against anyone connected with the administration of Buena Vista, including State Senator Buford Joseph. As she marched she repeated the words written on her sign:

P/Q—SHIT!

TO HELL WITH THEIR

PAY OR QUITS

WE WON'T PAY

AND

WE WON'T QUIT!

WE'LL BURN THE PROJECT

DOWN FIRST!

The chant "We won't pay and we won't quit" was taken up by everyone. On one side a group of teen-agers sat on top of cars, beating their heels on fenders. Others thumped with their hands. I recognized one car as Ben Hamilton's. Another group clustered across the parking lot, opposite the

155

office building. They were men. Men and boys. Black people—strangers who did not belong in the project. Like wild mushrooms after a rain, they rose from no place; only if one knew the poisonous from the pure was it safe to try them. Were these people Ernestine's outsiders? I turned to ask Tommy Gun about it. Loud catcalls, booing, and the crowd surging up the office steps stopped me. From where Tommy Gun and I stood, half-concealed by shrubbery, we could see the object of their anger. It was Ben Hamilton. He had come out to protect his automobile and found himself cornered. The women forced him back. His face muscles tightened. He blanched, then reddened. He raised his hands ineffectually. He tried to hold off the screaming tenants. They lowered their sign-poles and advanced like lancers in medieval paintings.

Tommy Gun shoved me aside. I heard him say, "Jesus Christ," as he moved toward the trapped man. He pulled, yanked, and elbowed his way to the base of the steps.

Piercing police sirens deadened the mob noise. Five black-and-white squad cars pulled in from Grand Boulevard and lined up antlike in a semicircle blocking the crowd in front. The last car was unmarked and I recognized it as Hank and Herbie's. Confusion spread as the police jumped out of their cars, clubs extended. Some wore riot helmets. Behind the police cars—following them—another car moved slowly with loud muffler-puffing. It was the battered old station wagon that belonged to Cameron K. Campbell, the project's seventy-four-year-old self-styled and perpetual candidate for office—any office.

Someone had conned him into the act. On the hood of his car sat Helen Jimmer. Like the masthead of an old sailing vessel, Helen leaned into the wind. Her legs straddled the hood and in one hand she held a bullhorn. Her actions separated her men's shirt and pants, exposing her navel, and in the deep recesses of her flesh, a jewel twinkled. Whatever she yelled was lost in the greater noise. Pied Piper-like, the slow-moving car trailed assorted kids and dogs. When it reached the other side of the parking area, the car was blocked by the police cars. A few policemen moved in to the station wagon. I turned back toward the steps where Ben had encountered difficulties. His attackers had retreated; the police cars had cooled down the crowd's anger. Tommy Gun stepped back also and moved next to me by the shrubs. We were standing close together when I saw Ben motion for me to come up the steps to him.

"Come on, Ben wants me. Let's shove our way through," I said to Tommy Gun.

He moved in front and spread his arms wide to open up a path. The crowd had thinned, chattering continued, but the immediate trouble appeared to have been stopped by the arrival of the law.

A vibrating explosion ripped through Buena Vista. Gunshots. More shots. Panic was instant. The strikers mobbed into a ball. I read the question in their eyes: Who? The cops or the tenants? I had the same question.

Activity surged from the police. White-helmeted men leaped across the tarred parking plaza with guns ready, aimed. Screams started as tenants resisted being pushed aside. More police moved in. The faraway whine of more police sirens approaching stirred greater fear.

The crowd parted and let the armed men approach the steps. I looked over at the place that the outsiders had occupied. Only a few were left. Where had they vanished to? I had no time to wonder.

Ben had disappeared from the top landing of the steps—probably made a dive for the safety of his office. Like him, I felt betrayed. I put my hand out to get Tommy Gun's attention. He was not there. Then words hit me like buckshot.

"Get your hands up, nigger! Up behind your head. Now!"

A riot-helmeted policeman, his face deformed like a gargoyle's, advanced on us, gun drawn, pointed. His plastic visor reflected distorted images. Behind me Tommy Gun froze, his hands folded, his fingers interlocked pointing upward, making a roof over his skull.

Three other cops rushed by me and threw the black man on the ground. One kneed him in the back as the other one snapped handcuffs on his unresisting body.

"One move from you, black boy, and you'll get a bullet in your head. You'll be a dead dog!"

A third policeman turned to me.

"Are you OK, miss?" The gentleness in his voice stunned me.

"OK, OK. I'm OK. What made you do that?" I was shaking. I pointed to Tommy Gun twisted awkwardly on the ground.

"Look at yourself."

I looked down and realized what caused their fear. It was the blood! It was the dog's blood that covered my dress and dripped down my legs. They thought Tommy Gun had hurt me; that the gunshots had found me as a target. I remember shaking my head and holding out my hands to prove I was all right. Unhurt.

I bent over the young man just as I had bent down to the wounded animal. One of the cops was still kneeling on his legs. Tommy Gun turned his face toward me; painfully he twisted his body. His voice was deadly. "One day the dogs will bite back, nigger-lady!"

The stock of the gun glanced off my hand before it smashed across his face. Pink flesh showed through the cut and welled in blood.

In horror I looked at the policeman holding the gun. He turned his plastic-encased head and got up, avoiding my eyes. I looked beyond him and realized that the scene had been witnessed by the silent crowd. The extra police cars had arrived and now the entire area was ringed. The silence hung like wet wash. It dripped drops of hate. Static from a police car radio cracked like castanets.

The sun was out strong. My eyes glazed. Forms moved like seaweed swaying in water currents before me. Sounds reached me muted.

A moan from Tommy Gun brought me back. His hands moved painfully. I reached over and pulled on the chain that linked the cuffs. A white rim showed where the metal bit into his wrists. Already the puffiness of swollen flesh almost hid them. I could not ease them.

Another man walked up. I saw it was Sergeant Fuller. He spoke to one of his men.

"Take him in."

I stood up. "What for? What for?"

"Resisting arrest."

"Arrest for what? He didn't do anything—we just walked up and they —the cops—jumped him."

"Move over, lady. We're taking him in. We've been trying to nail this son-of-a-bitch for a long time."

He shoved me aside. His face was grim. My heart pounded; I tasted the bitterness of injustice, the helplessness. Why couldn't I scream out that it was all a mistake? Why didn't I place my body over Tommy Gun's and fight them off? I was afraid—afraid of truth—of a dark uniform on a man who was badged with power? I could hardly hear myself.

"You can't!"

"Just watch us!"

Two policemen leaned over and pulled the black man up. Tommy Gun was bent over, still on his knees, when I heard it. First there was a single whistle, piercing, shrill—then more. They came from different directions, crisscrossing, closing in. The police hesitated, heads stiff, listening. Their eyes moved in one direction. I followed their glance.

Tommy Gun, the three cops, the sergeant, and I were the nucleus; around us were the tenants—women, children, a few older white men, all shifting uneasily under their dipping posters. Surrounding them were the riot police in their porcelain-white helmets and vampire-black uniforms. They looked like huge beetles; the guns held straight up were feelers exploring danger.

Encircling the spread-out police were hundreds of black people. The spores had multiplied, mushroomed, popped out of anger-earth.

Quietly, soft-stepping, swaying, they ringed the squad cars. Black beads around the neck of white fear. A scene frozen by a gigantic camera slightly off focus.

I heard the telephone ring inside the main office and then stop. Still the black people came—like jigsaw pieces on legs, they fit themselves tightly into the circle.

I looked over at Ernestine. She looked pinched and kept wetting her lips. Our eyes met for an eyeblink. I felt a shiver of understanding bind us. Then it was gone.

Steps grinding on the rough pavement made me turn to see Hank Garrison. He was coatless, his cotton shirt sweat-ringed under his armpits. The shoulder holster strap was a dark slash across his chest. He inclined his head as he neared me. His words were barely audible.

"If shooting starts, make it to the wall and fall flat."

He passed me and stopped where the sergeant stood. Over their heads I saw the police positioned with guns ready to fire. A few men fingered them like flutists reaching for the right stop.

I closed my eyes. Oh, God, let everyone keep their head, I prayed. I brought my folded hands to my lips. My fingers stuck; the blood, sweat—wet again—welded my hands together. The police raised their guns and pivoted. They moved their guns in an arc as if picking their targets.

Please, oh, please, God, don't let any cop press too hard or sneeze or stumble.

The sun made crosses as light bounced off the metal firearms. The ribbon of people moved like an ant-army. They squeezed and oozed past the black-and-white police cars, now emptied of men. The police calls bleeped and growled with garbled orders. One riot-dressed cop edged toward a squad car, but as he did, the ribbon of people split and re-formed. The car became inaccessible. The policeman backed up to join his buddies.

No one noticed another car that pulled in from Grand Boulevard. It purred to a stop behind the rows of people. A beefy man got out, a bullhorn in his hand. His police cap glittered with gold braid. In a harsh voice he shouted orders through the bullhorn.

"Everyone hit the deck! On your bellies! Hands behind your heads. On your faces! *Now!*"

No one moved.

In the still life the man picked his way toward us. Again he shouted.

"You have five seconds to comply with this order from the time I start counting. All resisters will suffer the consequences. This is your chief of police ordering everyone to hit the ground with hands behind heads."

Nothing happened. Now the numbers were called out.

"Five . . . four . . ."

Loud arguing started behind me and I saw Hank and Sergeant Fuller. The sergeant looked furious but did nothing to stop Hank Garrison from unlocking Tommy Gun's handcuffs. The blood was thick on the black man's face and he rubbed his wrists a moment after he stood up.

Hank shoved me aside and pulled on Tommy Gun to follow. They started walking through the striking tenants.

The counting continued.

"Three . . . two . . ."

The inside circle of riot police took aim, then hesitated as Garrison and Tommy Gun pushed into view. As the two men reached the black people, Hank stepped back and let Tommy Gun step ahead. The bristling blacks had moved menacingly toward Hank Garrison. Now they held back, uncertain.

Tommy Gun lifted his arms high over his head and made peace signs with both hands. The crowd saw he was free—no longer handcuffed.

A loud shout went up. The ribbon of people opened and separated so that both Hank and Tommy Gun could reach the police chief. Now a parade formed behind Tommy Gun and Hank Garrison. I followed the procession. I saw Hank lean over to the black man and say something. Suddenly Tommy Gun fused into the crowd. He disappeared. And with that, the people-packed area emptied. Just as when Billy Goochen was beaten and tenants appeared and then miraculously vanished, it happened again. Within moments the parking area was deserted. Only a few diehard rent strikers were gathering their signs with Ernestine Trotmartin. They formed a parade behind her and went back to the Action For Tenants office.

I walked up to Hank, who was talking to the chief.

"It was the only way to go, sir."

"Look, Garrison, I could bust you down to metermaid. Insubordination. When a sergeant in the field is C.O. and makes a decision, it's his responsibility and you P.R. men stay out of it."

I butted in.

"Please—Tommy Gun was with me. He protected me when bottles were pitched at me. They had no reason to arrest him."

I got a sour look. The chief pulled his lips tight.

"You're the woman that works here?" He knew the answer. "I admit we were in a helluva fix. You know that most of those bastards were armed—

I bet there's a regular arsenal in this snakepit!"

"When I heard that signal—the whistles—and then we were surrounded in a"—Hank snapped his fingers—"second. We were surrounded . . . outnumbered. I had to let him go."

"Guerilla warfare. Someone's training them." The older man turned and started back to his car. "I guess you did the right thing—this time, Garrison."

Hank and I watched as the last black-and-white peeled out. No one was left but us. It was high noon and the sun burned in August heat. Then we heard it. The unmistakable rapid firing of a machine gun. The shots echoed between the buildings; then, just as suddenly, they stopped. The long, low whistle that followed sent shivers through me. I felt Hank's hand on my shoulder. We were silent. Then Hank spoke.

"Your peacemaker has teeth of iron. One day they will have to be pulled."

Ernestine's rent-picketing was over—at least for today.

The rest of the day the staff wobbled like Jell-O through their duties. Each unexpected noise caused us to shimmy apprehensively. On the way to the maintenance department I passed Bernice bent over her desk. For once I didn't make a flippant remark as I saw her going through her stock of sympathy cards. She looked up at me as I passed.

Bernice should have been born a poodle; she had poodle eyes and that crinkly curled look, and I suddenly realized she usually wore some type of jeweled neck choker for decoration. Now her small kind eyes were red-rimmed. She shuffled through the cards.

"They don't make the right cards for the world we live in. Seems like they should have cards for different kinds of feeling sorry someone is dead."

I was determined not to sound maudlin. "Who kicked off now?" I asked.

"His real name was George but they called him Ape."

"Ape? Are you talking about Grace Smidt's boy?"

"Yes. George was not quite right. You know—he was backward." Bernice sniffed.

"What happened? I just saw him the day before yesterday. He was riding a minibike."

"That's what happened! He was riding the minibike on the freeway."

"And . . . ?" I knew already.

"He got hit." Bernice started to cry all over again.

That horror, on top of everything else, was too much. I saw the twelve-year-old boy's soft placid face with smiling eyes, heard the roar of the traffic. I burst into tears. Bernice came over to me. She put her arm around me and let me lean on her. Grateful, I was filled with love for this odd little person.

By late afternoon the office staff had left: Mattie pleaded a sick headache, Gloria a touch of the flu, Ben Hamilton suddenly remembered a dental appointment, and Bernice's favorite niece had a car accident, so Bernice rushed off. The maintenance men always left early because they started their day at 7:00 a.m. I was alone in the main office and had been pressed into setting the burglar alarm and cutting off the wheezing air-conditioner. The lights were already off, and there was a grayness about the place. I covered the typewriters, checked all the windows, and let the air-conditioner grind to a shaking stop. I dropped a pencil and it sounded like a steel beam.

Exhaustion draped me and forced me down into Mattie's chair. I leaned my head on my arms folded over her desk. The smooth cool wood felt soothing.

Bells knifed through my body as the telephone rang demandingly. I looked at it foolishly, numbly. I let it ring. Someone was checking up to see who was still in the office. My car! I remembered my car was at the drive-in across and behind the project. I was stranded here . . . alone with angry people . . . an arsenal of guns . . . windows from which arms threw out bottles. I would be an easy target again, a woman alone walking from one end of Buena Vista to the other.

The ringing stopped. I was looking at the black box when it started again. This time I picked it up, held it, said nothing.

A man's voice. "Hello? Hello? Who's there?"

Automatically. "Buena Vista Housing Project, may I help you?"

"Edith? Edie?"

"Edith Bentwood speaking." I remembered who I was.

"Listen, this is Hank—you know, Hank."

"Hank—Hank Garrison!" I felt weak. Relieved. For the second time that day I cried.

"What's the matter?"

"Nothing . . . nothing." I sniffed up.

"Are you all right?"

"Yes. No! I'm here alone and . . . oh, Hank . . ." Tears readied again. "My car—it's parked on the other side of the project."

"Stay there. I'll be off duty in thirty minutes and I'll pick you up. Don't try to get there alone. Don't try anything stupid."

I held on, enjoying the comfort I felt.

"Goddamn it! Do you hear me?" It was the cop again.

"Yes. I hear you and yes, I will. I'll wait for you."

It was forty-five minutes before he showed up. He pulled up in front, cut the headlights, and got out of his car. I flicked on the alarm and went to let myself out. As I was double-checking the door lock, Hank came up, bumped me. His hands turned me around. Unexpectedly his arms went around me and he pulled me close.

"Hey, watch what you're doing." He sounded gruff.

"I plan to . . ." I stood stiffly. I felt his arms relax and move down my arms. He stepped back.

"You ready?"

He drove slowly through the project. I was rarely there so late in the evening. I knew that most of the crimes happened at night, in the dark. Hank's car was a small compact, undistinguished. It attracted no attention as we passed the various parking lots. Tenants sat on the stoops and grass, drinking, fondling each other. Children ran barefoot. Loud music with heavy rock beats mixed with occasional cursing and yelling. Yellow light outlined movements. The day's bad dream was forgotten. The emptiness I felt contrasted with the aliveness I saw. Despite everything, the project had vitality, the energy of life being lived; tragedy, pain, a distortion of values, maybe, but under it all the immediacy of emotion gratified. As if Hank read my mind, he spoke.

"It's funny in a way."

"What's funny?"

"I wouldn't be any of these people for anything. Yet there's something to be said for the way they live. I guess it's their basicness—their immediate needs are all they care about. People like you and me, we plan—for vacations, for payments on our cars, what to eat for dinner a week ahead, our responses to people. We read books to convince ourselves . . . the 'I'm OK, you're OK' syndrome. When you know damn well nothing's OK. When you know it's all shit in a shell. What does it all boil down to?"

"Being responsible—to others and yourself—for yourself."

"To Master Charge?"

"You don't sound like an establishment cop!" I was surprised. His words didn't fit with the image of Lieutenant Hank Garrison. "If this looks so great to you," I teased, "why don't you quit and move into Buena Vista? Maybe you could qualify for welfare?"

"Or hit the road—hole up in the desert! But I've got two kids to support. I was married once." He looked sideways at me.

"Oh, no! I don't want to hear your problems. I've had my share of divorced men looking for a shoulder to dump their garbage on."

"Don't worry about this man. My wife died. Accident." He mashed the gas and we barreled around the curve.

We didn't talk after that. He pulled up to my car and waited until I got in and started up. Then he left.

Before I fell asleep, I remembered how good Hank's arms had felt around me. But who needs that? Involvement causes unhappiness, and besides, wasn't I involved enough with the project and its tenants? Anyway, that was a lousy thing for Hank Garrison to do—let me fall into a "bitchy" slot. He should have told me right away that his wife was dead. I wondered how old his children were.

20

The excitement over the aborted rent-strike picketing passed. Ernestine Trotmartin stacked her signs in the back room of the Action For Tenants office and indicated that they would be used again, and soon! She stayed closeted in her private office and, like the Pope, received only certain visitors. From my office window I could watch the comings and goings. Most of the outsiders who had caused the panic among the police melted back into the larger community. No firearms were found, and, except for a few strange faces and some hush-hush comments that made no sense to me, Buena Vista had a half-peaceful two weeks.

A visit from Hank Garrison and Herbie Brent ended in a standoff between us. The men insisted that much of the merchandise burglarized in the surrounding residential section ended up in the project.

"All you have is suspicions—no proof, no facts!" I insisted.

"Look, you're just a pigeon for all these crooks in here. You believe all the garbage they tell you . . . all the sob-sister stuff . . . all the con games and cover-ups! You're just a patsy for their perverted attitude on life—that the world owes them . . . ." Hank buttoned and unbuttoned his jacket furiously as he glared at me. When the one button dropped off in his hand, he angrily shoved it into his pocket. With a curt nod to Herbie to follow, he left.

Later that day I was checking out some supplies in the main office when the call came in. Mattie listened a moment, then held the phone away from her ear. I heard loud and colorful language. I laughed. Mattie's facial expressions showed pain and indignation until the screaming stopped and she hung up.

"That was Denise Dopplemyer. She says someone fire-bombed her place last night to cover up a burglary. You better go and see what's it all about," Mattie said.

Gloria heard Mattie and poked her head in.

"Ha! Dumpling Dopplemyer—no wonder she's upset. She's the biggest fence and pusher in the project. Guess someone ripped off her latest 'merchandise'! Serves her right. It's about time someone set that lard-bucket back on her heels!"

Mrs. Dopplemyer was not one of Gloria's favorite tenants. Denise, or Denny, as she liked to be called, had been one of my most faithful Take-It-Off Club ladies. She had been the treasurer because of her talent with numbers.

"I don't believe it—drugs, I mean. The only thing Dopplemyer pushes is food—into her mouth!" I answered.

"OK, smarty, don't listen to me! You'll find out!" Gloria drawled in her modified Katharine Hepburn twang. "Drugs—and God only knows what else!"

Bernice had walked in and listened. "We have to pray for those dear misguided people."

"Not even Billy Graham could help Denise Dopplemyer." Mattie scowled at Bernice.

Mattie's admission that her favorite stand-in for God was helpless in the face of Mrs. Dopplemyer's transgressions expanded into the accusation that poor Denise was in alliance with the devil. I had to defend my lady.

"Denise Dopplemyer has a lot of good qualities—she's friendly and cooperative and tries to help the youngsters. Why, just last week, Go-Boy told me she was trying to get him a job making deliveries. Some friend of hers owns a business."

Gloria jumped in like a lifeguard spotting a drowning man. Loud. "What's wrong with you, Miss Smarty, is that you swallow every damn fool story these people tell you. That's why you get along so good with them! You're *stupid!*"

I wanted to answer with something clever and cutting and true, but getting a back-handed compliment was better than further arguments with Gloria. I never won anyway.

Down to the Dopplemyer apartment I trotted, determined to prove my judgment was correct. My loud knock brought a thunderous "Come in!" so I pushed open the door and entered. The kitchen was spotless; chrome appliances filled the counters and utility table. Magnetized potholders dangled on the expensive side-by-side refrigerators. Stainless-steel cookware gleamed on the stove. Freshly starched curtains brightened the windows. No Denise. Then, she yelled again. "In here, in here."

I followed the voice into the living room. The lovely Denise was reclining on an imitation-brocade-covered sofa. Her bleached hair was rolled in pink plastic curlers and her bulk took up all the seating space. The room was stacked with televisions: small, big, portable, cabinet, wood, metal, plastic, Colonial, Provincial, Modern. There was a selection of brand names. At least twenty-five items piled up like egg crates.

I must have looked startled because she coughed importantly, lifted her thick ankles off the sofa, and patted the vacated seat next to her. I hesitated. I remembered a late, late, horror film I watched one evening after Johnny Carson had sunk his last putt. It dealt with a mountain of flesh without face or arms that smothered its victims to death by oozing its bulk over them.

"That's all right, I'll just stand." I smiled broadly to show we were good friends.

"Those son-of-a-bitches. Those son-of-a-bitches!" Denny flung one loose fat-skinned arm over toward the stairwell and front entrance. I followed her gesture. The front door, the floor, the wall leading up the stairwell were smoke-blackened. The door was smashed in and charred by fire.

"That's where those bastards threw the fire-bomb? And kicked in the door?"

"Hell, I don't care a shit about the goddamn door! It's what they ripped off after they got in! Three TVs and six tape decks and I don't know how many stereos, speakers and all." She spread her arms out to show the enormity of the crime.

I wanted to say, "Lady, you'll never miss them," but I didn't. Instead I waited for more information. It came.

"You can't trust a goddamn fuckin' son-of-a-bitch these days. Everyone's out to screw you. Nothing but a bunch of crooks!"

Mrs. Dopplemyer's righteous anger waited for me to agree. I did.

"You're absolutely right. Stealing from another person is despicable. Unforgivable."

Denny nodded. Her pink curlers trembled like blossoms in the wind. If Gloria Cogsville was correct about Denise, what I planned to say next should shake her up—curlers, fat, and fear. I spoke very distinctly.

"And next to stealing and making profits from it—next to that, the rottenest thing a person can do is encourage others to steal and . . . to deal in drugs."

Denise was silent for a moment. Nothing moved except her tongue. It darted in and out of her mouth, licking her lips and digging around her gums.

"Yeah, you're right, Miss Bentwood, dearie. It sure is a crappy thing when people screw other people."

Her choice of words told me nothing! Did she or did she not understand what I meant?

I leaned against one of the TV towers and watched Denny as she dug into a sack of potato chips, daintily ate some, and washed them down with orange soda. I was forgotten, half-hidden behind the door.

The sound of the kitchen door opening and then closing was followed by footsteps that stopped at the living room entrance. I recognized the voices. Concealed, I could not see them or they me. It was Dude Muggins and Freddie-O. Dude attacked.

"Listen, you jivin' broad, what in hell you pullin'? You goddamned fucked over us an' now you're bellyachin'! You don't cut us in—we cut you off!"

I heard the swish of his pool cue zing through the air. Freddie-O snarled. "Yeah, we take all the goddamn risks, maybe get busted—get our ass booted into the joint, an' a fat bitch like you sits on her tail and screws us outta our bread!"

I watched Denny. She rolled her eyes in my direction, made frantic hand-waving motions to shut them up. Neither boy picked up on her actions. They continued their complaints.

"Don't try to burn me or my brothers again, Lady Fuck-Up! Maybe you wanna pass that stuff on the street but don't deal us that crap."

Freddie-O took over for Dude. "You shaft us one more time, an' you get yourself some other boys. We fine young men are totally gonna crap in your playpen you pull that shit again. That shit you passed us was—shit!"

Sputtering, Denny's face ballooned red. "Shut your goddamn mouths, you shit-assed punks!" She King-Konged them with her voice. They crumbled at her next words. "Don't you idiots see I got company!"

They stepped into the room, looked where Denny pointed, and saw me. Freddie-O recovered first. Smiled his number-one con grin.

"Oh, hi, there! Mom thinks you're the most. Sure enjoys the Mothers' Club."

Clever! Very clever! I was up against a master. Honey Curtis, Freddie-O's mother, had come to the Mothers' Club only one time. The sadness around her eyes held pain-scars—layers and layers.

I looked at Denise. She picked up an emery board and sawed away at her tobacco-stained fingernails. She refused to look up. Dude edged himself backward, toward the kitchen door. Only Freddie-O, depending on his charm, pushed his luck with me. He did a jive rock dance step, snapped his fingers, swiveled his hips seductively. "Yeah, man, baby Bentwood, my old lady thinks you're cool!" Pop-pop, snap-snap, charm smile!

That did it! The popping of his fingers and the arrogance of his confidence triggered me.

"She won't think I'm so cool when I tell her what's going on—what I just heard. Don't you B.S. me! Stealing all those TVs and stereos and God knows what else and taking drugs as payment—messing yourself up! What's the matter with you? If you don't care about yourself, at least think about your mother and younger brothers!"

I stopped for breath. I wanted to slap his saucy face. I felt, rather than saw, Denny get up from her couch. She circled me and blocked me from the boys. She pulled her skirt loose from between her buttocks. Her five feet eight inches plus curlers towered over my five feet five.

"Who in hell are you accusing of being a thief? You got yourself some nerve coming in my house and trying to lay your shit on me. You talk about any drug crap, an' I'll have your goddamn ass. Ernestine's just laying for you—just waiting for you to fuck up. And what gives you the i-dea that these here TVs is stolen? Can you prove it? Hell, no!" Her sweaty face looked smug. "Matter of fact, these TVs are here being fixed. They're like being in a repair shop. That's right, ain't it, boys?"

She turned to Freddie-O. He was slouched against the wall, teasing his natural with that pronged comb.

"Sure is, Mrs. Dopplemyer. You are ex-actly correct." To me, "See, we is learnin' how to repair them for folks—free!" He gave a big horselaugh.

They had me. There was no doubt about it. Twenty-seven TVs in a welfare recipient's apartment would be no proof they were stolen. (I didn't even know what was in the bedrooms upstairs.) This was retreat time. Silence is golden, and in Buena Vista it's the only alternative to the screaming-meemies. I clamped my mouth shut and indicated by taking a step toward the exit that I wanted to leave. I was permitted to pass by the three others and hoped that my disgust was interpreted as dignity.

Once outside, I kicked two beer cans and stomped on a milk carton. The cans sailed through the air and clattered against an obscene-looking transmission coming from a disemboweled car-body nest. Vicious tentacles of cables reached out from its black and oily guts. A metal venus's-flytrap!

In frustration I stopped at this iron spider and addressed it like a black-frocked magistrate from Dante's *Inferno.* "So I know all that stuff is stolen —so what can I do? And dope—that fat slob is dealing in drugs and running a fence racket. And what can I do? Nothing! I can do nothing!"

My confessional was interrupted by a child's voice. I bumped him with my elbow as I turned.

"Will it talk back?"

"Will what talk back?" Cold and stern. That's me.

"That."

He pointed at my ominous-looking confidant, the brooding jungle of nuts and bolts. He was about seven. Chicano. Velvet-skinned. Marble eyes of wonder, not often seen in Buena Vista children.

Both of us looked intently at the transmission. If its cables had twisted or a greasy eye had opened from somewhere in its bowels of metal, neither the boy nor I would have been shocked.

"That?" I repeated.

"It's not saying anything." Disappointment in his voice.

"It's not hearing anything," I answered.

For a moment he was satisfied with a rational answer. Then, thoughtfully, he said, "If it don't hear, and it can't talk, and if it can't talk, and you know it can't hear to talk back, then why do you 'spect it to talk back to your talking?"

"Peter Piper picked a peck of pickled peppers, and if Peter Piper picks . . . What?"

We faced each other. I felt foolish.

"You stoned? Or something?" He squinted up at me trying to decide for himself.

"Stoned? I guess so." That word was as good as any to describe my gut feeling just then. Too stoned to think—my mind a concrete doorstop.

A knowing gleam and then he stage-whispered, "You better split . . . an' if you're holding, stash it. The cops is behind you." He spun around and ducked into one of the beehive doors.

"That kid rip off your purse?" a man's voice shouted.

I turned. It was Herbie Brent in the unmarked cop car. He was alone. Without Garrison next to him, the younger man seemed cut in two. I walked up to the car.

"Him? No. We were just talking to that." I pointed to the transmission. "He ran when he saw you drive up. Guess he doesn't like cops."

Herbie gave me a funny look. "Did you say you talked—to that junk?"

I couldn't stand Herbie on my better days. Today, not at all. "Why not?

I get as much response from a dead motor as I get from the great City of Crestview law enforcement crew."

"What's your beef?" He was mad.

"Just what I said. I just came from an apartment that has over thirty TVs, God knows how many tape decks and stolen stereos, plus the dame who lives there is running a fence operation and"—I paused to emphasize my anger—"plus she pays off her team of burglars with drugs! Drugs! What do you say about that?"

"You're talking about the Dopplemyer broad, huh? So what? Can you prove it?" His voice was Birdseye cold.

"Prove it? I'm telling you. I saw the TVs and I heard the boys talk about her cheating them on the quality of the drugs—hard drugs."

"Like I said, can you prove it?"

"No, I can't *prove* it! That's your job. That's what you get paid for!"

"Look, Miss Bentwood, my job is to uphold the law, and to enforce it. And until I catch those creeps in the act or have probable cause to enter, I've got less power than that talking transmission of yours." He pointed at the Metal Monster. "Trouble is, you bleeding-heart liberals, all-understanding those son-of-a-bitches who screw up our world, until you get a pet peeve, and then you think we should run around busting things up. We act illegal and a beef goes in to the chief downtown—we get our ass kicked like any company man."

"Where does the line form?"

Herbie flushed. Inwardly, I felt ashamed. I knew what he said was partly true. My silence indicated a truce. He eased the car ahead, then leaned out toward me again.

"I don't know what the hell Garrison sees in you. A good cop can get ruined by a radical dame like you."

He pulled away, leaving me furious, and yet a little pleased. He was wrong about a lot, but right about one thing. There was no chance that a "bleeding-heart liberal" and a cop could ever break bread, let alone share a bed.

Denise Dopplemyer was finally arrested for possession of stolen merchandise three weeks later. It created a lot of excitement when she was dragged out handcuffed. Then it was discovered that her hips didn't fit through an ordinary police car door. One seasoned cop strained his back trying to yank her in from the other side. A paddy wagon with double doors was called and Denise rode away in style. Her apartment was padlocked by the police, and a printed sign saying "Trespassers will be prosecuted" was pasted on to the glass on both doors.

The next day the police truck came to remove the stolen merchandise as evidence for the trial. It was gone! During the night the Dopplemyer pad had been entered and cleaned out!

A furious Sergeant Fuller came out with two detectives from the burglary section along with the fingerprint wagon. Hank stopped by my office on his way down to Denise's. Our conversation was strained until he fumed about the lack of respect the project tenants had for police orders. And warning signs.

"What did you think?" I said. "Certainly your guys didn't expect anyone would pay attention. Aren't you always saying how ignorant the tenants are? Besides, it was probably done by kids, and you know most of them are dropouts and can't read anyway, let alone words over two syllables!"

I suppose the glee on my face showed and we both began to laugh. It broke the ice. We rode down to the parking lot where Sergeant Fuller was pacing. The two detectives were telling him that without presentable evidence, the D.A. wouldn't file. The fingerprint man said it was useless to take prints.

"I can probably lift over fifty valid prints, but what would it prove? Nothing! Only that the lady had a lot of visitors, all living around here, all with legit reasons why their prints would be in there. Boys, you got a cold case!"

He packed up his gear and made a U-turn out to Flood Road.

Naturally, a ring of tenants watched the proceedings and a cheer went up when it was obvious that project cunning had outwitted police craftiness. I circulated among one group and nabbed Jet and Danny Gree.

"OK, whatd'ya do with the TVs?" I asked. "Who's storing the stuff?"

"Why, Miz Edie, you don't think we had anything to do with removing evidence!" Danny could have posed for a portrait of innocence betrayed!

"The pigs made assholes of themselves as usual." Jet's eyes were opaque behind pilot-type steel-rimmed shades. "They make a scene about piddlin' heists and let the big stuff slip by."

"What big stuff?" I spoke low.

Jet shrugged. I knew better than to push it. "Big stuff" meant only two things—hard drugs or guns. So what else was new? Still, the way Jet had said it made me wonder. Could he have meant something else? I was uneasy but, with no real facts, I buried his words and tone behind immediate situations.

Hank left with the other policemen. Three hours later Denise returned in triumph, released for lack of evidence. In addition, her benefactors and their girl friends had cleaned Denise's apartment after the "merchandise" had been removed. Joyce Franks, Hilda Franks's daughter, let it slip a few weeks later. By then, other crises at Buena Vista Housing Project made stolen TVs seem like a pimple on a person dying of cancer.

21

Voices below my window woke me up. Night darkness was moving over for pearl gray light. Saturday! I rolled over. The chattering continued, intruded, annoyed, and finally made me curious. Someone was packing for a trip down the coast. So all right already, leave! They pulled off in fat contentment.

I dozed, turned, and hid under the covers. Got smothered, slapped covers away from my head, and found out that I was awake for the day. Damn!

The pearl gray was pinkish; it rouge-rosed the sky. The idea of getting away, really away, from Buena Vista for a couple of days—just feeling free to wander—excited me. I got up.

I showered, had coffee, packed an overnight case, gassed up at the corner Exxon station, and took off.

A red light stopped me at the freeway ramps. South or north? San Diego or San Francisco? I turned north. I left the valley and stopped at Santa Barbara for eggs and more coffee. A poster stuck against the coffee-shop window urged me to experience Old World charm at Solvang. It showed a picture of a quaint European town. My old dreams came back. The slides in Renaissance Art II, the travelogues of Greece, and the lacy designs of the Alhambra. Heidi revisited and Rome experienced. Would I ever fall in love in Venice or sit on the steps of the Dam in Amsterdam? Could I begin a round-the-world trip by turning off Route 1 to head for Solvang, California? Why not?

It was nice. Small and expensive shops. Smorgasbord tables with millions of dishes, and shopkeeper ladies hustling Hong Kong-made Black Forest cuckoo clocks.

It was fun. I stuffed myself with heartburn dishes and bought a carved owl with glass eyes.

I pretended I was in another world—distant, different, delightful. But I wasn't. It was a bargain-counter, mark-down day and two-for-a-dollar dreams.

Saturday night I lay in my red-heart-decorated Motel le Quaint bed. The bleach odor of the pillowcase burned my nostrils and the shower head kept dripping in agonizing offbeats. I counted each moon-shaped headlight as the beam splashed into my room. Self-pity dribbled over me.

Would it always be like this? The sheets were rough. My toe found a knob of overwoven cotton and worried it. I lay dead center and let my fingers walk to the edge of the mattress. Space. Nothing but space around me. I was the kernel, the nucleus. Of what? Was Buena Vista the cross I had to bear? Holy Mary, Mother of . . . Hell, Lady, why didn't you have a girl? They wouldn't have nailed a female up on any cross. Think about what it would have saved the world! I didn't ask anyone to die for my sins. Hell, no! I was doing a pretty good job of living a dying life with no help from anyone.

I remembered Dellie . . . and the hurt of aloneness stung.

"Screw you! Get fucked!" I said aloud. And cried and fell asleep curled up like a mole. In a root cellar.

Knuckles rapped on my door. A voice asked if she could make up the room. I unwrapped sleep-strings. Wheels of her cart squeaked past my door, stopped. More rapping, this time on the door next to my room. I pictured a stack of toilet paper, slivers of soap, glasses bagged in waxed paper laid out like a surgeon's instruments . . . antiseptic sin-removers for motelectomies.

A murmur of voices; the pushcart wheels whined farther away. A haze of nostalgia seeped through my mind . . . pushcarts!

Cold . . . very cold winter days. Slip-sliding along icy pavements holding Mama's hand. My hand squeezed tight in rough woolen mittens against the mended gloves of Mama's. Fingers lumped into ice sticks. Snot frozen. Each sucked breath icy enough to hurt my chest. Gaudy neon lights blended into finger-paintings on snow-wet streets. Slush-soaked shoes took small hops to keep up.

The careful shopping from pushcarts manned by small, hunched men in tattered overcoats. Huge safety pins held the collars firm under stubbled chins. And the smells! Delicious chestnut smells, charcoaled and brittle, black-skinned. Newspaper cone with scorched nuts inside kept my hands warm. Chewing, I followed Mama. Satisfied with her bargains, she unfolded her oilcloth shopping bag and carefully stuffed groceries into compact arrangements. The large sack of potatoes was my responsibility. Clasping it to my middle, I staggered like a pregnant midget.

The chestnuts were long since eaten, but their earthy smell lingered on the way home. Mama and I walked silently back, casting our eyes downward to avoid the worst snow drifts. Besides, it hurt to move eyelids in the cold. Her booted feet paused; I knew we were home. Home meant an orange light. It shone through the etched-glass transom window of our front door —a friendly square, promising warmth and hot chocolate and maybe a game of Casino. Climbing the ash-spread steps, feeling pebbles through shoe soles, suddenly aware of torturous cold toes. And then the door opened wide. Orange light flooded out . . . embraced . . . soothed burning icy cheeks . . . unfroze stiffened fingers linked around the potato sack.

Years later, the smell of charcoal meant chestnuts sold from pushcarts, the memory of cold toes in wet shoes, and my mother's hand squeezing my fingers numb. The feeling of being safe . . . warm . . . loved . . . was acid-etched into my child's memory, and through it all shone the friendly orange light beckoning me home.

I fought tears. Opened my eyes into the klieg-light California sunshine. My fantasy-fog burned away. I felt good . . . great. Suddenly my head was together. I jumped up and started for the shower. Orange light was all around me. I just had to find the right door.

I checked out before twelve and headed back to Crestview and my project people.

Monday morning I was up early and into Buena Vista before eight o'clock.

At nine a call came from the local cable television station. The voice identified itself as program director. The girl asked for information on Cameron K. Campbell. I hedged. Information on any tenant was a no-no. Federal policy was very strict on confidentiality.

The girl grew exasperated. Finally she explained. The local paper had run an article over the weekend on Mr. Campbell as a declared gubernatorial candidate. The station felt his unique campaign deserved exposure and they wanted to do an interview with Mr. Campbell. They did not have his exact address or telephone number. Could I help?

176

"Well, it's true that Mr. Campbell is a tenant in Buena Vista but I don't think he's serious."

I was cut off by an ACLU-toned voice.

"The Fair Campaign Practices Law applies to everyone." The voice implied I was un-American.

"Fine!" (Didn't I allocate one dollar to the Presidential Election Campaign Fund on my income tax return!) "Great, I think it's a fantastic idea. Now, where and when are you planning this interview? I can't give out Mr. Campbell's address, but I can arrange for you to meet with him, perhaps in my office."

Sweetness and light took over and we agreed on a tentative date. My suggestion—conducting the TV interview in the community hall so that all the tenants could enjoy seeing one of their own gain recognition—was met with enthusiasm.

The voice became professionally efficient again. Also phony-baloney. "Fabulous! Terrific! We'll arrange to set up the taping directly at the base of operations. The mobile cable unit will handle it. Now, what we need is a full hall of Campbell supporters. You understand that authentic grass-roots support is what makes this a newsworthy item."

I was silent. Should I tell this gal that for every grass root there was a weed killer in the shadows? My silence was not golden to her.

"You *are* public relations for the project, aren't you? It *is* your job to coordinate, isn't it?" Her voice insinuated "death to the spoiler."

"Sure. Anything I can do to help."

"Great! We'll leave it to you, then, to educate the Campbell supporters into an enthusiastic spontaneous group. It takes a lot of planning to get that natural response, you know."

"Oh, it'll be natural."

"Fantastic." I was dismissed.

Did she realize that an enthusiastic spontaneous group in Buena Vista might resemble the storming of the Czar's palace? Audience participation in the project wouldn't include the friendly pap of "Let's Make a Deal."

Last week the project had been flooded with Mr. Campbell's campaign literature. He had come to my office and personally handed me the 2½-by-5-inch pink paper flyer. I picked it up now and turned it over. On one side was his name and the slogan "More for the Poor and Less for the Rich." Under that was a request for donations; his post office box number was listed. The flip side was an advertisement for a cough medicine elixir made in New Jersey.

Coordination was the keyword! Right? Arrangements to use the community hall, getting word out to the tenants about the television coverage, and contacting Mr. Campbell to let him know about the event. The last item was unnecessary.

My telephone rang. Mr. Cameron K. Campbell in his usual heavy Scottish accent was breathless and excited. Had I seen the news article? I hadn't? He'd run right over with a copy. I struggled to decipher his words from his burr. During a lull between sentences, I told him about the TV interview. That did it! His burrs sputtered and died. If it hadn't been for his heavy breathing, I would have thought we were cut off. Finally, a long "Ahhhhhh . . . !" told me he was still on the line. Carefully I explained it all. We both hung up with the understanding I was to come down to his place and make plans.

First, I went over to the main office. Ben Hamilton had to be informed. He knew about the proposed interview on television. He had referred them to me, he told me.

"I tried to tell that stupid producer that they were making fools out of themselves putting an old man like Campbell before the cameras," Ben moaned.

"Did you read the newspaper article on him?"

"Listen, this guy's a weirdo. Each time there's an election and Campbell sends his pink slips to the paper, some crazy reporter down there does a story on him. This time that jackass used a computer and came up with a prediction. Campbell got seven votes the first time he ran for some office. He got fourteen votes the second time and twenty-eight votes the third time and fifty-eight votes last time. So their calculations are that by the year two thousand fifty-six Cameron K. Campbell will be President of the United States. The whole thing is crazy—insane!" For once I agreed with Ben.

"Looks like there's nothing we can do to stop this publicity," I said.

"It'll be a disaster—but that's his funeral!" Ben sounded as if he wished the old fellow would need an interment instead of an interview.

As usual in Buena Vista, the word spread faster than free money. The project was tight with excitement. Youngsters fought to distribute the cough-medicine ad campaign flyers. Dumpling Dopplemyer had her hair bleached and set in wood-shaving curls. Margie Dunn replaced her broken front tooth (result of the Jordon-Dunn altercation). Even Gussie McClure washed her feet and dug out some real shoes in anticipation of being seen on television. Big talk from the teen-agers was how best to get the cameras to focus on them. Freddie-O threatened to appear nude as *Ebony* Man of the Month.

There were several telephone calls between the network, myself, and

Candidate Campbell before the date and time were confirmed.

Several days before the event, I was headed for the Tingle family apartment. Three previous attempts to follow up on complaints of smells from their apartment had fizzled out. Mrs. Tingle attended one Mothers' Club gathering. Her giggling and unkempt appearance led to empty seats on both sides. She came to the Take-It-Off sessions twice. Again, wide spaces between her and the other ladies.

To be honest, I just hated to tackle the Tingle situation. Was there a diplomatic way to tell a person, "Hey, baby, you stink?" It looked as if I would be forced to try today.

Halfway there, I was stopped by Vanessa Van Platzen. She towered over me; the Olympic Bronze Medal glittered on her bosom. Like a hypnotist's pendulum, it swayed on a level with my eyes. I fell under its spell.

"Hey, Miss Edith, honey, you been thinking about old Mr. Campbell and what could happen to him if this TV thing flopped and made him look like the old fool we know he is? I'm talking from personal experience when I say that it can crush you."

It was difficult to picture anything that would have the power or the nerve to crush Vanessa. She took my weak nod as meaning I acknowledged her wisdom.

"It'll break the poor old man's heart. We all know he's daffy, but it doesn't seem right the rest of the world should know he's nuts."

"There's nothing I can do, Vanessa. It's out of my hands."

"Miss Edie, you mean to say you can't come up with some ideas how we can help? Can't you just see what'll happen? Him stumbling over those TV wires with that old cane he uses, and his crooked old feet in them high-laced boots. Why, he can't even talk so that people can understand him good."

I never got down to the Tingles'. Vanessa turned me around and steered me into her apartment. A meeting was called of the members of the defunct Take-It-Off Club, plus a few other tenants. When the space was taken up inside and people milled around outside, Vanessa moved everyone out onto the grass. Standing on a wooden kitchen chair she boomed over the heads of the audience.

"This is bigger than just saving the old goat's feelings. They are trying to make fools out of all of us. Make us look like jerks . . . stupid . . . dumb! We ain't dumb!"

"Fuck 'em!" Someone yelled out the rallying cry.

"We may not be smart but we ain't dumb. We ain't educated but we ain't stupid! Now, what are we going to do to show them asses they are messing with dynamite when they try to screw the citizens of Buena Vista?"

"Blow them away!"

It was Freddie-O and his gang, who had come up to listen. He made a finger-gun and pointed it to his head. His mother was next to him. Honey Curtis slapped her son across the head. He ducked and gave her a horselaugh.

"Want we should rip off some of their gear?" This was Harry the Shoe. He took off his hat, bounced up and down, and waved it for attention. "Or maybe sweeten the gas tanks . . . fix up da tires? Huh?"

"That's amateur stuff—an' I'm a professional." Vanessa flexed her arms.

"What you got in mind?" Starlet Jones shouted.

"That's what I got Miss Edie here for." Vanessa deserved another medal for passing the buck as well as throwing the ball . . . or was it bull? She jumped off the chair and pulled me over, to climb up in her place.

"There is no way to stop the filming of the interview. The best thing to do is help Mr. Campbell make a good impression. You know—he'll have to wear a good suit and say something that makes sense."

"Why don't you write him a speech, Miss Bentwood?" Old lady Crowder was next to me and tugged on my skirt.

"Yeah, you got the gift o' gab, Miz Edith." Annie Flunk winked at the crowd and then at me.

Advice came from all sections. It was agreed that I write a speech. They would take care of his apparel needs, and everyone would attend the taping. Buena Vista would turn out in force to honor their political candidate. The mood was Buena Vista today . . . tomorrow the world!

If grass-roots support was the name of the game, Buena Vista tenants had the bullshit to make it grow! Unknown to Mr. Campbell, he had a party, a speechwriter, a P.R. organization, and a financial war chest to supply him with proper clothing.

That evening at home I labored over my first political speech. I tried it out aloud, revised it and re-revised it, until it sounded halfway professional. Meaning it said nothing in great language.

The next morning, after checking in with Bernice, I gathered my speech and headed for the Campbell apartment. I knew there was a Mrs. Campbell but had never seen her. Was she prepared for the glitter and excitement of political exposure, I wondered?

Their apartment was at the end of one of the larger buildings. A neat, grassy area, watered into a bright green, was planted with sturdy rosebushes that produced large flowers. A bird feeder was hanging from one of the silk trees. An oasis! I knocked and was greeted immediately by Mr. Campbell. He dragged me inside with a King Kong handshake.

I noted remnants of once-good furniture, a worn Oriental rug, faded oil paintings of misty landscapes, and a gallery of stern-faced family photographs covering a table. Hanging from large hooks bored into the ceiling were birdcages. In each were several birds hopping delicately in some ritual dance, scattering birdseed and loose feathers.

Through this forest of wire a diminutive woman advanced. Dresden-frail, a refugee from someone's glass menagerie, she dipped her delicate, veined hand toward me. This was Mrs. Campbell, or Birdie, as she insisted I call her.

While her bear of a husband and I talked about the coming event, Birdie fluttered around and produced cookies spread on hand-painted plates and tea in paper-thin china cups. Swollen birdseeds swirled in my cup as I stirred sugar lumps. I declined the cookies—fuzzy decorations indicated stray feathers.

The three of us sipped our tea as I explained the details of the arrangements. The Campbells' excitement exploded. Even the birds hanging over our heads picked up on it and bounced their cages like swaying blossoms. Cameron K. Campbell was a willing disciple and listened carefully as I explained how the project people were all behind him. When I brought out the speech, he was Eliza Doolittle to my Professor Higgins.

We worked all morning. Over and over, Cameron K. Campbell repeated the words; each time a few more burrs fell by the wayside, like seed scattered from a birdcage.

The last time, Cameron K. stood up, leaned on his cane, and, in almost understandable English, gave his talk. Birdie and I applauded wildly.

The event was Thursday at 2:00 p.m. By 1:00 p.m. the community hall was packed. The blue-and-white-lettered mobile TV truck was parked outside and gas-hose-sized cables snaked up the stairs and into the hall. Two men with snouted cameras perched on their shoulders shouted cryptic messages to each other. A grapefruit-butted girl swiveled her hipless hips as she took notes on a pad and looked important. A bored-looking older man in a wrinkled denim shirt clutched a Gucci tote bag and smoked a thin brown cigarette in a silver holder. The crew people deferred to him and I knew that he was The Director.

I decided to introduce myself and nudged myself into a face-to-face position. He turned red-rimmed puffy eyes on me and then looked past my shoulder as I talked. I was becoming gushy trying to hold his attention when a male voice sliced in.

"Hey, getta load of that fag! Hey, pussy, want to get it on?" I recognized Dude Muggins's putdown technique.

When the poor man finally met my eyes, I looked away. His hand tightened on the silver holder and a smokescreen choked my breath off as he exhaled into my face. So much for show biz! I backed away.

Portable lights were set up on the small stage at one end of the community hall. Three leather-cushioned chairs were placed on the stage in a semicircle. Little Swenson Mansfield discovered they rotated and he was wriggling them. A crewman came up and yanked him away. A low coffee table was placed in front of the chairs, with a tray, a water jug, and glasses.

I watched as a well-groomed young woman walked in and sat herself in one of the stage chairs. She glanced at the sheaf of papers in her hand, said silent words, checked back with her notes, silent words again. Then a brilliant smile (at nothing), a yawn, and she settled back, eyes closed. This must be The Interviewer, I decided.

Commotion, loud yelling, clapping, and car-honking outside made me run out to see what happened. Others already seated followed behind me, and we jammed the exit. At the top of the steps, I stopped. Wow!

A mile-long white Lincoln Continental glided to a stop in front of the hall. The rear door opened and out stepped Cameron K. Campbell, candidate for governor of the State of California. The old man had on a silk suit I knew must have been hot merchandise, probably ripped off from the best men's shop in Beverly Hills. He walked erect, leaning on a gold-knobbed cane. The high-topped shoes were gone. Polished pumps showed their tips as he moved up the steps. His usual scraggly hair was styled. Birdie Campbell followed closely in a long, elegant gown, like an animated bisque doll. In a state of shock, the crowd waited until both Campbells entered the hall. Then a rush as everyone crowded back inside. Me included.

The interview was a success. The ersatz Barbara Walters became enchanted with Cameron's slight Scottish burr. Birdie discussed her birds. She drew friendly laughs and catcalls when she said that if her husband were elected, she would make the governor's mansion open to all homeless birds.

The prepared questions on taxes, crime, and energy that the interviewer tried to get answers to were brushed aside by Candidate Campbell. Instead, like all seasoned politicians, he said what he wanted to get across. Cameron plowed through every word of the speech we had worked on. Once he started, nothing could have stopped him, not even an Andreas Fault earthquake. His closing remarks were met with wild applause, foot-stamping, and cheers.

Later, after the TV trucks pulled out and things quieted down, it was agreed by every tenant that that was the most outstanding event Buena

Vista Housing Project had ever witnessed. Everyone went home happy and proud.

The next day, Friday, I learned that Freddie-O, Vinnie Dunn, and Harry the Shoe had stolen the Lincoln Continental from the car-leasing service at the local airport. The silk suit came from a job pulled in Westwood the week before. Rumor had it that Tommy Gun had arranged it.

Birdie's dress was less fortunately obtained. Alpha Washington and Lisa Fritzle had "shopped" in a specialty shop downtown. Lisa got the dress out undetected, but Alpha had been stopped with a fur stole. The saleslady had grabbed at it just as Alpha got into the waiting car with Jet. After a tussle, Alpha managed to slam the car door on the woman's hand, and Jet roared away.

Both the getaway car and the Continental were ditched that evening across town. I struggled with myself. Should I forward the information to Hank Garrison? I decided not to; I rationalized. Nothing would be done anyway.

To Cameron K. Campbell's surprise, another article was run in the local newspaper. This time it mentioned the interview and gave the day and time it would run on the TV station.

Saturday night there were no fights, burglaries, rapes, beatings, stabbings, or holdups in the vicinity of Buena Vista. All the tenants were glued to their TV sets to see Cameron . . . and perhaps themselves. Law and order had come because of an old Scotsman's belief that in the United States anyone could run for office. Crime was postponed for one night!

22

Summer drew closer to Labor Day and the Buena Vista Housing Project looked terrible—ravished, ruined, raped. It never had had that Beverly Hills manicured look, but this was frightening. Like putting a rape victim on display for a Band-Aid commercial.

Buildings stood hollow-eyed with gaping holes. Unoccupied apartments were open to any desperate homeless person who needed a roof over his head and could stay hidden during the daytime. Rumors of squatters circulated the project. Glass from the smashed windows was scattered along the walkways and stoops. Plumbing fixtures were ripped out, and water flooded the lower floors, stagnating in pools on cement foundations. Children threw trash into the empty apartments, and dogs relieved themselves in piles and piss. Sacks of garbage drew glittering green flies. Spray-can art looped over inside walls, and all of the doorknobs and copper piping was stolen.

One day I held my breath and heel-stepped through slimy goo into one deserted apartment. I shoved a discarded pail under the dripping kitchen faucet, which tunneled into a trapless sink. The constant dripping had rotted away the wooden cabinet shelf, and when I kicked at a sack, a foul piece of meat rolled out, alive with maggots. I did an about-face and stormed into the maintenance department office.

Clarence Jackson, the maintenance supervisor, was talking low to one of the older grounds-crew men. From both men's manner I knew something painful was being said. A moment later the worker slid a ring of keys over to Clarence and left. His head was bowed and he dragged his feet, hesitated at the door, then gently let himself out.

"What's the matter with Joey?" I asked.

"Had to let him go." Clarence looked at the keys.

"That's what I want to talk to you about." I pushed my way past the half-door gate and sat opposite Clarence at his desk. "What's the score? This place is going to the dogs . . . and no cracks, please!" A tired smile had started on his face.

"You're right. I've been here twelve years and it just takes the heart out of me when I see what's happening."

"What is happening?" I asked.

"That's a good question for which I don't have a good answer. But something funny is going on. Like Joey here. He's a hard worker, knows the grounds. Gets along fine. He's the third man I laid off this month. I got orders to fire another nine. I don't like it . . . don't like it one bit." He sighed and picked up the key ring. It became a worry bead in his hands—back and forth—soothing regret.

"I just came from Building one-sixteen. The second empty apartment from the street side is a mess. Water is running and spilling down and the whole place is full of garbage. It stinks," I said.

"Tell me something new. We got about fifty-eight more like that."

"Why aren't they renting the places as they become vacant? Is it because your department can't keep up and get them ready?"

"Partly. But no. The word come down direct from the Big Man. Lottman sent orders not to fill the vacated units. So the next thing was—orders to lay off men, 'cause we got less tenants, he said. It don't make sense to me." Clarence opened his desk drawer and dropped in the keys, then repeated, "It don't make sense to me."

It didn't make sense to me either. It was Bernice who gave me some of the answers later that week. The Social Welfare Department called me to protest that one of their clients had been refused housing by the Buena Vista manager.

Mrs. Irma Mendoza with her two children had been evicted from a condemned one-room apartment. They were living in a car parked behind a motor repair shop, and using the rest room at the corner gas station. The social worker alternated between sarcasm and sympathy-pitches. I put her off as gracefully as I could and promised to get back to her later on with a solution.

Ben Hamilton was not in his office when I went over to the main office. Mattie and Gloria had left for lunch, so Bernice listened to my story about Mrs. Mendoza.

"I know, darling, but Ben stood right there and wouldn't let Mattie take an application from that dear woman with those dear children. And heaven knows, we've got plenty of vacancies."

"What in the world can I tell that social worker, then? How can I explain it to her so she can justify it to that poor woman?"

"Just tell her it's a new rule that Albert Lottman sent down in a memo."

"What memo—what new rule?"

"About rents. Lottman's memo said that because of the rent strike and all that commotion that Ernestine Trotmartin has made, the Board of Advisors okayed the rent increase." Bernice looked unhappy.

"To how much?" I asked.

"To a minimum of sixty-five dollars."

"I'm sure that this Mrs. Mendoza could pay that. It's still low considering it includes lights and gas. Even on welfare she could make it." I knew the amount that a family of one adult and two children received. I was doing some figuring as I talked.

"Poor thing! That's what she told Ben. She was crying and said one of the kids was sick from living in that old car."

"That's terrible! I don't understand Ben's attitude."

"It's the formula. See!" Bernice grabbed a housing application form and as she filled in numbers she explained them to me. A public housing project which received Federal money had to comply with a Federal law called the Brooke Amendment, named after Edward Brooke, the senator from Massachusetts. It said that a housing agency had to set its rent schedule at twenty-five percent of a family's income. After certain allowable deductions from the applicant's income, this net income was used as the basis for the twenty-five percent rental charge.

"But now with the new minimum that we are ordered to follow as equaling twenty-five percent of a person's income . . . see . . . ?" She made me watch as she jotted the equation down.

I understood.

If the $65 minimum rent was to equal twenty-five percent, then anyone who applied at the Buena Vista Housing Project had to have a net monthly income of at least four times that amount (or $260 a month) to qualify for an apartment. That meant that any senior citizen on Social Security with less than $260, or any welfare family of one, two, or three children, whose welfare grants did not reach $260 a month, would be ineligible for housing.

It sank in. I understood. I did not like what I understood. "That's not fair! Those are the very people who need places to live. That's crazy! First they make a rule to keep poor people out, then they fire the maintenance men who keep the place in shape, and then they say they can't rent the apartments because they aren't fixed up."

I was running around the office like a crazy person, pacing and slapping my forehead in frustration. Bernice ripped the form into tiny squares and held them over the wastebasket. Some fluttered in, some fell out onto the floor—like the poor who needed homes, I told myself.

Later that day I confronted Ben Hamilton in his office. I ranted about the vacancy factor, the vandalism, the layoff of maintenance men, and the increased rent. He reacted with his customary panic.

"I don't ask questions. Lottman says charge more, I charge more. I change our policy only when the Housing Agency does. Not before."

My prodding got nothing else out of Ben. Next I went to Gloria. A little soft soap about her efficiency induced her to open her account books for me. It was confirmed that Buena Vista was solvent—still making money, even with Ernestine's rent-withholding strike. I thanked Gloria and left. Why, I asked myself, was this happening? I was determined to find a way I could question Bert Lottman about it. Surely he had been ill-advised on the consequences of this policy. I remembered his intense words the day I was chosen for the position, his emphasis upon helping the low-income citizen to "acquire dignity, self-respect, a feeling of worth." I promised myself that I would do something about this situation. That made me feel better and I went about my project's business.

All that week I walked the project: female fights, kid hassles, parking lot arguments, two fire-bombings, one knifing—nothing very serious.

Unbelievable but so—the project got worse-looking. The grasses and shrubs grew wild, even in the areas still occupied. They crackled dryly as I shoved a path up to the doors. And the doors—some hung on one hinge; panes were cracked, jagged-edged. Not even the rented apartments were maintained now! Complaints of neglected plumbing problems met me at two out of five places.

It was time to confront Albert Lottman.

The chance for a meeting came when someone had to take the financial sheet showing the delinquent rents to the central office of the Housing Agency. I volunteered.

The drive up on the freeway gave me time to organize my comments, complaints, questions. My approach would be objective, calm, and concise. I blew it.

Ushered into the deep-rugged, walnut-paneled, slick-furnished office of the head of the agency, I sensed coolness in his greeting and smile. We both made a few polite comments before Bert Lottman pointedly asked what I wanted to talk to him about. He swiveled in his Eames chair, alternately chewing on his cigar and inspecting his cuticles. My description of the physical appearance of the project and my plea for staff to keep up with the grounds were met by curt remarks.

"There are things about running a Housing Agency that you don't understand. Asking questions to which I can only give you incomplete answers will just confuse you."

"But what about the sixty-five-dollar minimum rent policy? HUD says that only twenty-five percent of the income can be charged. All those empty apartments could be filled if—"

He cut me off. "Why don't you just do the best you can and let the more involved decisions rest with me and the Board of Advisors?"

I blabbered on. About the glass in the sandboxes, the sewer lines that backed up in the bathtubs, the heaters that didn't heat, stoves that never baked a cake—I found myself defending some of Ernestine's complaints!

He guided me to the door, gave me a pat on the back.

"You take things to heart . . . and that's fine. The tenants need someone involved and sympathetic to their problems. But the Board of Advisors and I don't." His look gave added meaning to his words. It said get lost!

Traffic was bumper to bumper on the way back. It gave me time to think. Dissatisfaction with one's self is bitter to take. I was angry at how I had handled the meeting with Bert Lottman. This professionally polite and manipulative man managed to reduce honest concern into a shrill female nag-session.

One question would not go away. Why? Why was this happening? Didn't the destruction of Federal property reflect on the man and agency delegated to oversee the housing of low-income citizens?

The answer came in broad headlines in the *Crestview City Press:* "Alderman Maxwell Oliver demands Buena Vista be razed!" The story continued:

> Oliver, running for re-election to the Governing Board, came out strongly for the total destruction of the low-income housing project. In vivid terms Maxwell Oliver stated, "Buena Vista is a blight upon this city. It is a hotbed of crime draining off city services that should be used for the taxpaying citizens of Crestview." Bolstering his reasons, the alderman cited the rent strike called by Mrs. Ernestine Trotmartin, a tenant, as a contributing factor in the high vacancy rate and vandalism of buildings. A recent discussion with Albert Lottman, head of the Housing Agency

delegated by the Housing and Urban Development Agency (HUD), says Oliver, indicates that the Agency's Board of Advisors is not opposed to the elimination of this project. "My election promise will be to close up Buena Vista, run the criminals out of Crestview, and return the property to those who will construct decent homes for the taxpaying public" is Candidate Oliver's election statement.

It went on to give a background of the project and more of Maxwell Oliver's campaign policies. I read it all. A picture of Oliver and Lottman and two members of the Board of Advisors was included.

When the evening television news picked up the story, all hell broke loose in Buena Vista!

The glove had been thrown down and Ernestine Trotmartin kicked it back into their faces! The project rose up like yeast dough in a hot oven.

The morning the blast against the project appeared, the tenants rang my telephone bell hoarse. Each one wanted to know what it meant. Would they lose their homes? Be put out? How could they pay the rent "outside"? Why? Why? Why?

I told them that I knew no more, no less, than they did. I lied. At least I had a suspicion, an ugly, rotten thought that had to be discussed. With the news article in my hand, I cornered Ben Hamilton in his office. A Band-Aid on his neck indicated either a shaving mishap or an attempt at throat-cutting. His blotches bloomed.

He tried to stop me from discussing the news but I insisted. "Look, whatever Ernestine Trotmartin's faults, she is not responsible for the empty apartments. The Board and Lottman are. You know it and I know it.

"I don't know anything. I don't want to get mixed up in it." He glanced at the paper as I shoved it under his nose, then pushed it away. It dropped on the floor. His distress was pathetic. I wouldn't give up.

"I don't get it. We both know that when they changed the rent base, it automatically made all women with up to three kids and on welfare ineligible for housing in here. That's why the place emptied. The twenty-five percent of their welfare grant doesn't equal sixty-five dollars. Someone's been feeding this Maxwell Oliver a lot of B.S. The rent strike has nothing to do with it."

"So what? Oliver and Lottman are buddies from way back—went to school or something. Anyway, they know what they're doing and I don't . . . and *you* don't!" He picked at the flesh-colored Band-Aid stuck on his neck.

Fear, apprehension, and anger became the glue which fused enemies into amicable comrades. Neighbors who slashed tires last night helped repair them the next. Big kids stopped mugging little kids and taking their lunch money. Grand Prix Papa, the project pimp, loaned his lavender auto to carry Ernestine Trotmartin, Annie Flunk, Mrs. Gomez, Mr. Tingle, Vanessa Van Platzen, and Cameron K. Campbell to the weekly Governing Board meeting at the Crestview City Town Hall. The Grand Prix bulged —not with brains or beauty, but with gut-determination.

The Council's thin veneer of political integrity was pricked and ripped open by Ernestine's blunt comments. Efforts to silence her were useless. She and her backers made colorful copy and newsworthy TV film. I, and most of Southern California, saw Buena Vista and its problems and people raise more dust than any wagon train ever led by John Wayne. Three nights running the TV networks featured different aspects of the controversy. The bleeper was overworked whenever Ernestine expressed herself.

The initial flurry of public attention lasted until the next sensational story broke. Buena Vista was soft-pedaled by Maxwell Oliver at the next two Council meetings. The *Crestview City Press* said Albert Lottman was unavailable for interviews. The Housing and Urban Development regional office spokesman was filmed in his office. With a tight smile, he tossed out HUD manual section and paragraph numbers of regulations and guidelines. The emphasis placed on the word "guidelines" translated the word into "Godlines," as if God's many mansions depended upon HUD approval. By now, I wasn't sure that God wasn't in cahoots with HUD! Was it possible that P/Q in God's manual stood for Poor/Quality? Certainly it would take a miracle for the tenants to triumph and Buena Vista to survive as a haven for the unheavenly.

Ernestine called an Action For Tenants meeting in the community hall for the next week. Reports filtered back to me from Amelia Goochen and Gussie McClure that the gist of the decisions to be voted on was that the tenants would unite and fight any attempts to evict them from the project or any "deals" to demolish Buena Vista.

Buena Vista skidded through the next days with a new low in ripoffs, robberies, and routine rapes. Tenants had worried expressions as they went about their nonbusiness days. Except for complaints about the noisy nighttime shootings, I suffered from a lack of high-level emergencies.

The front-page stories that blotted out the Buena Vista flap involved three bombings of local banks, a mysterious plane that dropped revolutionary leaflets on the outdoor political rally for Senator Joseph, and a shoot-out. The stories came together in a neat package when a stolen van was recovered in Crestview. Discovered inside were more flyers, a money sack from one of the bombed banks, a blue workshirt with identifying prison laundry marks, and evidence of other activities of the radical members.

Grim-faced local police and FBI men were interviewed on TV. Articles about the personal backgrounds of the suspected terrorists were published, and sightings of suspects were reported from Fryeburg, Maine, to Oceanside, California.

The morning that Big George, the project carpenter, dumped a handful of spent shells on my desk, the complaints of over a month became reality. Big George had been in two wars, and his limp and the lumpy scar on one side of his neck testified to personal experience with firearms. He explained the various kinds of ammunition to me. After he left, I set the shells up like toy soldiers. If only they could answer my questions . . . and quiet my fears!

Hank Garrison's voice interrupted. "Look at her, daydreaming again!"

Herbie and Hank made themselves uncomfortable on the loveseat. Herbie got smart about my not earning my salary. Then the questions started. They took turns and tried to disguise their concern. Had I seen any "strange" people in the project?

"Are you kidding? Show me any that aren't! *You* keep saying that they should all be in a zoo, so why ask a dumb question like that?"

Next, the subject of shooting came up. I relented and used my daybook records to trace the dates of nighttime complaints. Hank took down the information in his notebook. I had flattened my shell-soldiers when they walked in; they were concealed by my arm. Herbie spotted them when I opened my top desk drawer and began to shove them in. He moved quickly and held my wrist.

"Hey! Where the hell did you get these?"

"They grow on trees."

"You can't keep those—that's evidence!" Herbie picked one up, turned it over to Hank.

"The heck I can't! Finders keepers, stubborn mules are weepers!"

They looked disgusted. I was defensive. "You guys come in here, try to act so cool, ask me a lot of phony questions and expect me to jump. I've been telling you about the shootings and you gave me the brush-off. All of a sudden you're hot to trot—well, I'm tired of this cat-and-mouse bit."

"OK. What do you want to know?" Hank gave in.

"What's cooking? I mean—is Buena Vista being used as a training ground? And if it is, where're the machine guns coming from and who's using them? And why?"

"Finding those shells is the answer to your first question. Machine guns are war weapons. Next, they could come from any one of a dozen places. Three National Guard armories were ripped off in the last six months. And who's behind it? Misfits, bloodthirsty, trigger-happy criminals, with no respect for law or themselves. Sap-happy spoiled kids that want to save the world by ganging up with psychos."

Hank stopped. Frustration clogged his reasoning. Added a phrase. "They want to gang-rape the country."

Herbie was all business. The Federal men had gotten a tip that five members of the radical group might be holed up in the project. Again I was asked about strangers, squatters. With all the empty and open units, wasn't it possible that one was used as a "safe" house? Anything was possible, I told both men, but not probable. Secrets like that could not be kept, especially when a cash reward had been publicized. And squatters were commonplace. They came and left without anyone reporting them.

They left with the empty shells, after giving me a description of the fugitives reported in the local area. Two black men, Lincoln Bates and his brother Conroy; a black girl—daughter of a famous blues singer—turned radical; a white woman of about twenty-four and her child, a girl of four or five. Lincoln Bates was the man who had escaped in the county jail shooting. Pictures had appeared in the papers and on television. I remembered thinking they looked like a million other bedraggled people—ordinary, undistinguished. When I offered to ask around the project, Hank told me no, it might tip them off. I was to keep my eyes open . . . and ears . . . but keep my mouth shut!

23

Labor Day weekend always brought trouble. That's what Ben Hamilton told me. Weekends were bad enough but three-day weekends were disastrous in Buena Vista. Gloria and Mattie agreed.

"They go crazy every Labor Day. It acts like the full moon on loonies," Ben moaned.

"Ha! We're the loonies! We drag our duffs in here and work and they freeload on our aching backs. No wonder they celebrate Labor Day—our labor and their laziness!" Gloria was in top form. Even the heat couldn't dim her hostility.

On Friday the creaky air-conditioner creaked out. Heat layered, like stacks of thin quilts, choked our breathing, and burned our eyes. My thin cotton dress felt like a ski outfit; I plucked the damp fabric loose from my sweaty body. In slow motion the office staff got ready to close up the main office. I wished them a pleasant Labor Day weekend and returned to my office.

Halfway across the front parking area, several short explosive sounds stopped me. I stood still. Listened. Dulled vibrations died, only to be followed by more sharp cracks. I waited, trying to identify the direction they came from.

My feet burned. The thin-soled sandals I wore didn't protect me against the hot asphalt. The heat made the tar surface tacky. Each step forward caused a rasping sound. I decided the noise had just been backfire. When I reached my office, the telephone was ringing. "To hell with it!" I made no effort to pick it up. It was quitting time and I needed that long three-day weekend.

The telephone shrilled again. Again I let it die. The third time it screamed to be answered. I counted the times—six . . . seven . . . On the ninth ring I gave in. I picked it up.

Sadie Handle gasped her words out. I was to get down to area six. Area six ran along the freeway and contained the storage barn for the project, where the trucks, tools, and maintenance supplies were kept. Area six also was a trouble spot because of Ordie Durkee.

"Sadie, listen, it's after hours and I'm just leaving. Can't it wait?"

"No, it can't! You get down here right now, Miss Edith. Ordie Durkee is drunk and shootin' off his gun outta his upstairs window. He's gonna kill someone!"

"Call the police."

"What's the matter with you? You know damn well the cops won't come for hours. Besides . . . you think I want my head blown off when Ordie finds out I turned him in?"

"Look, Sadie, there's no way I can—"

Her voice cooled, grew mean, insinuating.

"OK, bitch! Goddamn phony . . . pretending you care about us tenants. Ernestine's got you pegged. . . ." She hung up. Hard.

Ordie Durkee was our resident drunk. Not the bimonthly welfare-check drunk, but the vanilla-extract, cough-medicine, hip-pocket-bottle drunk. He was white, in his fifties, and a former Crestview City employee who had held a responsible job until he drank his way into Buena Vista. Mrs. Durkee worked as a nurse's aid at a convalescent hospital for old people. Like a small gray squirrel, she scurried to her night-shift job, usually returning to the project the same time I reported to work in the morning.

My first run-in with Ordie came the day he locked Lisa Fritzle's youngest child, Jeff, in the abandoned ice chest in the storage barn. Lisa had gone crazy searching for her child. A teen-age posse was organized, but it was Clarence Jackson, the maintenance supervisor, who found the child. He was in the barn and heard a weak cry. Jeff was near death when Clarence finally yanked open the door.

That afternoon, after Jeff was declared out of danger, I made a call on Ordie. He answered my knock and appeared relatively sober. Once-good looks were buried under loose flesh, and a sailor gait helped keep him straddled so he would not fall. My accusations got me no place. He fended off attempts to shame him. I threatened him with the police. He got a bottle and offered me a drink. I declined. He drank alone. Frustrated, I was ready to leave when Ordie showed me his guns. Three loaded shotguns were ready; two handguns and boxes of ammunition were stacked next to pancake flour in the kitchen cabinet. His tongue was loose; he babbled.

Ordie Durkee made Archie Bunker sound like William Kunstler. He defended his guns by saying, "These guns'll make nigger blood run," if his "rights as a white man" are violated. He boasted about teaching Lisa's child a lesson.

"Damned half-breed pickaninny, that's all them half-nigger bastards are! Called me a dirty name, that coon did . . . me! A white man! Just let them try lording it over me. I don't have my guns loaded and ready for nothing."

The next day Hank and Herbie came in to the project. I explained about Ordie and his guns and what had happened to Lisa's boy. I insisted he should be arrested.

"You've got no proof," Hank said.

"What proof do you want? A dead child!"

"It would help." This from Herbie.

"Some day that crazy old drunk will kill someone and then what will you say?"

"Good! I'd tell him to do it again. Only I'd ask him to let me pick out the next victim."

"You're sick!" I told the young cop and turned away.

It was Hank who softened the explanation. A small child, frightened, was not a reliable witness. Suspicion was not proof. No D.A. would file on it. They left; I was furious. It did me no good.

So now I was on my way to stop Ordie Durkee from killing someone with his wild gunplay. Sadie's gibe at me had done the trick—as she knew it would.

Building #73 was down Greentree Lane. I reached the area to find a semicircle of tenants formed like an Indian powwow at both ends of the building, out of angle range of Ordie Durkee.

When they saw me, a cheer went up. It gave me false courage. I stopped at the corner of Building #73, poked my head around, and saw Ordie leaning out of his window, gun pointed. I yelled: "Mr. Durkee, oh, Mr. Durkee!"

Bang! Bang!

"Ordie—Ordie Durkee!"

He heard. Answered. Yelled. "What the hell you want, nigger-lover?"

"Put your gun away. I want to come in and talk to you."

Silence. I waited. "You hear me, Ordie?"

"You bringing the cops?"

"No. No cops. Just me, Edie Bentwood." I moved out so he could see I was alone. Ordie still pointed the gun out. "See—no cops!" I wiggled my hands, as if policemen could have hidden between my fingers.

"OK. Just you. Understand? And no cops! You can come in. Door's open downstairs."

"You promise to leave the gun upstairs?"

"I promise."

I walked to the Durkee apartment and pushed open the door. Ordie met me coming down the steps from the bedroom. There was no gun in his hands. But one look around the kitchen showed me two more shotguns plus the rest of his arsenal. I had really walked into it! I knew I better tread easy and talk sweet. I did.

I felt like seven Dear Abbys and two Jeane Dixons as I predicted he would be restored to his city job and said that his anger at "niggers" was understandable; that his "few" drinks every day were necessary for his arthritis; and that his wife, Ardis, didn't appreciate him.

I almost convinced Ordie to let me take the ammunition to my office for safekeeping along with the guns. I was reaching for one of the shotguns when his mood switched. He grabbed one handgun and pointed it. As he advanced, I decided it was time to get out. I was backing up and reaching behind me for the doorknob when the door opened and struck me in the back.

It was Mrs. Durkee. Her hands were holding a green wash-basket filled with laundry.

"Get out of the way!" Ordie waved his gun.

His wife shoved me aside and screamed, "You old fool! What in hell do you think you're doing?"

He pointed the gun at her, but she kept coming until the basket pressed against his waist.

"You put that damn gun down. You want to get someone killed?"

"Shut your mouth, bitch! I'm gonna get me a nigger-lover!"

I got out then. The last thing I saw was Ardis Durkee tipping the basket and dumping all the clean clothing on the man. He struggled to free himself as I closed the door and ran.

A few tenants came up to me, and I told them to stay clear of Ordie. Not to aggravate him. Maybe he would settle down. None of them looked too happy at my advice. Nobody had a better suggestion.

The Odd Fellows (as I had labeled Freddie-O, Dude Muggins, Harry the

Shoe, Danny Gree, and B.T.) clustered in their habitual way whenever there was excitement of any kind at Buena Vista. They blocked my path as I walked toward my office. This time Jet was with the younger guys. Dusk was settling over the project. They stood—posed. Their chiseled black features were polished—smooth wood sculptures. Noble primitives from a hidden African jungle . . . caged in this project jungle. Sudden grief for their loss of dignity sent a crazy kind of love-feeling through me. When Jet stopped me with his hand on my arm, I wasn't alarmed.

"Miss Edith, you gonna find yourself dead if you don't leave that honky alone."

"He's bad—bad crazy, he got no sense!" Freddie-O worried his hair with that comb.

"That man has got to go!" Danny Gree picked on a scab on his arm. "He been jivin' with us too long . . . way too long."

"Maybe so, but you better not help him along," I said.

"What you gonna do about the mother-fucker, Miss Know-it-all? Let him fuck up some more?" Dude Muggins poked his pool cue into the gutter and lifted a tin can. He spun it around on the tip. We all watched it. He let it fall. It clattered and rolled back down the gutter.

My encounters with the Odd Fellows usually progressed according to a formula made up of insults, arguments, and verbal jostling for points. Once that was out of the way, I would try to provide an opening for a surrender, a request for help with a problem, to protect them from losing face.

Tonight it was different. Their cockiness was gone. They were asking me for something . . . I wasn't sure for what yet. We stood like friends, troubled about a common matter. Even in my tired state, I smiled. So many things had changed. I made the first move.

"Listen, guys, I'm played out. Beat. Really. Maybe things will work out by themselves. If not, let's kick it around after the weekend. OK?"

Their faces told me nothing. I walked away from the group. Footsteps came up behind me. Jet walked at my side. We reached my office door. I had turned to thank him for escorting me when he put his hand over mine on the doorknob.

"What's your telephone number?" he asked

"My . . . phone number?" I stalled. Gave him my office number.

"Don't ragtime me. I need the number of your pad." His hand encircled my wrist.

"Why?" I hedged.

My home number was unlisted. Bert Lottman had advised me the day he interviewed me never to let tenants have my telephone number. I would be bugged to death about every little thing. Ben Hamilton warned me I would get abusive calls. Hank Garrison had a fit when he discovered I had told a tenant the street I lived on. He made me swear not to give out my phone number. He explained his concern by telling me that if they knew my street they would locate the building I lived in by spotting my car. Then by calling me and getting no answer, they could break in and rip off all my things. My memory bank punched out these warnings. Speculations ran wild through my mind. I watched his eyes as I repeated: "Why? What do you need it for?"

"Tommy Gun wants it. He said to tell you that things are gettin' tight —there's a lot of shit coming off the walls. Heavy shit. You read me?"

"Not really. If there's trouble, call the cops. That's their job."

"Fuck the pigs!" He dropped my hand, half turned away.

"You mean that the Mayor of Buena Vista can't handle his own . . . shit?"

"Man, I told him—I told Gun, you weren't nothing but a prick-teasin' white honky. You don't care a fuckin' fuck 'bout the project people. All you care about is settin' your rosy ass in a tub of bubblebath!"

"*Pink* bubblebath! Now let me go home!" I turned the key and pushed open the door. My purse and car keys were inside.

His voice was low and cold. We were enemies again. "Tommy Gun don't ask twice."

He pulled a knife and wiped it on his backside. No! This was too much. I let it all hang out.

I shoved Jet backward. "You get the hell away! You rotten black son-of-a-bitch! Think you can pull a damn knife on me and I'll cave in! Well, let me tell you something, no Little Black Sambo is going to melt down this tiger. You are barking up the wrong tree." I knew I was getting words mixed up. "I've had enough of your shit today . . . yesterday . . . last month. Why in hell do you think I stay around and take all this garbage if I didn't care?" I was crying now. "Care! It's jerks like you who don't care! And that fathead Tommy Gun . . . you just go back and tell him . . ."

He cut me off. Anyway, I was choked on my sobbing. Jet folded the knife blade and returned it to his pocket.

"Thing about Tommy Gun . . . he read me off—said I was asstail turned around 'bout you. Said you had soul. Said he hated to think a white broad could be trusted. Yeah, man. Said he hated to say it. But he did."

Jet was a dark cutout against a lighter background of dusk. His face was featureless. His voice was expressionless. "What you want I should tell the Gun?"

I gave him my number.

Nothing happened. Saturday night I had a date with a nice man whom I met at a city conference to discuss alternatives to public low-income housing. He was dedicated to computer programming, skin diving, and his beagle hound. He proudly showed me pictures of a low-slung, sad-eyed animal, and told me that he bred her twice a year. From the sale of the puppies he paid for his car license, a season's pass to the Rams, and a yearly plane ticket to the Midwest to visit his mother.

After the movie we discussed dog foods—the merits of canned versus dry—and the Rams' chances for the coming season. He tried his skin diving on me as we parked in front of my place. The picture of that poor pregnant beagle interfered with any response on my part. I almost broke two of his fingers before I eased myself out of his factory-equipped Pinto.

Sunday I drove in to Los Angeles to visit a rediscovered school friend from the East. The apartment was wall-to-wall everything. She and her husband bickered while I filled up on salted peanuts and good scotch. He told me he was "in pants," which I learned meant he manufactured them. I felt like telling him that he might be "in pants," but his wife wore them. On the pretext of showing me the 180-degree view of Hollywood from their balcony, the husband fumbled his words but not his meaning. It had to do (crudely) with his pants and mine making such beautiful music together. No doubt to zipper accompaniment.

Sunday night I went to bed early. I planned to get up early on Labor Day and beat the rush to the beach for a last suntan.

I heard the telephone ring. I couldn't move myself awake. It died out somewhere in my dreams. Then began again. I fumbled for the receiver.

When I answered it, a polite voice spoke. "Miz Bentwood, ken you come down here?"

"Who is this?"

"Don't make no difference, do it?"

"It sure does. Come down where?" Awake now, I tried to place the voice. I knew the "where."

"We got some trouble here in the project." It wasn't Jet's or Tommy Gun's voice. It continued. "That Ordie Durkee, he is gone crazy. He got Starlet's baby an' Jody Reedy and Honey Curtis's boy locked up in his apartment an' he's shootin' all over the place."

"He's got Freddie-O?"

"No, ma'am. Her second boy, Romeo, he's the twelve-year-old."

"Oh, my God! Why call me—call the police!"

"They come already, but they aiming to shoot up into the place and we is feared they'll hit one of them babies."

"Who gave you my number?"

"Tommy Gun. He say to call you. He say you know what to do. He say to tell you to get your ass down here." Dead silence on both ends. Then . . . "You coming, Miz Bentwood?"

"I'll come."

I splashed water on my face, yanked on blue jeans, and grabbed the first blouse I touched, an overblouse of tucked muslin. Holding tennis shoes in one hand, I ran barefoot to my car. The car clock read 1:00 a.m.

24

The parking lot by Building #73 lay spotlighted—like a grand supermarket opening. Shafts of headlights from police cars crisscrossed under the focused flood-spots. Figures crept molelike around the dark rim. Hushed voices crocheted a blanket of fear.

I left my car parked across from the activity on Greentree Lane. Soft-footed in my sneakers, I ran toward the scene. A few tenants recognized me as I got closer and opened a path. Blinded by the glare ahead, I ran into a barrier. A shotgun turned sideways barred me. The cop pressed hard, forced me backward. With both hands, I knocked the barrel aside. My action surprised him. I had time to give my name and position. The hand that held the gun dropped . . . slowly. He jumbled words out.

"Look, can you get the people to leave—get back into their places?" His eyes shifted towards the crowd. "They're hanging us up. What the hell are they standing around for?"

"They're scared. Afraid some trigger-happy cop will start shooting and hit one of the kids. Until they see the kids are OK they won't leave."

"If we nick a couple of them, they'll move . . . but pronto." Compressed lips. A loose finger itched the trigger.

A bulky form threw itself on me. It was Starlet Jones. Moaning, sobbing, she poured blame upon herself. If only she had not left Bitsy with Romeo as a babysitter! As we walked away from the policeman, I patted her back and tried to calm her.

We skirted the crowd. My eyes became acclimated to the glare. Honey Curtis and Jody Reedy's grandmother stood together. Jody was a polio victim. Her grandmother had raised her after the mother had abandoned the child. Jody was fourteen but looked half that age. Her mind functioned well, even if her legs could not carry her body. Jody was her grandmother's reason for living, and the project was used to seeing Jody in an old rattan baby carriage being wheeled by the old lady.

As I watched the trembling old woman with her gnarled, veined hands pressed to quivering lips, her fear became my anger. Goddamn that old drunk! I remember his hate-filled words. My mind turned them around. I hated him!

Starlet left my side and I drifted to another tenant circle. They made room for me.

"What started it?" I asked anyone.

"Damn mother-fuckin' shitass honky!" The voice was black. "Durkee's old lady started the mess. Three black chicks stalled their car in the parkin' lot and happened to cut off old lady Durkee's wheels. The chicks were hustling a jumper cable to start the car up, an'—"

Another voice picked the story up. "I was there. I seen it all. Miss Edith, let me tell it. Ardis Durkee come out to go on her night shift and she see her car blocked. She gets hot and runs her ass back in to that old fart, Ordie, He come flyin' out and him and Clarice—she been drivin' the car—get into a big fuss. Ordie screaming he's not takin' any sass from no nigger slut, and she better get the fuckin' car moved so's his old lady can get to her job."

Another voice took it up. "You taking too long, Esther. You runnin' off at the mouth. What happen was that Jet and Tommy Gun come along with cables, an' they jump the car. Tommy Gun sweet-talk the old fool, get him calmed down. After the old lady take off for her job, Tommy Gun slip Ordie a couple of bucks for a half pint an' it looks like things is cool, and then—"

The first voice took over again. "The old man hikes it down to the liquor store for his bottle and coming back into the project, he pass Romeo. Way he tells it, the kid pushed him—but we all knows Ordie is crocked all the time anyway. Next thing we know, he runs and gets a gun and tracks Romeo down babysittin' Starlet's Bitsy, so he grab Bitsy and make Romeo go home with him. An' that's when he nabs Jody."

I had heard enough. I felt sick. They told the rest of the details to each other. I listened.

Bitsy was wailing and screaming as Durkee and Romeo passed the Reedy apartment. The grandmother came out to see what was going on. She tried to take the little girl, Bitsy, from the man, but he punched her out. He saw a chance for easy pickings. Durkee told the boy to go inside, grab a purse or any money around. When Jody cried out, Durkee panicked and forced the twelve-year-old Romeo to pick up the crippled girl. He herded them all into his apartment.

"Romeo should have split and called someone," I said.

"Shit! The old coot had a thirty-eight poked in Bitsy's ear! What was Romeo suppose' to do?" It was Freddie-O at my side. His usual snotty manner was gone. I separated myself from the others. Freddie-O trailed me. I was looking for Jet or Tommy Gun.

A cordon of uniformed policemen held the large crowd pushed against the building across the parking lot from the Durkee apartment. The cops had drawn handguns and shotguns. Their heads were turned to the upstairs bedroom window. It was dark. Except for shuffling feet and murmurings, nothing happened.

I saw before I heard. Two cracks. The crowd sucked in breath loudly. Cops played musical chairs, prancing to the shots like gun-shy horses. Gunfire was returned by a kneeling officer. Bits of plaster fell from hits close to the Durkee window.

A scream—was it Starlet? People regrouped themselves. Voices became louder. Grumbling. Everyone listened intently.

A knot of men stood in the shadow at the far end. Police. Through an opening I saw Tommy Gun. Gestures of anger, argument, a few raised voices. I skirted the rear until I could overhear.

"Man, let me try." Tommy Gun, low and tight.

"No." An older voice. In charge.

"You start shootin', and he'll kill the kids! Man, you don't know this cat like we do! He's crazy wild when he drinks!"

"No one goes in there after him. Not as long as he's holding those hostages. Our sharpshooters will pick him off."

"Hey, man, listen to me . . . please! I'm telling you—"

"You're telling me nothing, black boy. I'm telling you. Run along."

Anger. Pent-up. Tommy Gun exploded. Attacked. "Run along, shit! You mother-fuckin', cock-suckin' bastard! What the hell your stinkin' sharp-shooter care about our kids—"

A young cop snapped his arm out toward Tommy Gun and bunched a handful of T-shirt in his fist. He dragged the black man off his feet by surprise.

"Listen, boy, if you goddamn people didn't live like animals, boozing it up and fucking your damn lives away, things like this wouldn't happen . . . and we wouldn't have to wipe up your fucking shit!" The youth in the cop's voice shook. It came out too loud—louder than he expected. The cop in charge tried to shut him up, but it was too late. The damage was done.

Catcalls started. Voices rumbled into drumbeats of anger. The crowd evolved into the beginning of a mob. It surged, broke through the line of police, was pushed back. The crazed drunk holed up with the three children was forgotten until the shooting started again.

Phizz . . . zing-zing . . . phizz . . . A child screamed.

Paralyzed, the people melded into clots. Action began from the police side. The men took position, guns aimed at the window. A light came on upstairs. Durkee paced. We saw Bitsy squirming in his tight grip, the handgun always pointed at the child's head. Now Ordie herded Romeo to the open window. I saw the boy's black arms dangling from the sill. His head rested on the frame. The gun pressed against his natty hair. He wept as he called out, "Mama . . . Mama . . ."

Honey Curtis rushed forward as her son called her. Two cops tossed her back into other women's arms. Banshee wails. Other tenants tried to break through, were shoved and cussed back. Police hunchbacked as they ran from one area to the other.

I stood alone, helpless. Haze steamed under the hot spotlights, became a scrim that diffused the scene. The cleared parking lot glistened like onyx as night dampness settled. I shivered.

A whispered conference took place on my left. The commanding officer and the young cop decided something. Now a bullhorn was brought in. The older man climbed on top of a pickup bed. His first words were garbled, like stones rolling down hill. The sound was adjusted. Orders were barked out. Ordie was to surrender by throwing out all his guns.

Ordie shot out the bedroom light as his answer. In the darkness a hand reached out and yanked Romeo from the windowsill. A loud thump and the hysterical crying from one of the children brought women screaming to the end of the police line. Stupp Hankerson hobbled to my side. For once he didn't smell like wine.

"Why the hell don't they send for Ardis? Mebbe she could handle Ordie . . . get him to give up!"

I felt a warm arm across my back. Annie Flunk squeezed me. She was dressed in a ragged flannel robe, linked by safety pins over her huge breasts, which jiggled as she heaved and sobbed.

"Oh, my God, Miz Bentwood, this is the most terriblest thing ever happen in Buena Vista. Oh, Lordy . . . you let that child Romeo off safe and I promise never to run him off again with my butcher knife!"

Junior Hernandez walked up with Dude Muggins. They greeted me with eye recognition. The bullhorn sent out threats, ultimatums. The window was a blackboard—smooth, empty.

"Where does Ardis work?" I asked softly.

"Don't know. We tried to think which hospital she's at, an' none of us women recall the name," Annie said.

Again the bullhorn orders came. Like a football team getting signals, the police repositioned themselves. I had a crazy desire to laugh, to yell out "hike," or "go-man-go!" Touchdown! Rah, rah . . .

The next shot smashed into the pickup. The second one hit the man standing on it. The officer went down with a grunt and curse. Three cops ran over but he was already climbing over the edge. The bullhorn hung shattered from his hand. His hand was mangled and he screamed as one of the men tried to remove the bullhorn handle from the broken bones. Someone hustled the injured man into a squad car. The motor caught and roared away.

The young officer took over. His face was ghostly as he stood in the hazy headlights giving orders.

"They oughta let Tommy Gun go in. He'd talk that mother-fucker out," Stupp Hankerson said.

"Oh, no!" That was me. "Ordie Durkee hates blacks . . ."

"Hates himself, Miz Edith. But he don't hate Tommy Gun. Tommy Gun and Ordie got an understanding . . . respect . . . that's it. Rotten as that old man is, he's got respect for the Peacemaker." Junior Hernandez said his piece and moved away from us.

"Hey, lady, you think you ken get the pigs to hold their fire?" Dude spoke into my ear. "Tommy Gun's making a run to get inside."

"God . . . I don't know . . . maybe he shouldn't . . . you know . . . if Ordie freaked out maybe he'd . . ." I didn't finish my fear.

"Mother-fuckers . . . if they'd get the hell away and let us take over—but no, *they* got to act the heroes, they got to get the headlines . . . all we suckers get is the headstones. You wait, woman, 'fore it's over there's gonna be some killing! Son-of-a-bitch!" He vanished into the dark.

Strange. Was this the same person who had stabbed Doug, let him bleed to death? Slammed Alpha against the wall? Ran drugs inside the project? When had he become a concerned citizen? Compassionate? Worried about a crippled white girl?

I was so tired. What time was it? In my rush to get there I had forgotten my watch. Now I looked around for someone who could tell me. A command post of some kind was set up by the younger policeman who had taken his superior's place. I pushed through to him. He didn't hear my first "Officer," so I tapped his arm. Irritation showed as he glanced down at me.

"I don't want to tell you your business, but I know these people—I've hassled Durkee myself and maybe if you pulled back your men and let Tommy Matthews up . . ." (I left out the "Gun" on purpose.) ". . . he has a way with—"

"Ma'am, the police have a way also and you're right—don't try to tell me my business. One man has been injured already. We're going in and take this bum."

"But—"

"And you get word to Matthews, one funny move by him . . ."

The shooting began again. The headlights of one squad car blacked out. Glass splintered, fell. Orders were shouted. Random fire struck the window area. The crowd responded, aroused. I watched as uniformed men crept behind cars; some crouched in shadows on the parking lot perimeter. All had rifles. Some had machine guns.

Then I saw it. A figure darted out, ran along the edge of Building #73 directly under the Durkee bedroom window. Half on hands and knees, it dog-paddled its way toward the Durkee door. I knew it was Tommy Gun. From upstairs, Ordie roared curses. Hit another car.

Now the police returned the fire. Shots sprayed the walls, window, ground. Everyone was yelling. Maybe no one noticed Tommy Gun. I had to tell the cop . . . make him hold fire. I grabbed his jacket. He knocked my clawing hand from his arm. I shouted over the bedlam. "Listen . . . tell them to stop shooting . . . someone's trying to get up to Durkee . . . Tommy Gun—"

"Shut up, lady! Get the hell away! Judson, get this dame the fuck away from here!"

The cop called Judson twisted me around and shoved me face forward into the crowd. I stumbled, hung on to someone. I knew I was screaming and cussing, but the noise was louder than my voice. I couldn't hear myself. I had to know if Tommy Gun made it inside. I forced a path to the edge of the milling people, and broke into the open. I stood at the end of the parking lot. Before me was a Ping-Pong game: bullets instead of balls.

I had a clear view of everything that happened. The area under Durkee's window was empty. Tommy Gun had made it! Gunfire still popped but suddenly it sounded one-sided. Ordie had stopped shooting back.

Why didn't the cops realize it? Stop? Wait? They continued, like mechanical dolls that had to let the spring run down. I saw a figure in the shadowed doorway of the besieged apartment. Impulsively, I moved toward it. I yelled. I waved my arms. The shape came into sudden light. It was Tommy Gun and he had Bitsy by the hand and Jody over his shoulder. I saw him squint, blinded by the floodlights, turn sideways. Our eyes met. I thought I saw him smile. He called out, "Don't shoot! Wait! Stop! Hold it!"

But they didn't. They shot him. I saw it. He dropped to his knees and knocked Bitsy back inside. He raised up, twisted, covered Jody up with his body. His hand was palm out, over his head—a flesh paddle to fend off the bullets.

I went crazy. Running and screaming, I hoped that when they saw a woman they wouldn't shoot any more. But someone did. It went past me and hit Tommy Gun. I hit the ground. My head turned toward one side and I saw him! The young cop who took over for the injured older man. He was half concealed, braced against a car fender. Horrified, I watched him pump out shots.

Something bumped me as I lay flat. A body rolled past, down the grassy incline. Another shot jerked it over. It fell, still, on the onyx-black asphalt.

He lay on his back. Palms up, slightly curled fingers. His blackness melted into the blackness of the ground. On the whiteness of his T-shirt a red blood-rose bloomed, its petals unfolding with each heartbeat.

The shooting stopped. I dragged myself up. Crawled. No one moved, came near. Someone turned off the remaining floodlights. The sudden darkness released tensions.

A crying child. Bitsy. Then Romeo ran out of the Durkee door. Honey Curtis wept over her son, dragged him away, Freddie-O at their side. Uniformed legs moved past me where I knelt by Tommy Gun's body. Others came close, knelt or squatted in a circle. I looked up once to catch and hold the eye of the young cop, the one who had called Tommy Gun "black boy," the one who had kept shooting—too long. He turned away first.

It was over. The three children were led off. Jody was carried home by Dude Muggins. The tenants faded quietly back to their homes. Only two police cars remained. The muted whine of an ambulance approached. When it left I would go also. I waited alone by the side of Tommy Gun. Someone approached. I looked up to see Ernestine Trotmartin. Our eyes met. I felt tears, struggled to keep them back. Her lips opened . . . said nothing . . . closed.

We watched the ambulance pull up and the men bring the stretcher over. Hands started to lift the body when Ernestine kicked them away.

Painfully she bent down, kneeled on one leg, and put her hand flat on the bloody shirt. For a second she held her hand still, then carefully wiped it across her garment. It left a dark slash across her breast.

The waiting men shifted their legs impatiently. The two police cars idled their motors.

She repeated her movement. Again she dipped her hand in Tommy Gun's blood. Suddenly, I sensed a special moment. I raised my eyes, looked up into Ernestine's face. I felt her hand move across my chest on my white blouse.

I stood up. Confused. Unhindered, the men hurried to take away their loaded stretcher. The police cars escorted the ambulance out of the project.

Ernestine remained on her knee. She tried to push herself up with her crippled hand; unbalanced, she fell back. I put out my hand. She took it.

I opened the car window as I drove home. A sherbet sunrise promised a beautiful Labor Day. The cool wind felt good on my face.

I never went back to bed. Instead, I showered and went out for breakfast. The beach was hot and crowded and I left early. In the evening I wrote out some bills and then did needlepoint while watching a TV police show.

I misjudged a stitch and jammed the needle into my finger. A bubble of blood formed, spilled over. I cradled my finger in my other hand and started for the bathroom and a Band-Aid. And then the tears came.

My soiled blouse lay on the floor where I had ripped it off. I picked it up and where the dried stain of Tommy Gun's blood slashed across its whiteness, I wiped my finger.

The newspapers told it all. Ordie Durkee was found upstairs with a broken jaw. He was transferred to jail and held on an assortment of charges. The next night the Durkee place was fire-bombed. Ardis Durkee, at work, was left with only the clothes she wore. Thomas Gunther Matthews's death was reported as an unfortunate accident caused by a citizen's refusal to heed the police's instructions. It was regrettable but unavoidable. Case closed.

A Labor Day editorial praised the chief and his men for saving three children. They cited it as proof that color or circumstances made no difference where police help was needed. Residents of Buena Vista should "take note" before they made unfair charges or complaints against the city police.

The project was grim: Like a high-flying balloon suddenly pricked, it snaked with a whine into shriveled deflation. Women sat on chairs placed on the narrow cement porchways, their doors open to allow September sun and air into the dank rooms. In small groups they sat . . . watching their children, stray dogs, ancient cars rumble down the project streets. Sammy the Breadman drove his yellow van into each area but few women trundled their way over to buy.

The weather continued hot. The sun dragged its way across the railroad tracks on one side and sank into the slimy flood-control ditch at the opposite end of Buena Vista each evening.

There was no funeral. Tommy Gun was whisked off from the morgue. Inquiries by Ernestine Trotmartin brought vague answers. Calls to the local newspaper gave no satisfaction. As noisy and public as Tommy Gun had been in life, in death he disappeared into silence.

It bothered me as it bothered the tenants. The release of tension, sorrow, anger, which a public occasion would have allowed, was denied. In its place remained an unreality . . . a feeling of being cheated. But then, the project people were used to that.

The memory of the trip I had made with Tommy Gun came back to me as I tried to calm down the Mothers' Club that Friday. Annie Flunk swore the cops had spirited his body away to conceal their repeated shooting at a defenseless man. She became so vocal, she had the other women incited to storm the Crestview City police station. Then I told them about Tommy Gun's father and what Tommy Gun had told me.

"Why stir up something you can't win?" I said. "Why destroy his father's life? He must have loved his son . . . he came and took Tommy Gun home."

"This was his home . . . we were his people . . . an' we're the ones that got the right to cry for him . . . not some ol' man sittin' high as a hog on a shitpile." Denise Dopplemyer blotted her damp forehead to cover up the wet, reddened eyes.

The last member of the Mothers' Club had gone when Hank Garrison pulled up in front of my office. He was alone and I watched his long-legged strides approach my entrance. We had not talked since the Labor Day violence. I was glad. I didn't think I could handle my feelings about that night with him. His first words told me I was right.

"You took one helluva chance coming down here that night!"

Sudden pain held me wordless. I refused to look at him, respond. He continued. "You realize that was a damn fool stunt you pulled!" He slammed his hand on my desk to make me look at him. "*You* could have been shot instead of that bum."

"He wasn't a bum!"

"You amaze me! What are you trying to do—make a hero out of a no-good black son-of-a-bitch? A parasite . . . a man who lived on women and children . . ."

He threw up his arms and started out the door. He turned, paced. "OK, you got your opinion and I got mine. He was a rotten, lying, stealing, dope-peddling bastard. He's dead, buried, and hopefully soon forgotten. The project is better off without him. He couldn't be trusted!"

"I trusted him . . . and he trusted me."

I covered my face so that Hank would not see me crying. All the events of that night and the days that followed finally broke me. I felt myself being lifted off my chair and pulled upright. Hank's arms went around me and I let them stay. My face was pressed into his damp shirt. The day's heat was still thick. The faint smell of after-shave could not cover the heavy odor of male sweat. It gagged me and yet made me grateful to be close to strength . . . a man's strength.

When I started sniveling and reached one hand back to a tissue box on my desk, he released me. After I had blown my nose and cleared the choke out of my throat, we talked about what happened. I told Hank what I knew about the "good" Tommy Gun and reminded him of the time when he had depended upon the young black man to put down a possible riot.

"I've done and said a lot of things in my life that I've regretted . . . and a lot of things I'm sorry I didn't do . . . a lot of nice things I could have done . . . and didn't. Words I should have said . . . and held back. Mistakes that have haunted me. But I'll always be glad that I came when Tommy Gun sent for me. It proved I trusted him . . . and he trusted me. Maybe it proved more . . . maybe it proved I trusted myself again . . . trusted myself enough to make the right decisions."

Suddenly, peace filled me. Drained now, I still felt vitalized. I could look Hank squarely in the face. Without tears.

"Edie . . . Edie . . ." Now it was his turn to stumble over words, feelings. "About what you just said . . . about being sorry that you didn't say or do the nice things . . . until it was too late. I understand . . . I know that . . . that haunting. Me, too. My wife . . . she used to ask me to stay home when I was off duty . . . spend more time with the kids . . . fix the sprinklers . . ." He rubbed his hand over his eyes as if trying to rub out the memories. "Now, when I take Dena and Eric to a baseball game or zoo or whatever . . . it's like I'm not doing it for the kids, but for Kathy . . . trying to make her feel good . . . now when it's too late. It was months after the accident before I could sleep in our bed. I'd pass out on the couch every night, trying to pretend that if I'd walk into the bedroom I'd find a lump on her side of the bed . . . her robe kicked onto the floor." He stopped talking.

"It would be nice . . . I think it would make Tommy Gun feel good

. . . even laugh . . . if he knew we both learned something from him . . . from his dying." I said it lightly, smiled, felt content about my words. "Maybe . . . but still—it was a damn fool thing you did!" This time he did leave.

25

The momentary contact between Ernestine Trotmartin and me the night Tommy Gun died evaporated under the continued agitation she created among the tenants. The more tenants who withheld their rent payments, the more often Ben Hamilton broke out in blotches and went home early. Ernestine's rent strike was effective.

The Tingle matter finally came to a head. On Monday, the following week, a call from Charles Tingle's teacher left me no choice. Soft-spoken, concerned, she asked me to check on Charles. Why wasn't he in school regularly? He was such a bright, sensitive, and handsome ten-year-old. He had real potential. She repeated it, "real potential." Since there was no telephone number listed in the school file, would I mind . . . ?

That same day Mr. Gilsworthy dropped by and gave me the blue copy of the Health Department citation he had issued on the Tingle apartment. Mr. Gilsworthy was within a year of retiring as inspector for the city. His 1952 suit was shabby but his mind was sharp. He came right to the point. He pinched his nose. Said one word. "Christ!"

Building #107 sat behind an obstacle course of twisted car frames, pools of drained oil, assorted trash, soiled paper diapers, and dog piles. I hopscotched my way to the Tingle door. Knocked and waited.

A puppy ran up and slobbered on my shoe. A larger dog was chained—tangled—to the clothesline pole. Each time it struggled, the collar choked it. I was bending down to unwind the chain when my knock was answered by a raspy voice speaking over my head.

"Yeah?"

The freed dog beat it to the far side. I stood up.

"Mr. Tingle?"

"That's me."

Mr. Tingle cracked the door a foot wide. He leaned against it, fumbling with his zipper. Matted hair, watery blue eyes, stubby reddish eyelashes, chicken-necked, and hollow-chested, Mr. Tingle was no centerfold. Even by man-hungry Buena Vista he'd been labeled a reject.

To save him embarrassment while he finished dressing, I looked down. The gray cotton pants sagged in greasy folds to his bare feet. One big toenail was broken—bruised purple. White flesh showed through encrusted dirt.

Something smelled terrible! The man shifted one foot, then lifted his leg.

"Son-of-a-bitch."

The puppy had wiggled up the stoop. Mr. Tingle's foot caught the dog under the soft belly and kicked it into the air. I gasped. The bundle of black-and-white fur slammed and slid down a car. It lay there. I wanted to kick Mr. Tingle into the air . . . high!

He scraped his foot on the edge of the doorjamb. He grinned at me with stained teeth. "Used to be a real hell-raiser playin' football back in Arkansas."

I tried to smile . . . couldn't.

"Used to kick pretty good."

I couldn't stop myself. "What did you practice with? Babies?"

"Hee, hee! That's real good, never thought of that." His breath forced me backward. "Naw! I don't believe in kickin' kids."

What did he believe in, I wondered? Not soap and water, that was obvious.

"Mr. Tingle, I'm from the office and I'd like to talk to you and Mrs. Tingle."

"Sure thing—but you gotta understand, the place ain't been picked up yet this mornin'. Beverly Suzanne's kinda pukey the last couple of days."

He pulled open the door and stepped aside. Beverly Suzanne must have been more than pukey the last few days. From the stench, something had died, and not gone to heaven yet! No one, absolutely no one, could live in this dump. Yet here they were—both parents under thirty, already with four children. One look at Beverly Suzanne confirmed that a fifth was on the way.

She was sloppy fat. Wads of flesh flapped under her arms. Her breasts lay flabby and pendulant over her protruding stomach. The muumuu she wore showed antique food stains. Barefoot like her husband, she had surprisingly small feet, but they were no cleaner than his. A scarf of lilac toilet tissue cocooned the curlers in her hair. With one hand she tucked up a loose section.

"You'll have to excuse my appearance . . . I mean . . . I hate to be caught with my hair in curlers." Her voice was sweet.

"She's from the office." Papa Tingle pointed at me.

"Why, sure, Miss Edith an' I are old acquaintances. Isn't that right?"

I bobbed my head in agreement. Tear gas would be an improvement in the Tingle townhouse. A rummage sale gone mad! The floors were deep in soiled clothing, sheets, trash and broken toys. Like cherries on a sundae, curled dog messes topped the piles. Eau-de-urine scented the air. Rotted food dribbled out of garbage sacks. Cockroaches waltzed over grease-laden pans heaped on the stove. The dinette table was piled with trash. Catsup glued the pages of Felicia Moxie's "Family Planning Guide."

Beverly Suzanne tiptoed delicately around rotted garbage.

"I guess we better go into the parlor, since the kitchen is kinda messy this morning. I been feeling under. I'm four months along." She patted her stomach.

Parlor! A faded, soiled couch missed a cushion. Its bare springs coiled menacingly. Curled around the impaling metal, a cat nursed her litter.

I took out the Health Department citation and wondered how I could tell these people that their home smelled like a toilet . . . because they used it for a toilet . . . all over! I could see and smell dried excrement caked on the cement floor. Ringed marks looked like old urine puddles. A dull thump followed by a scream and topped off with uninhibited sailor talk postponed my task. Daddy Tingle ambled to the stairwell and shouted up.

"You goddamn kids, cut your horseshittin' around. We got company. An' don't let me hear any of that goddamn fuckin' language again!" Daddy T. looked my way and winked! "Got to keep the kids on the straight an' narrow. Let them know who's boss!"

A herd clumped overhead and pell-melled down the steps into the living room. Three children entered.

I recognized Charles from seeing him around the project. He stiffened, then backed off a step. He tucked his rumpled shirt into the too-short pants.

"Don't get riled up, Charles. She's not from the school," Beverly Suzanne said.

I picked it up. "You're supposed to be in school?"

"I wanted to go . . . I *was* going but . . ." Charles looked at his mother, walked over to pull a kitten away from the mother cat. I watched this handsome boy gently fondle the small animal. I looked at the other children. How insane! Such beautiful children born to parents who didn't know or care.

Charles's sister was about eight. Also with that reddish-blond hair, creamy skin, shadowed deep-blue eyes. Tear-tracks remained on her face. The baby she was carrying death-gripped her neck. She pried his hands loose, yanked his arms away from her neck. "Tiddily, stop it!"

The baby set up a howl. It was a boy; its bare buttocks were red, blotched with dried feces. He also was a picture-book child: blondish curls, forget-me-not blue eyes, trembling rosy lips.

"Cut that damn squalling! Tiddily!" his father ordered.

The baby coughed down a sob, buried his face in his sister's neck, whimpered.

"He seems to have a diaper rash," I said.

Beverly Suzanne cocked her head. Her manner said such a thing could not even be considered. I felt foolish, like a tourist in a foreign country unable to communicate. All eyes were fixed on the baby's rump.

"Is Tiddily the baby's nickname?" I broke the silence.

"It's his real name," Charles said flatly. "Go on, say it! It's a stupid name for a kid! Dumb . . . dumb! Who the fuck would name a kid that . . . only nuts—jerks!"

He dropped the kitten, turned, and lifted a pile of dirty clothes bunched into a corner. From under the mess, he dragged out one sock and a pair of shoes. He held up the sock. A turd hung down.

"Shit! Why in hell don't you ever wash?" He flung the soiled sock at his mother. It fell short of her foot. "You bitch about the school getting on your case, but you don't do a damn thing to help." He grabbed an armful of soiled garments and tossed them up. They scattered. "Now you know why I don't get to school! 'Cause of her! She! She won't wash us any clean things. Just this rotten stuff is all I have to put on . . . or not go at all. She's a pig!"

The father reacted to the outburst. He slammed the boy across the head. The child fell. The man grabbed him upright and held him captive while he punched with the other hand. Grunts followed each blow landed. The family stone-eyed the scene. I was horrified. Would I dare interfere? It ended as suddenly as it started. Charles crawled into the kitchen and escaped outside.

"Respect. That'll teach him," the man said. He rubbed the knuckles of his punching hand. Blew on the reddened skin. "I don't believe in kickin' kids." He looked at me to make sure I picked it up. "But that's one kid oughta have his ass kicked. Talking the way he does!"

He got no pleasant agreement from me. I stated my business coldly. "I have a copy of the health citation given you last week. Your home is unfit and a health hazard. Unless you clean it up, I will have to report it."

Mr. Tingle jumped as if I had struck him. His wife whimpered. "Oh, yeah? What in hell you government people expect? Look at these dumps we hafta pay rent on! Then you want us to sweat an' keep 'em up for you."

"When you moved in here the place was painted, floors waxed, plumbing inspected, and appliances all in good working condition. Now look around!"

"Yeah, well you jus' look at this here stove." I followed him into the kitchen.

He stood in front of the stove and kicked it. White chips fell off. He shoved some pots aside and wiggled the burners. "Crap. Loose. That's what you call a stove? You expect my wife to cook on loose burners?"

"I can't cook on loose burners," Beverly Suzanne echoed behind me.

"In fact"—Mr. Tingle got huffy—"in fact, I'm not paying rent till you get my wife a new stove."

He walked away and found a ripe banana under something. As he peeled it, he waited for my reaction. None came. He tipped a dinette chair and let the trash on it slide onto the floor. Sat down and munched on a banana hunk.

"That Ernestine's got the right idea. From right now, I'm joinin' her rent strike."

"That's your choice. But the rent strike has nothing to do with the city Health Department. You have to clean up."

I looked around. The girl had placed Tiddily in a food-encrusted high-chair and given him a cup of dried cereal. He knocked it over. She was feeding a half-eaten Twinkie to the returned puppy. Jimmy, the four-year-old, wandered in holding a kitten by its head. The animal dangled helplessly. I rescued it.

The scene before me was an Italian movie working overtime to show life at its seamiest. But this was sunny California, the land of Dial Soap, the Rose Parade, Disneyland for kids, Leisure World for oldsters, and Singles for the Swingers!

To hell with public relations. I took a stand.

"I'll give you until tomorrow to clean up this apartment."

He considered me . . . went back to the banana. Peeled it down and took another bite, masticated open-mouthed, then swallowed. We were horn-locked; only one of us could survive!

Eyeballing me, Mr. Tingle eased himself off the chair, groaning as if in pain. He picked up two overflowing sacks of garbage and went outside. Beverly Suzanne watched with big eyes. The little girl grabbed a smaller bag and followed her father. I turned to the lady of the house. I commanded, "Clear off the washer and start some laundry."

Beverly Suzanne—stunned—padded obediently to my directions. She dug out a box of soap powder, collected the dirty laundry, sorted the colors according to my orders, and set the dial on wash.

Mr. Tingle marched in and out until all the garbage was dumped. To the slush-slush of the washing machine, he swept and mopped the floors.

It was like watching windup dolls, each rotating in his own orbit. They ignored me. Some half-dimmed memory of what a home should be filtered back from the past. I left.

The next morning I pulled into the Tingle parking lot before going to the social service center office. After all, I had promised Charles's teacher to get him back into school.

The kitchen door was half open as I walked up the path. Inside was a family scene. Tiddily, his blond ringlets flattened with water, was properly diapered and sat happily in a scrubbed highchair banging a spoon. A pleasant gulp-gulp of perking coffee combined with the smell of bacon. Mr. Tingle and the other two children were seated around the table. The early morning sun slanted across the yellow plastic tablecloth. The mother cat and her kittens were bedded in an empty tomato lug and shoved into a corner. Beverly Suzanne was shoveling scrambled eggs onto plates. Her robe was clean and her hair combed.

I hesitated. No use inspecting . . . things had changed! I backed up quietly, only to be bumped from behind. It was Charles. He was carrying a loaf of bread in a sack. We exchanged looks. His eyes shifted away first, toward the scene I had just left, then came back to my face. He blinked and I felt moisture gather in my eyes.

"Thanks . . . thanks." He rushed past me and into the kitchen.

I noticed his clean shirt, pressed pants, and socks. The fact that one was blue and the other green somehow didn't matter. With a little luck—and lots more prodding—the Tingles would make it!

Like a crazy fool I sang loudly all the way to my office. "Oh, what a beautiful morning. Oh, what a beautiful . . . !"

It didn't last long!

26

October's Indian summer days brought swarms of green horseflies along with buckets of political rhetoric. The mourning that drenched Buena Vista after the sad Labor Day weekend drained away; edginess sat like an eagle ready to swoop down and claim a victim. Something was up!

Persistent rumors of night-long shootings came from various tenants who refused to give their names when they called. The time I stayed late to complete a report on tenant participation in social programs, my concentration was broken by whistles—human whistles. First long . . . echoed . . . then a pattern of shorter notes . . . repeated by a chorus from outposts someplace within the project.

I got up and listened by the open window. The next time the pattern changed: a counterpoint to the first. It came back to me: the morning when the bottles were pitched at me—the near riot . . . At the end, when it was over, came the whistles.

The hot air of the approaching Election Day blew politicians into the project. After all, there were close to a thousand potential voters nested in the swampland of Buena Vista. Their votes, if captured, would help return Maxwell Oliver to his high-backed upholstered chair in the City of Crestview's Town Hall. They could also help send Senator Joseph back to Sacramento for a fourth term.

The *Crestview City Press* announced that Oliver and Joseph had scheduled a joint appearance and a special pre-election tour of the Buena Vista Housing Project on Friday—before Tuesday's election. The article noted their "intense concern" for the problems and needs of low-income voters. It was "highly possible," according to Alderman Oliver, that recommendations emphasizing the "good" elements might result in canceling the demands to demolish and sell the "surplus" Buena Vista land. That's what the newspaper said.

The story was received with mixed comments by the tenants. Few believed, fewer trusted, and most razzed the intentions of the politicians. Still, there was an element of hope that a measure of cooperation on the part of the project people might influence the decision concerning their homes. A hurried Action For Tenants meeting was called by Ernestine Trotmartin. Saving the project was the goal!

Ben Hamilton drove up to the central office for a meeting with Bert Lottman. He returned gloating. The thirty-day eviction notice would be up next week. Ernestine would be out!

The procedure was to have the local sheriff's department tack a three-day notice on her door. After three days, if she was still in the project, all her belongings would be put outside and the apartment locked up.

For Ben it was Christmas, Easter, St. Patrick's Day, and the Fourth of July all at one time. Halloween was set aside for Ernestine; she was the witch!

Ben's only disappointment was that Ernestine's eviction was ordered delayed by Bert Lottman. The three-day notice would not be posted until after the November election. Ben confided to me that Maxwell Oliver was in Senator Joseph's back pocket and that both men were "old and very good" friends of Lottman. Once they were reelected, Ernestine's big mouth couldn't stop the machinery that would close the project. With her out, the tenants would not present any problem. For once, Ben did not stuff licorice balls, and his rosy face was clear of blotches.

The tenants' meeting was in session when I entered the community hall. I sat near the back. Confused thoughts, angry feelings, and helplessness took turns: A decision had to be made by me. But what? Where did loyalty begin? And to whom?

Ernestine rapped the gavel. The motion was made by Amelia Goochen, seconded by Sadie Handle, and passed with a show of hands. The tenants agreed to put on their best front for the visiting men. Committees were appointed to clean up parking lots; mothers were told to have their kids cleaned up; the teen-agers were ordered to weed and trim and to wash smut from the building walls. "Operation Impress" oiled its gears, and all the tenants pulled together.

The next days saw feverish excitement. The senior ladies promised to clean up and dress all the babies in the project while their mothers washed and ironed outfits for the older children. The few able-bodied men, under the leadership of Mr. Tingle, moved the heavy auto wrecks and parts out of the parking areas. The young boys washed windows for the older tenants. The older boys—including Dude Muggins, Harry the Shoe, Go-Boy, Jet, and assorted outsiders brought in by Freddie-O—cleaned out the vandalized units, rehung the doors, and boarded up smashed windows. (No one questioned where the truckload of plywood that was used came from.)

Even Grand Prix Papa imported three of his "ladies" and set them to housecleaning for those women who needed an extra hand. Stupp Hankerson shaved and had his hair cut. Otis Dawson stayed sober. Raquel Mansfield swept out her apartment and removed George Wallace from her wall. Lisa Fritzle offered to play "God Bless America" on the yellow-and-orange-enameled upright piano which stood against the wall in the community hall. She drove Gloria into a migraine as she practiced for the reception in honor of the candidates. Lisa's "God Bless . . ." sounded a lot like "The Saber Dance" to me, as I passed the open doors of the hall.

I was on my way to Mrs. Hupp's to check out her leaking water heater when I did a Jack Benny doubletake. Who was that? The person approaching me looked familiar . . . I couldn't believe it! Flo Bunsey, the project dyke, pranced toward me in a flowered dress and anklestrap shoes! Face to face, she greeted me with a tooth-rattling slap on the back.

"Howya, Bentwood? Fooled ya, huh?" A horrible wig concealed her usual mannish haircut. She did a slow model turn with exaggerated movements.

"My kids flipped when they saw me this morning. You shoulda seen them! Their eyes bugged out like blisters. How do you like it?"

"Gee, Flo, you look . . . absolutely . . . really—"

"Great! That's what they said—sen-sa-tion-al! I'm lookin' so good, I might even go straight after this!" A poke in the ribs demanded I agree with her new femininity.

"What about Cissy Bee? She like it?" Cissy Bee was the other half—Flo's "roommate," a vapid, blond girl whose husband was in for life.

"Cissy Bee screamed like a plucked canary!" Flo's elbow winged in my direction for another poke, but I sidestepped out of range. "Yeah, like Ernestine laid it out—all us tenants got to show some style. We gotta convince those assholes we ain't no different from them. Class—that's what we gotta aim for. That's why I figgered it wouldn't be no good for anyone to get ideas . . . you know . . . maybe stigmatize—that's the word, ain't it? Means bad-mouth ya, right? Anyway, the mos' important thing is to keep our places in here . . . keep the project open. Well, we don't got no other home but Buena Vista. Wouldn't no one else take us in . . . me and Cissy Bee."

I watched her walk off, sailor-gaited, the bright flowered skirt riding her haunches like a horse-drawn cart. Her feet wobbled, ankles twisted twice. She stopped, pulled the heeled shoes off and continued barefoot up Greentree Lane. So much for sex change!

The day for the scheduled political meeting arrived. The Buena Vista Project residents were prepared. A last-minute sweeping of the community hall was finished. A spraycan-painted sign on a torn sheet was tacked over the double doors, saying, "Welcome." Rows of chairs faced the speakers' platform. The untuned piano blossomed next to the platform in waxed orange-and-yellow glory.

Everyone was ready at two o'clock. Buena Vista sparkled with trust. Even Ernestine Trotmartin subdued her usual loud and colorful phrases.

They came in several large cars. The usual eager, too-smiling, eye-shifting young male aides escorted Oliver and Joseph as they pulled up to Buena Vista. A modest group of reporters, some with tape machines, positioned themselves along one wall inside the hall. A toss of a coin decided who would give the signal. Romeo Curtis won. With a two-finger whistle he let Lisa know when to start up the music.

Under Lisa's ump-pa-pa technique, an off-key Strauss waltz ushered the startled politicians in to make their pitch. A restrained Ernestine welcomed them. Her presentation was orderly and direct in defense of keeping Buena Vista operating. Once I caught her looking at me. I grinned back. Even the applause from the tenants lacked the catcalling and vulgarity that always erupted at tenant meetings.

Senator Joseph addressed the crowd first. Later, Maxwell Oliver skirted his former demand to close the project. Instead, he praised the tenants for their interest in their homes.

"Both Senator Joseph and I are vitally concerned with each and every one of you. In fact, it is because we feel that you are entitled to live in decent, pleasant homes and crime-free neighborhoods that we plan to make every effort to see that you can." Loud applause. "Being poor is no disgrace—living poorly, is!" Big hit-the-bull's-eye smile. "When I am reelected, one of the first goals I will put my shoulder to . . ." Slight sideways turn, one shoulder hitched forward. ". . . is to solve that problem for deserving citizens like you tenants. Where else but in this great country of ours does each one of you have the right . . . " Meaningful pause. ". . . the duty to vote into continued office the man who has pledged to serve you . . ." Benevolent look at closest children. ". . . and your children, the future leaders of our nation! Not only that but . . ." Lost place. ". . . but as Senator Joseph so well expressed it, Up for the people! Up! Up! Up!"

Lisa mistook Alderman Oliver's "up-up"s as the signal to start the music. Her first shattering off-key chord of "God Bless America" stunned the speaker into silence. The ticky-tack piano sounded organlike under the Slavic girl's fingers. The audience changed from a restless, apprehensive crowd into a unit of togetherness. Vowed enemies sat next to each other, exchanged smiles, sang the words. Rival teen-agers stood peacefully, knives folded, fighting fists relaxed, lips curved in comradely grins. Mrs. Dunn offered a tissue to wet-eyed Mrs. Jordon as her sniffing added to the music.

The song ended with a boisterous clapping. I turned to watch in shock as a small army of boys from seven to ten marched past me in rank and file from the hall's entrance. The group was led by Billy Goochen carrying an American flag. They wore identical T-shirts silk-screened "Buena Vista Boy Patriots" across the front. On the back in lavender letters, "See Grand Prix Papa for Service" advertised their sponsor! They marched up to stand next to Oliver and Joseph. The flag dipped, was jerked up by Grand Prix Papa, who trailed behind his charges. Dressed in tight leather pants and matching jacket, he vaulted onto the platform and took stage center. He raised his hands as if conducting. The tenants understood and rose. Like a cresting wave of seaweed, they swayed as they again sang "God Bless America" to Lisa's untuned piano. By now most of them knew the words. Some bellowed, others went sour on the top notes, several voices cracked. The last three words brought the house down and ended in a wild clapping. They were "Home, sweet, home."

I waited, watched, as the audience began to leave. The "Boy Patriots," ordered by Grand Prix, still stood at attention. Tenants filed out to be met at the steps by the younger male aides. Into the hands of each adult they crammed leaflets that showed their man's picture and pertinent facts about his career. With knowing smiles and winks, they tried to entrap the tenants into secret commitments to vote for their candidates.

The hall emptied quickly. People drifted off toward their apartments. The aides went over to the cars, talked as they waited. Their bosses had disappeared. Probably making a tour of the project, I decided.

I was heading for my office when I remembered that maintenance had to be informed about two sewer stoppages. I cut around the side of the main office. Parked in back was a car with an out-of-state license. That puzzled me. It was a blue-and-white Nevada plate with a rim that identified it as coming from Las Vegas. The sleek Mercedes-Benz, as out of place in Buena Vista as a Neiman-Marcus outfit, was pulled close to the main office back entrance. Conversation drifted out through the open window of Ben Hamilton's private office—hard, mean voices, relieved by gruff laughter. I recognized Buford Joseph's voice and Maxwell Oliver's higher-pitched tone. The third man's words sounded like an Eastern twang, clipped, nasal.

Uncomfortable at being an eavesdropper, I continued for a few steps. Then something that was said made me turn back and listen. The words were clear and unmistakable. Buford Joseph spoke.

"Hell, people like these don't care where they live. Long as they got a place to booze it up, collect welfare . . . and fuck! Like you said, Nick, it's a crime to waste seventy-eight acres of prime land on scum!"

They laughed. Nick? My mind rolled over the name. Came up empty. Now it was Maxwell Oliver speaking.

"You've got to admit we've got it down pat! Handled it first rate. Never gave any of those rabble-rousers an opening to pin us down. Generalizations! That's the secret to getting votes. Do a Jerry Brown . . . say everything . . . and nothing!"

"You talk too much." This was a new voice . . . Nick's? "This deal isn't chickenshit. This deal has got to go . . . move. Understand? The boys want this pigpen emptied out . . . enough so the HUD people are convinced to dump the damn project. Write it off. Our people are ready to move in with an offer."

The scraping of a chair indicated that someone moved. A shadow showed against the screened window. I moved a few steps back. Joseph's voice carried out louder now.

"You think the tenants will buy it? I mean . . . can we keep them snowed? That woman . . ." His voice drifted. Had he moved away from the window? "That fat nigger dame that's been screwing things up—can you shut her up?"

Oliver answered. "Trotmartin? She's on her way out. On the skids! Eviction! P/Q notice went out thirty days ago. Hamilton's got orders for a three-day eviction notice right after the election's over."

"What about Lottman?" Buford Joseph sounded worried. "He's been making noises like he doesn't go along with . . . the deal."

"Albert Lottman don't have no choice. He bellyaches, we lean on him a little. The man's got too much pride—those ex-Marines got steel balls, but even steel can be softened!"

"Main thing now is to keep it under wraps . . . you know, stonewall it!" Maxwell Oliver coughed out a nervous laugh. "Can't have this deal backfire, can we? You big boys don't fuck around, do you?"

Was this said to Nick? Was he one of the "big boys"? Nick responded.

"Maxie's got the message. We sponsor you, baby, you better play the game . . . by our rules!"

"Right!" Joseph was the shaky-voiced one. "Nick's right! It's their ball game. When they pay, they own the ballplayers! Right, Nick? Right! And they make fucking sure they win. I know. It was touch and squeak last time around for me. That half-baked kid who declared against me in the runoff last time. Almost knocked me out. Mother-fucker just about grabbed my seat. But the boys here . . . they took care of him, right, Nick?"

"Unfortunate thing happened to his wife on the way to his first election. Cops found couple of ounces of hard stuff on her when they made a traffic stop." This was the Nick character talking.

"Sure cut into his votes! Pays to have connections." Joseph's words were triumphant; his tone was anxious.

I'd heard enough. I moved away from the window toward the entrance to the maintenance office. Confusion stalled my mind. A voice calling my name brought me back. It was Bert Lottman. He came out of the maintenance office as I pushed open the door.

"Edith . . . Edith? If you're looking for Ben, I sent him to the bank." He unpeeled a fresh cigar.

"No." I fumbled for a sensible attitude. "No, I was just reporting a smelly situation." I caught myself. "Pipes backed up, I mean."

"That reminds me. Before I forget, Monday I'd like you to report at the central office . . . early. Wanted to talk to you about setting up an improvement program for Buena Vista. I'm sure you have ideas . . . valuable ones." He smiled a plastic recruitment grin at me, noticed his unlit cigar, and added, "Got a match?"

"No, I don't smoke."

"Smart girl!" he said and headed for the other building.

Later on, sitting at my desk, I tried to evaluate the conversation I had overheard, tried to put things into perspective. The more I attempted to clarify my thoughts, the muddier my feelings became. One thing came back to me: Lottman appeared to be a victim and not a participant in whatever shady business was going on. And Ben? Ben was just floating on top, like a leaf at the mercy of any ripple.

Monday! I put my meeting with Lottman on my calendar. Was this a clever way to get me out of the way before the Tuesday election? Not take a chance I might tip off tenants not to vote for Maxwell Oliver or Buford Joseph? Should I have mentioned to Bert Lottman the conversation I had overheard? Eavesdropped on was more accurate. Eavesdropping is unethical. So is lying and cheating, murdering hope and raping trust. And if Lottman really was under pressure, my confiding in him wouldn't do any good. Might even make things worst. No. The war to save the project was my war. I cleaned my desk up and went home. It was Friday, and I had plans.

That weekend I packed my paints and drove up to Big Bear. I had to get away—to think, to retreat back into sanity. The cabin I rented had a fireplace. After spending the day sketching and laying in a background for a landscape, I picked up some Colonel's chicken. Later, I fell asleep in front of the fire.

The next day I finished the picture. A sociable couple in the next cabin, along with a pleasant man and his two children (he explained it was his weekend for visitations), and I rented a boat and took turns rowing on the lake.

The November air was cold and my cheeks stung from the wind and sun when I returned to my cabin. The man (Clifford was his name) brought over a bottle of wine, and when his kids went to bed, we sat and drank and talked. He was a salesman for aircraft tools and traveled to various Middle Eastern countries. As he described the places he'd been to, the sights he'd seen, the funny or unpleasant situations he'd encountered, my old dream of prowling the corridors of museums, galleries, and palaces came back. He spoke well and wanted to stay with me, but his breath was sour, and his hands were damp when he pushed them under my blouse. He took rejection well, and we said a friendly good-night.

That night I woke up. In my nightmare I was freezing. I was in a boat rowing, and the water was rising over my ankles. Hands reached up through a hole in the boat's bottom. Like long white snakes they tried to drag me down. They coiled around my legs and, when I used an oar to hit them, the oar turned into a gun and I was shooting wildly at the bottom. Suddenly the black water turned red and Tommy Gun's face rose from it. His eyes were closed but his mouth was wide open and his features contorted. His scream was silent. It turned into the song that Carl and I danced to before our marriage. Two figures appeared swaying on the red waves. They multiplied into a string of paper-doll cutouts and chain-circled around my sinking boat. I heard myself scream for help as they sank, sucked in by a whirlpool. In the center of the rushing water, Hank Garrison's face appeared. I felt water reach my chin, then my mouth. I woke up. The taste of blood was on my tongue. I put my hand to my lip and it came away bloody. I had bitten myself. I was still freezing.

27

Election Day came and passed. Cameron K. Campbell did not get elected governor of California. His votes multiplied to 368, which moved the timing for his presidency up at least twenty-eight years! He carried the clipping which showed the returns and pulled it out for anyone who would look and listen. Senator Joseph was shown on all television channels being congratulated. Maxwell Oliver's picture was in the local paper along with the other local winners.

The tenants settled down, believing their homes were saved and satisfied that they would be supported by the elected official for their district in getting some improvements for Buena Vista. I struggled with myself. Should I spill the information I had overheard? How much? When?

The indecision sent me into my root cellar of despair. Going to Bert Lottman was useless. Ben Hamilton was helpless, and I . . . ? I decided I was spineless. It made me uncomfortable, unhappy, and irritable.

Then a weeping woman with five gray-skinned, shivering, rumply-dressed children made the decision for me. She arrived in a banged-up, sputtering, and clanging old station wagon whose original color was concealed by patchwork and rust.

Hidden behind a file cabinet where I was reviewing some tenant files, I heard Mattie refuse to take an application for admittance to Buena Vista. The woman sobbed and pointed to one of the children who coughed wildly.

Mattie stood her ground and the woman was at the door herding her bunch out when Ernestine walked in.

She blocked the entrance, swung her arms wide, and bellowed, "What the fuck's going on here?"

The poor woman shriveled against the wall; her children huddled against her like little mice.

"I need a place and she—that lady—says she don't have no room."

A banshee yell for Ben Hamilton, and Ernestine shoved Mattie aside with her good arm and barged toward his office. The frightened woman and Mattie were joined by a curious Bernice and Gloria. I tiptoed around the files and left by the back door in Bernice's office. Discretion is the better part of valor, and this time I didn't want to wait around. I hurried back to my own office.

Ten minutes later a noise made me look up. It was the pile of junk driven by the woman. I watched as she went into a parking area down Flood Road and disappeared from my sight.

Two minutes later, a crash, a slam, and a curdling war whoop sent me scrambling into the front room of my social service center.

Ernestine Trotmartin had come to visit!

We eyed each other in silence; her yell dwindled to a rattle. Marching before me, she stalked into my back office. I followed. Ernestine refused the loveseat but I settled myself behind my desk. The unexpected appearance of my number-one antagonist left my knees shaky. With no introduction, Ernestine launched her anger.

"That goddamn prick, Hamilton, what the hell's he think he's pulling? That woman living in a motel room with five kids! Six people in one stinkin' room. An' that shitass says he can't 'accommodate' her family. Accommodate, balls! You know what's going on?"

She faced me. Watched my struggle as I avoided her eyes, fiddled with stuff on my desk. Buena Vista was peaceful now. Should I stir up things with my eavesdropping information?

"What's the matter? You gone deef? Or you gone honky-yellow?"

The pitiful picture of the children floated before me. The harsh, smug voices of the men plotting to betray the project people, the memory of Tommy Gun and his death . . . all passed before me. The sound of the coughing child . . .

"What's going on?" Ernestine spoke calmly; her anger was gone.

Still, I hesitated.

She turned her back on me, faced the wall.

"It's time you decided which pot you're goin' to piss into!"

She was right. The moment of truth—corny but true—had walked right up to me, punched me in the face, and dared me to back down. The Buena Vista tenants had no time left for "please"s and "thank you"s. The politeness of my world did not work in theirs. I felt released . . . light-headed . . . as I began my recital.

I told her of the conversation I had overheard—not all, but enough to let her know that Buena Vista could expect no help from Lottman, or Joseph and Oliver. I hesitated, not sure where Lottman fit in, then reminded her that her P/Q notice time was up. Next, she would be served the three-day quit papers.

She blew up! A whirlwind, a riptide, a revolution in Cuba was less violent than Ernestine Trotmartin faced with the doublecross! Hercules in chains was an uncomfortable youth next to Trotmartin betrayed. I watched her storm out. She headed toward the homeless family parked down Flood Road. I held my breath. Had I done right in telling her? Ernestine unleashed! My God, I wondered, what will happen now?

The waiting was short.

Ernestine swung into action on three fronts: Word spread that she had settled the family as squatters in an empty apartment. Next, there were rumors of a giant rally to plan strategy to save the project. And lastly, Ernestine defended herself against eviction.

Call it instinct, ESP, or just plain shrewdness, but the day Ben Hamilton got word to the sheriff to serve the three-day notice, Ernestine went into court and got a restraining order against the management.

The court reporter for the *Crestview City Press* picked it up and ran an article on the hassle between the project tenants and the authorities. The legal action was filed by an Annamaria Guido, attorney for the Legal Aid Society. The brief claimed that Ernestine Trotmartin and Does I through XX had been denied due process. They were entitled to their day in court to defend the claim that the rent had been withheld because the public agency had not provided "safe, sanitary, and decent" housing units.

The day the lawsuit was served on Ben Hamilton, he ran into an ice-cream truck on his way home. No one was hurt, but he had to pay for all the melted ice-cream bars, snow cones, and assorted frozen items knocked onto the street.

I stayed in my office, away from the main office, for two days. Then Bernice called and insisted I have lunch with her on the third day. Between bites of chow mein and egg roll, I learned that Bert Lottman was furious and that Ben Hamilton was in danger of losing his job. According to Bernice, Ben was blamed for having waited too long to serve the three-day notice, despite orders from Bert Lottman not to contact the sheriff. After Bernice read her fortune cookie, she pursed her bee-sting lips, and confided, "Albert Lottman is a damned liar! You know, Edie, people think I'm stupid, but I just play stupid. You just wait."

She saw my puzzled look.

"You know, I have just another six months before I retire . . . then it won't matter. But someone should investigate—check up on Gregory Land Company."

No matter how beguilingly I phrased my questions, nothing else could be dragged from Bernice. She refused to tell me why she mentioned Gregory. We all thought of her as a nut. Maybe we were wrong. It looked as if she was the squirrel—and we the nuts!

Thanksgiving was a week away and I was flooded with pleas for extra food. Appeals to local merchants brought a few turkey donations. Baskets of canned goods came from community neighborhood centers. Complaints of food stamps stolen from tenants became common. Three project kids were nabbed shoplifting food, fed by arresting police when they claimed hunger, and released.

The heroic project-wide cleanup job lasted only a short time. The project slipped back into its usual pattern. The parking lots again became dumping areas for old cars and tires; grimy oil pools collected.

The number of unoccupied units grew and vandalism increased. The commercial lawn mower broke down and Ben Hamilton said it was beyond repair. A request sent up to the central office for a purchase order on a new one came back with a memo from Lottman saying that funds were not available.

Sad was the word for Buena Vista. The lawns looked shaggy. The tenants looked shabby. The project was in shambles. The Thanksgiving Day holiday turned out to be a turkey for the project.

The unlikely combination of Judy Nickel, the project's Avon Lady, Carmen Sanchez, our Latin Mother Earth, and Flo Bunsey, our Butch, cornered me in my office the Monday after Thanksgiving. Judy Nickel was a walking advertisement for femaleness, Flo Bunsey, a living "What is it?" in twenty questions. The flowered dress was gone, the wig discarded; only the monster-crushing slap on the back was familiar. Carmen interjected with Spanish as Flo Bunsey exploded.

In outraged tones I was told the story. Mrs. Moreles had squeezed and saved to have a small turkey for her children's Thanksgiving feast. Just before it was ready, the stove blew up! Turkey was plastered over the kitchen walls.

I had the choice of being dragged immediately to the Moreles apartment or rushing down alone. I rushed.

My knock was answered by a weak, "Come in."

Disaster! Wall-to-wall turkey, gravy, giblets! Any area that wasn't laminated with fowl was peppered with beans. The half-sized gas stove was disemboweled, metal slivers speared into wooden cabinets, pots had shattered bottles and glasses.

Little Mrs. Moreles stood between the living room and the kitchen. Clustered around her were the six kids. The patience that comes from enduring constant injustice showed in her resigned look.

"Ah, Missus Edith, the Blessed Virgin send you to us. Please to help." The children all followed their mother's lead and hastily crossed themselves.

"Wrong, it was Judy Nickel, Carmen Sanchez, and Flo Bunsey." Credit due to those who deserve it!"

"You get me another stove, missus?"

"Of course! Haven't you reported it to maintenance? They'll come down, clean up this mess, and bring you a new stove."

I went closer to the remnants, tried to see from which section the explosion began. They watched me, big-eyed.

"Too bad you didn't report something was wrong before this happened. You must have suspected something was wrong."

"I did! I did!" Mrs. Moreles was bitter. "I tol' Meester Ben seex times dat da stove don' cook right. Dat a leakin' from the gas make a bad smell. 'Ho-K, Missus Moreles,' he say, 'I sen' Big George down.' But Big George no come. I sen' da keeds up, an' Missus Mattie say not to pest them. Even my Maria got hurt when it fly apart."

I looked over at nine-year-old Maria. She held her arm out. A makeshift bandage had slipped and an ugly gash showed.

"Mama told me to stir the bean an' I was just standin' there by the stove when . . ." Maria made a circle with her arms to show the explosion. "I got hit by something."

"Missus, we got nothin' to cook on. Meester Ben, he say he got no more good stoves to give out. How'm I gonna fix to eat for my keeds?"

"Of course there are stoves! The storeroom is filled with stoves that were taken out of the empty units. You must have misunderstood, Mrs. Moreles!"

"I no make mistake. You ask the keeds." Young heads nodded in agreement. "Meester Ben no wanna give stove 'cause I go to Town Hall that time wit' Missus Ernestine. Please, you help get me stove?"

"Don't worry. I'm going right up to the office and make sure you get a decent stove before the day is over . . . and get the maintenance crew to clean up."

Tears rimmed the woman's eyes. She grabbed my hand and pressed it to her lips. She was small; her head only came up to my chin. I patted her on the back, resisted an urge to embrace her, cuddle her, tell her everything would be "Ho-K."

Anger built up with each step I took. If Mrs. Moreles's story was correct —that Ben Hamilton knew about the defective stove—then his refusal to repair it was criminal. Why in hell didn't he send her a stove to replace the wrecked one?

Ben Hamilton sensed something was up with me when I stamped into his office without my usual polite knock.

"OK, now I want to know what's this about no stoves available? And why didn't you send someone down to fix Mrs. Moreles's stove before the damn thing exploded?"

I went on to describe the kitchen—the ruined turkey, the beans shot around like bullets, the havoc! He grinned foolishly.

"What's the matter? Beans always cause explosions! Happens this time it was external instead of internal."

"I'll tell you what's the matter. This incident might explode in your face if Mrs. Moreles takes this to the newspapers—or to court! One of her children was hit! Or doesn't that interest you? Someone could have been killed!" I was screaming.

Mattie ran into Ben's office as our voices got louder.

"Let her try to sue—she doesn't stand a chance in court. Your Bean family hasn't paid rent for a month and so she's technically an illegal tenant and squatter! Squatters have no rights. In fact, let's get Gloria to bring in her rent records."

He pressed the intercom and gave his orders to Gloria. She came in, an over-aged Mouseketeer in a too-short skirt. Her Living Bra bust heaved with excitement as she plunked the yellow rent-pay cards in front of Ben. "Here it is! Just like I said—she's ready for a thirty-day P/Q notice!"

"That's not fair!"

"Maybe so—but it's legal!"

"How about the Sanchezes?" Mattie never forgave the Sanchez family for the ever-continuing illegal "cousins."

"Sure. Let's P/Q them, too. No rent paid there for months. Right, Gloria?"

"Absolutely." Gloria hammered another stake into her heart. "Then there's Sadie Handle and Annie Flunk and . . ."

"Annie Flunk has been after you to fix her tub for two months. I know, because I've been down there. She can't use it, because the drain is stopped up."

"Niggers don't bathe anyway, so what difference does a tub make!" Gloria and Mattie retreated.

An octopus of hate strangled my reason. It was all a game . . . a rotten way to zero in on defenseless people. Rents were delinquent for various periods of time long before—and after—I came to Buena Vista. Gloria fussed but accepted installment payments to apply to overdue rent accounts. She, as well as Ben and Mattie, knew that the Housing Agency was not lily-white in fulfilling the basic legal requirements of a good landlord. Faulty equipment, bad plumbing, and sloppy grounds care would not have passed any real inspection. In addition, Ben's timidity was fanned by the hot wind of Ernestine's mouth. Rather than tangle with her, he had chosen to ignore her enormous past-due bill. Until now!

Now things were changed. Salmon's legal brain had devised retribution against the most vocal complainers: eviction on a mass basis. No quarter given!

I ranted at Ben Hamilton. I threatened him and Bert Lottman and the two-faced politicians and finally warned him that the tenants would unite and fight.

"It won't help. It's cut and dried, Edith. You don't understand that little people—poor slobs like these tenants—don't stand a chance against big men like Lottman and the Board of Advisors with politicians they own. I learned a long time ago that if you rock the boat, you can drown. There's always someone who will pull the plug and sink you."

Ben got up, turned his back to me and stared out of the window as he continued. He was a different man, serious, soft-spoken. "I hate this job, but I need it. It's turned me into a rag. They use me to wipe up their rotten shit. I know better . . . but I don't do better. I can't fight it. I do a lot of pretending just so I can stay alive—not destroy the one little part of me that still breathes. I admire you. You'll never play their game . . . or let them make a loser out of you."

The sadness in his eyes startled me as he turned to face me again.

"Oh, you might not win, but you'll never lose, either. You should know . . . I want you to know that if Lottman . . . suspects you, I can't protect . . . can't help you. See, he's owned also!"

The haggard expression stopped the angry words I had prepared as he talked. Ben Hamilton represented to me a weak, shallow, inadequate person. A man with no backbone, an emotional floater. Bland. Now fear showed in his eyes; his hands shook. He was terrified! Why?

"What did you do before you came to Buena Vista?" I asked.

He fumbled for his chair, pulled it away from the desk, and dropped down into it. Leaning his bent elbows on the desk, he spoke in muffled tones through his fingers. The wisp of hair across his bald head was damp with sweat. Ben looked old, much older than his age.

"I was brought up in a service family—Navy. My parents expected me to follow that life, but I couldn't. I tried, but I didn't have it . . . whatever it took to succeed. So then . . . then . . . after I dropped out . . . I tried other things. Went in for medicine . . . but . . ." He moved his hands away from his face but kept his eyes hooded with his eyelids. "I got married but that didn't . . . She left me. Seems that anything . . . everything I've tried . . . I flopped in. This job . . . it's the first one that's lasted . . . so you see . . ." He looked straight into my face.

I struggled to feel something—pity, anger, disgust. Nothing. Somewhere along the way Ben Hamilton canceled out of life.

"I see," I said and walked out.

It did not take long for Mrs. Moreles's P/Q notice to bring action from Ernestine. Later that day the flyers had already gone out for an Action For Tenants meeting. The wording left no doubt. War was declared—no holds barred. It read:

LET THE SHIT HIT THE FAN

LOTTMAN

OLIVER

JOSEPH

IT'S OUR TURN TO CRAP

ON YOU

28

Word of Ernestine's latest tenant meeting reached the police community relations department. They sensed that Ernestine's lawsuit and the notice carried in the newspaper of new tenant unrest spelled trouble.

Herbie and Hank Garrison visited me the day after the news of Ernestine's AFT meeting appeared.

"My God, this place is raunchy! Even those people deserve something better than living in this garbage heap!" Herbie Brent pinched his nose.

"Coming from you, that's almost a love letter," I kidded the young cop.

"Not really," Hank added. "Remember when we asked you about machine guns . . . and/or strangers?" His voice was tight. I nodded, wondering.

"Well?" This from Herbie.

"Well . . . I remember. What else do you want me to say?" I asked. I knew what they wanted to know . . . but most of what I knew was hearsay, or shots in the dark. "All I know is that when I stay late, I hear shots . . . but then . . . they could be anything."

"Machine gun?" Hank pinned me with his eyes.

"I wouldn't know," I said. "What's it all about anyway?"

"We're not at liberty to tell you." The official Lieutenant Garrison spoke.

"Well, neither am I . . . at liberty. I've got work to do."

They took the hint and left. I left my office and started down Greentree Lane to answer a wild call for help from old Mrs. Fisher, who claimed someone had thrown a dead cat into her car.

I had just stepped off the curb when Tank, Ernestine's twenty-year-old son, tore around the curve in his old VW van. He skidded toward me. I jumped back, heart pumping, glad to be alive. Immediately, I saw the unmarked car with Herbie driving, whipping around and speeding after Tank. Good, I told myself. It's time that maniac was stopped. His reputation for barreling over everyone certainly justified his name, Tank. I knew he worked part time as a laborer whenever a job was available, and disappeared for days when he wasn't employed. The paradox of his personality appeared in the concern and gentleness he showed his mother, Ernestine. The times I had seen them together, I'd been struck by the devotion of son toward parent. His driving was something else. I hoped Herbie would give him a ticket for reckless driving.

After I settled Mrs. Fisher's dead cat problem, I returned to the social service center. Later that afternoon I noticed Tank's van speeding down Flood Road. Damn! I was tempted to call Hank and complain. I put it off.

The next day Ernestine Trotmartin, dressed in a mechanic's jumpsuit and swinging a stillson wrench, stormed in at the exact moment when the twelve o'clock whistle sounded from the chemical plant in the neighborhood, spoiling for me the sack lunch I had just opened. She shouted over the noon signal. "I'm giving you a chance, honky! A chance to prove Tommy Gun wasn't fucked when he give out you weren't jus' another mother-fuckin' cock-sucker!"

Was there an answer to that? I didn't have any. I waited; she paced. Stopped. Glared at me. I bit on a raw carrot, chewed. Ernestine yanked the only straight chair in the office away from the wall and jammed it close to my desk. She sat down and leaned her bulldog face halfway over to me.

"They got Tank!" she said.

"Who's got Tank?" Ah-ha, I thought, some cop had the sense to stop his crazy driving!

"The pigs—the narcs! They bust in an' drag him away last night."

"What for?"

"I told that goddamn kid of mine to stay clear of them fools. Those fuckin' crazy fools will do you in, I told Tank. But what the hell, kids don't listen no more!" She was yelling again.

I yelled back. "Calm down! Tell me . . . what did Tank do?"

"Maybe it's my fault! I was sorry for the kid . . . but I told Lincoln to stay away from my place." She stopped cold. "Forget what I said. Thanks anyway . . ." She braced herself, was half up, when I stopped her with my next words. Suddenly I knew—Lincoln . . . Lincoln Bates, the escaped terrorist!

"They're here, aren't they? Someplace in Buena Vista."

I spoke low. Her voice was low as she answered me. The coarseness was gone. "I never expected to ask you for help . . . but I don't have any choice. You're right. Lincoln and Conroy Bates and the others . . . we've got to get them out of the project! Tank was going to drive them out tonight and take them to a safe house."

Her look asked if I knew what a "safe" house meant. My nod told her I did.

"The narcs took Tank's VW. He don't have any dope in it and they'll have to cut him loose . . . but they must be on to something. We can't wait until the pigs get wind. They'll rip the project apart . . . kill anything that moves . . . call it unavoidable accidents—like when Tommy Gun . . . Unavoidable—shit!"

She was right. It would be all over the moment I called Garrison. The project would swarm with police squads—only this time they would bring in the Federal men. Their image was already tarnished by the cleverness of the hunted group which had avoided capture for so long. Would they control their eagerness to punish? What answer did I have for Ernestine? None.

At best, it would be a nightmare that Buena Vista and her people would never recover from. They were untouchables already, and the stigma of a raid which produced the capture of the underground terrorists would swallow up the good tenants along with the bad. Those who wanted to eliminate the low-rent project would have ammunition to back up their position.

Go slow, Bentwood, I told myself. This true confession may be a ploy for a righteous con job. Making me a party to crime information could involve me as a conspirator. Damn her!

"Why are you telling me this? If Tank is clean, he'll be cut loose and then it's up to him what action he takes. Why involve me?"

"They got seventy-two hours to hold him . . ." She stopped.

"I don't know what you're getting at." Now I was angry. "Either lay it out or get out!"

She crumbled. Trotmartin the Terror became the woman. "I've got the little girl, Wendy, hid in my place. See, Lincoln carried her over because she was sick. Her mama is white but Conroy Bates is her daddy. I took her to the emergency hospital as my granddaughter. They said Wendy had a fever and stomach virus. She had shit so much, she would have died without medicine."

"I still don't see . . ." I pressed.

"When they bust in to take Tank, Wendy was asleep but they saw her. After Tank was gone, one of the narcs stayed and asked me questions about Wendy. Now, if what I said don't jive with what Tank will say . . . well, it won't take them long . . ."

"What are you asking me to do?"

"After they turn Tank out, the bastards will move in . . . make it look like Tank turned stoolie. It'll be a bloody mess. If the Feds don't cut Tank down, the underground will. It's Tank's life that's on the line . . . maybe mine . . . even the kid's if they bust in shooting."

"That's ridiculous! No one's going to come in shooting if they know a child's inside!"

"We need a car to take them out. Tonight." Her meaning was clear to me.

"You must be kidding! You want me to drive these . . . ?"

"If the cops are watching, they won't think anything about you working late . . . leaving a little later. You got the only car that can pass through."

Madness.

"I can't. No way! Besides, where would I take them?" My mind juggled fear, despair, and horror.

"All we need is your car. You drive out and pull up by the back end where the opening is in the flood-control fence. Just walk away, like you got a flat. Next morning your car will be parked by your house. You don't know nothing."

But I did!

"You're asking me to aid criminals escape!"

"I'm asking you to stop killing. Once they're out of here, at the safe house, the women and kid will surrender."

"And the Bateses?"

"They'll have to settle their own shit."

"You're asking the impossible."

"I'm asking you to save Buena Vista," she said and walked out.

The day dragged. I waded through my duties as if slogging across mud flats. Each time the telephone rang, I jumped. Twice the police black-and-white cars cruised by my office; each time an urge to run to the john came over me. Once I broke into wild laughter when my radio played a jazzy "Jailhouse Blues." Later I found myself crying unexpectedly.

238

A trip to the main office helped distract me. Gloria's ranting about the past-due rent accounts and Mattie's description of Mr. Campbell telling her he felt in his bones that he would be elected in the next governor's race relieved my tension.

At five o'clock the staff went home. Except me. I moved in a fog, doing unnecessary things. It was dark when I parked my car next to the flood-control fence and threw the keys on the floor mat. The short walk to the bus stop seemed like a cross-country mile. At first I ignored the car which slowed up at my side. A soft voice called me. It was Dude Muggins. Numbly, I walked over. He was sent to take me home. Arrangements had been made, he said. The late model sports car screamed GTA. I thanked him but took the bus.

The next morning I came out to go to work—and found my car parked neatly in front, the keys hidden under the mat, the gas tank full. A wash and wax job glistened—no fingerprints left there!

I felt relief. Obviously everything had gone well; the project image was saved. No one was really harmed. In fact, I comforted myself, a peaceful surrender and low-key solution without violence would now be possible.

We all saw it. Two days later, on national television and in Living Color, the "safe" house became Castle Conflagration. Combined law enforcement agencies staked out the small frame house in the nondescript integrated neighborhood. Directors orchestrated the spectacular for utmost dramatic impact. Vengeance was the ticket, bought with money passed over the counter of cruelty. The best seats were next to Death.

Two men, two women and one child died.

The city police chief blamed the Federal agency. The local FBI man said the Treasury Department's Gun Control Division had relayed "bum" inside information about the child, Wendy. She was reported left in an apartment at a public housing project (unnamed). It was too bad. "Regrettable" was the word used. If only they had surrendered (the stern-faced men sighed). Chances were offered (they cleared throats). The fire was their own fault (eyes ice-glazed).

After everyone went home that night, the eleven o'clock news showed fire hoses washing the ashes of the dead into the sewer.

No one connected Buena Vista with the holocaust. Tank was released the next day. I called in sick. When I did go back to work, Ernestine and I passed each other in the project but we didn't speak. If it had happened in Buena Vista, it would have been worse. Ernestine and I both knew it; there was nothing to talk about.

An unspoken sadness smogged Buena Vista after the horror of the Bates deaths. Tenants refused to talk about what they thought or knew; an unseen gag sealed mouths.

I dreaded the next confrontation with Hank and Herbie. My rationale for my actions held up as long as I ignored a small but worrisome guilt.

It was with trepidation that I watched the unmarked car pull up in front of the social service center. As soon as they walked in, I sensed something was wrong. A separateness, hinged on anger, showed in their body English. Herbie flung himself over the loveseat, not leaving any room for Hank. Hank yanked out the straight chair and straddled it.

"What's up?" Hank asked.

"Not much. What's up with you guys?" I tossed back.

"Why the hell doesn't the damned Housing fix this place up . . . cut the grass . . . rent the goddamn units. All those kids out there . . . living in joints worse than in here . . ."

"Yeah, Herbie's got a personality change lately. He's mellowed!" Hank's tone was joking, but his eyes were questioning as he glanced at his younger cohort.

"What's the matter? Been to see the Wizard for a heart?" I kept it up.

Herbie got red-faced, then clown-white. His breath came in hard gasps. He wet his lips, started to speak, stopped. Then a stream of obscenities that were new even to my tuned-in Buena Vista ears spilled out, like water breaking through a dam.

I was stunned. Hank acted as if shot in the belly. Neither one of us interrupted. Herbie's words strung out such hate, outrage, and fury that I could not understand the meaning, only the anger. That terrified me. I heard Junior Hernandez's and Jet's and Tommy Gun's and even Freddie-O's voices in my mind—they made an obbligato of whispered encouragement. Herbie terrified me.

When Herbie gulped for breath, Hank moved toward the young officer, hand outstretched, murmuring softly. It did no good. His hand was knocked aside, and Herbie slapped my office door open and ran out. I heard the car start and roar away.

Hank reacted. He sat on the loveseat and buried his head between his hands. My body ached; I felt physically beaten. Finally he spoke.

"I'm sorry. I don't know what's wrong with the guy. He's been acting" —Hank groped for words—"insane. Crazy. Forgets things. Moody. When I try to talk to him he clams up."

"He's probably had a fight with his girl friend . . . or maybe he's got bills, or the flu . . ." Why did I defend Herbie? Hadn't I hated his attitude for almost a year?

"No. He's got women lined up like bowling pins—knocks over a different one every night, one by one."

"Drugs?" I said it hesitantly.

"Now *you're* crazy! Herbie would never fool with drugs. No. Something's happened to him . . . but he won't talk about it."

"You don't think he's flipped? Dangerous? I mean having a gun and all?" I expected an angry denial. None came.

"I don't know. I wish to God I did. You know, I feel responsible for the guy. He's my partner."

He got up, walked to my desk, grabbed the phone. "I'll call downtown and have a squad car pick me up. OK?"

I nodded and listened to him make his call. He finished but kept looking down at me. "Edie, if Herb comes back, talk to him. You know . . . you're good at that. Maybe he'll open up to you."

"So you've finally decided I'm good at something!" Maybe I could get a smile from the troubled man.

Instead, Hank came toward me, close, and let his hand slide from my hair until it rested around my throat. "Wouldn't be surprised if you were good at a lot of things!" He bent over, kissed me, and walked out.

Hank was correct. Herbie Brent came back. I was returning from Mrs. Crocker's apartment—someone had cut her screens up—when I saw the familiar unmarked car pulling up in front of my office. He called over to me as I crossed Flood Road to my office. He sounded harsh—fury still colored his words. My heart pounded. With a shock, I realized I was afraid! Afraid of a policeman! Momentarily, I understood the panic a tenant felt —poor, black, white, or Chicano—when powerless against power.

I dragged my feet. He called again. Urgency in his voice.

It was a somber man who asked me to get into the car. He looked haggard, drained, as he drove out of the project and down Grand Boulevard. I said nothing as he pulled up to a small neighborhood Mexican restaurant and parked.

It was cave dark inside. Regular mealtime was over and, except for two men at the far booth, we were the only diners. A pudgy waitress took our order and came back with steaming coffee. Herbie stirred sugar into his cup, kept on stirring.

"I want to apologize. I don't know what happened to me today." He kept his eyes on his stirring. "Did Hank say anything after . . . after I left?"

"Not much. Except he's worried about you," I said. "Cops are supposed to stay cool—you know, be stable—not . . ." I let it hang.

"And I blew it."

"I can't answer that. Everyone has a different fuse. You know, what sets me off might not throw you. The crazies come with assorted reasons. Maybe you had a reason . . ." I left an opening for him.

"I've been thinking about quitting—resigning from the force."

"I thought you liked being the law-and-order man?"

His hands became the centerpiece of the table. They were flesh ropes, knotted into a ball.

"Law and order. That's a joke. Look . . . I believe in law. In law with order. Not murder. Not viciousness. Not maiming. Not retaliation for a wounded ego." Again, that bitter, hard, unripe-apple sourness.

The waitress came with our tacos and refried beans. The oval plates were steaming; we were warned not to touch them. Suddenly I was hungry, annoyed I had to wait.

Herbie continued. "Remember that shootout? And fire? The one where those two blacks—brothers—the Bateses, and the others and that"—his voice sank—"that kid?"

Remember? Could I forget? My hunger disappeared. Did Herbie suspect my role in it? I hedged. "The one we saw on TV?"

"They never had a chance . . . that little girl . . ."

"Wendy—her name was Wendy," I said. My eyes watered.

"I killed her."

Herbie's words forced my eyes to meet his. I shivered. "What do you mean?"

His eyes looked sunken, dark-circled. "Our department was called up that night. I was there. I saw it. They killed those people. They wanted to kill those people. All that stuff on television they said were lies. They lied to the newspapers, to the relatives. The whole fucking bunch of cops—the Federal goons—they covered up. It wasn't true that they refused to surrender. They tried . . . God, how they tried! One of the Bates brothers came to the window and waved a kid's shirt at the end of a broomstick. He kept yelling they wanted to get the child out safely. He kept screaming out her name—Wendy." His voice broke, then continued. Softly, so only I heard.

"I saw a Fed man lob in a grenade. It wasn't tear gas. It was shrapnel. I stood next to him—I saw it go in. Then he handed me one, and I tossed it. Just as I let go I saw her . . . the woman . . . the kid's mother with the kid in her arms and then . . ."

Herbie slid his hands across the table. He pushed the food platters aside and folded my hands between his. We sat, our hands praying.

"I saw that baby ripped apart." Now the tears came. Tight sobs and loose tears fell on both our hands where Herbie laid his head over our entwined fingers.

Now I had to tell him. To let him know that he was not alone in his guilt. In a rush, I saw my role in what had happened. Could I be less honest than he? I pulled my hands away. Forced him to sit up. My voice started unevenly.

"Herbie, listen! Do you know how the Bateses and the others got to that house? The house where they . . . died?"

His look told me he didn't understand what I was getting at.

"I helped them. I let my car be used to take them out of the project." He stared at me.

"Someone . . . someone came to me and said they were squatters in Buena Vista. The Federal men—Treasury men—found out and were going to use pressure on one of the tenants. Were going to set them up. So we—the other person and I—decided it would be bad . . . just bring down more disgrace and complaints against Buena Vista people if it was known that the project was used to hide fugitives."

"Did you know where they were being taken?"

"No. Only that it was to be a safe house." I stopped. Now my tears came. "I must have been crazy—not thinking straight! All I could think of was saving the tenants further shame . . . even death. I was afraid that the cops —even you—might use the raid as an excuse to shoot others . . . after Tommy Gun and what was said to be unavoidable but wasn't. It's just that I care . . ."

He was my comforter now. "It probably was the right thing you did. No matter where it happened . . . it wouldn't have made any difference. Maybe some lives were saved—maybe letting your car be used to move them out of the project was the right thing to do. I guess it's something we will have to live with and wonder about all our lives. Just you and me." He repeated softly, sadly, "Just you and me. Just us!"

We left our cold food untouched. Herbie drove me back to Buena Vista.

29

The emptiness left by Tommy Gun's death hung heaviest over the young men of the project. Jet tried to assume leadership, but he lacked Tommy's qualities. Surprisingly, it was Danny Gree, the chain-wielding youth who had almost killed Billy Goochen, who started a new trend among the youngsters.

Football season was over and with basketball taking over the sports interest, Danny Gree's lackadaisical attendance at practice led to a constant chore for me. Every day I had a call from his coach, and every day I scoured the project for six-foot-four Danny and shamed him into reporting back to school.

Then suddenly calls from the coach stopped. I was glad. But I wondered —had Danny been dropped from the team or what? I found out when I opened the Crestview City evening paper and saw Danny's wide, white-toothed grin and sweaty face, and his skinny frame in a basketball T-shirt. The headline stated "Project Boy Hot." The article described Danny's ability and said that he had been scouted by four top-ranking schools, three in the Midwest and one near Crestview. The State University was half an hour's ride away. Its team was not considered in the same class as the others, but since Danny Gree was a local boy, the offer had been made. They did not expect him to accept. The other schools had prestige, big names, and a record of wins. It would be crazy for Gree to accept less than the best offer, the writer said.

Yet Danny turned down the other offers; he elected to stay in Crestview City and play on the local college team. The announcement was made in the Crestview City Sunday newspaper.

Monday morning Danny came into my office. Hunched over in his usual posture, he shuffled his huge feet, kept zipping his jacket up and down. I waited for him to tell me what was on his mind. Finally, "You see the papers, Miz Edie?"

"Sure did." I grinned back.

"Bet you were surprised."

"Nope, not really." I played a game.

"Shit, woman, don't cattail jive me . . . you *were!* It took the wind right outta you!"

"I see you got plenty left . . . wind, I mean . . . hot air!" I decided to help him out. "That was a nice thing you did, Danny."

"Ya, well, it weren't so much . . . not really. I almos' didn't . . . you know . . . decide to stay aroun' here."

He straightened up, waved his hands in a broad sweep.

"But then, ya know, my ma's here . . . and my friends . . . and besides . . . Tommy Gun . . ." He stopped. Started again. "Tommy Gun and me . . . we sometimes talked . . . rapped, you know how it is. It's kinda like I'm stayin' on account of Tommy Gun."

"Like a memorial to him?" I said.

"Whatever! He always said that if you believed in sumpin', you fuckin' better never cop out on it, 'cause you'd be crappin' on yourself. I figgered, what the fuck. So's State U. don't have no star players, but maybe I kin help . . . change things. It don't take but one dude to change things sometimes."

"And you're going to be that dude?" I was so proud of him. Mist fogged my sight.

"Shit, why not? Hell, look at you . . ." Embarrassed, he cut his eyes away. "You stuck it out . . . even with all the crap you got . . . an' some from me. Fuck, lady, you made a change, an' you're jus' one lousy broad."

No lover ever spoke sweeter words. I choked up. Danny cleared his throat, and after a weak "See ya," he left. I wanted to dance . . . rent a plane to spell out the words in the sky for the world to see. Finally, without "please"s and "thank you"s I crawled out of the root cellar to find love!

Danny kept his word to Tommy Gun. After school he organized all the project boys over ten into basketball teams. As I drove home in the evenings, I saw groups of kids tossing balls into the playground hoops. Among them, Danny Gree stood out like the proudest tree in the forest.

The appointed day for the next AFT meeting came. Tenants turned out en masse. Ernestine was in super form. She waved her copy of the lawsuit filed by the Legal Aid attorney, Mrs. Guido. Mrs. Guido was thin, with clever bony hands, lank brunette hair which she kept shoving behind too-big ears. Dressed in an out-of-date tweed skirt, tunic top, and greenish nylons, she looked like a bargain-basement Peter Pan from New Jersey.

Her legal advice to the tenants was to put their withheld rent into an escrow account. That way, she explained, with her fine Italian hands racing down the law book, they would show good faith. Good faith would prove to any court that they were honestly protesting intolerable conditions.

"Intolerable conditions are *prima facie* evidence that the Housing Agency is not abiding by the Federal guidelines as set down by the Housing and Urban Development Department."

The complicated phrasing went over the heads of most of her audience, but they recognized her sharp tone directed toward their enemy, the Housing management. They loved her for that and stamped and shouted "right on" until she finished.

Ernestine took over then. In her usual language, she told the tenants about the doublecross and warned that they should expect renewed efforts on Maxwell Oliver's and the Housing Agency's part to discredit the people and pressure the outside community to eradicate Buena Vista. This time there was no singing of "God Bless America." The goal was to hang on by their teeth to the only homes they could afford. Ernestine's suit against eviction was one tactic; others had to be found. The meeting ended with the election of a committee to collect past-due rents and open an account for escrow deposits.

Ernestine's eviction was postponed. Silence from Alderman Oliver and Senator Joseph, along with the approaching holidays, put the rent strike into the background. Still, an uneasy expectancy of retribution by the power structure kept the tenants subdued.

Christmas straggled into Buena Vista. The Mothers' Club went into a frenzy to finish various handmade projects as gifts. Whenever I left my office, someone was sewing or painting plastic molds or making candles and was unwilling to leave. Of necessity, I left the door open to accommodate my ladies.

Late one afternoon, ten days before Christmas, I returned to find the rooms empty of Mothers' Club members, but in my private office, Amelia

Goochen waited. A misshapen sweater was folded double over her emaciated chest; torn hose were twisted on her spindly legs—Ichabod Crane in drag. A wild-eyed fear completed the picture.

Her grief was sparely worded. Celia, her hope, her joy—Celia was pregnant. Dreams of Celia's future success hardened into boulder-sized sobs. I let her recover before asking questions.

No, Celia would not say who the boy was. Yes, she was too far along for an abortion.

There was nothing else to say. We sat across from each other; our mind-wheels were stuck, like Celia, in a mire of helplessness, and we could find no solution to pry Celia out from the rut. Amelia pleaded with me. Would I talk to the girl? Her anxiety about the father of the child prompted a suspicion in me: Amelia knew, but hoped against hope that her fears were wrong. Before she left, I promised to find an opportunity to draw Celia out.

Celia passed my office each morning and afternoon as she walked to high school. It would be easy to step out and call her in on some pretext. Yet I made excuses not to. There was a sadness about this small-stepping girl who wore starchless country-flowered dresses and dark-toned hose when other teen-age girls wore breast-filled knitted croptops, jeans, and flapping sandals. A limpness, a setting-apart that didn't enhance . . . that made her clownlike, a baggy, sapling-legged caricature. White-faced and owl-eyed as a mime, she silenced her existence away. She frightened me.

Easy as it was to ignore Celia Goochen, it was impossible to avoid some member of the Curtis family any week. If it wasn't Freddie-O, it was Romeo, or Mac (for Macbeth) or Lear! The youngest boy, Puck, was an unknown quality so far. Did Shakespeare know he was godfather to black children living in a Tempest where a Midsummer Night's Dream usually turned into a nightmare?

On a mid-morning walk past the Curtis encampment I heard echoing screams, high-pitched and female, as an obbligato to male rumblings and funky cusses. I knew it was Freddie-O and his mom, Honey Curtis. Freddie-O had turned seventeen a few weeks earlier at a bash that probably set back the community merchants' profits for six months, shoplifting being the highly developed art it was among the junior set in the project. I walked away from their voices thinking that Freddie-O was getting unbearable— too big for his britches!

How much too big I learned that afternoon.

I was Scotch-taping my latest lopsided Santa Clauses onto the wall when Honey Curtis walked into my office. Freddie-O, spring-bouncing on the balls of his feet, swiggled hipless after her. Honey's face was grim,

Freddie-O's cocky. I stepped back to view my wall collage. Mrs. Newton's kindergarten class must have used a bale of cotton. Each Santa Claus had a frothy cotton beard—some were stringy, like porcupine needles, twisted with paste; others hung spun-thin in wispy cloud formations. Every face had round black eyes and a red nose.

As the three of us faced the wall, I felt the unexploded tension between the mother and son. I positioned a professional smile, sat down behind my desk, and looked up. I wished I had idiot cards before me like those bright gals on television commercials.

The contrast between them was glaring. The boy wore his usual dirt-stiff jeans, and a faded orange T-shirt with blotches of white where bleach had attacked. The printed picture across the front showed a monstrous motorbike. Her knife-pleated red miniskirt umbrellaed taut-fleshed thighs. A slinky white turtlenecked jersey molded her pointed breasts. Slender café au lait fingers worry-rubbed cherry-red plastic beads which hung looped to her navel. A smooth-haired wig topped her chiseled features, and dark glasses with red frames hid her eyes. She removed her shades as she sat down on the loveseat facing me. Freddie-O slouched, thrust his pelvis forward, and puffed his already bushy Afro higher with his metal comb. As I watched her it was hard to believe this doll wasn't on the cover of *Ebony* but was the mother of six husky boys and supported them on welfare.

"I have come to discuss my son with you, Miss Bentwood." Her tone was dry.

"You mean Freddie . . ." (I caught myself—left off the O.)

"Yes. I want you to understand that I do not approve . . . absolutely do not approve of my son's actions."

That left a big opening—what—which actions? I only nodded. Finally she looked at her son.

"Tell her what you've been doing."

"Ah, Mom." Charm oozed, rippled, shivered its way from a wide grin, past the motorbike chest, swelled his penis, and arched his sandaled feet. "Ah, Mom . . . !"

"Ah, Mom, nothing. You tell her or I call your probation officer." Honey drummed on the red plastic handbag on her lap.

"I didn' do nothin', 'cept maybe mess around a little."

"I'll say you been messing around. More than a little bit, I'd say though." She turned back to me. "You been talking to Amelia?"

"Mrs. Goochen?" I asked. No. Please, say it isn't so!

"Celia's ma. She been in to report on Freddie?"

"My mom is getting weird. She's just some chick, Celia is. Kinda weird, too." Freddie examined his pants zipper. "Celia's mom got no cause to tattle on me."

"Has Celia?" I got into it now.

"Depends. Me, I'd say she got no complaint 'bout nothin' I done." His sly smile told me all I needed to know.

"She's pregnant, Miss Bentwood, and so is Tami Jewel . . . and Sugar-Jean Latimer."

Was she trying to run down all the project girls who had been indiscreet . . . or knocked up, in the vernacular of Buena Vista?

"What about it, Freddie?" I turned to the boy.

"What about which one?" he asked.

"Which . . . one? You mean you're responsible for all of . . ." I let it hang. I felt myself blush from the all-knowing, lusty grin from the youth. It was a triumphant, male look, the "look, Ma, no hands" bellow of a five-year-old. Births from random relationships were common among project women. Mixed racial combinations caused no discrimination against any child. When my flush cooled, I found my voice, and my old standby.

"We seem to have a . . . a problem," I announced.

The problem would be Celia's mother. I remembered her hopes for this child. Also her bitterness against the black boys who had attacked Billy with that biker's chain. And now, to have her serious, studious daughter . . . attacked! That's the way she would see it when she found out that Freddie-O was responsible. Found out for sure, instead of just dreading the truth.

"You think Amelia knows about Celia and . . . ?" I pointed my chin at Freddie.

"You're damn tootin' she knows! That little bastard, Billy, smashed all my windows last night. Him and that Mex, Jesus—Christ, what a name for a kid—egged my car. Ruined the paint!" Honey Curtis's crossed legs became a pump handle, pumping anger from the well of her frustration.

"Did you call the police?"

"Po-leece! Shit!" She snapped open her red purse and shut it with each word. "You think I'm fool enough to call the pigs and have that trash bomb me out after the cops leave?"

It was an old story. I didn't even respond indignantly any more. I went on to the next girl.

"What about Tami Jewel?" I asked.

"Her mama don't care. Pearl Jewel's already got Tami her own welfare file and check coming. She's glad 'cause it'll bring in another couple a hundred every month, and when the baby comes, they get extra food stamps. She's not sweatin' it." Honey stopped pumping her legs and snapping her purse. She was back to lacing the red beads between her fingers.

Tami Jewel was a skinny fourteen-year-old, the product of a part-black, part-Mexican mother and a white father. She had reddish hair, dark skin, and Negroid features. Usually I saw her dragging two or three of her half-sisters and brothers around in a Safeway shopping cart, the latest baby in the small seat and the kids of stand-up age crowded like bundles of broccoli in the wire well.

I stalled, rubbed my eye. A nickelodeon scene flickered past me—a choo-choo train of rusty Safeway carts holding infants newly born, each with a welfare check attached to the umbilical cord. Celia . . . Tami . . . Sugar-Jean—sweet names, sweet young eyes, soft cheeks, doomed to lives of rusty wire cages.

"Latimer? Sugar-Jean? Old Hattie Latimer's granddaughter?" I addressed Honey.

"Slut, nothing but a slut! Grand Prix's been after her to join his girls. Least, I can give her the smarts for turning him down . . . rate she's putting out, she'll own him!" Her tone gave no credit.

I looked at the young male, smoothfaced, picking away at his nails with the prongs of his metal comb. School dropout, ripoff artist, con-kiddie, and now father-to-be—not once, but three times!

"I'm throwing him out. That's something I *can* do!"

Freddie looked cunningly at his mother.

"Bullshit! Then your welfare check'll be cut—and you know that don't go over no-way! No more fancy shoes or honky wigs! You want I get out? OK. Shit, I'll go sack down with Tami Jewel's ma."

"I'd kill you 'fore I let that slut bed my kid—that no-good, low-down, cock-sucking black bitch!" Honey's praying hands turned into claws.

"Now, that ain't no way for you to talk 'bout Tami's ma, seeing as you two ladies gwina be grandmammys together!"

"Shut your goddamn fuckin' mouth, black boy. I'm not going to own up being kin to any bastard. Black or white!"

Honey jumped up and tackled her son. Her nails raked his cheek as the slap twisted his face aside. She sank her other hand in his Afro and tried to hold him for another blow. But the boy grabbed her wrist and freed himself. He spun her around and dropped her back on the loveseat. Then, instead of backing off, he advanced, eyes narrowed. The comb in his hand was sharpened on his backside like a knife being honed. His forearm twitched as the muscles lumped and flattened. He stopped just short of where his mother sprawled.

Suddenly, he brought his arm up, and the metal teeth bit into the frizzed hair on his own head. He tugged it through and free. The comb slipped into his back jean pocket again. He kicked at the straight chair by my desk and it teetered, then dropped back on the floor. Now he reached the door, turned.

"Get fucked!" he told his mother.

He was gone.

I looked over at the woman . . . like wax, like a melted wax candle of different colors, all run together. Then Honey moved, sat up, adjusted her wig, untangled the red beads.

"I shouldn't have said that. It wasn't right."

A hesitancy in her voice told me more was coming. I said nothing. Sat still. Waited. It came out in soft tones . . . sad. In quivers of monotones.

A sigh, like a November wind stripping last summer's remaining leaves, blew fluttering words—leaves, life-dried. Dead.

"He don't know who his father is. I don't neither. I don't even know what he looked like—his face or eye color. Sometimes when Freddie was little, I'd look hard at him. You know, like you check over the stuff they call 'irregular.' Like you make sure you get the best of the mistakes."

Her hands lay quiet now in her lap, the red purse forgotten on the floor. Then her hands twisted, dug into the red pleated skirt at her crotch. A guttural groan ended in quivering words.

"I was fourteen an' staying with my auntie outside Little Rock an' it was a long tote home after school. Roads out our way weren't tarred and the white boys used to race their cars . . ." She let her words drift . . . stop . . . before she picked up again. "There was three of them, an' they messed over me. All of 'em messed over me."

I turned my eyes away and saw an early string of Christmas lights outlining a window of one apartment across Flood Road. Bulbs from three sockets were empty already. I wondered if Freddie-O had swiped them.

"I hadn't yet turned fifteen when . . . when he was born. So . . . I never did know. I used to watch from my auntie's porch for that car to come by. I used to make up things to say, case I could run out and stop the car. I never did see it again. It never came by our street again. It got so's every time I set my eyes on that kind of car in town, I'd run over to see who's driving, but it weren't no use. It almost got so's in my head it was the car that gave me that baby. At least I could recall the car, where I never did recall the . . . their faces . . . any of the faces . . . any of the three faces. So you see why I shouldn't have said what I did to Freddie. I had no right, did I, Miss Bentwood?"

"I think Freddie . . . your son . . . knew how upset you were. It was honest anger. It happens to all of us sometimes." I felt inept.

"The other boys had a proper daddy. He used to clean up the high school in town. Mathew Luke was a janitor and I had it good 'cuz he didn't carry on about Freddie. Seems like Mathew Luke felt he hadda hurry with baby-making since he was fifty-six or so and I was just sixteen. That man was crazy 'bout naming the kids after Shakespeare . . . an' he did, go crazy. One day he come home and half beat me and Freddie to death. Then he broke into the schoolhouse and poured gas around and set it on fire."

I could see the bruised girl and terrified child.

"They put him away because he burned half the school down. That's when me and the kids came out here. I wanted it better for them."

When she came in I thought Honey Curtis was a shallow, self-centered, and uncaring mother. I had new respect for her.

"That's why I got so nasty to Freddie. It's just because I didn't want him to mess over some other little girl like I done been messed over. He's a good boy, Freddie is." She was pleading. "This place, this project, it's no good. No good for kids at all. You seen it, Miss Bentwood, they all turn rotten. But I don't have enough money to move. Here I pay forty-three dollars a month with my lights and gas paid. You tell me—where can I move with six kids for that on my welfare check?"

I couldn't tell her.

The dark glasses came off when the tears started. It was the frightened fourteen-year-old girl I saw after she had been let out on that dirt road to walk her painful and shamed way home.

Now I was at her side, holding her swaying body against me. Her arms encircled my waist and we leaned on each other. Her crying stopped and after a moment, I stepped back.

Honey Curtis stood up, adjusted her dark glasses over tear-red eyes. I handed her the red purse.

"Thanks, thanks for everything." She started out, looked back. "Freddie is a good boy. I really do love him. You think he'll be OK, don't you?"

I let my head drop and Honey interpreted it as a yes. She left. I felt rotten. Freddie was not a good boy. Freddie-O Curtis was headed for trouble.

It came sooner than I expected.

Five days before Christmas, I opened the morning paper and headlines told about two youths who had held up a liquor store. One was black, one white. A clerk was shot and was lingering near death in the hospital. The report said that the clerk had pulled out a gun and shot back. The white boy died in the ambulance. The other boy had stood his ground and when the police pulled up, he shot at two cops. One died. So did the black youth. The reporter gave the names of the policemen. Also the names of the two criminals: Mansfield, also known as Go-Boy, and Fred Curtis, both from the Buena Vista Housing Project. The story went on to say that the youths had told the clerk they just wanted money to buy Christmas presents. My hand shook as I put down the paper. Driving to work, I remembered what Honey had said only a few days ago about looking this misborn child over —this irregular piece of goods. Freddie-O Unknown was not a good person. He lived an ugly life. Had his mother ever told him he was loved?

But she had loved him . . . and in some crazy way, so did I. I started to cry. The day was gray; unholiday traffic jammed the streets—the shoppers would come later. But Freddie-O and silly, stupid Go-Boy had not made it to Christmas.

My car windows were up and I first said it softly, "I love you." Then louder, until I was screaming, "I love you, I love you, I love you" and stopped only when my throat rasped from the strain.

Was I trying to make up to this black child for all the "unlove"? Or was I trying to prove to myself that my tongue had not unlearned those words?

The shopping center I drove past had light poles twined with fuzzed silver garlands, which made me think of Freddie-O and how he teased his hair into a halo.

I stopped crying as I pulled into my parking space at the project. Suddenly I started to laugh! That damned Freddie-O! Probably teasing his Afro into a halo right now someplace! And enjoying the con he'd pulled. After all, he had left part of himself in the bellies of three girls. And I was glad!

Honey Curtis came in to say good-bye the day she left to take Freddie-O's body back to Little Rock. The other boys were slicked up, impatient, scratching shined shoes against brown legs. They were leaving for "home," Honey said. Her auntie had died and the house passed on to her. It wasn't much but there were kinfolks around to help with the boys. She had put off returning but she had settled it in her mind—it was the right thing to do. I hugged the two smallest boys, and squeezed Honey's hand.

"You'll let me know, won't you, about the babies, I mean. Freddie's babies when they get born. I'm intending to send a little something to the girls . . . in Freddie's name." They left. I watched as they poured into the old station wagon piled high with boxes. It took off with a whine and then a roar. I went back inside. It was two days before Christmas.

Celia Goochen came into my office that same afternoon. She was showing already. Instead of the sad face I expected to see, I saw a warmth, a confidence that never had seemed part of this shy, quiet girl. She pulled out the straight chair and sat next to my desk.

"Miss Bentwood," she started. "I know Mama came in to see you. But I want you to know it's right between us now. I'm talking about . . ." She looked at her lumpy waist. "If it's a boy we're going to call it after my brother that was hurt in Nam."

She looked away, out of the window. Dusk made the lights show up on the Christmas trees set up before the project windows.

"If it's a girl, I'm going to call her Fredia."

"That's nice. Different," I said.

"Merry Christmas," Celia said as she went out. I watched her walk down the sidewalk and disappear into the darkened alley between the buildings.

The Mansfields took Go-Boy's body up to Lancaster, where the family had relatives. Only one car with tenants drove up to attend the funeral. The season of joy had little room for sadness.

30

Christmas Day fell on Thursday. I had put in for time off on Friday, so that I would have a long weekend away from Buena Vista.

The maintenance crew gave their usual "X-Eve Bash" in the storeroom back where stacks of broken screens were layered against the wall and cartons of broken locks, odd plumbing parts, and cases of toilet scum-remover were stored. The office staff was invited and everyone brought fixings. My assignment was to bring chips and three dips.

It was a gray day, almost Down-Eastern: damp, cold, yet without the hope of snow to whitewash the grime. Someone noticed the unmarked car that Hank Garrison drove pulling up at my office. Unwillingly I left the maintenance quarters. The two plastic foam cups of screwdrivers I had drunk had been mostly vodka, and, while steady, I was light-headed. Taking another drink, I told the others I'd be right back.

The rawness of the late afternoon air made me shiver as I ran toward the car. Hank and Herbie got out and moved to the office door. A shout from me and they waved back. They waited until I unlocked the door, then trailed me inside.

I felt silly and acted giddy. "Merry Christmas and may the mice in your attic scare the hell outta Santa Claus!"

"Don't you mean bats in a belfry? Your belfry?" This was Hank Garrison.

"Hold it! I'm going to revise that. May all you rat-finks end up holding the bag . . . and I don't mean Santa's!" Even I knew that didn't make sense. "I am not drunk," I announced.

"C'mon, let me lead you into the Casbah and sit you down on the loveseat!" Hank said.

My arms were taken and I felt myself shoved onto the lumpy couch cushions. Herbie sat next to me and I noticed a box in his hands. He poked it at me.

"Sober up, you closet alkie. Drinking on the job can get you canned!"

We all laughed. Hank leaned against my desk, shaking his head, while Herbie was trying to force my fingers around the gift-wrapped box.

"Finally, she's acting human!" Hank said.

Despite their smiles I felt something serious. A "shall we tell her now or wait" look passed between the men. The haziness simmered into uneasiness. No use trying to act the lady drunk to keep up the mood. I stopped. I took the gift from Herbie.

"OK, guys, what is this, a time bomb?" I still tried for fun and games.

"Nope, it's a Christmas present, a thank-you gift, and a going-away offering." Herbie sounded happy-sad.

"The police department cannot fire me!" This was the funny me again.

"Herbie's leaving the department," Hank said.

The box felt heavy on my lap. "You kinda Trojan-horsed me!" I held it up and looked squarely at Herbie.

My voice sounded scratchy to me when I spoke. Quick blinking kept wetness from becoming tears. "It couldn't happen to a nicer guy!" I told him.

The feeling between us showed because Hank sharpened his tone. "Don't tell me that you two had something going that I don't know about?" He wanted to sound clever.

"Coming . . . and going," I said.

Laying the present aside, I leaned over and kissed Herbie. His arms went around me and for a moment his head lay on my shoulder. I knew if I touched his hair, I would break down.

They left soon after. I stood in the doorway and waited until Herbie's last wave was cut off as they turned onto Grand. He had kept his word, made good on his vow, followed through on his commitment to his conscience. My mind went over the many arguments we had had, the insults we traded, the anger we showed. As I closed my office door I knew that something precious had developed, something which could never be rooted out from our memory: understanding . . . trust . . . and the acceptance of shared responsibility.

More surprisingly, I thought—maybe I could trust a man again. Because of Herbie Brent, ex-cop.

I had planned to spend Christmas Eve alone, but when Hank called, my new trust invited him over to watch me open Herbie's present. It was after ten o'clock when he rang my bell, a bottle of wine in one hand and a small trimmed Christmas tree in the other. Dena, his nine-year-old kid, had fixed it, he said, as I made room on the table for him to steady it on the plastic stand and hook up the tiny lights.

"Yeah, when I told Dena I was going to see a friend she asked me if my friend had a tree. Since I wasn't sure, she said I had to take this one."

"You'll have to thank . . . Dena for me." Steady, I told myself.

He fussed with the wine cork. "No big thing. It was an extra one." I knew he lied, but I didn't accuse him.

"It's so damn hard to get a babysitter these days. Have to hock your bank account," Hank complained.

We settled on the couch and watched celebrations on TV, drank wine, and ate the leftover dip on broken chips.

The little Christmas tree blinked its minute lights off and on. The forced "specials" on the TV screen showed stars with their families—children of all ages—singing carols. The American Dream of yearly togetherness splashed like acid across me. I glanced at Hank. His face was bland as he sipped the red liquid. Only his lips moved—he was biting them.

"Christmas is for the birds!" I wanted a light response.

"Maybe . . . birds in a nest . . . safe . . . warm. What's so bad about them?"

He made me uncomfortable. How did he know I felt so separate, so . . . nestless? I passed up the chance to answer. He never noticed.

"After Kathy . . . went . . . Christmas was torture. I dragged through it for the kids, but I hated it. It took me almost four years until I felt good about it. I still hate parts of it . . . like Christmas morning opening presents. Dena and Eric have each other to get excited with, but I miss . . ." He paused, then turned straight at me, looked in my eyes. "It's the little moments . . . the pleasure of exchanging glances . . . knowing both of you read each other . . . the completeness."

"Buying a section of turkey instead of the whole bird." I felt his . . . my pain.

"How about coming over to my place tomorrow morning? Helping the kids open presents? I'll pick you up at seven . . . eight?"

"That's pretty early for company, isn't it?" I controlled the tremor in my voice.

"God, they have me up at six. You can have breakfast with us. I make the best frozen waffles on the block!"

"OK, if you let me pour the syrup!"

It was late. I was wine drowsy when I remembered Herbie's box.

It was professionally wrapped with clusters of bells and grinning angels in gold foil. I removed the figures carefully and insisted Hank take them back to Dena. Under the folds of tissue paper, a gauze-lace robe and gown shimmered in muted colors. As I lifted them out, I glanced at Hank. He was grinning but I pretended not to see. Magnin's was not cheap and this was their best.

A card fell from between the folds. I opened and read it aloud, "Try it . . . you might like it . . . again! Herbie." I knew I blushed when Hank took the card from me and haw-hawed like a donkey. I accused him of collaboration, but he denied it.

"Still, the boy may have a good bit of advice there!" Hank rattled the wrapping into a ball, walked into the kitchen to dump it into the trash basket.

"Not this year!" I yelled out to him.

He kissed me lightly when he left. At the door he pulled on a strand of my hair, tucked it behind my ear.

"Don't forget—next year is only a week away! I'll see you at seven tomorrow."

My five days off during the holiday went quickly. The day after Christmas Day I left for San Francisco, where I had made reservations. For three days I explored the city. Sunday I flew home.

I heard the telephone ringing before I got my apartment door unlocked. Dumping my bag and purse, I ran for it. The ring died in my hand.

After unpacking, I took a long shower, and again I reached the telephone too late as I stumbled, wet, with a towel turbaned around my hair.

Well, whoever it was would call again if it was important, I told myself. The phone rang again. It was Hank Garrison and, if it was important, I never found out.

"Where the hell have you been?" he started. "Shacking up with some jerk? You damn women, never consider others—"

I hung up. Mixed feelings—gladness that he was jealous, anger at his assumed right to question me—kept me awake.

Monday I went back to work.

Tuesday I got a picture postcard from Herbie. He sent it from New Mexico "on the way home," except he didn't say where home was. He made a crack about my using his present. I tucked the card, glossy side up, in my bottom dresser drawer under his gift.

Wednesday Hank Garrison called me at work and asked if I had seen two teen-age girls floating around the project. They were runaways. Thirteen and fourteen years old and ripe. Would I check out Grand Prix Papa's stable? Then he apologized, after a lot of throat-clearing, about the phone call. In return I told him about getting a card from Herbie. Our careful, modulated voices did not cement the cracks in our relationship. I declined his invitation to join him and his kids on an outing to Disneyland that weekend.

Politics had been shoved off the front pages by the holidays, which also postponed Ernestine's locking horns with the Housing Authority, more specifically with her arch enemy, Bert Lottman.

The huge dump trucks that emptied the project's trash bins scattered discarded Christmas tree tinsel over the parking lots. Remnants of December twenty-fifth hung on at Buena Vista. Most tenants had a fetish of decorating their windows with spray-can snow in snowflakes, snowmen, and sometimes just squiggles. The enthusiasm did not extend to removing their artwork. The project seemed to be living under Pennsylvania Dutch hex signs, but instead of warding off evil, these markings appeared to draw the devil closer.

The children dragged themselves back to their classrooms. Everyone looked tired and drawn. There was a ring-around-the-collar griminess about the place during January. Even the crimes were uninspired. I found the teen-age girls, but not under Grand Prix's care. Instead, old Mrs. Reedy, Jody's grandmother, had taken them in, and both girls helped her with Jody. When the Juvenile authorities came to get them, the girls cried. One of them yelled that her folks were always gone and she wanted to stay with Mrs. Reedy. The other girl just cried and said she was tired of seeing her mother and third stepfather fighting all the time. Later I found out that both youngsters came from exclusive country club homes across town.

The dullness vanished, however, the day Maxwell Oliver gave an extended TV interview. Buena Vista Housing Project, he claimed, was an eyesore, a slum, a breeding place for crime. The lazy, unworthy tenants were cheating the good taxpayers by refusing to pay rent. Blown-up photos of the dilapidation were displayed in his office against the waxed pecan paneling. The project looked blitzed!

Maxwell Oliver, with his best side toward the NBC cameraman, announced dramatically that, after talks with Housing Agency's Albert Lottman and State Senator Joseph and intense discussions with the Washington Office of Housing, the decision had been made to demolish Buena Vista. Its seventy-eight acres would be used for parks and private, "reasonably priced" homes. "Good" tenants would be encouraged to buy the homes and establish a positive way of life for themselves and their children. The price range would be $40,000 to $50,000, Oliver explained. On the reporter's question of how poor people could buy those homes, Oliver hedged. He went on to another point in the plans.

"The City of Crestview, because of my efforts, will get permission to purchase the Buena Vista `Project acreage for five dollars an acre." He folded his glasses and indicated the interview was over. He brushed aside the next question, "Alderman, are we given to understand that seventy-eight acres will be sold for three hundred and ninety dollars?" All channels carried Maxwell's death warrant for Buena Vista that night. Morning papers picked it up.

One man's death sentence is another woman's passport to life. Ernestine Trotmartin puffed up like a Goodyear blimp. And when she blew, she rocked the city like an earthquake of 7.9 magnitude on the Richter scale.

This time a meeting was unnecessary. By word of mouth the announcement chained the tenants into a common attitude. In drab winter clothing they gathered, like sparrows flocking to a crumbled cake, to each parking lot. As the groups got larger they merged and finally ended up blocking the end of Flood Road and filling the huge parking area in front of the main office.

I watched from my office door, as upset as any of my project people, feeling frustrated, furious . . . and helpless. How can one fight city hall, state government, and the big boys in Washington?

I was to find out.

All day long my phone was silent. No complaints, no problems, even no crime reports. It rattled me so, I found myself close to tears, like a child who imagines her mother doesn't love her any more. Why was I being ostracized? I was doing a private soap-opera hand-wringing scene when Ernestine arrived in my office. She confided in me. Her plan was simple. March on Town Hall the day of the weekly Governing Board meeting. She laid out her strategy. Contact all television stations, the Los Angeles papers, and Bert Lottman.

None of these tasks was left to me. Bert Lottman got the news from Ben Hamilton, who overheard two maintenance men discussing the scheme. I was relieved. I knew that, if I had had to explain to Ben, my voice would have revealed smug satisfaction at the unfavorable publicity that would be heaped on Lottman and his cronies.

Maxwell Oliver took care of the news media. Evidently, a call from Lottman had alerted him and, ever the profile-boy, Oliver contacted the TV stations and newspapers. Thursday's meeting was guaranteed full exposure. The day started out sunny. I woke up to an early alarm-clock setting. Weather in Southern California is moody: February can be like July and June like November. Thursday was glorious. I raced into clothes, gulped coffee, and ate an English muffin while driving to the project. It was just 6:00 a.m. as I pulled in behind my office. Already the parking area was crowded with tenants, dressed in garments that looked like flags of every country: bright, gay, and festive. Signs reading "Save Our Homes" were ready.

The meeting did not begin until nine, but a three-mile walk by people of various ages and physical handicaps through morning traffic dictated an early start. For those who could not go on foot, Grand Prix Papa loaned his lavender car. Infants were in strollers, and a few grocery carts had been sneaked into service for toddlers.

Blacks were mixed with whites. Chicanos brought along their guitars. The music blended like the people: mixed tunes, gay and loud.

Since my official day did not begin until nine, I offered to use my car for anyone still needing a ride. Lisa Fritzle accepted my services because her left leg was in a cast. She and Betty Lou Lupke had had a fight and Betty Lou had been beaten up. Two days later, while Lisa was standing on a stool outside her apartment, washing her windows, Betty Lou came along and kicked the stool. In the fall, Lisa broke her leg. With Lisa came her two youngest kids. Last was old Mr. Gunnersohn, the project inventor, deaf and half-blind, who could pull out creased and soiled letters signed by top men in automobile and oil firms. Mr. Arthur, as everyone called him, would tell how he had been swindled by these men, who had stolen his inventions. Despite his occasional mind-wandering, I was inclined to believe him. Today, Mr. Arthur wore his Scot's cap and plaid plus-fours, which he informed us he used to wear when playing golf with Walter Chrysler. Mr. Arthur admitted to being eighty-six, but that number was probably another of his inventions.

The tenants' march attracted the expected attention. Television portable trailers were parked at various stops along the route to Town Hall. Cameramen darted for angles, while young men who looked like copycat editions of Robert Redford poked mikes at fringe walkers. The pace was brisk and they ran to keep up and get the last words of each remark.

I idled the car at a funeral speed behind Grand Prix Papa. Before the crowd reached the downtown section, an escort of city motorcycle cops on Harley-Davidsons, dressed in black leather outfits, cruised alongside the marchers.

The closer we got to Town Hall, the louder the music became. Whining children were slapped into silence. Some tenants straggled in irregular columns. Heading the group, Ernestine marched with her arms swinging in Marine drill precision, her massive chest heaving, as she led her followers up the whitewashed steps of Crestview City's Town Hall onto the polished marble floor of the lobby. Except for the women who had children in strollers, the tenants ignored the elevators. The army coiled like a multicolored snake up the fancy staircase with its cast-iron railing, and tramped up to the fourth floor and into the auditorium.

The Governing Board was in session. The curved public seats were sparsely filled until Ernestine's group marched in. Immediately the three hundred seats were taken. More tenants lined the side walls and filled the back area, jammed four and five deep. Mothers parked their strollers in the hallway and stood with infants in arms.

The chairman, a wrinkled old man with a gold chain across his vest, rose like a scarecrow from his place at the podium. He fluttered his hands trying to quiet the room down. The sweaty, tired people did not want to be put down. Children yelled; mothers threatened; youths screamed out four-letter words. The chairman sank back into his chair. With a hopeless look, he motioned to Maxwell Oliver to take over.

A pasty-faced Maxwell Oliver stood up with bureaucratic bluster, holding his mike close to his lips. I noticed his hand. It shook.

"Please"—the word blasted out— "let's have order . . . everyone sit down and be quiet!"

"*You* sit down . . . on your fat ass!" Ernestine's voice had its own built-in electronic system. It was called righteous indignation. She moved up front. Her wildly designed and dyed dashiki sleeves were wings of a new-type American eagle.

"You goddamn crooks . . ." she began. "You mother-fuckin' bastards—"

"Out of order . . . out of order . . ." The chairman gaveled desperately.

"Out of order. I'll tell you who's out of order—you and those other tit-sucking jerks with you!" Ernestine was warming up. "Who the hell you think you're kidding, selling off our land—poor people's land—for five dollars an acre?"

She was tight up against the wooden separation which divided the audience from the official area. Several of the aldermen sank back, stunned;

some leaned their heads on folded arms on the table. Maxwell Oliver stood still. Again the chairman rapped, his voice squealing. "You're not recognized, madam. We're behind the rail . . . we're behind the rail!"

"You mean this shitty fence here?" Ernestine kicked at one of the rungs holding up the railing. It hung, then fell. Snickers, laughs started from the tenants. With one hand held behind her, Ernestine indicated they should be still. They shut up.

"So! I'm not recognized! Well, you better take a good look at me, all of me, and there's plenty for you to feast your eyes on, and you better scan those behind me, 'cause you are sure as hell gonna recognize us—all of us! But you might be right about one thing. You don't watch out an' that there rail you so hot about just might turn into a jail after we get through with you, bum!"

At that, Maxwell Oliver sat down, hard.

The rest of the meeting was shown on television that night: Ernestine's remarks about "poor" people buying $40,000 houses; the accusations that Senator Joseph was involved; that someone was getting a payoff for handing over Federal land so that private developers could profit . . . it all came out clear. Clear and loud.

It did no good.

31

High spirits walked with the tenants on the way to the meeting; the walk back to Buena Vista was quiet; steps dragged and hope was at half-mast.

The evening *Crestview City Press* carried the story of the city officials' actions after Ernestine Trotmartin and her entourage left. Discussions by the aldermen centered on honor. Commitments had to be honored—to the Housing Agency (Lottman's name was mentioned), to the local Housing and Urban Development department, and to the "good" citizens of Crestview, who wanted to get rid of the eyesore labeled "Buena Vista." The needs of the low-income tenants were not mentioned. Finally, a vote was taken. Buena Vista was to go!

A brief mention that night in the evening TV news, a short paragraph the next morning in our regional edition of the *Los Angeles Times,* and Buena Vista was forgotten, replaced by the latest sex-thrill murder and Washington investigation.

Defeat depressed the people in the project. Even sex appeared to be affected. During all of March no attempted rapes were reported and, when Grand Prix Papa came into my office, he complained about business. It was so bad that he couldn't even trade his lavender car in for a new spring model.

"The old paint job ruins my image—purple's out this year," Grand Prix Papa said. "It's the bronze jobs moving in, taking over the field. Sharp, man, sharp—I need to hustle me new wheels!"

I nodded, as if that was the most important change affecting the world. He had something on his mind. I waited.

"It don't make sense pulling down this place. What's gonna happen to all the people—they ain't got no money to find them decent places to live. It ain't right." Grand Prix Papa crossed his skinny legs in their suede pants and twisted the many rings on his nervous fingers. "We gotta do something."

I looked at the concerned face of the pimp. The world was upside down! The people's representatives were trying to displace the poor and helpless; and the despised symbol of everything evil and rotten, the lowest creature on the rung of society, a pimp, cared and worried!

"We gotta do something." He looked straight at me.

"Maybe . . ." I stopped. "There's no way without money."

"Money ain't so hard to come by."

"Perhaps if money could be gotten . . . allocated by the Federal Housing Agency—HUD—to fix up Buena Vista . . . clean it up, put in new kitchens—"

"Overhaul is what you mean, like a dame that's played out and gets a face lift. That's what you're talking about! Face-lifting the pads in here!" He got up, excited. Narrow eyes became wide. Wonder of discovery split his brown lips apart. His smile dazzled. "For a broad, you got balls! You know helping the tenants is gonna get you fired? You'll get dumped by Lottman. It's past time we fuck around with local pricks. It's the big shits we got to bugger!"

After Grand Prix Papa left my office, Hank Garrison walked in. The contrast was too quick for my muddled mind to digest. I began to laugh hysterically, choked. Not mad or crazy but helplessly confused. Hank watched, then yelled at me to shut up.

"What you need is a vacation! Lady, you're going bananas!" He pulled me over to the couch and made me take a stick of gum that he held out.

Chewing it, sucking out the sweetness, I told him about the conversation with Grand Prix Papa and his scheme. Hank's reaction surprised me, even pleased me.

"He's probably got the right plan. The only way to deal with little crooks is to deal with big crooks. And Washington is the place to do business under that circumstance."

Then he explained. If pressure was put on in the correct way, the pus would pop out of the pimple. Scandal in Federal funding and land-grabbing were the last things any politician needed in an election year. National nerves were raw, and backlash from minority groups could catch on and spread. Low-income housing was a big sore spot anyway. Not even Washington could take a chance.

"Ernestine Trotmartin could be the sandpaper to open the wound." Hank ended with, "They just might throw her a couple of million to modernize Buena Vista—going through the right local channels, of course."

"You mean Oliver and Lottman?" I asked.

"Depending on the stink the Dragon Lady makes, I'd say Lottman would be looking for another soft job. And ol' Maxie Oliver will do as the big boys tell him. He's ambitious. He's got to lie low when he's causing hot spots on their fur."

"You really think it might do some good, sending Ernestine?" I asked.

"Can't do any harm, can it?"

"You're not such a bad guy after all!"

"Try me . . . you might like me!" He stood up, patted me on the head, left.

The word spread that there might still be a chance to save Buena Vista. When the Mothers' Club met that Friday, Carmen Sanchez, Sadie Handle, and Geneva Lane said that Ernestine and Grand Prix Papa were mighty thick these days.

"Honey"—Geneva paused in her macrame knotting—"Miz Edie, honey, Grand Prix been yakking about getting money to fix up the project. He been beatin' in everyone's ear that you done tol' him money could be gotten from the govern'ent. That so?"

I hedged. Explained about getting an allocation from the Federal Housing Agency in Washington. Without using his name, I added the comments that Hank Garrison had made about pressure and politics. The women listened intently. I looked around at the seventeen ladies: flat-nosed, pugnosed, Latin eyes, freckled Irish skin, old veined hands, overweight bodies. They asked questions that proved that they understood the complications. Dishonesty was what they had lived with all their lives and chicanery was a familiar tactic.

"What we need is a delegation to send to Washington," Vanessa Van Platzen said as she bit a strand of macrame rope in two. "Like Welfare Rights, and oil companies, and all them other big-shot companies. Lobby —that's the scam. We gotta lobby!"

"Yeah, we got rights. Where me and Mr. Tingle and the kids gonna find a place when they tear down Buena Vista?" Beverly Suzanne had her last baby sleeping in a stroller. The Tingles were one of our few "intact" families in the project; most of the others were fatherless. Since that fateful day when

I had shamed them, the Tingles had become one of our best families.

"It cost money, lots of money, to send people across the country—plane tickets and food and motels . . ." Amelia Goochen said.

"We'll just have to raise it. Have a rummage sale," Starlet Jones suggested.

"Shit, that's no good. Who wants our old stuff! No. We'll have a fair . . . a carnival with booths and games and food and soda pop!" Annie Flunk clapped her hands in delight.

A vote was taken; the carnival was approved. Ernestine was consulted, along with Grand Prix Papa, about who should be part of the delegation to Washington. It was decided three tenants should make the trip: Mr. Tingle, Carmen Sanchez, and, of course, Ernestine Trotmartin. That decided, the date for the carnival was set for the week before Easter, three weeks away. The Washington trip was planned for the week after Easter. That meant we had to forestall for at least one month the final approval from the Federal Housing Department, both locally and in Washington, to demolish Buena Vista.

I stayed out of the strategy. Grand Prix's remark about my being fired worried me. Jobs I could get, but my life was tied in with the project. With the people. My people.

I decided to play it cool, remain on the sidelines, let the tenants do their thing. News came to me via the grapevine, the washline, and Bernice's coy remarks.

Legal Aid's Guido solved the postponement problem. She had filed a writ for an injunction against the City of Crestview, claiming that the aldermen had no authorization to make decisions pertaining to Federal public housing lands.

The next day Senator Joseph said in a speech in Sacramento that public monies should not be used to fund agencies that fought the government. He mentioned Legal Aid offices that were "used by ill-advised citizens to hold up progress," and he implied threats to investigate the background of the "eager beaver" lawyers who were costing the taxpayers millions by bringing misguided lawsuits. The local paper made headlines out of his complaint, and two conservative judges concurred in somber TV interviews. After that, the ACLU demanded and got equal time to champion the right of Legal Aid to enter the controversy. In the meantime, the carnival plans were proceeding.

Celia Goochen and Sugar-Jean had their babies two days apart. Celia named her girl Fredia, as she had promised. Sugar-Jean had a boy and, for whatever strange reason, named the boy Peace. Tami Jewel had lost her baby in the fifth month, which had caused her mother practically to disown her—it meant no extra welfare money!

The Mothers' Club met three times a week now, and items to sell were made with feverish concentration. The macrame bunch went at it with such vim that one day Starlet Jones got her curlers hooked by an extra enthusiastic casting of the rope and almost hung herself. Her rouged cheeks turned from pink to purple. It took three glasses of grape Kool-Aid to bring back her blushing rose complexion.

Harry the Shoe and Dude Muggins cornered me when I was on my way to answer a wailing complaint from Gussie McClure that the men in her attic were coming down at night and eating up all her grated-carrot-and-raisin salad. Padding like a big-bellied penguin, Harry the Shoe stumbled over his feet in the too-large brogans. His hat with the wide black brim bobbed and flared like Dracula's cape. It slid over his eyes, and he almost tripped into my arms. I bent double to see his face as he spoke.

"Miss Social Lady, me an' Dude want to help out on this here carnival."

Harry, usually the silent member of the team, had a surprisingly deep and mellow voice. To oblige me, he unflapped his shoes and leaned backward before I broke my back reducing my height to his size.

"That's great!" I told them both. "See Grand Prix or Mr. Tingle."

"Nope, Madame Society." (My title was being elevated.) Harry leaned so far over that I put my hand out to hold him upright. Even Dude jumped behind his buddy to act as a backstop. "We got stuff for to sell, but we don' want it be ripped off 'fore the carnival."

"What kind of 'stuff'?" A picture of being booked for allowing baggies of cocaine or heroin to be peddled over the counter at a booth buckled my knees.

"Heavy stuff . . . like tapes for cars and houses, an' maybe fancy car wheels, and hardly used sewing 'chines, an' chewelery—purty rings and stuff like that. Heavy stuff, you get da ideer?"

Who's kidding who? Did I get the "ideer"? You bet your walking catfish I did.

"Hold it, fellows! You're not suggesting that I let you store stolen merchandise in my office?"

Harry the Shoe looked doubtfully at Dude. The big words confused him. "She saying no?" he asked Dude.

"She's just askin' a question . . . like how much muscle we gonna use."

"Shouldn't you worry, Mrs. Director. We need more muscle, we get." Harry flexed his arm and a melon rose under his shirt sleeve.

Dude and I exchanged a long look. Garbo and Gilbert's most passionate eyeballing was less intense than the emotions that vibrated between honky and blackie. I cleared my throat first; Dude spoke first.

"Harry don't jive, we stay on top of the shit. You play it cool an' nothin' will come down on you. We is dis-creet! Fact is, you don't open the door to the room, you don't see nothin'."

Here I was, standing in the bright California sun—me with a university degree, able to name every painting in the Louvre, the Metropolitan, the Museum of Modern Art, J. Paul Getty's Garage Collection, and the British National Gallery, me who knew the shoe size of each angel painted on the Sistine Chapel ceiling—making a deal with a murderer and thief, scheming to store illegally gained items in the building owned by the Federal government and, to top that, implicitly allowing this "heavy stuff" to be resold. Maybe Hank Garrison was right. I needed a vacation. I *was* going bananas . . . in fact, right now I felt like a whole fruit salad! Maybe the men in Gussie's attic had room for one dame!

They were waiting for an answer. I copped out. I walked away.

I also made sure no one opened that back-room door from the next day until carnival day. Each time I passed through the small hall into my office, I skirted that door as if it were red-hot molten lead—sizzling—straight from hell!

Ben Hamilton buzzed me on my hot-line a few days later and asked me to come over to the main office.

For once he wasn't reaching for a licorice. He looked ragged; there were hollows around his eyes and he needed a shave. He paused, then spoke hoarsely. "What's going on? What's going on? This place is driving me crazy! Lottman calls me and says I'm supposed to get hold of the judge and have the injunction set aside. I'm no lawyer. What does he expect from me? It's too much . . . it's all too much! Oh, my God . . ." He tossed himself into his swivel chair, which tilted dangerously.

Finally, after he chewed up the candy and appeared rational again, I told him about the carnival and the plan to send three tenants to Washington to plead the case of the about-to-be-ravished housing project. The march on the Town Hall had brought trouble to him, Ben told me. Lottman had blamed him for not keeping his ear to the ground. The poor man moaned, "What does he think? That I'm an Indian? I put my ear to the ground and these savages will scalp me!"

I hated to tell me that he was correct. Ben Hamilton never "got it on" with the tenants, had no "soul," no "balls." That was Grand Prix Papa's description of the project manager.

"You've got to stop it—this whole crazy scheme. If you don't, it'll mean our jobs . . . my job!"

His whimpering blew it for me. I let it fly. "It's their homes . . . their place. Where else can these people go? You know damn well those crooks are out to fatten themselves on this land . . . and a hell of a lot you care! Bullshit!" (I shocked myself; retreated.) "Baloney! Where's your compassion? All you care about is this lousy job and you know what . . . ?" He looked up. "You're even lousy at it . . . completely, unequivocally incompetent, inadequate, and a total flop!"

The words relieved some of my anger. I left. Behind me I heard a feeble, "I'll report you to Lottman. I'll report you're uncooperative!"

Report away, I thought to myself! To the open-mouthed Gloria, Mattie, and Bernice, who stared as I left, I said one word. "Shit!"

The carnival took shape; I made no pretense of staying out of the preparations. What will be, will be . . . and after the session with Ben I knew the die was cast, the fat was in the fire, and the shit (my shit) had hit that ever-revolving fan! All I could do was wait and see where and on whom it landed. And how much.

Buena Vista became an anthill of activity, not all legal. The local chamber of commerce was quoted in the local paper as saying that shop owners had experienced a wave of shoplifting—tape stores, car-parts dealers, and Singer Sewing Machine store managers were hit hardest. J. C. Penney was losing big. Sears had a group of security men at every exit. Getting out was like trying to leave the U.S. Mint with a shopping bag!

Back at the project, each parking lot had an organizer. Groups were formed to supply and deliver certain products for individual booths. Sadie Handle volunteered to set up a fortune-telling tent.

"I'll fix myself up . . . you know, with junky beads and gypsylike raggedy clothes," Sadie told me as I walked past her apartment.

"Fantastic!" I said, leaving out the observation that her ordinary outfit already filled the bill.

The Take-It-Off Club ladies gathered in memory of old times and re-named themselves the "Cookie Jar Ladies," which was more sensible and accurate anyway. They were making cookies and cakes for their booth, named, of course, "The Cookie Jar."

Each hour saw a new talent added to the carnival: A taco stand blossomed; two illegal Chicanos would be troubadors playing their guitars; Jet, Danny Gree, Buttons Lewis, and B. T. spoke up for an African booth they promised to keep free of drugs; Judy Nickel offered to donate all her beauty samples and man a "Beauty Tent" and "Makeup Studio."

Grand Prix Papa's idea of a massage parlor was turned down, but his girls were allowed to conduct a "Car Wash Massage Parlor." His Boy Patriots, with Billy Goochen leading, would give a patriotic salute before the official opening of the carnival.

Tenants who usually stayed behind tightly barred doors emerged. Enthusiasm bean-sprouted, internal project crime fell to zero, and the police started to worry.

Stupp Hankerson volunteered to run the soda-pop stand, with Gussie McClure to dish out hot dogs and spread mustard. Mrs. Anne Windsor, who claimed to be related to English royalty and was the Buena Vista horticulturist, condescended to open "Ye Royal Shakespearean Pot-Plant House." Jars, cans, bottles, and cartons were prepared with offshoots of her many vines, slips from succulents, and seedlings of vegetables and flowers. Lady Anne, as she called herself, had lived in Buena Vista for twelve years and her end-cottage garden challenged any Bel-Air landscaping for lushness and beauty.

Everything was going so well that something had to go wrong. It did. It went wrong when Hank Garrison drove through the project and stopped me as I walked toward maintenance. It went wrong when he said, "Customers . . . the public!"

"Customers?"

"That's right. Who's going to buy all that crap? The tenants? Your friends won't make a dime if you can't get the public—the outside community—to bring their wallets."

"So?"

"So who even knows about this . . . this shindig?"

"Posters. We'll make posters and get a notice in the paper."

"Won't work. Isn't enough. Who in their right mind would come into Buena Vista, let alone with folding money, and that's what it's going to take. You just don't have what it takes!"

"That's a low blow!" I said.

"Hell, you know what I mean! You have to have an attraction, something big to bring the outside people inside . . . like circuses have—a barker!"

He was right, of course. I wanted to scream and stamp my feet like a kid having a tantrum. All that work!

"It's your fault," I stormed. "You cops give this place a bad name. That's why people are scared to come into Buena Vista."

"Hey, you know better. What's the matter with you—got blinkers on? You know the kind of crude that hibernates in here."

"Then why did you try to help? You started me thinking about Washington and pressure!"

"Maybe I got blinkers on, too. You know that old chestnut . . ." He gave me a funny look. Started the car up. Then, "Too bad you can't get someone to do a benefit . . . throw a five-hundred-dollar-a-plate hot-dog lunch or get Bob Hope to do an Easter program in war-ravaged Buena Vista." He took off.

I turned back to my office.

For almost an hour I sat behind my desk trying to decide how to change the situation. Finally I made several telephone calls. To each person I said that an emergency meeting had to be held.

After Ernestine, Grand Prix Papa, Jet, Starlet Jones, Amelia Goochen, Annie Flunk, and Mr. Tingle arrived, I told them the bad news. Reactions varied from cussing to moaning to crying to threats of revolution NOW! It was the first time Ernestine appeared stymied, and that depressed us even more. Gritty gloom settled like sand after a windstorm: it buried hope.

A noise at the front door; then Carmen Sanchez's singsong voice. "Hello, there, why no one send for me to come to meetin'?" She came into my office and was met by grunts and dark looks.

"Vot the hell is matter? You all lost your last enchilada?" She got no laughs. "Someone die, no?"

"Almost you are right. We been buried . . . alive!" Grand Prix Papa said.

In broken sentences punctuated with "fuck"'s and "shit"'s, Carmen got the story. She pulled her rosary beads out of her apron pocket, dumping clothespins, soiled Kleenexes, and loose change onto the floor. Religion was on nobody's mind, only hot revenge! God had been invoked, but only to damn! Now Carmen prayed.

"Oy, Saint Anthony, c'mon, we need your help. Mary, most Holy, Mother of God, you tell Saint Anthony we gotta have his help. We is in beeg trouble down here, we hafta find some vay to make carnival happen beeg."

No one objected to Carmen's pleading. We were still numb. She quieted down into a silent prayer with an occasional eye-raising toward the ceiling.

Starlet Jones noticed it. "You getting like Gussie? Think you got a man in the attic?"

A dirty look from Carmen stopped anyone from smiling. Carmen's faith didn't need even a mustard seed. "Go ahead, you 'merican citizens, you make ha-ha on me, but I tell you, Saint Anthony he never let me down. You see, he help."

"We need money, not miracles," Annie Flunk said. "Enough to get Ernestine, Tingle, and you to Washington."

"Maybe I could borrow . . ." Carmen hesitated.

"From Saint Anthony?" Jet mocked.

"No. From my sister's 'usband's cousin."

"The President of Mexico?" Jet again.

"From Carlos . . . you know Carlos . . . Sharlie." And Carmen named one of television's biggest singing and comedy stars.

"C'mon, Carmen, shuck the shit!" Annie Flunk said.

"Charlie Castrias is your sister's husband's cousin?" I asked.

"Sí, Carlos stay wit' me when he come up. He was jus' leetle boy . . . so high . . . maybe twelve. Long time ago. Sure, Carlos is Buena Vista boy— for five years he live here, then go to New York. Always crazy for the singing and dancing. Lots of jokes he tell also."

They all thought I was insane when I got up, screamed, and gave Carmen a big kiss. "That's it! We'll get Charlie Castrias to come. Project boy makes good! He'll be the barker . . . the shill. He'll bring in the bacon!"

"Suppose he won't come?" This was Amelia, always dour.

"We'll make him an offer he can't refuse!" Grand Prix Godpapa said.

"You speakin' 'bout that skinny no-account bastard used to steal my car and ditch it outta gas?" Annie's eyes grew big.

"That's the keed!" Carmen verified.

"Oh, he'll come, fuck yes, he'll come when ol' Annie call that boy!" Annie settled it for us.

I was delegated to make the call to CBS. The others draped over me like weeping willow trees as I was transferred from extension to extension. Finally the "Charlie Show" producer got on the line. My stumbled explanation brought a few bored grunts. I rushed my words, made no sense.

The pained expression on my face triggered Carmen. She yanked the phone out of my hand. In a furious combination of Spanish, Mexican, and project English, Carmen made her point. It probably sounded as if the Mexicans, Cubans, and Puerto Ricans had joined forces and taken over Los Angeles. The producer gave in.

Charlie Castrias was paged in the rehearsal studio. We knew when he got on the phone to talk with his Tía Carmen, his second mama, his familia! Carmen's gestures and excited Spanish, ending with emotional tears, indicated success!

Sure, Carlos can come down for the carnival. OK if he bring special girl star of the show, maybe few other amigos? Make celebration maybe? It was all settled between them. I whispered the time and date of the affair to

Carmen, who repeated it to her famous relative.

When Carmen finished talking, an unspoken signal started us laughing and crying, arms went around each other, kisses were exchanged. And repeated handshakes with me sealed the celebration.

Later that day I felt so good, I put in a call to Hank. He had a right to know that his criticism and concern had set off the spark we needed for success. He was out, so I left a message for him to call.

After I got home that evening, he called me. I was still on a high even though I was exhausted. His offer to bring some pizza and a pie sounded good. I accepted.

32

The word spread. Charlie Castrias and members of his show would appear at the Buena Vista Housing Project carnival! His past residence at the project was exploited by the producer's public relations firm as a good promotional ploy. Spot announcements blared on evening news programs and Charlie was interviewed on several talk shows about his rise to success.

Finally carnival day arrived. A rising sun washed over an exceptional California morning. It began at 5:00 a.m., as if God had set an enormous alarm clock.

The arrangements were to start early setting up the booths. I arrived at my office just as the exodus began from all the apartments. Tenants streamed out of each door. Wooden frames jack-in-the-boxed over the grassy areas. Sheets, blankets, and bedspreads were draped over the structures. I even recognized drapes out of some of the living rooms. Large cardboards were being lettered for signs by those children who could spell and print well.

Gussie McClure arm-wrestled with sacks of day-old hot-dog buns donated by the local bread manufacturer. Stupp Hankerson forgot about his leg and slushed a washtub of boiled hot dogs over to his booth and set it on top of a hotplate. Electric connections spider-webbed the needed power through pieced white, brown, red, and green extensions. Some tenants used Christmas lights to jazz up their booths.

Garage sale leftovers I had collected were put in a fenced yard as "Antiques." Dude and Harry the Shoe played it cool and got Billy Goochen and Lisa's oldest boy to man their "Mag-Wheel Booth." Harry the Shoe sat cross-legged underneath the counter inside the booth and grabbed any money either kid took in sales, while Dude kept a lookout for cops.

Sadie Handle stole the show with her fortune-telling tent. She recruited two teen-age girls—the now unpregnant Tami Jewel and one of Carmen's many relations—who did a Little Egypt number in front. Inside the darkened space, Sadie hummed tunes from *Fiddler on the Roof.* As customers spread silver on her palm, she read fibs on theirs.

Helen Jimmer surprised everyone by setting up a goldfish game. Jars of faded fish were placed in rows, and for twenty cents a throw with clotheswire hoops, one could win a prize. The prizes were wrapped in yards of tape, discouraging immediate discovery. Her bulk, in a makeshift clown outfit, defied recognition.

The advertising paid off! Crestview City citizens jammed the project. A raucous crowd milled from booth to stall. Three trips were made to the Safeway store close by for additional hot dogs. Stupp and Gussie were outdoing everyone, and some smart aleck dubbed them Sonny and Cher!

Ben Hamilton locked himself in his office—despite my assurances that he would not be scalped. Bernice and Gloria poked heads out of the office door, then ran back into Ben's cage. I saw three heads in a huddle through the lopsided broken blinds over Ben's windows, a lot of wig-wagging, then nothing.

Denise Dopplemyer had been elected keeper of the cash. Chuckie and Alfred from maintenance had made a platform and donated an empty nail barrel, hammered shut except for a slit in the top. As money was taken in, runners were sent to Denise, who stuffed it into the barrel.

Hank Garrison came up behind me and pointed. "Isn't that like getting the fox to mind the chickens?"

"The fox is reformed, for today, and the chickens will turn into vultures if a dime is missing!" I answered.

There were several black-and-whites in the project, but they kept a low profile. The entrance from Grand Boulevard was guarded by two motorcycle cops, sweating in the hot sun. I knew they were there to escort the celebrities as they came off the freeway down the street towards Buena Vista, so I kept an eye on them.

I didn't have to!

A three-toned horn blasted through the crowd noise. Again and again it was repeated until everyone realized "they" were here! The motor cops jumped on their wheels and rammed down the street. The expectant audience parted, making a passageway. Giggles, excited voices, squalls from kids who were pushed out of their choice observation spots by older kids. Hank elbowed me to a spot which gave us a clear view.

Here they came! Boop . . . Boop . . . Beeeep!

Leading the procession, a sparkling gold-bronze Grand Prix! A horn, the size of a trumpet that Gabriel would have been happy to blow, kept pumping out the three notes. Driving it was a grinning Grand Prix Papa. In the back seat sat a gussied-up Carmen, with Carlos, the ex-project kid. Next to him was a famous blond who had wiggled and bumped on many television shows. Behind the bronzed job came a long line of limousines—studio cars.

Grand Prix Papa swung around twice before finally pulling up in the cleared space. With all the aplomb of a presidential chauffeur, he ushered Carmen and Carlos out.

"Pimping profits must have picked up!" I indicated Grand Prix Papa's new car to Hank as we watched another carload of lesser stars and semi-stars and hopefuls pile out.

Success is too mild a word for the carnival! Hollywood has not yet invented descriptions to fit it. Exhausting? Yes! Like staging the Russian Revolution for a Bicentennial Minute! But that day gave the tenants of Buena Vista a lifetime feeling of accomplishment.

By dusk the outside community had left. The limousines crawled worm-like back up the freeway; reporters and cameramen dragged themselves off. Tenants dumped the last boxes of garbage into the trash bins. The last sheets and drapes were folded, the booths dismantled.

The moment of truth came. How much money had been taken in?

Vanessa Van Platzen heaved the barrel over her head and settled it on the tailgate of Mr. Campbell's old station wagon. With Denise in charge, we counted.

An anvil chorus of voices intoned every counted coin and bill. Finally, when the last rattle of money was dumped into Denise's lap, a victory yell went up.

One thousand, seven hundred and ninety-three dollars and thirty-four cents!

Enough for three plane tickets, hotel, and meals!

The cheers would have made Tinker Bell's light glow for a trillion years in Never-Never Land!

That same evening, with my office crowded with listening tenants, plane reservations were made for the three travelers. Exhausted, we all went home.

During the next week, the Buena Vista Housing Project hung on silken nerve threads. Ernestine, in a new dashiki and with an apple-green tote bag, was given last-minute instructions of what to do and say. Mr. Tingle, through his son, sent word he wanted me to come speak with him and Beverly Suzanne.

A dejected family greeted me. Tingle had no decent pants, jacket, or shoes. The starched gray work pants and faded shirt from Grant's did not look like garments to wear to Washington. Mr. Tingle sat with knees spread apart, hands clasped between them, head to chest, eyes on his dirt-stained scuffed buckskin boots.

"Miss Bentwood, I'd be a plum disgrace to everyone if I went lookin' like this . . . like some cleaned-up wino straight from a free mission meal. I jus' can't go nohow!"

"He want you should get someone else, Miz Edie!" Beverly Suzanne was near tears. She sucked her lipsticked lips.

"Pa, you gotta go . . . I been telling all the kids. You gonna jack-off, let us down? You gonna be a LOSER?"

The boy screamed out "LOSER" at his father again. It sent a shiver through me . . . like watching the flag carried in a parade. This was it. I knew that what happened next would be the most important minute in this family's future.

The man worked his bone-thin hands like gears trying to mesh, shifted his shoes, then raised his head to look full into the eyes of his oldest son. He spoke low.

"Shut your filthy mouth! You ever call me a loser again an' I'll beat the crap outta you, young dog!"

Then the father jumped up, grabbed the boy . . . and for a moment we women were afraid for him. But the father drew the child close, one hand on his gold-flecked hair, the other around his shoulders. He buried his son's face in his chest.

"Your ol' man ain't no loser. Screw what I'm wearin'! It's what I'm gonna do that's the 'portant thing . . . what I'm gonna say!" He turned to me. "That's right, ain't it, Miss Bentwood?"

He didn't wait for my answer.

"It ain't my pants that got the brains, it's m' head!"

He released Charles, who stepped back, eyes snapping tears away. "Pa, you're the greatest! Folks are gonna think you're the smartest man in the whole world!"

"Fuck the world—the world don't matter, jus' so's you keep that in mind 'bout your daddy."

Soda-pop was offered and I accepted a can. Tingle got a pad, borrowed my pen, and with my help wrote down points that he decided would carry weight in saving his home territory. He shook hands importantly when I left, as befitted a man off to deal with professional scoundrels.

Later that day a frantic call from Ben Hamilton came over my hot-line. "What are they up to? What are they up to?" he sputtered. "They're holed up in the AFT office. What is that Ernestine plotting now?"

Before I could say a word, Ben demanded I come over to his office immediately. There was no use arguing.

Once in his office, I became the calm eye in the center of a cyclone. Ben whirled his arms and circled my chair as he rambled on about Bert Lottman. The head of the agency, Ben reported, was furious. The local Housing and Urban Development Agency was stalling. Their permission to demolish the Buena Vista Project was held up because of "those damn trouble-making tenants."

"Lottman wants us to shut the tenants up." Anxiety raised his voice. "I tell you, Edie, there'll be repercussions—our heads will be knocked together if those rabble-rousers aren't stopped. You've got to check out what's going on with Trotmartin and her bunch!"

"You're putting me in a rotten spot. After struggling for more than a year to get accepted, now you want me to become a snitch—to spy on them!"

"You! You in a rotten spot? What about me? I've got Lottman on my neck . . . and that's not all—Maxwell Oliver's aide called me and . . ." His voice was rubber-band tight. He stopped.

"Relax . . . OK." I didn't want to be responsible for his stroke. "I'll find out if there is anything the Action For Tenants want to share with you, or Lottman. I'll level with them . . . tell them you need to know what's up . . . but I won't lie."

As I walked toward the AFT office, I reviewed what I knew. With the carnival profits, the trip to Washington was a foregone conclusion. But how and when to see the people who could help? I sensed that the gathering involved some plan to set up proper channels to meet the right connections in Washington.

I was right. When I shoved my way into the AFT office, our defeated gubernatorial candidate, Cameron K. Campbell, was on the telephone to the HUD Washington office. Surprisingly forceful, he introduced himself to the startled minion at the other end as a presidential candidate in the next national primary. He got him what he wanted: an appointment with the top management official in the Housing and Urban Development Department. Next, a call to the Justice Department resulted in another firm commitment from a deputy D.A. to set aside time for the California delegation. Lastly, a call to the office of the junior senator from California, Mark Balance; an aide guaranteed a hearing. To each person at the end of the line, Mr. Campbell carefully spelled out the names Trotmartin, Sanchez, and Tingle as the authorized representatives of the Buena Vista Housing Project.

I kept in the background, still confused about my role. Loyalty and self-preservation made uncomfortable bed-partners. I left and returned to Ben.

"Well?" Ben demanded when I walked into his office. "Did you straighten them out?"

"Our tenants are so straight that if Lottman knew, it would blow his mind."

"I don't follow you." Ben showed his fear.

"The Housing Agency—the whole bunch may be in for a shock. Their scheme to tear Buena Vista down may get them into hot water. Ernestine is taking the tenants' case to Washington—to HUD, the Justice Department, and to Senator Balance."

Ben let loose a primal scream, then flopped into his chair. I gave him time to calm down.

Questions about the events of the last few months stormed my reason. I wanted answers. Still, I hesitated, afraid to let on to Ben what I had overheard the day Senator Joseph, Maxwell Oliver, and "Nick" had talked in his office. However, my questions spilled over: What did Ben know about any plan to sell off the project land after the buildings were demolished? Who had set the price of five dollars per acre for prime property in the middle of a large city? And who decided who could buy it at that price? Oliver's statement that $40,000 to $50,000 houses would be built for low-income tenants didn't make sense. Rents of even $65 were hard for some tenants to make now. I ended with the basic question: Why would Albert Lottman urge the destruction of a large housing project, an action that would reduce his own importance and authority?

Ben, pale, still in shock, silently shook his head, as if he wished he could bore his way out of his predicament. He bowed his head, fingers interlocked in a praying clasp. His words came out piecemeal, flat.

"There's a deal. Lottman's in a bind . . . under pressure. That's what I hear. He owes . . . not money . . . but favors. He got his job through some connection he had with Joseph and Oliver on another deal. It's all mixed up with a big contracting firm. I don't know . . ." His voice faded.

"So?" I hoped I sounded encouraging. "Where does Buena Vista fit in?"

"It has to do with political contributions . . . under the table . . . to Oliver and Joseph. I guess this company wants a payoff and the seventy-eight acres of Buena Vista is the honey pot."

"How do you know?"

"I don't know for sure. It's just that some . . . people . . . men . . . have been into the project looking around. They asked a lot of questions . . ."

I remembered seeing Ben with two rough-looking men and one handsome, silk-suited older man. They had driven by me in a Mercedes. I had wondered and had noticed their license was from Nevada. Suddenly I remembered the strange man's voice the day I overheard Joseph and Oliver talking in Ben's office. Could there be a connection?

Nevada brought only one place to mind: Las Vegas! Visions of gambling tables, millions of electric lights shaming the sun and lavish shows passed in review. The contrast to Buena Vista was ludicrous! Or was it? Ben's silence brought me back. I made a few comforting noises . . . waited. He continued.

"After they left, Lottman called down. He was excited . . . almost hysterical. He was so upset he forgot how much he was talking . . . telling me. He wanted me to repeat every word they said. He kept asking, 'And what did the big boys say then?' He called them collectors. Collectors for the 'company.' "

"What company?" I asked.

"Lewiston Development Company. Harold Lewiston's some big wheeler-dealer, I guess. Got his finger in lots of pies." He panicked. "But, please, don't let on I gave you any names!"

My mind went back to what Oliver had said about "playing the game by their rules." It fit in with Ben's information . . . Joseph's remarks about a "deal." What deal, I wondered. And now, Albert Lottman's anxiety . . . the men in the silver Mercedes. I got goosebumps: What was I getting into? Rather, were the tenants, Buena Vista, even Ben and I, part of a bigger plan? And how far did it go? Something was still missing . . . but what? Of course —the Board of Advisors. Albert Lottman could not move without the approval and consent of the Housing Agency's Board of Advisors. Appointed by the Los Angeles County Board of Supervisors, the governing board for the county, the Board of Advisors were respected businessmen. My thoughts became vocal.

"Ben, I think you've missed the fact that Lottman has to take any proposal to eliminate Buena Vista to the Board even before the Federal housing people are approached. And Oliver and Joseph have no power over the Board of Advisors."

"They don't, but others do." He waited for a beat of five, then added, "Let it alone. There is nothing you or I—or the tenants—can do. Sure, maybe they can delay . . . aggravate Lottman, scare him, worry Joseph and Oliver . . . but in the end . . ." He got up, turned to the window, and clammed up, never finished.

I left; puzzled, dissatisfied, angry.

Later that week, the project turned out to see the travelers off. Ernestine, in her new paisley-patterned dashiki, carried a battered suitcase in her good hand and an apple-green plastic tote bag over the other arm. I knew the bag was filled with Buena Vista news clippings and tenant petitions. Next to her was Carmen Sanchez, brilliant as a bird, in a flounced tiered skirt trimmed with coarse white Mexican lace, a red satin bodice, and a fringed shawl. Her black hair was skinned tightly back on her small head, and she clutched a discolored canvas G.I. zippered bag and a small transistor radio blaring Spanish guitar music.

Mr. Tingle was dull as a judge by comparison, in his starched gray cotton pants and a faded rayon shirt patterned in small pink sea-horses sailing upside-down. Only his hat was new. An imitation Stetson, its brim dipped crookedly giving him a recycled Hoot Gibson look. A neat, brown-paper carton tied with old Christmas ribbon held his extra clothes. They left for International Airport in Grand Prix Papa's new bronze car, trumpeting down Flood Road.

God, I loved them all!

Then came the waiting.

Buena Vista throbbed with excitement, hope, anxiety. My rounds through the project the next few days were punctuated by constant stops from tenants who passed me on the way or called sharply out of doorways or windows.

"Heard anything yet, Miz Edie?" Annie Flunk poked her head between wet sheets and oversized underpants as she hung her wash out. My negative nod drew a frown from her and she ducked back behind a mammoth muumuu.

Four days after our ambassadors left, a terse telephone call came from Ernestine to the AFT office. Sadie Handle answered it and reported back to the project. She quoted Ernestine.

"We got the mother-fuckers locked in the ball park, the score's even, but the game ain't over yet!"

There was much debate over what she meant. It was decided by Annie

Flunk and Denise Dopplemyer that it sounded encouraging. I wasn't so sure, and I told them so.

Jet and Danny Gree came in at the tail end of the meeting.

"Fuck, man, you gotta keep the faith—gotta keep believin' things are gonna come down right-on! You gotta keep the vibes vibratin' . . . you dig?"

They all agreed they "digged." I still had reservations, but kept silent. Wait and see was my game plan.

The day for the return of the travelers came, and Grand Prix Papa was sent to pick them up.

Since the conversation with Ben Hamilton, my imagination hula-hooped in my brain. The implications of shenanigans would not fade. I fixed myself a can of soup that evening and, while eating, I divided a sheet of paper and made two columns. One was headed "what I know" and the other "why." By the time the last soda cracker was eaten, I was sure there was a pattern connecting the deterioration of Buena Vista with the political pressure to eliminate the low-income tenants and dispose of the seventy-eight acres of land to a private developer. The only problem was the "why" side.

Ben's rambling information was not proof of any wrong-doing. Besides, the salvaging of the Buena Vista Project for the low-income people was my only concern. Let the wheeler-dealers do their thing, as long as "my" project was saved! I decided to keep my mouth shut. First, I'd wait to see how Ernestine, Carmen, and Tingle made out. Perhaps all this other stuff was talk . . . just talk. There was nothing to worry about, I told myself as I got into bed.

Not yet, anyway.

33

It was Friday that our ambassadors returned. Close to the time for their arrival at the project, the tenants assembled. In clumps, they chatted, in high spirits. Pell-mell—people, dogs, kids on bikes and skateboards, stiff-kneed senior citizens with canes, maintenance crews wheeling their Cushman scooters like high-strung racehorses—everyone gathered to get the word.

I watched from my office window; the car had to pass on its way down Flood Road toward the community hall. A repeated honking of a three-toned horn was the signal. The bronze Grand Prix glided in from Grand Boulevard past my window and swung around to stop in front of the community hall steps. I hurried over. A wild cheer greeted Ernestine as she stepped out. Carmen and Mr. Tingle followed to the same rousing welcome. A path was made and they were allowed to climb to the top step. With immense dignity, like some Roman conqueror, Ernestine lifted her large fleshy hand for silence. She got it. With her two cohorts on either side, she began her performance.

"Let me tell you sumpin', those big shots in Washington are for shit! They're nothin' but puny minds . . . tight as an arse. You face up to them, and they shrivel like a sizzling piece of bacon! They did a mighty lot of sputterin', but we got them to own up on the facts.

"When we got finished with those mothers, they were pea-green in the face. Hell, the whole bunch are so fouled-up, it's a wonder we ain't all back livin' in caves. Anyway, we found out it ain't legal to sell off Federal low-income land to private developers as long's there's livable housing on it. That means no asshole Alderman Maxwell Oliver or Senator Joseph or that shit-faced Lottman is gonna screw us around!"

Wild cheering!

"Shut up!" Ernestine bellowed. "Now, it ain't all sweetness and cream puffs. We did the best we could, me and Carmen and Mr. Tingle, but we still got problems."

Various tenants shouted out questions; others showed concern by their low-keyed murmuring.

"That Washington housing bunch are gettin' pressure from our local rat-finks who wanna tear down the buildings that been bust up and messed over."

Loud "no, no"s and "screw them"s and angry grumblings.

"Hold your water . . . it ain't all that bad! We still got a chance. Hell, we had a pitch they couldn't shut their ears or eyes to! There we were, big as life! One nigger bitch, one Mexican cockroach and one Arkansas razorback. Now, don't you know they knowed if we got our shit together, they better not crap on us! An' they took that into consideration . . . *big* consideration."

Everyone laughed big!

"We got a long row to hoe. We gotta stop them from tearing down *any* of the buildings, 'cause if they got a right to cut down on the number of pads for poor folks, then it ain't much of a step to shove us into a little corner and declare part of Buena Vista is surplus land. That's what these pricks call it—'surplus land'! Fuck their surplus land. The only thing they got to worry about is surplus people who need decent housing . . . cheap!"

Ernestine's voice gave out. Mr. Tingle stepped forward.

"We had a right good meeting with the young dude, Senator Balance. We informed him we got over seven hundred votes tied up right here in Buena Vista an' he recognized our position after that. What we aimed for him to do was to get those Washington housing pricks to throw us some bread to fix this place up . . . not tear it down." Mr. Tingle puffed up, grinned, and blushed as screaming approval greeted him.

Now Carmen Sanchez jumped into the act with her two cents. She held up six fingers, spread wide apart and started counting them off—uno . . . two . . . up to seex!

"Seex million . . . seex million! We as' for seex million dollars to feex up da project! Gut! Huh!"

That did it! A snake dance started up; the tenants went wild. Everyone hugged. The oldsters banged their canes and a couple of car radios blared assorted music.

Ernestine was swamped for more stories about her trip. I watched as the Tingle family walked back to their building. Mr. Tingle looked ten feet tall and Charles's face made the sun appear pale as he looked adoringly at his father. Carmen had a mob around her, mostly the "visitors" she put up in her apartment. Guitars were brought out and a dance session started.

It was after hours already when I returned to my office, exhausted from happiness. The rest of the staff were gone.

During the homecoming reception, I had noticed Ben Hamilton peering out of his window, but he had stayed concealed during the meeting. Tomorrow I would be questioned by him for information that could be relayed to Lottman. While I was musing on what I would report, the front door creaked, and I heard someone enter. Momentary fear returned—it was night . . . I was alone. Then calm took over. What did I have to fear? No one—not one tenant—would hurt me. I had earned my stripes. They were *my* family . . . and I? Was I a part of theirs?

A weary Ernestine stood before me. It was the first time I had seen her deflated, unready to spew out challenges in her usual street language.

"You busy?" she asked.

"About to go home. Why?"

"Things aren't as good as I made out . . . about saving the project."

"That figures!" I said. Waited for her to unburden herself.

"See, this dude at HUD told it right. There's no way this mother-fuckin' bastard Lottman can sell off the land Buena Vista is on, 'long as it's got these buildings and apartments on it. It's Federal land . . . set aside for poor people . . . an' Washington HUD ain't allowed to OK any sale."

"Doesn't that protect Buena Vista then?" I asked.

"It would . . . except . . ." She stopped.

I picked it up. "Except that the project is being emptied—first the maintenance is cut down, then the units are vandalized, and then a whole building is declared unfit because there aren't enough workers to repair them. Right?"

Ernestine nodded. We were on the same wavelength.

"Then comes the rent increase . . . the sixty-five-dollar minimum." I let her pick it up from there.

"You got it together, Bentwood! They schemed it . . . that mealy-mouthed Maxwell Oliver and that ass Buford Joseph, along with that mother-fucker Lottman. The whole bunch of crooks are in cahoots! They get the project empty enough, they can petition HUD to declare this housing ain't needed, seeing so many apartments are vacant . . . unused!

"That's when they'll move in . . . like vultures. Five dollars an acre . . . crap! You wait . . . there's a nigger in the woodpile an' he ain't black, he's yellow—stinkin' rotten asshole yellow!"

Ernestine was her old self again. She was pacing in the small space of my office; then she stopped, leaned over my desk, her fists hard against the scarred wood. Her eyes pinned mine.

"What are we going to do about it, honky?"

My previous happiness was drowned under the woe Ernestine deposited on me. To struggle so long—the protests, the march to Town Hall, the effort to raise money with the carnival, the trip to Washington—all for nothing? Finally to have won Ernestine's trust and now . . . to sense the rug was being pulled out . . . slowly sliding away under the feet of the Buena Vista tenants. My mind raced. I wanted to come up with a solution, had none. Tommy Gun! He flitted through my mind. What would Tommy Gun have done? Suddenly, I knew. Intimidation! That was Tommy Gun's weapon. Well, maybe I could use it! I stood up, took both of Ernestine's hands in mine.

"We're going to do something!" I told her. "We may have a problem, but nothing that can't be solved."

We walked out together. She waited until I was ready to leave in my car. As I drove out, Ernestine made the age-old, triumphant gesture of a fighter: palms clasped together, high over her head.

My mind spun as fast as the wheels as I drove home. Could I make good on my promise? What *was* the solution I could come up with. Intimidation was great . . . but I had to have an angle. I had nothing . . . only doubt, suspicions, and anger—hot, hot anger.

It was Grand Prix Papa who gave me the angle. The next day he swaggered into my office. He carried an ebony cane topped with a silver knob and did a routine, tap-dancing around it à la Fred Astaire.

"OK, Sammy Davis, Jr." I had to laugh at him. "I've seen your dance, now what's your song?"

"Sweet, sweet, oh, how sweet it is!" He flopped on the loveseat, legs extended over the arms of the couch at one end, head cradled on a bent elbow at the other.

"You seen Junior Hernandez's new wheels?"

He didn't expect an answer: I didn't give him one. I knew Junior was driving Grand Prix Papa's old lavender car.

"Yeah, man, that Junior's got himself a sharp-looking pair of wheels . . . paid cash, too!" He looked slyly at me to see if I picked up his meaning.

I did. Junior's money had come from the aborted Federal drug ripoff.

"Junior was lucky he didn't get a sharp bullet in the rear that night. And . . . oh, yes, tell Jet he can get his cap!" I pulled out the woolen knit headgear from my bottom drawer and held it up. Gussie McClure had brought it in. She had found it in her kitchen that night.

"What really made me mad is finding out how rotten you all are," I continued. "All of you—you come in here and bellyache about the cops, about how terrible things are in here, and then you use Buena Vista for a drug depot. Instead of helping your people, trying to keep the kids halfway out of the drug scene, what do you do?" I shook my head.

Grand Prix Papa doubled up; he roared, twisted, slapped his legs, banged his silver-knobbed cane on my wall. Then sat up. "What happened the night the Feds came . . . well, you might call it a case of a hen sittin' on the wrong eggs! Can't fuck a stone . . . you dig what I'm tellin' you?"

"You trying to tell me that it was a set-up? That it was a cross-up? That there never were any drugs—that it was a double ripoff?" I strained to keep from smiling.

"The Feds were rutting like a moose smelling a bitch in heat, so . . . we decided to oblige. They wanted to score, an' we wanted to score. Now it was a case of who outscored who!" He started to laugh again, slapped his hand against my desk, almost doubled over. I pulled my face straight.

"About Gussie . . ." I started.

"Gussie's a good ol' gal. Those men in her attic sure do help out sometimes!" He knew I understood.

"I'm going to have to tell Garrison," I threatened.

"Fuck, that dude don't care as long as it weren't his outfit that got ripped off! Besides, show me where's the proof?"

Suddenly, he got serious.

"You hear they transferred that broad from Legal Aid? That Guido or sumpin'. Yeah, the Man-in-Charge—one of those shitass politicians—put on the ol' heat. Ernestine called this morning an' they said Guido was workin' outta San Jose now."

This was bad news for all the tenants, who had counted on Mrs. Guido's protection through the court with the thirty-day injunction soon to expire.

"Think you kin pull some ropes, uh?"

"Any ropes I could pull would just tighten the noose," I told him.

"What about if you went up to old Bertie Boy, you know . . ." And now he leaned forward, his lean body tight against the sharp edge of my desk. "You know he ain't much better than any two-bit hustler on the street that knocks over a liquor store . . . 'cept the hustler points a piece at the dude's head, and your boy, or boys . . . they do sumpin' worse. They blast into the guts . . . into the place where you live, you dig? They use their fuckin' power and the fuckin' law to ruin the brothers an' sisters and the kids. You take away a dude's pad, put him on the street . . . then what kin you expect?"

"Except that a gun kills! The loss of a home is only temporary," I protested.

"A quick hit is less bad than a long-dying death. That's what makes a dude cash in—when all the doors close an' there's no fuckin' hope. Look around you, Miz Edie. Check it out! These folks that squat in here . . . shit, the roof over their heads been raining piss on them *all* their lives. It's time dat some of that piss falls on the Power-Boys."

"What can I do? You don't think Lottman or Maxwell Oliver or Senator Joseph cares what I think or say."

"What you need is a crowbar, lady. You know, when I was growing up my folks lived on the outskirts o' Dallas. Now Dallas is a fine city, but our street, down where the niggers lived, there weren't no hard-top roads. Come winter an' the rainy season, we kids used to carry our shoes in hand till we waded through the mud onto the main drag. Some of us used to carry a rag to wipe the dirt free 'fore we put on our shoes, such as they were, 'fore we walked into the school.

"Times I 'member when mud stuck 'tween my toes, an' I'd sit in school and when my feet sweat, the dirt loosened—made mud—and I'd squish my toes 'round the mess. My mama used to wonder why the fuckin' shoes never lasted. I coulda told her . . ."

I noticed for the first time that he had specks of gray in his hair.

"Us nigger kids used to pick up change doin' yard work for white folks. We'd walk us to a ritzy section of town, sometimes along Turtle Creek or Inwood Road, an' go to the back door and as' for work. That's how I learned about crowbars. See, I hired out to do the digging work on a fancy landscaping job for some rich mother-fucker. He had imported this big rock he wanted placed just so. I was breakin' my ass trying to jar it, roll it into place. No way! No way could I move dat mother! I looks up and sees this white dude laughing his fuckin' head off an' he goes into the garage and comes back with this crowbar. As easy as cold clabbermilk goin' down your throat on a hot day, this dude tips the rock over usin' that damned crowbar. I learned from that honky—you kin move anythin' or anyone to your way o' thinkin', so long's you got the right crowbar . . . an' ain't afraid to use it!"

"That's great, but I don't have any crowbar," I said.

"Then you gotta come up wit' one!" And Grand Prix Papa took off.

Driving home that evening, I remembered his words. Maybe if I searched, I could find a crowbar. First the crowbar—then the intimidation!

That night I lay awake going over the scraps of information I had about Oliver, Joseph, Lottman, and the progression of events which had led Buena Vista Housing Project and its tenants into a shambles. The proposal to sell off the seventy-eight acres after the project was demolished seemed to be the key or payoff. If I was on the right track, I would have to find the connection between Alderman Oliver, Senator Joseph, and—yes!—the Board of Advisors, and Lottman's place in all this. But something was still missing. Ben's statement about pressure . . . whose pressure? And why? For what? The seventy-eight acres, of course! It always came back to that. To that and the "collectors" from Nevada. My thoughts were already fogged with sleep. One word remained—money! Whose?

34

The next morning I called in sick. Bernice took my call and started to cross-examine me. Her tone said she hoped I was ill enough for her to send me one of her get-well cards. I shut her up with a curt, "Bernice, I'm just under the weather." After all, I had taken only three days' sick leave in almost a year and a half at Buena Vista: two days for a flu bout and one day for an impacted wisdom tooth. After I convinced her that I was not going to die, she hung up. I dressed quickly, got into the car, and headed to Los Angeles on the freeway. My first stop was the Registrar of Voters Office, where records of political contributions were filed.

I found the office hidden in an old, weather-stained brick building tucked away near the fringe of Chinatown. A creaky elevator clanged past the second floor and stopped at the scuffed linoleum third-floor entry.

The over-disinfected smell that old buildings seem to acquire gagged me for a moment. I found myself in a high-vaulted room with grimy plaster molding that swirled in baroque designs around the top edges of the walls. A scaffolding of pipes hung three feet below the ceiling. Ghostly tubes of fluorescent lights cast a cold, harsh glow. My reception from the staff was just as cold, just as harsh.

Behind a linoleum-covered counter was a line of old scarred desks. Seated behind the desks were middle-aged women and one rail-thin black girl (pressure from Equal Employment Opportunity?) who finally acknowledged my presence. My request to inspect the campaign records of Maxwell Oliver and Buford Joseph caused a blank stare, then a frown, and finally a conference with "Miss Elvira." Miss Elvira sat at the center desk and had three telephones. Tucking in a strand of her marceled hair, she advanced on me in her Kosy Komfort shoes, Roto-Rooting me with her eyes, from my plain red pumps up to my layered gypsy-cut hair. Her over-rouged cheeks were soft, her eyes hard, and her tone sharp.

I repeated my request.

Her answer was a crooked forefinger indicating I should follow her back past the gray steel files, a Berlin Wall of bureaucracy. I was assigned a metal table and chair, and three thick volumes were stacked in in front of me. Finally Elvira spoke.

"All right." (She really meant it wasn't.) "You can examine these records here. Only here. You are not to remove, mark on, or tamper."

"I never tamper." I hoped I sounded salty.

She Kosy Komforted away, back to her wooden tank.

I opened my yellow legal pad, got out my pen, and started.

Six hours, a huge headache, and a desperately empty, growling stomach later, I dumped the records on the lovely Elvira's desk and left. Despite my physical misery, my mental attitude was cheering, skipping, and chuckling. I had found a crowbar . . . or at least the handle. My hours of checking and cross-checking turned up interesting information. Donations to both Oliver and Joseph had come from two specific housing construction companies. In addition—and this is what puzzled me—three members of the Housing Agency's Board of Advisors also were large—unexpectedly large—contributors.

My drive home was filled with speculation about what it all meant. I got home, undressed, and showered, and while I waited for the oven to heat a TV dinner, I consulted the memos I had made. Gilbert Builders and Lewiston Development and Engineering Company appeared in several ways. There was a $10,000 item from Gilbert Builders to Maxwell Oliver. A $25,000 donation from Fred Gilbert, $5000 from Helen Gilbert, and two smaller sums of $1000 and $2000 from Jerry and Debby Gilbert all went to Senator Joseph. Nice of the kids! Lewiston Development and Engineering Company was even more generous. They had splurged—$45,000 at one time to Joseph and another $15,000, under Lewiston & Lewiston Systems, Incorporated, to Oliver. I had copied down most of the larger contributors' names, but none intrigued me as much as these two. The oven buzzer went off, indicating that Chin Lee's Chinese dinner was ready to eat.

I sat at the breakfast bar and unpeeled Chin Lee's foil. The steam glazed my eyes. The shrimp were soggy and the rice mushy, but I was hungry. I ate. Later, the fortune cookie crumbled in my hand as I tugged out the paper slip. The writing was faint—thin words in red ink. I spoke them aloud: "You must follow the path chosen to its finish." That did it! I had received my mandate. Now let the cookie crumble . . .

I took off another sick day.

The next two days produced a tour de force in bureaucratic doubletalk. I went from the Department of Corporations to the City Clerk, to the Board of Franchise, to the City Business License Department. Each time I circled downtown Los Angeles for parking places. Each time I ended up paying the gouging parking-lot prices. The merry-go-round of information- and documentation-gathering finally showed a trend. It involved the two public servants, Maxwell Oliver and Buford Joseph, and, surprisingly, the same members of the Housing Agency's Board of Advisors. A cross reference of corporate files showed officers of the Gilbert and Lewiston organizations were also members of the Board of Advisors. In addition, the Gregory Land Company listed Buford Joseph as a vice-president. So Ernestine wasn't wrong about the $250,000 playground contract! There were other connections: The name Nick Falwayer showed on two corporate officer lists as treasurer. His home address was given as Las Vegas. The Falwayer name was often in the news. Recently, I remembered, he had been questioned by a Federal Crime Commission concerning union pension funds and Las Vegas casinos. Ben Hamilton's words replayed in my ear: the three men, the frantic Lottman asking questions. And the Mercedes from Nevada. I wondered if the strange man's voice I heard that day in Ben's office could have been Nick Falwayer?

What did I have? Where did all these pieces fit in? Was it merely a coincidence that some of the Advisors who voted on issues concerning Federal housing property were also involved with large construction outfits? Was it wrong? Was it illegal? And why was Buena Vista so important? Where did my housing project fit in? And Lottman—his name never appeared on any records. Still, he must be involved—under pressure! Maybe he was only a puppet, but someone had to pull the strings. Why? And who?

I spent that night putting my notes in order. I drew a chart, with all the companies, names and connections cross-matched. It made an ugly map: conflict of interest, undue influence, huge Federal contracts, pressure to sell so-called surplus land for a pittance! Whatever one wished to call it, it smelled! The *future* of Buena Vista was undoubtedly involved; had there also been "arrangements" in the past?

It was after 2:00 a.m. when I finally fell into bed. Sleep came on my last thought: Hank . . . check with him about Falwayer . . . and that Mercedes and . . . I slept.

I returned to work the next day. Three days is the maximum time off for sick leave without a doctor's certificate.

Routine problems took up my morning. Bernice trotted over to feel my head in case I had fever. I did—the fever to get answers. I considered sharing my discoveries with Ernestine, then decided against it. I had to be careful, sure. Great harm could be done if I was wrong. Suspicions were not facts. Even if I was correct, my investigations could backfire. After all, my main goal was to help the tenants of the project keep their homes, to save them from being put out on the street in a city where low-income housing was nonexistent.

Toward the end of the day, Hank Garrison walked in. He was excited, and in his enthusiasm ignored my serious attitude.

I half-listened as Hank began to describe a new policy that the chief of police of Crestview planned in response to the increased crime in Buena Vista's neighborhood. He was also getting a new partner, Wendel Ray, a young black rookie.

"Plus two more men will be assigned. Walk a beat. That'll stop some of the violence and crime."

"Really?"

"Christ, you're sour today!"

"I have problems."

"Don't we all? Bad night?" Hank smirked.

"Real bad." I stopped playing our usual love-hate bicker role. I handed him the chart I made last night. "Have you heard of Nick Falwayer?"

He didn't answer. His face showed concern as he took minutes to look over the information. I pushed. Asked again. "So? Give out!"

"Why? Where does Falwayer fit in?" His tone was cautious.

"It's just that I've come across some . . . some odd things in connection with what's happening to Buena Vista."

"Like what?" Hank was all business now.

"Like large—very large—amounts of money being contributed to Oliver and Joseph. Like some members of the Housing Agency's Board of Advisors voting on contract jobs involving Federal money to outfits on which they are directors. And there's more . . . other things I don't understand. And Falwayer's name keeps cropping up."

He handed me back the chart. "Leave it alone. A smart dog doesn't waste his time digging up a rotten bone."

"How does he know it's rotten until he digs it up? Besides, you haven't answered my question. Nick Falwayer?"

I had never seen Hank Garrison reticent before. Or uncomfortable. He was both.

"Edith, my God!" He stopped, started again. "You goddamn women . . . always shoving your nose in stuff that doesn't concern you!"

"What rabbit ran over your liver? Who rocked your gallstones?" I was mad. "You sound like the high and mighty Albert Lottman. Both of you disgust me!"

"OK—OK! You want it straight? You got it, baby! Nick Falwayer is a front man for many organizations, some legal, some not. Most of them have hidden records and intertwined relationships and lots of political clout. He's dangerous, and he's connected with even more dangerous men. Powerful men. Now are you satisfied?"

"No."

"What else do you want? Your head blown off?"

"I want to know how I can help keep Buena Vista open, stop the project from being torn down and the land sold!"

Ten minutes of silence followed as Hank again studied the information I had outlined. I waited impatiently.

"If it were me . . . if I wanted to muzzle . . . queer a deal . . ." He looked directly at me. "With stuff like this"—he waved it—"you could shut up an elephant."

"Are you talking about . . . blackmail?"

"Of course . . . blackmail would be wrong!" He held up his fingers in the famous Nixon pose and wagged his head. "But you could call it . . . friendly persuasion!" He grinned widely.

"Or a crowbar!" I grinned back. "Maybe I'll follow Grand Prix Papa's advice! Rock and roll Lottman into place with my crowbar!"

"Someone's going to rock and roll you into a nuthouse. How in hell did you get so hooked on this place . . . these people? Don't you know yet they're all losers? You better split before you really bomb out. I've been telling you to get away, take a vacation!"

"Don't worry about me. I'm not the type to crack up!"

He groaned, walked over, squeezed my shoulders, and placed a kiss on top of my head. "Just take care . . . you wacky dame! Hear?"

He left.

My depressions usually come when I am caught in indecision. The past months had me seesawing, high moods and low—very low—days. My rational, selfish motivation—protecting my security, my position—conflicted with my inner eye, the eye that all of us have, or should have, when a choice is necessary between expediency and integrity. The paycheck I took bound me to protect the distributor of my salary, to be loyal, to be a team player. The trouble was, I wasn't sure I was on the right team.

My smugness at uncovering the details of possible high-level illegalities and the pleasure I would get from shoving my information under the patronizing nose of Albert Lottman and his team players Oliver, Joseph, and the Board of Advisors evaporated as I contemplated the consequences to me if it backfired. Hank Garrison might be right: Men like Falwayer don't fool around with nobodies like me who throw blocks into their plans.

I vacillated, lined up all the possible actions I could take, reviewed the chart, played devil's advocate with myself—and came out with one foot in heaven, the other in hell. My butt was glued to the fence: I was pulling a Ben Hamilton and I despised myself. Cornered, trapped, and scared, I was in a root cellar of my own making. Only I could shove open the door. Only I could decide when to walk out into the light, to feel the sun, and to watch red and gold leaves against the blue autumn sky.

I was wrong. The decision was made for me by an old lady and a crippled child.

35

A restless night followed my conversation with Hank. I woke with a head-ache—unusual for me. Even strong coffee failed to end the throbbing. No matter how I tried, I couldn't ignore my nagging conscience. The hot potato in my hand had to be unloaded . . . but when and where?

As I drove to work, I decided to postpone any confrontation with Lott-man until official news concerning Buena Vista's future came down from the local Housing and Urban Development Department. After all, so far only statements by Maxwell Oliver and Buford Joseph had got the head-lines; official orders were lacking. I would wait. I didn't feel good, but I *did* feel better as I unlocked the door to the social service center.

Twenty minutes after I got to the project, the hot-line rang. It was Ben Hamilton.

"Immediately . . . get over here!" He hung up.

Now what? Knowing his low tolerance under pressure, I trotted over to the main office.

He was beside himself. Almost incoherently, he blurted out his distress. Lottman had called him at 8:01 that morning and demanded to know who in hell was prying into public records. He, Lottman, had received a call from Senator Joseph. The Registrar of Voters office had reported to the state senator that a woman had demanded to inspect political contributions reported by him and Alderman Maxwell Oliver.

"That's ridiculous!" I said. "Why would some clerk make it their business to contact a senator?"

"If they got the job through him, they would. Some woman down there is a cousin or sister-in-law or something!"

My friend Elvira Kosy Komfort, no doubt! I dropped the subject. Ben continued.

"Lottman wanted to know if anyone from here had gone into Los Angeles the last few days. Thank God, I could say no!"

I kept my mouth shut.

"You were home, weren't you? Sick?"

"What do you think?" Scornfully ambiguous, that's me!

"That's what I told him." Ben leaned his elbows on his desk and massaged his forehead with his fingers. "Edith, it's getting too much . . . much too much!" He looked up pitiously.

"You can say that again!" I agreed as I eased myself out.

The afternoon was worse than the morning. It began with a telephone call from the Department of Public Social Service, Child Protection Division. A sweet-voiced girl identified herself as Miss Stevens and said she was assigned to the Reedy case. She informed me she was recommending that Jody Reedy be removed from her grandmother's care.

From that tragic night when Tommy Gun was killed, old Mrs. Reedy and Jody had acquired a new protector—Dude Muggins, the crude, jivin', practically illiterate black youth, killer, thief, fornicator, you name it! Dude Muggins appointed himself as a guardian angel to the two females, one old, one young. Now, hearing Miss Stevens, I tried to blot out frightening conclusions. "I don't understand. Why would you recommend that action?"

An inner vision pictured the slow-walking old lady wheeling the old-fashioned wicker baby carriage with the crippled child in it. I knew it would destroy her if the granddaughter were taken away. The girl was all she lived for. And what would it do to Jody, whose mind was well even though her limbs were twisted?

I cursed Dude Muggins! While afraid to mention his name to the social worker, I was sure he had something to do with her interference. The horrifying word "rape" raced through my mind. No! Not even Dude would . . .

"It wasn't an easy decision, but the last time I made a home visit it was obvious that Mrs. Reedy couldn't cope with the physical needs of Jody. Jody will just have to be removed to a state facility." Miss Stevens reinforced her position.

"No. No, you can't do that." I groped for potent words, persuasive reasoning. "You don't understand. It would kill the old lady."

"It's the child that the department is concerned about, Miss Bentwood. You are dealing with Child Protection, you know!" Miss Stevens's back was up.

I tried again, knowing that it was useless, knowing that one small deformed child and a life-tattered old lady were no match against bureaucracy. "If you feel Mrs. Reedy needs help, couldn't a homemaker or the public nurse stop in to give a hand? It would be cheaper than institutionalizing Jody."

"That's out of the question. I appreciate your concern, but I'm sure Mrs. Reedy will adjust to our plan for Jody when she sees it's all for the best." Miss Stevens softened, wavered a bit. "You see, Mrs. Reedy hasn't long. She's sick. Terminal."

"Terminal . . . cancer?"

"This way Jody will be spared."

I was silent so long, Miss Stevens shouted into the telephone, afraid we were disconnected.

"I understand . . . but are you sure? I mean . . . is it . . . is the cancer diagnosis definite . . . really"—the word stuck—"terminal?"

"Oh, yes, no doubt at all. And soon." Her voice had that "case closed" tone. She became business again. "The reason I called was to see if you'd arrange for Mrs. Reedy to get transportation to visit Jody once a week after she is moved to the state facility—at least until . . . until, you know."

"Sure. No problem. No problem at all." We hung up simultaneously.

I sank back into my chair. Drowning . . . I felt I was over my head . . . that something was holding me under. My chest felt tight . . . struggling to break open. It was the same feeling I had had that year I was seventeen. On a windy summer day a group of us had gone sailing. Salt spray dipped over our tanned bodies; we played the touching games that teen-agers practice on each other. Then carelessness interfered and we tipped, floundered into the cold ocean water. Everyone laughed and grabbed onto the boat edge. Except me. My foot got caught and tangled in the lines and I was dragged under. I remembered that desperate sinking sensation before my boyfriend dived under and released me.

"No problem . . . none!" My eyes filled: I winked them open and shut. A trip to the bathroom and cold water splashed on my face helped. I returned to my office and stood at the door looking at my desk. It was piled with notes, unfinished records. Overloaded. So was my head . . . and suddenly my life.

Everything was scrambled, reversed. Bad became good, right was not as right as wrong was right. Fragments of the past year's events nipped at my memory with tiny cat teeth. Whatever stability I had was in shreds. I had to get away. Hank was right. I had to escape, even if only for a month. Away . . . far away . . . to another world, different, unknown, but safe with unemotional strangeness.

I sat down at my desk, searched through the yellow pages, made my call. A man answered, "Fun Time Travel Agency."

"Hello, I'm interested in making reservations for a tour—a trip to Europe, maybe London, Rome, Florence . . . and Venice. Absolutely Venice."

I hung up. It was done. My escape was planned. I wrote a memo to Ben Hamilton, requesting vacation time to start in three weeks. He could not deny me: I had time on the books. I walked it over to his office to get his signature of approval.

He tried to argue. "Wait until winter. Things aren't so hectic then. The cold and rain keeps the tenants calmed down . . . not so aggressive."

"Listen, Ben, if I wait till winter, I'll be taken away—in a basket! Now sign!" I handed him my pen. He signed.

The next day I received the confirmation of my reservation. At lunchtime I transferred funds from my savings account to my checking account and picked up my tickets. I had a giddy feeling; a dream was finally being fulfilled. My next duty would be to tell the tenants I would be away for a month, starting in three weeks. I shoved the chart and notes into my top desk drawer under other papers and purposely ignored them.

I told myself that nothing would happen—could happen—soon to Buena Vista. If I had to disclose the information about possible wrong-doing, there would be time when I returned.

It was Dude Muggins who jolted my complacency. Swishing the bushes with his ever-handy pool cue, he stopped me on Greentree Lane. "What the fuck's goin' down at the Reedys'?" A branch snapped off and he kicked viciously at it. "Some suckers gwanna get his ass kicked they mess wit Jody an' her grandma!"

"Hold it!"

"Hold nothin'! Shit! What's that white honky doin' packin' Jody's duds and actin' like big shit with the old lady?"

"She's probably from the Department of Public Social Service—Miss Stevens. Jody's going to be placed in a state facility . . . probably Fairview Hospital for exceptional children," I said.

"The hell she is? What's the matter wit you, Miz Edie? How come you

let them take Jody! Shit, I kin help the ol' lady. I been doin' it since
. . . you know . . . since Tommy Gun." He stopped.

"You've been a good dude . . . Dude. I really can't figure you out,
knowing all the other things you've been into."

"Yeah, well. We is forgettin' about what's done run down the river. That
Jody . . . that kid—you know she's smart! She might not walk or hitch up
her pants alone, but she's got a brain. Y'know she's been teachin' me
. . . yeah, yeah! She kin read like a professor, know dat? Hell, Miz Edie,
you gotta stop dem from movin' her outta Buena Vista. Locking her up with
dumdums! I . . . I need her."

Miracles are not confined to cathedrals; they also occur in housing
projects.

I told him. About Mrs. Reedy and that she didn't have long. That
transferring Jody now would be kinder. She would have a chance to adjust
instead of witnessing her grandmother getting sicker.

Dude Muggins kept slashing at the shrubbery, head down. His eyes
narrowed. A pulsating throb centered in his mid-cheek as he clamped his
jaws together.

"It ain't fair, Miz Edie . . . a little kid like Jody being stuck in a place
where no one really cares. She'll die there. It just ain't fair." He looked up
and his eyes—those hard, coal-black eyes, those eyes that had calmly witnessed stabbings and beatings and mayhem—wept. Large messy tears cas-
caded down his face, detoured over a razor scar, gathered at the corner of
his thick lips. He used his hand to smear them away. Like a small boy, he
sniffed up his nose, rubbed his eyes. I was watching Dude Muggins become
again that small black child, unhappy, puzzled, asking why his world wasn't
"fair."

"Fair? What's fair, Dude?" Softly I said it and touched his arm. "I'm on
my way down to Mrs. Reedy's. Come, go with me."

We found Miss Stevens just leaving in her shiny red Mustang. She was
young and blond and picked her way carefully through the trash of the
Buena Vista parking lot. When she saw me, she stopped and called my
name. I acknowledged her and we met halfway.

"It's all set. I'll have the van from Fairview pick Jody up tomorrow.
Maybe if you're around, it might make things go smoother."

"Maybe," I said.

She glanced at Dude standing near the Reedy back door. I could see her
apprehension, read her mind, feel her fear. "He . . . that man . . . he came
in while I was packing the kid's stuff. He's got a knife!" Miss Stevens
shivered. "How can you work in a place like this? Aren't you afraid you'll

be killed? God, this dump shouldn't be named Buena Vista; it should be called Vista Horror!"

There was no use giving her an answer; she didn't expect any. She drove away as Dude and I entered the Reedy apartment.

Jody was propped up and tied into her oversized highchair. A yellow ribbon held her soft brown hair off her milky-skinned forehead. Her expression changed when she saw Dude. He sat next to her on the dinette chair and patted her thin listless arms. He uncurled her crippled fingers and massaged them around his rough black ones.

Mrs. Reedy turned from the sink where she was washing dishes. She looked the same as ever except for a grayish pallor. I knew that complexion. I had seen it on my mother—first gray, then with an undertone of green, sallow, signifying death was reaching out. Her white hair, still well-groomed, was fluffed out, but her movements as she turned to us were jerky, as if any movement pained. Her smile was bright, her teeth artificially even. She dried her hands on her apron, then held one out for me to shake.

"Jody's pleased you come down to tell her good-bye, Miss Bentwood. And you, too, Dude."

She led me to a chair, sat down next to me.

"I've been telling Jody how nice the hospital will be . . . lots of other children, and games and fancy food . . . Jell-O. Jody loves Jell-O, don't you, darling?"

"I don't want to go. Grandma, Grandma, don't send me. Dude, please . . . Miss Bentwood, please . . ." Tears overcame her.

We adults exchanged glances, each of us caught in our special agony. Mrs. Reedy turned her head away from Jody, looked sideways at me. She silently formed words: Should I tell her? I stared at her, felt water gather in my eyes, coughed, became busy, avoided reaction. She turned to Dude, who also looked away.

"What's the matter with everyone?" Jody's voice trembled. "I'd rather die than leave you all. I'd rather die than be sent away. Why do you want to leave me alone? Don't you love me any more? Dude . . . Dude . . . who's going to teach you? Read to you?"

"There's no other way, honey." Someone *had* to answer the child. I did. I explained about her grandmother. It was the hardest thing I ever did. When I finished, the four of us sat still, silent, spider-webbed together by grief. It was Jody who brought us back.

"If God wants my Grandma, then he should want me too. Let him take me—let me go with you, Grandma! He should know better than to leave a cripple alone, with strangers, with no one who loves her."

Oh, Jody, who knows why he paints our lives with certain colors . . . dips his brushes in pots of pain or pleasure?

"Sometimes God's a mother-fucker!" Dude's voice rasped like the old Dude: coarse, deadly, the street-runner returned. "Listen, baby, whatever you want . . . well, ol' Dude'll see you get it! I promise."

He jumped up and ran out the door. There was nothing else to be said or done. I leaned over and kissed Jody's tender cheek, patted Mrs. Reedy, still slumped on her chair, and left.

I searched for Dude as I walked back to my office, but no one reported seeing him. The sadness followed me home.

That night I showered . . . rubbed suds over my body, watched the water run smoothly over my breasts, down my thighs, swirl around my feet. The picture of Jody's deformed limbs returned. Suddenly, I became angry—angry that I ignored my body's needs . . . cold-storaged my emotions . . . wasted my sexuality. A new appreciation of my own possibilities for living contrasted with the agonizing fate before the deformed child. Jody's cry—"I'd rather be dead!"—didn't sound so wrong. I would rather be dead, too, if my future were nothing but pain and aloneness. Aloneness . . . that was the nail that crucified. I stepped out and folded myself into a bath towel. Grief for Jody and what she had to miss and grief for myself for what I had programmed myself to deny sent a somber Edith Bentwood to the telephone. Dena answered and said her daddy had gone out. I was stunned. Suddenly, I knew what my feelings were about Hank Garrison. I needed him as Dude needed Jody: someone to give to.

The next morning I started down to the Reedy apartment to meet Miss Stevens. After all, I had promised her, and besides, it would help Mrs. Reedy to have someone with her after Jody was taken away. I dreaded being a witness to the parting, but there was no way out.

Approaching me on Greentree Lane was Judy Nickel. In a flapping housecoat and lugging a cardboard carton, she yelled at me to stop. She puffed herself calm before she spoke.

"Something's wrong down at Mrs. Reedy's. I went down to give Jody some of my discontinued Avon samples—for a going-away present—and no one answered! You know they'd be up on a day like this, Jody leaving an' all! I'm scared for them. Do you think something's happened?"

"No, no, of course not!" I dismissed a quick fear.

"Anyway, I stopped in at Annie Flunk's an' told her to call the medics . . . just in case . . ." Her worried tone and frightened eyes demanded action. I started to run toward the Reedy parking lot.

Before I reached the Reedy apartment, a police car passed me, and then an ambulance. My heart sank. Those two vehicles coming in together always meant bad news for the project. I blanked my mind, refused to consider what they might find.

The paramedics found them together on the bed. The small apartment was spotless: not a dirty dish, not a soiled garment. Two people, embraced in death. Two faces, one smooth with unlived life and the other creased by sorrow and pain, lay on a hand-embroidered pillowcase with a crocheted edge.

The police entered after the ambulance took Mrs. Reedy and Jody away. They found four transparent sandwich bags, each twisted at one corner into a small pouch. I recognized them: That was how "nickel baggies" of "reds" were sold. A red capsule remained in one baggie, as if Mrs. Reedy, in her last act, wanted to make it easy for the authorities: to tell them how she and Jody checked out on the world.

I waited until everyone had left the apartment and then locked it up. Suddenly, I realized Dude Muggins had been absent from the crowd that had gathered, as usual whenever something happened in the project.

I felt drained as I started down Flood Road toward the main office. I wasn't sure what would happen to the property left in the apartment. Ironically, it would probably go to Jody's mother, the mother who left her child. Maybe in the Reedy file a name of another relative was listed. I hoped so.

From no place, Dude Muggins appeared at my elbow.

"Here." He thrust an envelope at me.

I took it and kept walking.

"It's from Jody's Grandma."

I kept walking. My head down, watching my feet take steps. "You got the reds for them, didn't you, Dude?"

"I . . . I promised Jody . . . she'd get her wish. No way I could cop out, you dig?"

"You could be held . . . supplying drugs that caused two deaths."

"You tell me I done the wrong thing an' I'll turn myself in, Miz Edie. So go on . . . tell me."

I was drowning again . . . all that weight on my chest. Who was I to say what was bad or better? If I couldn't decide on my own life, how could I rule on others? I walked past the main office, toward my office. My silence was his answer. He left me at the door and disappeared behind the building.

Once inside, at my desk, I opened the envelope. The handwriting was spidery, words misspelled:

Dear Miss Bentwood. I am writing this to thank you for all your kindnes to my grandauther and me. We talked it over and Jody and me desided we rather be together. We no we done the rite thing and God will forgive us. And God wil love Dude becas he done it with love. Yours truely, Gertrude Reedy.

I carefully folded the narrow blue-lined tablet paper and placed it in my wallet behind the small picture of my mother and me, taken when I was twelve. I stood tall and thin next to her seated in a lawn chair. Her lap was full of flowers and I was dressed in my confirmation dress. The letter made a small bulge but I pressed it smooth and returned the billfold to my purse.

Courage takes many forms. Gertrude Reedy and Jody had the courage to leave this world together because they knew it was the best thing for both of them. The loving thing.

They took a stand and followed it through. I took a stand on Buena Vista —to save it—and I backed away. No more!

I opened my top drawer, pulled out the notes and chart. I reached for the telephone, dialed the central office. I requested an appointment with Albert Lottman for the following afternoon. There was no turning back! Tomorrow I would confront Lottman on his home base!

36

I dressed very carefully the next morning. It was getting warmer every day. The usual spring days, cool in the morning, turned blazing by noon. I chose a cotton dress which had a light sweater to match. Instead of letting my hair loose, the way I usually wore it at the project, I pinned it into a French twist. It gave me an older, more businesslike appearance.

There was a nervous quiver in my middle area as I went about petty duties in the project that morning. I had Amelia Goochen come in and we went over the craft supplies to see what had to be reordered. Later, Raquel Mansfield barged in, complaining about plugs. It seemed that whenever she plugged in her toaster, all the lights blew out. Judicious questioning revealed that she used an extension cord that had four other appliances plugged into one outlet. A call to maintenance to replace a fuse satisfied her and she left.

Time crept. I was jumpy. I rehearsed what I planned to say. Consulted my documentation. Had butterflies in my stomach and jelly in my knees. When Amelia went home for lunch, I locked up and went over to Ben Hamilton's office. I caught him just as he was getting into his car, and hailed him to wait.

He was going to have lunch . . . did I want to join him? This had never happened before. Surprised, I accepted. He pulled into a Denny's and we went in. While we waited for our order, I told him I was going up to talk with Lottman—to ask about "certain information." His reaction knocked over a metal cream pitcher. The white liquid dripped toward me and I slapped my paper napkin over it to soak up the fluid.

"I won't back you up. I don't know anything. You'll be fired. There's no use in being hasty . . . rushing into things. Lottman will suspect me . . . think I gave you tips . . . egged you on." His face grew red and still he rambled on in a hoarse whisper.

"Shut up, Ben," I hissed. "Shut up! No one is going to implicate you. This is my party . . . all mine . . . something I have to do. Someone has to take a stand, and I guess I'm elected."

"Have you told Ernestine what you know?" He settled down to an acceptance of my determination.

No, I told him, I hadn't. He sighed, relieved. Power in her hand was dangerous, he insisted.

We ate our hamburgers and fries and parted, I toward the freeway and the central office, Ben back to Buena Vista.

Clutching my notes in a manila envelope, I was ushered into the same plush office with the same calm yet precise, military-type man seated comfortably, rocking gently in his Eames chair.

He made small talk to which I responded in tight stiff phrases. Finally, an impasse was reached. He leaned forward, removed the cigar from his mouth, and pointed the end toward me. "You." He impaled me on that "you." "What's on your mind that you needed an appointment with me?"

I laid the manila envelope on the desk, drew out my chart, which had the names, addresses, and the crisscrossed connections. He held it between thumbs and forefingers, like hot metal or something dirty. He stopped rocking. His cigar was shifted from one side of his mouth to the other by his rabbit-pointed teeth, which nibbled as if eating an ear of corn.

My heart pounded. I had a pressing need to run to the ladies' room. My fingers stiffened around the chair arm. I waited. He turned the paper over, placed it face down on his blotter.

"That all?"

"Not quite," I said.

"What else?"

"Falwayer."

The name acted like a needle. I watched Albert Lottman as he jumped, rose halfway out of his chair, then sank back. He removed his cigar and tried to lean it against an ashtray. It rolled over and tipped. The ashes scattered. He tried again to brace it. His hands trembled and he ended by laying it across the silver tray.

"It's all a bunch of nonsense. You know that, don't you?"

He knew that I knew it wasn't. I said, "Then it doesn't matter if I tell Ernestine Trotmartin, does it?"

He also knew that I knew that my information in the hands or mouth of Ernestine would open up a can of worms.

We squared off, our eyes locked. I had seen fear in tenants' eyes, but this was different. The fear in this man's face was a coward's panic. What other hidden evil was he involved with, I wondered? Like a Chinese dragon, he seemed to have a long tail of misdeeds twitching behind him.

"Oh, Mrs. Trotmartin, she's a difficult lady to deal with." He wet his lips. "There's no use getting her mixed up in policies that can be settled on a higher level. In fact, Senator Joseph and I contemplated withdrawing the suggestion to demolish Buena Vista. Even the Alderman agrees that the City of Crestview has been too critical of Buena Vista. The Board of Advisors discussed a new proposal to upgrade the units. Put in better kitchens, replace plumbing. They asked me to prepare a request for modernization funds—six million."

He leaned forward, intimately extended his arms across the desk, reached for the manila envelope under my hand. At the same time, he patted my arm.

"That make you happy? Satisfy your concern about the future of Buena Vista and its tenants?"

I allowed him to remove the balance of my notes. It was over. The crowbar had done its work. At least for now! I agreed to let him keep my "ideas," as he called the information I had gathered. I had complete copies at home. We parted after a handshake. I knew I had won only a partial victory. Yet now I could leave for my vacation with certain knowledge that Buena Vista's demolition was canceled—at least for the time being.

That afternoon, after I returned to the project, Hank and his new partner, Wendel Ray, cruised Flood Road. They stopped the car when Hank spotted me walking back from Carmen Sanchez's.

Carmen had overloaded her apartment again with "cousins." Gloria screamed at me to do something . . . anything . . . get rid of them. Usually Carmen's visitors included women with lots of children. This time I noticed there were only men. Grim, silent-faced men. Without guitars. They eased into the other rooms when I entered. No one was drinking beer and the ever-blaring Spanish music radio station was turned off. Carmen greeted me cordially, but I sensed a reservation as she offered me coffee. When I declined, she appeared relieved. We discussed the problem. She assured me, "You no hafta worry, Mees Edie . . . all be gone. Cousins not come visit again for much time. Everything be fine. I promiz you, dey all leave end of week."

I sensed something was going on, but what? It was still on my mind when Hank insisted he had to talk to me. While he parked, I unlocked the door. We all went back into my office.

Guns! What did I know about guns coming into the project! What kind of guns? All kinds! He drilled out the questions.

"This is about the millionth time you have quizzed me about guns!" I said. "Sure, there're guns. Anyone over six has a gun! You know that . . . and I've told you about hearing shots that sounded like machine guns . . . but not recently. Things have been cool lately."

"Well, it's heating up!" Wendel Ray said. "Three National Guard armories were broken into within the last month—one in Compton, one up north near San Jose, and one last night in Glendale. Enough ammunition and guns were ripped off to start a small revolution."

"So what has Buena Vista to do with that?" I asked.

"Word came down that the project is being used to harbor gun runners and that the stolen firearms are stashed someplace inside Buena Vista." Hank was uptight, cold-angry.

Memories of my first meeting with Tommy Gun and Jet returned. Their words about a "marshmallow roast" had chilled me then.

"Whose . . . ? What kind of a revolution?" I pressed.

Hank sat down heavily and said with a weary voice, "That's the hell of it . . . we can't figure out if it's blacks against whites, whites against blacks, Mexicans against gringos or against each other! It's one helluva mess! All we know for sure is that Buena Vista is armed to the teeth!"

"Couldn't it involve politics? The tearing down of Buena Vista? Rebellion by the tenants?" I said.

My mind raced. Perhaps I should take Ernestine into my confidence? Clue her in on the tactics I had used with Lottman? Show her the information I had? Prove that Buena Vista was safe for now? Calm down heated tempers, violent tenant reaction. I wavered, confused.

"I don't think so," Hank said. "It's bigger than that."

We had ignored the young cop. Wendel Ray had remained quiet, listening to Hank and me. Now he interrupted. "No one asked me, but on the street in Watts and Compton, and in the East L.A. barrio, there's rumors—"

Hank interrupted. "There's always rumors. We need facts! When you've been on the force as long as I have, you learn to ignore them. Forget them! Rumors and a dime get you a phone call!"

Ray clamped his lips together; even under his black skin, a flush of resentment showed. The older man's putdown hurt. "Yeah, well, I was on the street before I went through the Academy. Maybe you twenty-year men got years on us new black cops. But we got something you whites don't have —we've got that third ear, that ear that hears unspoken words!"

"And what unspoken words does your third ear hear?" Hank's sarcasm stirred anger in the black rookie.

"Shit, man, why don't you open your eyes? Being a cop should make you aware of who goes to jail . . . what color skin most of the prisoners are . . . the percentage of minorities in all jails . . . prisons. When the S.W.A.T. teams go on a raid, isn't it usually a black dude who gets cut down in the line of duty? And is a cop ever found responsible for negligence? Hell, no!"

Hank and I were backed up by Ray's passion. His words were violent and yet pleading. "You can't tiptoe around whites and smash your gun butts on black or Chicano heads without them finally rebelling. I've been to too many jails, too many court hearings, trying to get my friends, even relatives, sprung loose. They know money is what oils the prison locks. Well, maybe guns will also!"

Hank moved quickly, grabbed the slender man in an iron grip, spun him around. "You telling me that the hardware we're tracking is going to be used for raids on California prisons?"

"That's what the street's been whispering into my third ear."

Hank released his hold and Wendel dropped onto a chair. Sweat polished his dark skin. He buried his face in his hands. For a second, Hank stared; then awkwardly he put his hand on the young man's back.

"Look, I'm sorry . . . I got out of line with you. Shot my mouth off. Guess one's never too old to learn. That third ear, does it tell you anything else, partner!"

At the word "partner," the rookie looked up. "Shove it! I don't pay attention to what a honky says anyway." His eyes smiled. The men made their peace.

They left, but I had a suspicion I would hear more about the guns. I was right. That evening Hank called me at home.

Word had come in about another gun heist. This time it was a large warehouse of surplus arms at the Marine base. Hank said he was working a double shift: the captain had put him on the case. The third ear indicated the guns were stashed inside Buena Vista. His question to me was "Where?"

"There's over two hundred empty apartments in the project," I told him. "Some are boarded up, all have attics . . . lots have squatters living in them. My God, it would take a house-to-house search. Besides . . ." I stopped.

"Go on!"

"If the guns . . . if you *are* right, the guns could be hidden in the occupied apartments also. Wouldn't you need a search warrant?"

"Yeah. Yeah." Defeat in his voice. "Yeah, we would, but *you* wouldn't! Hell, you can get into every damn door in that place."

"They love me!" I said dryly.

"Me, too! Love you if you'll get your duds on and meet Wendel and me out there."

I didn't answer. Three "hello"s later, I did. "What would I have to do?"

"Go door to door. You know which apartments are occupied, which are empty, where the squatters are. You just come right out front . . . tell them what you're looking for. Level with them. Explain that if the ammo is not surrendered, we'll have no choice but to go in with full force . . ." Hank paused. Repeated. "Full force."

"Which means . . . ?" Chills started.

"People are bound to get hurt . . . lots of people."

The Bates shootout floated before me . . . Herbie Brent's anguished face.

"OK," I said and hung up.

We found the stuff.

It took all night. My knuckles were raw from knocking on doors, my feet cold from the night mist as we shuffled through wet grass. As usual, the word spread as soon as we finished at the first building. Lights went on all over the project. People answered their doors with grim faces, and when they stalled me with useless talk and inconsequential conversation, I knew it was to give other tenants time to maneuver. Time to dispose of incriminating evidence.

Hank Garrison and Wendel Ray stayed behind me, waited at the end of each walkway leading up to each door. Restrained, quiet, respectful, they let me dictate my own pace.

It paid off. Toward the end, we stumbled over boxes of ammunition tossed from upper windows, crates of guns, now cracked open, spilled rifles, machine gun sections, ammo belts.

No one emerged from any building—strange for Buena Vista, where tenants usually swarmed like flies to fruit. Ernestine helped. When I reached her door, she demanded to know what was up. Her eyes told me she knew already, but I went through the motions of telling her. As I talked, she kept her eyes on the two dark forms waiting behind me.

"You trust the pigs?" she asked.

"*These* pigs." I told her. "Remember when you asked me to help . . . keep Buena Vista from becoming a battlefield . . . help Tank?"

She nodded.

"Well, now, I'm asking."

She considered me. Then, "Right on, nigger-lady!" She reached for a jacket, struggled into it. Closed the door behind her. With Ernestine beside me, we canvassed the rest of the project.

Trucks came. Notified by Hank, the police moved in to load the stolen firearms. The grounds of Buena Vista were piled with weapons like droppings from some huge dog, like macabre cornstacks in the graveyard of hell.

Four arrests were made. Junior Hernandez's lavender Grand Prix had a back seat filled with shells. A "cousin" of Carmen's was caught jamming out of the project in a van filled with guns. Two other men, both black, both strangers to me, drove into Buena Vista with a camper. The low-key activity had not warned them of the investigation. Inside the camper was part of the Marine warehouse haul.

That was all. It was finished. Buena Vista was freed of guns . . . for a while.

Hank Garrison and Wendel Ray had done a night's work. So had I. On the way back to my car, I told Hank I had taken his advice. I was leaving next week for a vacation. I was going to Europe.

That Friday at the Mothers' Club meeting, I announced my vacation and told them where I was going. The idea of Europe brought only vague recognition. Disneyland, Las Vegas, Bakersfield, even Chicago were within their scope of familiarity. London, Paris, Rome, Capri, Innsbruck didn't register. My being unavailable for a month did. Each came to me in private, pressed my hand, wanted reassurance I would be back. Tied me to them by their need.

Time galloped! Time dragged! I had misgivings. I ached to be leaving. My actions became mechanical as I moved through my daily routines. Sudden bursts of humor and extra devotion to my dearest tenants followed.

My tickets lay in my desk top drawer and I pretended daily to find them under my hand. My behavior finally caused Hank Garrison to ask me what the hell was the matter with me?

Finally! The last week passed.

Departure was Saturday morning. By Friday, everything was packed, my plants farmed out to my neighbors, the paper canceled, the refrigerator emptied of spoilable food. Bills were paid up, booster shots taken, passport tucked in a new purse. I was ready!

The Mothers' Club was to meet on Friday again. I tried to cancel it, since

I was anxious to get away early that afternoon. They wouldn't hear of it! I gave in.

They started coming at one o'clock. Before I realized it, the office was jammed with tenants. Young, old, the best, the worst, cold-blooded, warm-blooded, mixed-blooded, mixed-up! In Annie Flunk's big black hands was a huge white cake decorated with roses, a blue icing ribbon, a gaudy picture of a smiling airplane, and a florid scrawl spelling out, "We Love You, Come Back Safely."

The cake was eaten, the last good-bye was said. I tidied up my desk, emptied the wastebasket, wiped the bathroom sink clean, and cried a little. Then I drove home.

Last-minute packing kept me busy. Later, sitting quietly with a towel around my freshly washed hair, my year and a half at Buena Vista passed through my mind. Faces and feelings. Events zoomed into focus, faded; people took their place: Freddie-O, Lisa Fritzle, Ordie Durkee, Denise Dopplemyer, Starlet Jones, Jet, Dude Muggins and his Jody, Ernestine, and Dellie. And Tommy Gun.

My hair was dry. I was brushing it when my doorbell rang. It was Hank with a bottle of champagne.

We woke up to a dazzling June morning. I opened my eyes first. The sun played shadows on the white ceiling. A lone fly buzzed against the screen, shattering silence. Sounds long forgotten echoed in my ears. I was twelve again. Lean as beef jerky, I was lying in my bed of childhood dreams, expecting life to be wonderful.

It was.

I moved my leg. Touched Hank's.

My trip began.